Walter Benjamin and Berto

Erdmut Wizisla

Walter Benjamin and Bertolt Brecht

The Story of a Friendship

Translated by Christine Shuttleworth

VERSO

London • New York

1 3 5 7 9 10 8 6 4 2

Verso
UK: 6 Meard Street, London W1F 0EG
US: 20 Jay Street, Suite 1010, Brooklyn, NY 11201
versobooks.com

Verso is the imprint of New Left Books

ISBN-13: 978-1-78478-112-5 (PB)
ISBN-13: 978-1-78478-113-2 (US EBK)
ISBN-13: 978-1-78478-114-9 (UK EBK)

British Library Cataloguing in Publication Data
A catalogue record for this book is available from the British Library

Library of Congress Cataloging-in-Publication Data
A catalog record for this book is available from the Library of Congress

Typeset in Ehrhardt by Kitzinger, London
Printed in the US by Maple Press

Contents

List of Illustrations

Publisher's Note

This work, which began as a doctoral thesis in the former East Germany (the German Democratic Republic), was completed in 1993, three years after German reunification. The author substantially rewrote it for publication in 2004. This English-language edition has, with the author's agreement and participation, in turn been modified for a further new readership. The intention is to make it available to an English-reading public, including those who know German but who prefer to read a substantial study like this one in their own language, or – even if English is not their first language – in English rather than in German. This means that, where published English translations of books, articles or poems exist, such sources are quoted and/or cited. This involves primarily the work of Benjamin and Brecht themselves, but also that of Theodor W. Adorno, Gershom Scholem, and Hannah Arendt among others. In all these cases, quotations in this edition have been taken wherever possible from the published English-language source, to which reference is made. Where translations of passages quoted do not exist, they have naturally been translated, but the German reference has been retained. This also applies to any secondary literature, whether quoted or mentioned. In one or two cases, reference to a standard English-language work has replaced or supplemented an original, untranslated, German-language secondary work (see the List of Works Cited, p. 222).

The German edition contains a section (in the first chapter) of detailed discussion on the debate, dating from 1967, about the initial republication and publication of Benjamin's work in Germany from the mid fifties. This politically founded controversy, albeit generally conducted in scholarly and philological detail, remained a parochial, inner-German affair. None of the books and, mainly, articles referred to in this respect in the German edition is available in English. Consequently, all material pertaining exclusively to this past controversy, as well as some other references that refer to exclusively German philological matters, has been omitted.

Chronology of the Relationship

23 June, Frankfurt   In a review in the *Frankfurter Zeitung* of *Gedichte, Lieder und Chansons* by Walter Mehring, WB refers to BB as 'the best chansonnier since Wedekind'.

24 June, Berlin   WB tells Scholem in a letter that his 'very friendly relationship with Brecht' is based 'on the well-grounded interest one is bound to have for his present plans'.

30 August, Berlin   In an article in the *Frankfurter Zeitung* on a conversation he had had with the radio broadcaster Ernst Schoen, WB reports that Schoen has interested BB in working on radio features.

Summer/ Early Autumn, Berlin   Ernst Bloch persuades WB to 'formulate his Brecht-spell'.

18 September, Berlin   WB writes Gershom Scholem that 'not much honour accrues' to *Happy End*.

20 October, Berlin   Première of Karl Kraus's post-war drama *Die Unüberwindlichen* ('The Invincibles') at the Volksbühne. In the 1 November issue of the *Literarische Welt*, WB reviews the play, which initially BB was going to direct at the Theater am Schiffbauerdam.

1930

18 April, Berlin   In a conversation with Siegfried Kracauer WB confesses to being very taken with the recently published first volume of the *Versuche*. He drafts a commentary on it.

25 April, Berlin   WB and BB's plan to 'annihilate Heidegger' in a critical reading-group fails because BB is away.

24 June, Frankfurt   WB gives his radio talk 'Bert Brecht' on Südwestdeutscher Rundfunk.

6 July, Frankfurt   WB's 'From the *Brecht-Commentary*' is published in the *Frankfurter Zeitung*.

September   WB, BB, and Herbert Ihering plan to edit a journal for Rowohlt. In discussing its programme they agree on the social role of intellectuals, develop educational ideas, and devise a catalogue of writing styles. The work is to develop in three stages: 'i) creation of a capitalist pedagogics, ii) creation of a proletarian pedagogics, iii) creation of a classless pedagogics.'

8 September, Berlin   According to Ernst Rowohlt WB, BB and Herbert Ihering are ready to work on the journal, whose general position is moving 'sharply left'.

Autumn, Berlin   BB sees the following as editorial directors of the journal: Herbert Ihering, WB, Bernard von Brentano, and himself.

3 October, Berlin   WB informs Gershom Scholem that he and BB have formulated the principles of *Krise und Kritik* in the course of long mutual discussion. He feels in a position to overcome the 'immanent difficulty of any collaboration with Brecht'.

10 November, Berlin   WB mentions 'current really tumultuous discussion' with BB.

21 November, Berlin   *Krise und Kritik* editorial committee meeting between Ihering, WB and BB.

26 November, Berlin   As on 21 November, between the same members plus Ernst Bloch, Siegfried Kracauer and Gustav Glück.

December, Berlin   In a conversation with BB, WB considers resigning from *Krise und Kritik*.

1931

5–6 February, Berlin   WB tells Scholem that his interest in the situation in Germany does not extend beyond the small circle round Brecht.

6 February, Berlin   The *Man is Man* production at the Gendarmenmarkt Theatre provokes a debate about BB's theory of epic theatre. WB, who was at the first night, defines its principles in his essay 'What is Epic Theatre? (1)'.

13 February, Berlin   *Krise und Kritik* editorial committee meeting at BB's flat, with Ihering, Brentano, Alfred Kurella and Armin Kesser. For the first issue, planned to appear at the end of March, Kesser agrees to reply to Alfred Döblin's pamphlet *Wissen und Verändern*.

Mid February, Berlin   WB resigns as co-editor of *Krise und Kritik*. The first proposed articles gave him substantial cause for concern; they departed from the agreed position; none could claim 'expert authority'. Nevertheless he is ready to collaborate as an author.

March, Frankfurt   WB submits 'What is Epic Theatre?' to the editorial board of the *Frankfurter Zeitung*. The article is accepted, and then in the Summer rejected.

3 March, Berlin   An agency report in the newspaper *Tempo* announces the new journal *Krise und Kritik*. It is to appear in Berlin, published by Rowohlt, from 1 April, edited by Herbert Ihering in collaboration with BB and Brentano.

7 March, Berlin   Images from the Schauspielhaus production of *Man is Man* come to WB while he is experimenting with hashish.

11 March, Berlin   BB announces at a press conference that he is going to edit a journal with Herbert Ihering under the title *Krise und Kritik* whose main focus will be critical.

23 March, Berlin   *Krise und Kritik* editorial committee meeting with BB, Ihering, Brentano and Kesser. The journal is now due to appear on 1 October, with a deadline of 15 September.

3 June, Le Lavandou (France)   WB visits BB and his circle: Elisabeth Hauptmann, subsequently to be replaced by Carola Neher, Margot and Bernard von Brentano, Marie Grossmann, and Emil Hesse-Burri – plus Lotte Lenya and Kurt Weill from St Tropez. Collective work is done on *St Joan of the Stockyards*. Conversation about Trotsky who, according to WB, BB thinks is the greatest living European writer.

6 June, Le Lavandou   BB, who appears to be 'devouring' *The Great Wall of China*, which has just appeared posthumously, surprises WB by his 'overall positive attitude to Kafka's work'. In a conversation with WB, BB announces that Kafka is a 'prophetic writer'.

8 June, Le Lavandou   Lively discussion between BB and WB on the difference between living and inhabiting (*das Wohnen*), in the course of which they try to develop a 'typology' of different kinds of habitation.

11 June, Le Lavandou   In conversation with WB and Wilhelm and Marie Speyer, Brecht talks about his childhood.

12 June, Le Lavandou   Discussion as to whether there is now a revolutionary situation in Germany; BB confesses to being shocked by his conviction that one will still have to wait years for it.

15 June, Le Lavandou   WB, BB and Carola Neher drive to Marseilles with the Brentanos; the Brentanos go on to Paris with WB; BB returns to Le Lavandou with Carola Neher. Discussions about epic theatre, Strindberg, Georg Kaiser and Shakespeare.

9 August, Frankfurt   In his review of Heinz Kindermann's *Das literarische Antlitz der Gegenwart*, WB refers to BB, Kafka, Paul Scheerbart and Döblin as authors in whom the most important characteristics of contemporary literature are discernible – the fusion of great poetic achievement with that of an ordinary writer.

September/October, Berlin   In his 'Little History of Photography' (published in the *Literarische Welt*) WB quotes from BB's as yet unpublished '*Threepenny Opera* Trial'.

1932

5 February, Berlin   WB's article 'A Family Drama in the Epic Theatre' appears in the *Literarische Welt* on the occasion of the world première of BB's *The Mother*. WB begins by quoting from BB: 'Brecht has said of communism that it is 'the middle term'. 'Communism is not radical. It is capitalism that is radical.'

July, Leipzig   WB's 'Theater und Radio', as well as BB's 'The Radio as a Communications Apparatus' appear in the *Blätter des Hessischen Landestheater Darmstadt* (special number on theatre and radio).

Autumn, Frankfurt   In a discussion on literature against war between Joseph Roth, Friedrich T. Gubler (from the *Frankfurter Zeitung*) and Soma Morgenstern, WB expresses the view that the influence of anti-war novels is exaggerated, and that a poem like BB's 'Legend of the Dead Soldier' is more effective.

1933

25 February, Cologne   The *Kölnische Zeitung* prints WB's 'Short Shadows II'; in the section 'To Live without Leaving Traces' in it, WB quotes 'a neat phrase', 'Erase the traces!', from Brecht's *A Reader For Those Who Live In Cities*.

28 February, Berlin   BB emigrates, initially to Prague.

17 March, Berlin   WB emigrates to Paris.

4 April, Paris   Brentano brings greetings from BB to WB.

19 April, San Antonio (Ibiza)   WB refers to Brecht's poetic cycle *Die drei Soldaten* ('a children's book') as 'an enormously provocative and simultaneously an outstandingly successful work'.

29 September, Sanary-sur-Mer   Eva Boy van Hoboken, BB and Arnold Zweig ask on a picture postcard about WB's plans for the winter. BB asks if he is coming to Paris.

20 October, Paris   WB refers to his agreement with BB's output as 'one of the most important and strongest elements' of his whole position.

End of October / beginning of November, Paris   WB, BB and Margarete Steffin stay in the Palace Hotel, Rue du Four. There are daily, often long, meetings. Discussion on the theory of the crime novel gives rise to a plan to write one together. A plot is devised and motives established. WB gets to know BB's *Threepenny Novel*. Steffin completes the typescript of WB's *German Men and Women* for him.

12 November, Paris   In the Deux Magots restaurant, Hermann Kesten reads WB, BB, Klaus Mann, Siegfried Kracauer and André Germain his review of Heinrich Mann's polemic against Hitler, *Der Haß*.

Beginning of December, Paris   Through the Dutch painter Anna Maria Blaupot ten Cate, WB offers BB's plays to the Stedelijk Theater in Amsterdam.

7 December, Paris   WB makes plans to have his library moved from Berlin to BB's home in Denmark.

19 December, Paris   BB and Margarete Steffin leave for Denmark.

30 December, Paris   WB is invited to Denmark by BB. He writes to Gretel Karplus that he dreads the Danish winter, 'and having to rely completely on one person in Denmark, which can very easily become another form of loneliness', and having also to rely on a language he doesn't know at all.

30 December, Paris   In a letter to Gershom Scholem WB says that Paris is like a dead city for him after BB's departure.

1934

15 January, Paris   WB attends a meeting about the cover for Brecht's volume *Lieder Gedichte Chöre*. Elisabeth Hauptmann advises BB to make corrections to the volume only via WB.

5 March, Paris   WB plans a series of lectures on 'L'avant-garde allemande' in which each subject – the novel, the essay, the theatre and journalism – is explained through one representative figure: Kafka, Ernst Bloch, BB and Karl Kraus.

15 March, Skovsbostrand (Denmark)   WB's books arrive.

28 April, Paris   WB plans to deliver his essay 'The Author as Producer', written in 1931, as a lecture at the Institute for Research into Fascism. He considers it analogous to the essay 'What is Epic Theatre? (1)', respectively for literature and the theatre.

4 May, Skovsbostrand   BB tells WB in a letter that WB's essay 'The Present Social Situation of the French Writer' reads 'splendidly and says more than a good 400-page book'. BB reinvites WB to Denmark.

6 May, Paris   WB reads the manuscript of BB's *Roundheads and Pointed Heads* with pleasure.

21 May, Paris   WB tells BB in a letter that he considers *Roundheads* 'uncommonly important and a complete success'.

Beginning of June, Paris   In a response to a concerned inquiry from Gretel Karplus, WB says in a letter to her that his relationship with Brecht belongs to one of the few in his life which have made it possible for him to maintain some kind of pole to set 'in opposition against his original self'. WB begs his friends to trust that these ties, however obvious their dangers, will bear out their fruitfulness. His life, he writes, like his thought, moves from one extreme to another; he wants to bring things and thoughts considered incompatible together.

20 June, Skovsbostrand   WB arrives in Denmark and lodges with Frau Raahange, immediately next door to BB. He follows closely the completion of the *Threepenny Novel*. Hanns Eisler arrives on 5 July and plays through the music he has composed for *Roundheads and Pointed Heads*.

3 July, Svendborg (Denmark)   WB visits BB, in hospital with a kidney problem since mid June. They have a detailed discussion on WB's 'Author as Producer' essay. BB counts himself among the high bourgeois writers who, like the proletariat, have an interest in the development of their means of production.

5 July, Svendborg   Conversation about Kafka, about whom BB says that he foresaw certain forms of alienation that arise as a result of humans' coexisting, 'i.e. GPU methods'. BB distinguishes between two literary types: the earnest 'visionary' and the not wholly earnest 'level-head', under which type he counts himself.

4 August, Skovsbostrand   Conversation about Kafka between WB, BB and Hanns Eisler.

29 August, Skovsbostrand   Long and spirited debate about WB's Kafka essay, which Brecht accuses of encouraging 'Jewish fascism' and increasing the obscurity surrounding Kafka instead of dispelling it.

19 September, Dragør (Denmark)   WB visits BB and family, and Karl Korsch. Joint work, possibly on a prose satire around Giacomo Ui (*Wenige wissen heute*), or on a didactic philosophical poem.

28 September, St Louis, Missouri   Elisabeth Hauptmann tells BB in a letter that WB regards *Roundheads and Pointed Heads* as well structured and opportune for the bourgeois theatre.

2 October, Skovsbostrand   WB returns from meeting Gretel Karplus in Dragør and Gedser.

3 October, Skovsbostrand   BB leaves for London. His last talks with WB concern, inter alia, Hasek and Dostoyevsky.

20 October, Skovsbostrand   WB goes via Paris to Nice.

26 December, San Remo, Italy   WB works on his review of BB's *Threepenny Novel*.

1935

7 January, San Remo   WB tells Theodor Adorno in a letter that he feels *The Threepenny Novel* 'is a consummate success'. In a letter to BB he refers to it as 'highly durable'.

6 February, Skovsbostrand   Helene Weigel sends WB reviews of *The Threepenny Novel*. BB urges WB to hurry up with his own review, which Elisabeth Hauptmann is awaiting to send to America.

26 February, San Remo   WB writes to Gustav Glück telling him he cannot go to Denmark because of a meeting in Paris with members of the Institute for the Study of Fascism.

February / March, San Remo   WB tells Asja Lacis in a letter that his *Threepenny Novel* review will appear in April: 'I think the book will take its place in world literature alongside Swift.'

March / April, Amsterdam   Klaus Mann returns WB's *Threepenny Novel* review, already set up in print for *Die Sammlung*, because he refuses the fee asked for by WB.

20 May, Paris   WB asks BB for help with the publication of his *Threepenny Novel* review. His judgement of BB's 'Five Difficulties in Writing the Truth': [it has] 'the dryness and therefore the preservative qualities of an out-and-out classic work'.

20 May, Oxford   In a letter about WB's *Arcades Project*, Adorno warns that he would 'believe it to be a real misfortune if Brecht were to acquire any influence upon this work'.

25 May, Paris   WB points out to Werner Kraft that BB's 'Five Difficulties in Writing the Truth' 'is a classic piece, and the first perfect example of theoretical prose I know from him'.

6 June, Prague   Wieland Herzfelde tells BB about a very interesting, fairly lengthy conversation with WB in Paris over art historical and theoretical questions, about which they to a greater extent agreed.

16 June, Paris   BB arrives with the Danish writer Karin Michaelis to take part in the International Writers Conference for the Defence of Culture. For WB who meets them at the Gare du Nord, seeing Brecht is the most enjoyable – virtually the only enjoyable – aspect of the whole conference.

June, Paris   BB asks Lisa Tetzner to look for a Swiss publisher for WB's *German Men and Women* – which he refers to as 'a very flattering collection for Germany'.

15 September, Thurø (Denmark)   Margarete Steffin tells WB about BB's work and plans. She begs him to try to get BB's article 'Alienation Effects in Chinese Acting' published in France.

Beginning of October, Paris   WB calls 'Alienation Effects in Chinese Acting' 'an excellent piece' and the *Lehrstück Horatians and Curiatians* 'the most perfect of its kind'.

16 October, Copenhagen   Steffin asks WB if he would write a foreword to a collection of BB aphorisms, and asks him for advice on what texts about BB should be included in a publicity leaflet for the Malik edition of BB's collected works.

28 October, Paris   WB interprets the *Horatians* play as 'an outstanding implementation of certain techniques of Chinese theatre'.

1936

Replying to a remark by Werner Haft about BB and Heine, WB replies that for Brecht you must look towards a hitherto little explored tradition, in Bavarian folk poetry and in the didactic and parable sermons of the South German Baroque.

April, London In a letter to WB, BB expresses himself 'enthusiastic' about his essay 'Problems in the Sociology of Language', pointed out to him by Korsch: 'It's written in a grand style, it gives a broad view of the material, and shows that present-day scholarship should be approached with reserve. That's just how a new encyclopaedia should be approached with reserve. That's just how a new encyclopaedia should be written.' BB invites WB for the Summer.

28 May, Paris WB writes to tell Margarete Steffin in London that he sets much store by publishing the German version of his 'Work of Art' essay in *Das Wort*.

20 July, London BB asks the French publisher Éditions Sociales Internationales to discuss a new translation of *The Threepenny Novel* with his friend WB.

28 July, London BB and Margarete Steffin return to Skovsbostrand.

3 August, Skovsbostrand WB arrives at BB's. Revision of the 'Work of Art' essay, whose reception by BB 'is not without resistance, even clashes'. A week later WB reports thus on the project: 'But it was all very fruitful and led to several remarkable improvements, without in the least affecting the works's essence. The length must have grown by about a quarter.'

9 August, Skovsbostrand WB and BB ask Willi Bredel, co-editor of *Das Wort*, for an extension of the deadline for the manuscript of WB's 'Paris Letter'. Time had been lost writing 'The Work of Art in the Age of its Technological Reproducibility', in which BB had been engaged.

13 August, Skovsbostrand WB asks the Swiss theologian Fritz Lieb for a copy of Lieb's essay 'The Bible Message and Karl Marx', because he sets much store on introducing it to BB.

5 September, Skovsbostrand WB writes to Willi Bredel to say that it is Brecht's special wish 'that the title of "Paris Letter" is preserved'. When WB received this commission Brecht told him that 'he was particularly attached to the classic literary genre of the "Letter" report'. In a postscript BB himself added: 'the Paris essay is simply written as a letter and therefore quite informal in composition' – it was good for the journal regularly to have such letters.

Mid September, Skovsbostrand WB goes via Paris to San Remo.

4 November, Paris WB sends Margarete Steffin his *German Men and Women*, and asks if the editors of *Das Wort* had yet given an opinion on the 'Work of Art' essay, whose publication there was supported by BB.

Beginning of December, Skovsbostrand   BB urges WB to write another 'Paris Letter'. He still has no news from *Das Wort* on the acceptance of the 'Work of Art' essay. He asks for a copy of André Gide's *Return to the USSR* as well as news of its reception.

12 December, Paris   WB tells Steffin that 'party members'' shock' over Gide's book knows no bounds. He would send a copy.

1937

Beginning of March, Skovsbostrand   In a letter to the American set designer Max Gorelik, Brecht lists WB's 'Work of Art' essay among works to be collected by the Diderot Society.

22 March, Svendborg   Margarete Steffin asks WB to pass on BB's suggestion for the foundation of a Diderot Society to Jean Renoir and Léon Moussignac.

28 March, Moscow   Willi Bredel informs WB that *Das Wort* wants 'for the moment to distance itself' from the publication of the 'Work of Art' essay; because of its great length it could only be done in instalments, which would be a pity.

29 March, Paris   Letter from WB to BB to say that a new French translator has been found for *The Threepenny Novel*. He pronounces the call for the foundation of a Diderot Society 'excellent', but doubts if French readers would be able to obtain access to the founding principles. WB reports his finishing the Edvard Fuchs essay and his discovery of Carl Gustav Jochmann.

9 April, Svendborg   Letter from Steffin to WB to say that BB 'will in no circumstances let his Jochmann article escape from *Das Wort* and its famous cultural heritage'. He would understand if WB, after his miserable experiences with the editorial board, were disinclined to send anything else, and he fears WB will associate him, BB, with the board's sloppiness, but BB never writes to them without reminding them to write to WB.

April/May, Skovsbostrand   BB asks WB about the Paris cabaret Die Laterne, where Helene Weigel might one day play.

BB writes a letter (probably unsent) about Benjamin's Fuchs essay: 'There's not a bit of ornament, but the whole piece is graceful (in the good old-fashioned sense), and the spiral is never prolonged by a mirror. You always stick to your subject, or else the subject sticks to you.'

3 July, Moscow   Fritz Erpenbeck, for the editorial board of *Das Wort*, returns WB's *Threepenny Novel* essay: too much time has elapsed since the book's publication.

Around 12 September, Paris   BB and Helene Weigel arrive in Paris.

September, Paris WB visits rehearsals of *The Threepenny Opera* at the Théâtre de l'Étoile, co-directed by Brecht. Under the influence of the first night on 28 September, or early in October, WB writes a French text on the play's sources and characters.

October, Paris BB directs *Frau Carrar's Rifles* in the Salle Adyar, with Helene Weigel in the title role. WB introduces BB to Fritz Lieb at the first night.

WB plans to be in Denmark for Christmas, also to fetch his books.

6 October, Paris The writer Jean Cassou, editor of the journal *Europe*, asks WB for a note on *The Threepenny Opera* production.

3 November, Vienna Helene Weigel tells WB she is coming to Paris on 12 November and asks if he will have time for her.

November/December On behalf of BB, Steffin asks WB for two essays on the occasion of the publication by Malik of Brecht's *Gesammelte Werke* – one on the great characters in Brecht's plays (from Kragler – *Drums in the Night* – through Galy Gay, Peachum and so forth, to Callas in *Roundhead*) – and a second on the great plots.

9 December, Moscow Fritz Erpenbeck asks WB to review BB's *Gesammelte Werke* for *Das Wort*.

1938

1 February, Svendborg Margarete Steffin repeats BB's wish for WB essays on BB's characters and plots.

February/March, Skovsbostrand/Moscow BB and Erpenbeck repeatedly press WB to write about Brecht's volumes of plays, or at least to say something definitive about the suggestion to write about them.

12 March, Skovsbostrand BB asks WB if his review of Anna Seghers's novel *Die Rettung* ('The Rescue') wouldn't be suitable for *Das Wort*.

May, Paris Helene Weigel attends rehearsals for seven scenes of *Fear and Misery in the Third Reich* (current title: *99%. Images from the Third Reich*). WB greets her with tulips and collects from her everything he can of new material by BB. He is enthusiastic about BB's 'Lao-Tsû poem'. The director Slatan Dudow bans all guests from rehearsals.

21–22 May, Paris WB attends rehearsals of *99%* in the Salle d'Iéna.

30 May, Skovsbostrand Steffin tells WB in a letter that BB asked him to write something about the production 'so that he can hear an expert verdict'. Asked by the Danish police about WB's planned stay there, BB says that no long-term decision has been made, but he reckons on about two months – 'it is an ordinary holiday visit concerning nothing in particular'.

22 June, Skovsbostrand WB arrives at BB's and takes a room in the neighbourhood with an orchard owner called Thomsen. He makes notes on subjects for discussion: Virgil and Dante, Marxism and its interpretation, the dying-out of the state, and Soviet literature.

29 June, Skovsbostrand Discussions between WB and BB on epic theatre, logical positivism, and the 'purges' in the Soviet Union.

30 June, Prague / Zürich / Paris Under the title 'Brecht's One Act Plays' the *Neue Weltbühne* publishes WB's review of 99%.

1 July, Skovsbostrand Renewed discussions about political persecutions in the Soviet Union and the disappearance of Ernst Ottwalt. Margarete Steffin reckons Tretyakov may well not still be alive.

3 July, Skovsbostrand Discussion about Baudelaire.

20 July, Skovsbostrand In a letter to Kitty Marx-Steinschneider WB writes that he must, for all his friendship with BB, be careful to carry out his work on him in total isolation. His work contains 'quite particular elements' which BB will not be able to assimilate. BB recognizes the line now promoted by Soviet theoreticians 'as a catastrophe for everything we've committed ourselves to for 20 years'.

21 July, Skovsbostrand WB notes down BB's opinions on the publications of party theoreticians like Lukács and Kurella, on armaments in the Soviet economy, and on Marx's and Engels's relations with the working-class movement. A BB sentence: 'Personal rule reigns in Russia.'

24 July, Skovsbostrand Discussion on BB's poem 'Der Bauer und seine Oxen', on his attitude to Stalin, on Trotsky, whose writings prove that there is suspicion enough for a sceptical view of Russian things. Should that suspicion one day be justified, said BB, 'one must fight the regime – and, what's more, do so openly'. However, 'unfortunately or thank God', the suspicion is not yet certain. Renewed discussions about Lukács, Andor Gabor, Kurella, on Marx's writings, Goethe's *Elective Affinities* and on Anna Seghers.

25 July, Skovsbostrand BB notes that WB's Baudelaire studies are 'useful to read', but he criticizes the concept of aura as 'pretty gruesome mystique'.

28 July, Skovsbostrand BB challenges the editorial board of *Das Wort* to confirm WB's contract, evidently for his 'Commentary on Poems by Brecht'.

29 July, Skovsbostrand BB reads WB 'several polemical exchanges with Lukács' and asks if he should publish his own 'disguised yet vehement attacks'. These are 'questions of power' says BB. He himself has 'no friends' in Moscow, and 'the Muscovites themselves don't have them either – like the dead'. Discussion about fascism, provoked by the question whether BB's 'Children's Songs' should be included in *Gedichte aus dem Exil* (provisional title for the *Svendborg Poems*). At this point in the conversation WB 'felt moved by a power' in BB 'that was strong enough to be a match for fascism'.

Beginning of August, Skovsbostrand   BB says that in Russia a dictatorship rules over the proletariat. WB compares the organism of what BB calls the so-called 'worker-monarchies' with 'grotesque natural phenomenon', like the emergence of 'horned fish or other monsters of the deep'.

3 August, Skovsbostrand   In a letter to Max Horkheimer, WB describes his and BB's attitude to the Soviet Union, which is *still* an 'agent of our interest in the coming war', albeit – because of its victims – 'the most costly imaginable'. BB does not ignore the fact that the present Russian regime with all its horrors is the most arbitrary, without any justification, and that BB's friend and translator Tretyakov has probably been executed.

13 August, Skovsbostrand   In his *Journal* BB comments on WB's statement that Freud thinks sexuality will one day die out completely.

End of August, Skovsbostrand   WB changes address because children's noise disturbs his work. 'There are in fact no comfortable living possibilities here,' he writes to Gretel and Theodor Adorno.

Mid September, Copenhagen   WB spends ten days in Copenhagen organizing a manuscript of his Baudelaire studies. On 29 September he returns to Skovsbostrand.

End of September, Skovsbostrand   Fritz Sternberg comes to visit BB for a week.

4 October, Skovsbostrand   Letter from WB to Adorno: 'The more natural and relaxed my contact with Brecht has been this past summer, the less equitable I am about leaving him behind this time. For I can see an index of his growing isolation in our communication.' In this isolation WB recognizes 'the consequence of the loyalty to what we have in common'. He has seen almost nothing of BB's *Caesar*, because almost any kind of reading was impossible while working.

About 16 October, Skovsbostrand   WB leaves Denmark. Just before, he had got ready 'the several hundred books' kept at BB's for carriage to Paris.

6–8 November, Jerusalem   Scholem reports to WB on his journey to the USA; the members of the Institute for Social Research are 'keen and very outspoken anti-Stalinists', and he 'found not a good word to be heard said' about BB.

December, Svendborg Margarete Steffin tells WB that she wants to make a copy of BB's Caesar novel for him. Following which she asks WB to write to BB in detail.

12 December, Skovsbostrand BB is very interested in why the Institute for Social Research rejected WB's Baudelaire. Steffin writes to WB: 'Brecht sends his heartfelt greetings – he's eagerly awaiting your work on his poetry volume!' (i.e. *Svendborg Poems* and WB's 'Commentary').

1939

February, Skovsbostrand BB asks WB about Margarete Steffin, and if part of the rejected Baudelaire is suitable for *Das Wort* – 'that would be really good and interesting'.

26 February, Skovsbostrand BB notes that 'Benjamin and Sternberg, very highly qualified intellectuals, did not understand [the Caesar novel] and made pressing recommendations for more human interest to be put in, more of the old novel!'

20 March, Paris WB sends BB and Steffin his 'Commentary on Poems by Brecht' to forward to *Das Wort*. He considers the 'commentary' unfinished, but cannot get down to its planned completion in the immediate future. WB thanks BB for the offer to contact *Das Wort* about the Baudelaire studies, but cannot accept it because a new version of one section of it is supposed to appear in the *Zeitschrift für Sozialforschung*.

End of March, Paris WB is among those who receive stereotypes of the proofs of BB's *Life of Galileo*.

23 April, Basel The *Schweizer Zeitung am Sonntag* publishes BB's 'Legend of the Origin of the book *Tao-tê-Ching* on Lao-Tsû's Road into Exile' (first publication), with WB's commentary, in the same edition as Fritz Lieb's resistance article, 'Warum wir schießen müssen'.

3 May, Paris WB tells Lieb in a letter how very pleased he was by the appearance of the 'Lao-Tsû' poem and his commentary. He asks for confirmation that the main aim of such a publication must be 'to see that it gets into the hands of the right people – that's what I intend'.

Mid May, Pontigny (France) During a stay in the study centre in a Cistercian abbey in Burgundy, WB arranges for German and Austrian members of the International Brigades who had fought in the Spanish Civil War to act in scenes from BB's *Fear and Misery in the Third Reich*.

Mid May, Lidingö (Sweden) Steffin reports BB's enormous pleasure at seeing WB's beautiful commentary to his poem, and that it was published in Lieb's newspaper also pleased him.

Mid June, Paris   WB asks BB to send his 'Commentary to Poems by Brecht' to *International Literature*, Moscow; it was difficult to act on his own behalf.

Mid June, Zürich   The journal *Maß und Wert* publishes 'What is the Epic Theatre?(2)' anonymously in its July/August number, alongside an essay by its editor, Ferdinand Lion, based on an uncompleted dialogue with WB, which rejected Brecht; the number also contains the 'Sermon on the Mount' scene from *Fear and Misery in the Third Reich*.

22 June, Lidingö   BB doubts if the outcome would be entirely happy if he committed himself to the publication of WB's commentary to his poems. He's prepared to do it, but he did not have any success 'even with his own' journal (*Das Wort*). Margarete Steffin writes: 'Brecht smiled wanly when he heard that you expected anything could come from his recommendation.' She asks if WB had received the *Svendborg Poems* volume and what he thought of it.

August, Lidingö   Steffin admits to WB that 'to be *honest*' she did not like the essay 'What is the Epic Theatre ?(2)' in *Maß und Wert*, and neither did other friends – which could only mean BB and Weigel.

16 August, Küsnacht (Switzerland)   Bernard von Brentano writes in a letter that WB, whom he had met in Paris, was in a bad way, and that he hadn't been able to help him. 'Despite his material misery I found him as fresh and lively as ever. What asses those people at *Maß und Wert* are not to make continuous use of such a mind as that.'

4 September, Paris   France having declared war on Germany the day before, WB, like many other emigrants, is interned, at first in the Stade Colombes in Paris, then in a camp in Nevers.

1940

Spring, Paris   In connection with his theses 'On the Concept of History' WB repeatedly quotes texts by Brecht. He intends to send Brecht a copy.

5 May, Paris   WB tells Stephan Lackner that he is seized with unease when thinking of Brecht.

14 June, Paris   Just before Paris is occupied by German troops WB leaves town with his sister Dora.

June, Helsinki   BB asks Fritz Lieb about WB; he has 'heard nothing from our friend Walter since the previous summer'.

22 September, Basel   Lieb writes to WB that BB in Finland is asking after him; the postcard does not reach its destination.

26 September, Port Bou (Spain)   WB takes a lethal dose of morphine in a hotel in this Spanish border town.

1941

August, Santa Monica, California   Günther Anders brings BB, just arrived in the USA, the news of WB's death. BB reads 'On the Concept of History' and feels that 'the little treatise' might have been written after reading his Caesar novel. He calls the theses 'lucid and clarifying (despite all the metaphor and Judaism)': one thinks 'with horror about how few people there are ready even at least to misunderstand something like this'.

In memory of WB, BB writes the following poems: 'Casualty List', 'Where is Benjamin, the Critic?', 'To Walter Benjamin, Who Killed Himself Fleeing from Hitler' and 'On the Suicide of the Refugee Walter Benjamin'.

1942

August, Los Angeles   In a conversation with Adorno BB speaks of WB as 'his best critic'.

Los Angeles   BB and Soma Morgenstern 'often speak about Walter Benjamin', of whom – as Morgenstern reports – 'he speaks no ill – rather of me'.

11 February, Los Angeles   Max Horkheimer suggests to Leo Löwenthal that, in the planned Institute for Social Research memorial volume for WB, perhaps a couple of pages of BB could be included: 'You know that Brecht was an intimate friend of Benjamin.'

1946

15 October, New York   Hannah Arendt tells BB about a plan for an English-language edition of works by Benjamin to be published by Schocken Books, New York. She asks him for suggestions, an essay on WB and the manuscript of 'Conversations with Brecht', which Brecht had previously shown to Heinrich Blücher.

1948

April, Zürich   BB writes to the theologian Karl Thieme that he has heard that WB recited the Lao-Tsû poem several times by heart in French internment camps. 'But he himself found no frontier guard to let him pass.'

1955

Summer, Berlin   In a conversation between BB, Werner Kraft and Peter Huchel, talk turns to the literary estates of Georg Heym and WB. BB showed 'profound interest in both and expressed the wish they be published, no matter whether in West or East'.

Time chart and map of Benjamin's and Brecht's main locations in Europe

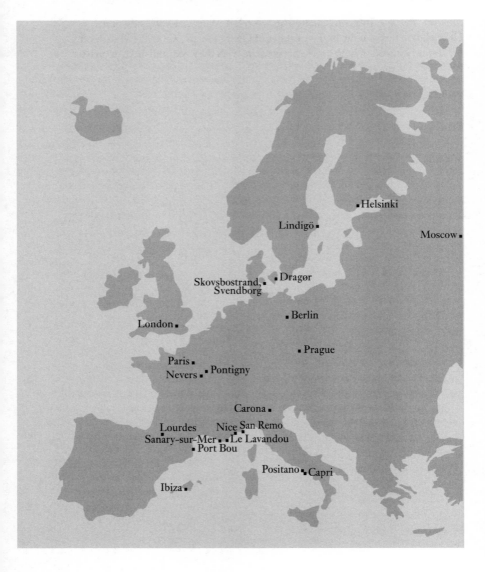

	Bertolt Brecht	Walter Benjamin
1924 Summer	Positano	Capri
1926 November	Berlin	
		Moscow
1927		Berlin
1929–30	Berlin	
1931 Summer	Le Lavandou	
1933	Prague	Paris
	Vienna	Ibiza
	Carona	
	Sanary-sur-Mer	
October–December	Paris	
	Skovsbostrand	Paris
1934 June–October	Skovsbostrand & Dragør	
	London	Paris & San Remo
	Skovsbostrand	
1935	Moscow	
	Skovsbostrand	
June	Paris	
	New York*	Paris
1936	Skovsbostrand	
	London	
August–September	Skovsbostrand	
		San Remo & Paris
1937 September–October	Paris	
	Skovsbostrand	Paris
1938 June–October	Skovsbostrand	
		Paris
1939	Lidingö, Sweden	
		Pontigny, Burgundy
		Nevers (internment camp)
1940	Helsinki (Marlebäck)	Paris
		Port Bou via Lourdes upon fall of Paris
September		Death

* Brecht was in New York from October 1935 to February 1936

I
A Significant Constellation

May 1929

'I have made some noteworthy acquaintances,' Walter Benjamin wrote on 6 June 1929 from Berlin to his friend Gershom Scholem in Jerusalem. 'To name one, a close acquaintance with Brecht (about whom and about which there is much to be said). To name two, an acquaintance with Polgar, who is now part of Hessel's intimate circle.'[1] This was the first hint of a friendship which, in the years that followed, many of Benjamin's friends and associates were to find disturbing. In his next letter, two and a half weeks later, Benjamin gave his correspondent some indication of what he had to say about Brecht – he had apparently forgotten his earlier letter:

> You will be interested to know that a very friendly relationship between Bert Brecht and me has recently developed, based less upon what he has produced (I know only *The Threepenny Opera* and his ballads), than on the well-founded interest one must take in his present plans.[2]

For Scholem, who had been a friend of Benjamin since 1915 and a regular correspondent of his since his own emigration to Palestine in 1923, this news could only be a fresh source of danger to a plan for which he himself had smoothed the way. Since 1927 Benjamin had been contemplating the idea of an extended stay in Jerusalem as a language teacher, with a view to finding out whether there were any prospects for him in the humanities faculty of the Hebrew University there. It was only in May 1929, precisely at the time he was getting to know Brecht, that he began to take Hebrew lessons in Berlin, thanks to a grant Scholem had obtained for him from the University of Jerusalem. However, he gave them up after only two months. He kept finding new reasons to delay his journey: work projects which could not be interrupted, such as his *Arcades Project*, and finally the demoralizing process of his divorce from his wife, Dora, and his hopes for a future with Asja Lacis who, however, was never able to make a commitment to him. Scholem's expectation that his friend would become geographically as well as intellectually close to him was finally destroyed when Benjamin told him on 20 January 1930 that his aim was to 'be considered the foremost critic of German literature.'* It would certainly not be

---

* See Scholem, *Benjamin*, pp. 137ff. for the background. For the letter see *Benjamin Correspondence*, p. 359. Significantly, this letter about Benjamin's plans to give up learning Hebrew and turn to German literature was written in French. Scholem entitled the chapter in Scholem, *Benjamin* on Benjamin's Jerusalem plans 'The Failed Project'.

wrong to see this statement in the context of Benjamin's meeting with Brecht. Brecht's texts and programmatic statements, his whole field of activity in fact, represented the strongest challenge Benjamin had ever faced, and gave him the opportunity to concentrate on a major focus of his work up to that time. Political developments, however, naturally hindered his plans. In the years leading up to the seizure of power by the Nazi Party, the platform opening up new fields of cultural research in Germany's Weimar Republic was narrowing into a defensive bastion. 'I cannot expect much of the German situation,' wrote Benjamin to Scholem in February 1931. 'My interest in it does not go beyond the fate of the small circle around Brecht.'[3]

Such was the statement of a critic whose stature was recognized not only by the initiated. Hannah Arendt disagreed with Scholem's view that Benjamin had been 'the subject of an esoteric whispering campaign' on the part of his friends. To her, Benjamin's reputation appeared more solid, 'even more solid than the aura created around his name by Benjamin himself and his tendency towards mystery-mongering'.[4] Admittedly, between 1933 and 1955, when the first collection of his writings was published in Germany, his name, as Scholem remarked, was 'as thoroughly forgotten as any in the intellectual world'.[5] Before that time he had been known, at least among the educated public, as an academic, critic, writer and writer for radio. Benjamin's books and translations, his essays and reviews in the fields of German and French literature, literary studies, philosophy and other works, written since the failure of his plans to qualify as a university lecturer in July 1925, were published during the Weimar Republic by publishers, magazines, journals and newspaper arts sections whose status testified to their quality. Among these were the publishing companies Rowohlt, Piper, Kiepenheuer, and such established periodicals and newspapers as *Die Literarische Welt*, the *Frankfurter Zeitung*, the *Weltbühne*, the *Berliner Börsen-Courier*, the *Neue Rundschau*, *Das Tagebuch*, *Die Gesellschaft*, and *Der Querschnitt*. His lectures and radio features were broadcast by the Funkstunde Berlin and Südwestdeutscher Rundfunk in Frankfurt. Benjamin had thereby at least come fairly close to achieving his ambition to become recognized as the foremost critic of German literature; in 1933, according to his wife Dora, he had been described as 'the best living writer in the German language' by editors, 'but', she added, 'only those editors who happen to be Jewish'.* Contemporary reactions

---

* Dora Sophie Benjamin to Scholem, 29 November 1933, in Benjamin/Scholem, p. 89. She referred to the same conversation in her statement that, at a gathering, the prevailing opinion was that Benjamin wrote 'the best German of all persons living' (Dora Sophie Benjamin to Walter Benjamin, 7 December 1933 (WBA 17/05), in Geret Luhr (ed.): 'was noch begraben lag' in *Zu Walter Benjamins Exil. Briefe und Dokumente* (Berlin, 2000, p. 37)).

confirm that his opinions were respected.* Hermann Hesse was among the readers who were impressed by Benjamin's style. His comment on *One-Way Street*, one of many such tributes bestowed on its author, was used by Rowohlt Verlag for publicity purposes: 'In the midst of the gloom and ignorance seemingly characteristic of our recent literature, I was surprised and delighted to encounter something as intense, composed, lucid and clear-sighted as Walter Benjamin's *One-Way Street*.'†

Such understanding was not always extended to Benjamin's writings, as was shown above all by reactions to his book *The Origin of German Tragic Drama*, like *One-Way Street* published by Rowohlt.‡ 'Benjamin was an outsider in a dual sense,' Scholem later appositely remarked, 'in regard to scholarship (which in large measure he has remained to this day) and in regard to the literary scene.'[6] Benjamin's sense that he was approaching a turning point in his life, which had made the idea of a future in Palestine positively attractive, was based on his impression that he was not rooted in any one of his spheres of activity. Conscious of this, early in 1928 Benjamin referred to his study of

* Three examples: first, the view of Benjamin's work expressed by the translator Richard Peters was certainly not an isolated one. On 18 May 1928, Benjamin had reviewed Peters's German edition of Leopardi's *Pensieri* in the *Literarische Welt*, criticizing the fact that Peters had not referred to a more recent translation by Gustav Glück and Alois Trost. In a letter published by the *Literarische Welt*, together with Benjamin's response, Peters wrote that Benjamin's criticism was 'all the more painful for me, because I retain, as always, the greatest possible admiration for you personally as well as for your literary achievements' (*GS* III, p. 120). Second, the *Literarische Welt*'s esteem for its author could be seen, for example, in an editorial comment on a partial publication of Benjamin's article on Goethe for the 'Great Soviet Encyclopedia', in its issue of 7 December 1928 (see *SW*, vol. 2, pp. 161–87 for this text). This (partial) version, on Goethe's politics and attitude to nature, represented 'in our opinion the most intelligent and thorough analysis we have ever read of this problematic, decisively important as it is for German intellectual history – and expressed in the most concentrated form'. Finally, Max Rychner, the editor of the *Neue Schweizer Rundschau*, in its February 1931 edition referred to Benjamin as a 'critic of high intellectual status'.

† *Die Literarische Welt*, 1 June 1928, quoted here from the facsimile in Brodersen, *A Biography*, p. 147. Benjamin commented drily: 'Since we are speaking of such voices, I would like to tell you that Hermann Hesse commented in a very friendly, specific and unprompted manner on *One-Way Street*. This one swallow – nebbich (poor thing) – *is* already summer for us' (Benjamin to Siegfried Kracauer, *GB* III, 2 May 1928, p. 372).

‡ Significantly, Hans Heinrich Schaeder, an Orientalist, and Werner Milch, a critic on the popular daily, the *Berliner Abendblatt*, both wrote disapprovingly, the former recommending both books 'to all adherents of the intellectual outsider', and the latter referring to the *Tragedy* book as 'altogether personal scholasticism, obscure to the point of incomprehensibility', and Milch 'recommending' both books 'to all lovers of clever outsiderism' (Scholem, *Benjamin*, pp. 148 and 154). It is interesting that approval and disapproval were based on similar grounds; the perceptions coincided, but were differently interpreted.

Baroque drama, which had met with a lack of understanding at the University of Frankfurt, as the conclusion of his work in the field of German studies. *One-Way Street* was to conclude a 'cycle of production' in which he also included his *Arcades Project*. This could be designated the literary or creative area.[7]

Hannah Arendt called Benjamin an '*homme de lettres* whose home was a library that had been gathered with extreme care'.[8] He was a collector who for years had not needed to make a living by writing. Despite a series of violent conflicts between father and son, his studies, and work on his doctoral thesis had been financed by his father, who had prospered as an auctioneer and partner in the antiques business of Lepke in West Berlin. On the death of Emil Benjamin, Walter had decided to realize his inheritance. By May 1929, however, this fund had been almost entirely used up, not least as a result of commitments incurred during his divorce proceedings. Scholem in Jerusalem commented on this period of 'crisis and change':

> Something that remained astonishing in this year of the greatest excitements, upheavals and disappointed expectations in his life was his capacity for concentration, his openness to intellectual matters, and the harmoniousness of style in his letters. There was in him a store of profound serenity – only poorly described by the word *stoicism* – that remained untouched by the awkward situations in which he found himself at that time and the upheavals designed to throw his existence off course.[9]

In his early writings, Benjamin, who owed his decisive impulses to his adherence to the German youth and student movement, had supported an idealistic concept of culture. Now his writings were free from esotericism, even from the hostility to his readership that he had proclaimed in the first half of the nineteen twenties: 'No poem is intended for the reader,' he had written in 'The Task of the Translator', in 1921, 'no picture for the beholder, no symphony for the audience.'[10] And in the 'Announcement of the Journal: Angelus Novus' in the following year, he had declared that criticism is not to 'instruct by means of historical descriptions or to educate through comparisons, but to cognize by immersing itself in the object'.[11] 'The critic is the strategist in the literary struggle,' Benjamin now announced in *One-Way Street*, and: 'He who cannot take sides must keep silent.'[12] At the beginning of this collection of aphorisms and treatises was a section called 'Filling Station':

> The construction of life is at present in the power far more of facts than of convictions, and of such facts as have scarcely ever become the basis of convictions. Under these circumstances, true literary activity cannot aspire to take place within a literary framework; this is, rather, the habitual expression of its sterility. Significant literary effectiveness can

come into being only in a strict alternation between action and writing; it must nurture the inconspicuous forms that fit its influence in active communities better than does the pretentious, universal gesture of the book – in leaflets, brochures, articles and placards.[13]

Much earlier, Benjamin had already found his path into politics, encouraged by the theatre director Asja Lacis, to whom he dedicated *One-Way Street*. His relationship with this 'Russian revolutionary from Riga', he had written to Scholem from Capri in the summer of 1924, was 'absolutely for the best in terms of a vital liberation and intense insight into the actuality of a radical communism'.[14] Such was the expression of a link between politics and life which was to remain an essential element of Benjamin's relationship with communism. What interested him was a politics which took account of and supported the individual search for happiness; he could be enthusiastic about the Revolution because, as the Surrealists said, it promised 'liberation in every respect'.[15] The 'communist signals' from Capri, Benjamin testified, 'at first were indications of a change that awakened in me the will not to mask the actual and political elements of my ideas in the old Franconian [i.e. old-fashioned] way I did before, but also to develop them by experimenting and taking extreme measures'.[16] His statements over the years that followed confirm the importance in his life story of his 'conversion to political theory' and his 'attempting to leave the purely theoretical sphere'.[17] For a few months Benjamin considered joining the German Communist Party as a logical next step, but during his stay in Moscow in early 1927 counter-arguments prevailed: 'To be a communist in a state where the proletariat rules means completely giving up your private independence.'[18]

What was Brecht's situation in May 1929, and what plans of his were of interest to Benjamin? The 1st of May 1929, Berlin's so-called 'Bloody May', was a decisive date in Brecht's political biography. The sociologist Fritz Sternberg, also experienced in literary matters, whose courses on Marxism and the humanities Brecht attended, described what took place outside Karl Liebknecht House, the headquarters of the German Communist Party, near the Volksbühne theatre. To prevent clashes between Social Democrats and Communists, each of which was planning a May Day demonstration, the Social Democrat chief of police, Karl Zörgiebel, had issued a ban on public meetings. The Communists demonstrated against this, often only in small groups, which were, however, repeatedly dispersed by the police. Brecht was watching this from the window of Sternberg's apartment. Sternberg recalled later:

> As far as we could make out, these people were not armed. The police fired repeatedly. We thought at first that they were firing warning-shots. Then we saw several of the demonstrators falling, and later being

carried away on stretchers. At that time, as far as I remember, there were more than twenty dead among the demonstrators in Berlin. When Brecht heard the shots and saw that people were being hit, he went whiter in the face than I had ever seen him before in my life. I believe it was not least this experience which drove him ever more strongly towards the Communists.[19]

Brecht's sympathies, like Benjamin's, were with the Communist Party, to the extent that it was the most radically anti-bourgeois and closest to the masses. 'He was not uncritical,' wrote Sternberg, 'but he took the view that any faults could be corrected'; he had hoped 'for leadership of the German left from below'.[20]

If there was in Benjamin, as he wrote to Max Rychner in 1931, total negation of the 'complacency of bourgeois scholarship',[21] there was the same rejection in Brecht of the complacency of bourgeois theatre. What happened on 1 May 1929 that distressed Brecht so deeply came at the high point of his career and certainly had little to do with his plans at that time. At any rate, he left no doubt that the resounding success of *The Threepenny Opera* the year before already pointed to the overdue transformation of the theatre. His plays were to bring to the stage events and material of contemporary significance, whose meaning would be accessible to 'an audience with sharp senses, who know how to observe'.[22] He expected an audience who could adopt a 'cool, investigative, interested attitude, namely, the attitude of the audience of the scientific age'.[23] To do justice to his ambition as a playwright, he had for some three years tried to establish insights into the workings of capitalist society, and had studied Marxist dialectics and sociological and economic theory, discovering in them problems he had already been concerned with in his plays: 'When I read Marx's *Capital*, I understood my plays,' he noted around 1928. Marx, he said, was 'the only spectator for my plays I'd ever come across'.[24]

Brecht's plans in May 1929, on which Benjamin had his eye, revolved around the artistic development of 'didacticism' – on the one hand, in the direction of the great documentary-epic stage play, on the other in the direction of collective forms, involving and mobilizing the public. In his reply on 31 March 1929 to a questionnaire addressed to dramatists and theatre directors in the *Berliner Börsen-Courier*, Brecht wrote that 'to comprehend the new areas of subject-matter' involves the representation of new relationships, which for their part 'could only be simplified by *formal* means': 'The form in question can however only be achieved by a complete change of the theatre's purpose. Only a new purpose can lead to a new art. The new purpose is called pedagogics.'[25]

In July, Brecht's *Lindbergh's Flight* and a 'Lehrstück' (didactic play), the later *Baden-Baden Lesson on Consent*, were to be performed as part of the 1929 German Chamber Music Festival in Baden-Baden. The 'Lehrstück' aimed 'at a collective artistic exercise', Brecht explained. It was 'performed for the self-orientation of the authors and of those actively participating, and is not meant to be an experience for all and sundry'.[26] And a note on *Lindbergh's Flight* recorded that the play 'is valueless unless learned from. It has no value as art which would justify any performance not intended for learning'; it was 'an *object of instruction*'.[27] A shorter version of the 'Lehrstück' for radio, *Lindbergh*, had already been published in April as an expression of Brecht's interest in radio, which his work was intended to change, not just serve. He was concerned with 'a kind of resistance by the listener, and for his mobilization and redrafting as a producer'.[28] Also in April, Brecht and Weill had completed the first version of the opera *The Rise and Fall of the City of Mahagonny*, whose première on 9 March 1930 in Leipzig caused one of the greatest theatrical scandals of the Weimar Republic. The notes to *Mahagonny*, published in *Versuche* in 1930, compared the epic and dramatic forms of theatre and became a programmatic text for Brecht's dramatic theory.[29] Brecht's change of direction – completed during his work on *The Measures Taken* from Spring to Autumn 1930 – towards Leninism, that is to the dictatorship of the proletariat and the proletarian revolution, resulted in a change of his planned activities, whose focus was now on changing the world.

For the financial leeway necessary for his 'Lehrstück' experiments, Brecht had to thank his contract with his agents, Felix Bloch Erben, of 17 May 1929, which assured him a monthly advance of 1,000 gold marks, excluding the takings for *The Threepenny Opera*, which was successively performed at the Theater am Schiffbauerdamm and in Vienna, Leipzig and Stuttgart. In April 1928 Brecht and Helene Weigel had married; in the *Berliner Börsen-Courier* the playwright had described her as an actress 'of this new sort',[30] that is, of the epic theatre.

Brecht was surrounded by an aura of controversial popularity; whatever he did or wrote attracted attention – positive as well as negative. At the centre of interest was the stage work of the Kleist Prize winner of 1922, especially when he was directing himself, but the publication of his *Hauspostille* (*Devotions for the Home*) in 1927 had also received much attention. Since 3 May 1929 there had been notorious accusations of plagiarism against him. The Berlin critic Alfred Kerr had made himself their spokesman in his polemic 'Brechts Copyright'; Benjamin was soon to be one of the few who angrily rejected these attacks.

At the première of *The Threepenny Opera*, Lion Feuchtwanger had described the thirty-year-old as a 'descendant of German Evangelical peasants, wildly attacked by German nationalists': 'He has a long, narrow head with protruding cheekbones, deep-set eyes, and black hair growing over his forehead. He emphasizes his internationalism, and from his looks you might take him for a Spaniard or a Jew – or both.'[31]

His manner was considered provocative and his public statements sometimes came across as harsh. Bernhard Reich, who thought 'the shape of his head gave him a dynamic expression', traced the 'inner drama' of his conversations with Brecht:

> He spoke very quietly, but he made claims, expressing these claims in paradoxical formulations. Absolutely categorical. He did not argue with replies, but swept them away. He made it clear to his partners that he, Brecht, regarded all resistance to him as hopeless, and that he gave them, the partners, the friendly advice not to waste their time and to capitulate right away.[32]

The closer acquaintanceship between Benjamin and Brecht of May 1929 was already the second attempt at an approach. That this was momentous compared with the first was a matter for Benjamin of an existential dimension. Now, in a letter of 10 November 1930, he was able to draw the attention of his friend Theodor Adorno to 'the resounding echo of the extended and extremely stimulating conversations' with Brecht.[33] The thematic palette of these momentous conversations included the new theatre, the cinema, radio, the political situation, particularly the necessity of a revolution and the fight against fascism, the role of intellectuals, the question of radical thought, and the function of art, particularly its aesthetics and technology.

What Benjamin had written to the art historian Siegfried Giedion on 15 February 1929, thanking him for his book *Building in France*, applies to his own relationship with Brecht: 'Your book represents one of the few examples of what almost everyone has experienced: that before contact with something (or with someone: text, house, person, etc.), we have a premonition that it's going to be of the utmost significance.'[34]

This was to prove true for Benjamin's encounter with Brecht. It reminded him of an important and constantly recurring 'constellation'.[35] This was the configuration of non-accidental but specific (and in this case favourable) circumstances, in a combination of uniqueness and predictability, and in the expectation that the effects of the resulting experiences and attitudes were not limited to an individual level but bore common features with the constellations of heavenly bodies. To this extent the meeting between Benjamin and Brecht was more than a phenomenon of their own biographies.*

> * The previous sentence is a paraphrase of the beginning of an essay by the critic Max Kommerell, 'Jean Paul in Weimar', to which Lorenz Jäger drew my attention. According to Kommerell, the writer Jean Paul's stay in Weimar could only be described by the word 'constellation', where the coincidental and the statutory were hardly to be distinguished. The term expressed 'where each person stands in relation to others, and all to all – at this time of high consciousness and most acute reflection' (see Max Kommerell, 'Jean Paul in Weimar' in his *Dichterische Welterfahrung. Essays*, Frankfurt, 1952, pp. 53–5).

A Quarrel Among Friends

'You have got into bad company: Brecht plus Benjamin,' the poet and critic Johannes R. Becher warned Asja Lacis.[36] Such warnings are likely to have been the exception in Brecht's communist circle of acquaintances. Brecht, who was hardly influenced by the opinions of those around him when it came to personal relationships, presumably never had to justify his friendship with Benjamin. It was different for Benjamin: above all it was his friends and acquaintances who observed and commented on his relationship and developing collaboration with Brecht with suspicion and an unreasonable lack of understanding, and in some cases with malice. Among these were Gershom Scholem, Theodor Wiesengrund-Adorno (who called himself simply Adorno after emigrating to the USA), Gretel Karplus (later Adorno's wife), Ernst Bloch and Siegfried Kracauer.

Benjamin's most important statement about his relationship with Brecht is his reply to a letter from Gretel Karplus, which was typical of his friends' objections in its tone and the specific reservations it expressed. On 27 May 1934 Karplus had written to him:

> I view your move to Denmark with some anxiety, and today I must touch on a most delicate subject. I would prefer not to do this in writing but I am forced to do so. You of all people, who never uttered a word of complaint about my apparently leaving you in the lurch by not coming, who always understood my commitments and never stood in my way, have every right to ask me how I can allow myself to cross the border imposed on us and interfere in your personal affairs. Certainly you are right from your own point of view, but I also have objective things to defend in you, and I will try to do so as best I can. We have hardly ever talked about B. Admittedly I have not known him as long as you have, but I have very great reservations about him, only one of which I would like to mention, of course only as far as I can recognize it: his often palpable lack of clarity. At the moment it is less important for me to discuss him in detail than to say that I sometimes have the feeling that somehow you are under his influence, which could be very dangerous for you. I vividly remember an evening of discussion at Prinzenallee about the development of language and your agreement with his theories, when I thought I sensed this particularly strongly. I have been at great pains to avoid this topic, because I think this relationship is a very emotional one for you and perhaps represents something quite different, but here too any further comment would be too much. And he is, of course, the friend who has given you most support in your present

9

difficulties. I understand very well that you need this contact to escape from the isolation that threatens us all, but which I would consider possibly the lesser evil for your work. I know I am risking a great deal, perhaps even our whole friendship, by writing this letter, and only our long separation could have moved me to speak out.*

This letter from Gretel Karplus reiterates the arguments of other critics of this relationship, chiefly those of her subsequent husband. The friends who were concerned about Benjamin's association with Brecht made no secret of their political and personal reservations. They believed it their duty to shield their friend from this dangerous influence, and they assumed that Benjamin was emotionally dependent on Brecht. These critics expressed their warnings in emotional terms; they suggested that the stakes were very high. They gave the impression that Benjamin needed to be 'rescued' from Brecht. This was the result of a higher interest; the aim was to defend 'objective reality'.

Benjamin usually met such reproaches, when they came to his ears, with confessional clarity. It is not by chance that letters in which he referred to his 'decisive encounter with Brecht'[37] and proclaimed his solidarity with him were directed at precisely those friends who had been particularly dissociating themselves from his contacts with Brecht. Benjamin's reply to Gretel Karplus is of the same exemplary value as her letter. To answer her letter, he said, he had had to keep his distance, from this letter and from his current work. Not everything she said was wrong, but not everything spoke against his approach to Brecht.

> What you say about his influence on me reminds me of a significant and continually repeated constellation in my life...
> In my existential economy, a few specific relationships do play a part, which enable me to maintain one which is the polar opposite of my fundamental being. These relationships have always provoked more or less violent protests on the part of those closest to me, for example at the moment my relationship with B., and to a less marked degree that with Gerhard [sic] Scholem. In such cases I can do little more than ask my friends to have confidence that the rewards of these connections, whose dangers are obvious, will become clear. You in particular must realize that my life, as well as my thought, is moving towards extreme positions. The distance that it asserts in this way, the freedom to juxtapose things and ideas that are considered irreconcilable, achieves its character only through danger. A danger that generally seems obvious to my friends only in the form of those 'dangerous' relationships.[38]

* Karplus to Benjamin, 27 May 1934, GB IV, pp. 442ff. The following unpublished sentence follows in the original letter: 'Forgive me, if you can, if I have gone too far' (WBA 2/12ᵛ).

Benjamin was well aware of the significance of his encounter with Brecht for his life and writing. He could not be surprised by his friends' critical emphasis. In reply to their reservations he stressed that he knew about the 'limits' of Brecht's significance for him; Brecht, as he wrote to Adorno in May 1935 with reference to the *Arcades Project*, had infused his work with 'problems', but not with 'directives'.[39] Where his friends sensed difficulties, Benjamin was aware of a complex coherence: the 'dangers' and 'rewards' of his 'connection' appeared ambivalent. Benjamin rarely expressed it more clearly than in this personal reflection: the original aspect of his thought included precisely the attempt to link together opposing positions.* The unspecified but obvious dangers consisted, one can assume, in the failure of his attempt at linkage and in his consequent adherence to one of the positions designated as extreme. Benjamin saw the rewarding aspects of such relationships as the opportunity to explore with individuals on equal terms attitudes and positions which formed alternatives to those he had previously adopted, and to sharpen his thinking. The fact that Benjamin went out of his way to explain this important aspect of his attitude to Brecht rules out any posthumous belittlement of Brecht's significance for him.

Benjamin refrained from minor mentions of Brecht in letters to individuals whom he knew to be critical of Brecht.† This is significant in the draft of a letter of July 1938 to Friedrich Pollock, the administrative director of the Institute for Social Research. In describing the course of his day, which he organized so as to 'allow an optimum amount of time for my work', he crossed out passages in which he at first revealed that he spent the whole day at the Brechts' house, took his meals there, and that Brecht was his daily chess partner.[40] These were not corrections of style, but examples of his placing limits on a description which might be read at the Institute from the point of view of financial sponsorship. This tactical selection – Adorno described it as an adaptation to his correspondent, a 'certain diplomacy'[41] – by no means contradicted his self-revelation; both were ways in which Benjamin was able to react to reserve and hostility.

The opinions of particular importance in the discussion of his relationships were those of Scholem and Adorno. From the start, Scholem's reaction to the intensive contact between Benjamin and Brecht was restrained. He had only a moderate interest in Brecht. Benjamin positively urged Scholem to read some

* Burkhardt Lindner was the first to point out – in 1978 – the programmatic character of this passage of this letter to Adorno: it read 'like a previously absent declaration' (see Burckhardt Lindner (ed.), *Walter Benjamin im Kontext*, Königstein, p. 7).

† For instance, when he informed Scholem, Gretel Karplus and Adorno that he was to lecture in Paris on the German avant-garde, he omitted to mention that his topic was Brecht (see Benjamin to Scholem, 3 March 1934, Benjamin/Scholem, p. 99; to Gretel Karplus, 9 March 1934, *Benjamin Correspondence*, p. 435; and to Adorno, 9 April 1934, Adorno/Benjamin, p. 41).

works of Brecht's, only to wait in vain for Scholem's assessments.* In retro-spect, Scholem acknowledged the significance of the friendship for Benjamin and referred to the fact that Brecht had

> for years held Benjamin spellbound and fascinated. Brecht, after all, was the only author in whom he was able to observe the creative processes of a great poet at close quarters. Also, he had much in common with Brecht's at first strongly anarchistically tinged brand of communism.[42]

With Brecht, 'an entirely new element, an elemental force in the truest sense of the word' had entered his life at that time.[43] But Brecht's part in Benjamin's attempt 'to incorporate historical materialism in his thinking and work, or even to harness his thinking and his work in the context of this method', was acknowledged by Scholem with an aggressive undertone:

> Brecht, the tougher of the two, left a profound effect on the more sensi-tive nature of Benjamin, who had nothing of the athlete in him. That it was in any way for Benjamin's good is more than I would dare to claim. Rather, I am inclined to consider Brecht's influence on Benjamin's output in the thirties baleful, and in some respects disastrous.[44]

The increasing severity of Scholem's disapproval of Brecht can only be understood on the basis of its displacement function. In the person of Brecht, Scholem, a Judaic scholar and researcher into mysticism, was attacking an intellectual-political development of Benjamin's – that is, the decrease in the

---

* Benjamin repeatedly complained that Scholem did not write to him about Brecht's texts. And Scholem expressed his 'reservations concerning several books that Benjamin had recommended especially to me, reservations that I had expressed by prolonged silence in my letters. For example I regard Brecht's *Threepenny Novel* as an altogether inferior product' (Scholem, *Benjamin*, p. 208). Scholem's reserve also emerges from the correspondence between Benjamin and Kitty Marx-Steinschneider. Benjamin had met Kitty Marx-Steinschneider in Berlin in 1933 shortly before her emigration, and on that occasion had lent her the proofs of Brecht's *The Mother* (see *Benjamin Correspondence*, p. 412). When he received them back, Benjamin wrote: 'But above all I now want to thank you for kindly returning the Brecht and Musil volumes. Actually I would have liked you to have written me a few words about both of them. But I can easily get over my disappointment as far as the second item is concerned. Less so with regard to the first; perhaps also because, after a hint from Scholem that I seem to remember, I had noted that he too had got down to reading *The Mother*. So in this case your silence would have an echo, perceptible even across the distance of an ocean. I would appreciate it greatly if you could give me any information about these uncertain presumptions' (Benjamin to Kitty Marx-Steinschneider, 22 August 1933, *GB* IV, p. 281). In her reply of 14 September 1933, she wrote: 'Your assumption that he had read *The Mother* is only partly correct. I did give it to him for this purpose, but took it away again when he told me that he had begun it, but did not intend to read it to the end' (WBA 91/5ᵛ–6).

metaphysical, Judaic-theological, and the increase in the materialist tendency in his work – which he considered to be harmful to him and therefore tried to discourage. Benjamin, Scholem said, was 'Janus-faced', with one face turned to Brecht, the other to him.[45] Scholem's discouragement of Brecht represented an attempt to gain mastery over Benjamin's thinking. Adorno, in a transferred sense, saw it this way too. After a meeting with Scholem in New York in 1938, he wrote to Benjamin that Scholem was 'obviously bound to you to a quite remarkable degree' and that he counted 'anyone else who crops up in this connection, whether it is Bloch, Brecht or whoever, as one of the enemy'.[46] When, in 1968, a violent debate ignited about an edition of Benjamin's work that would do him justice, Scholem hinted in a letter to Adorno, as though it went without saying, that the 'lack of sympathy for Brecht's influence on Benjamin' was something they had in common.[47] Adorno and Scholem had agreed, in what Hannah Arendt described as a 'depressing manner', that his friendship with Brecht had had a bad influence on Benjamin.[48] In Brecht and his friend's involvement with him, Scholem was attacking the whole movement – Marxists, communists, anti-Zionists – who had lured Benjamin away from him. Asja Lacis, too, who claimed to have dissuaded Benjamin from emigrating to Palestine, was part of the personal environment that had brought Scholem's resistance into play.* The Stalinization that was intensified in the Soviet Union after 1933 also played its part in encouraging Scholem's 'anti-Marxist instincts'† and transferring them to Benjamin.

In their correspondence about historical materialism in the spring of 1931, Benjamin's work 'in the spirit of dialectical materialism' had already moved Scholem to the reproach that Benjamin was 'engaging in a singularly intensive kind of self-deception'.[49] To him, Brecht was the instigator of these aberrations, and Scholem perceived Benjamin's friendship with Brecht as the exact opposite of his own relationship with him:

> * See Asja Lacis, *Revolutionär im Beruf*, p. 45: 'Once he had a Hebrew language textbook with him and said he was learning Hebrew. Perhaps he would leave for Palestine. His friend Scholem had promised him a secure existence there. I was speechless, and then we had a violent argument: the path of a normal progressive person leads to Moscow, but not to Palestine. I can say with confidence that it was thanks to me that Walter Benjamin did not leave for Palestine.' Scholem's aversion to Asja Lacis, whom he had never met, was openly expressed in the following letter extract: 'How Benjamin could be taken in by a pretty fiend (*Aas*) like Asja Lacis is among the unanswered questions of his biography, perhaps even, as you suggest, among the least interesting of these.' In his anger, Scholem could not even resist a primitive pun: 'Asja = *Aas? Ja!*' (Scholem to Walter Boehlich, 12 October 1980, in Scholem, *Briefe III*, Munich, 1999, p. 215).
> † Werner Kraft used this phrase after a conversation with Scholem on 26 September 1934 in Jerusalem about 'B[enjamin]'s Bolshevism' (see Geret Luhr (ed.), 'was noch begraben lag', pp. 192ff.).

For a long time I could have only a vague notion of what we now know from Brecht's complaints in his *Journals* about Benjamin's 'mysticism in spite of an unmystical attitude' and his perennial 'Judaisms': namely, that what attracted me so much in Benjamin's thought and tied me so closely to him was precisely the element that Brecht was bound to find annoying about him.[50]

On the political plane, Scholem found in Brecht no explicit statement against Stalin – which reads like a roundabout accusation that Brecht was a Stalinist.* Despite Scholem's enduring commitment to Benjamin's work, he had a blind spot in the total lack of understanding he brought to the latter's relationship with Brecht.

Benjamin had no illusions about Scholem's attitude to Brecht. In a letter to Gretel Karplus he complained about his friend's lack of solidarity: accounts of his own hopeless situation had brought to light in Scholem 'a reaction whose wretched embarrassment (not to say insincerity) gave me not only the saddest idea of his private nature, but also of the moral climate of the country where he has been formed for the last ten years'.[51] The depth of Benjamin's bitterness is seen in the next sarcastic turn of phrase, in which he gave vent to his feelings about Scholem's aversion:

> It is probably not going too far to say that in my situation he is inclined to see with pleasure the avenging hand of the Almighty, whom I have incensed by my Danish friendship.†

The personal and political distance that characterized the relationship between Scholem and Brecht did not at first exist between Adorno and Brecht. Adorno's objections arose from other sources, and yet each expressed himself quite similarly in both style and content. In the late nineteen twenties Adorno had frequented the larger circle of Brecht.‡ He had described the 'hollowed-out simplicity' of *The Threepenny Opera* as 'classic', but the work itself as 'functional' (*Gebrauchsmusik*).[52] In April 1930, in an enthusiastic essay on *Mahagonny*, welcomed by Benjamin, in the journal *Der Scheinwerfer*, Adorno had

---

* See ibid., pp. 212ff.: 'Afterwards I was quite surprised when it turned out in New York that unlike Brecht the Institute group – especially the Jews among them, who constituted the overwhelming majority – consisted with a few exceptions of passionate anti-Stalinists.' See also Benjamin/Scholem, p. 236, 6–8 November 1938: 'By the way I also found all the Institute members whom I got to know to be diligent and very outspoken anti-Stalinists, great and small, and I didn't hear a single thing said about Brecht.'

† Benjamin to Karplus, after 3 December 1935, *GB* V, p. 205. Brecht was then living in Denmark.

‡ See Ernst Bloch's recollection: 'Benjamin had the best reputation in our small circle of friends: Adorno, Kracauer, Weill, Brecht, myself and a few others' (*Über Walter Benjamin*, with essays by Adorno, Bloch, Scholem and others, Frankfurt, 1968, p. 22).

publicly stood up for the controversial opera by Brecht and Weill.* But in the course of the nineteen thirties he developed an initially veiled, but increasingly severely expressed, criticism of Benjamin's relationship with Brecht, which – as in the case of Scholem – involved the rejection of elements of Benjamin's intellectual development. Adorno was also haunted by the unexpressed concern that Brecht could become his rival with Benjamin. While fundamentally endorsing Benjamin's philosophical approach, he found fault with the concrete use of the materialist method, with which he was familiar, in his friend's work, as 'undialectical' (above all the theory of the dialectical image), and a 'simplification'.† In 1938, referring to his work on Baudelaire, Adorno had made this criticism: 'Your solidarity with the Institute, which pleases no one more than myself, has led you to pay the kind of tributes to Marxism which are appropriate neither to Marxism nor to yourself.'[53]

'What drew Benjamin to dialectical materialism', wrote Adorno in later comments, 'was no doubt less its theoretical content than the hope of an empowered, collectively legitimized form of discourse', a 'need for authority in the sense of collective legitimacy', which was 'by no means foreign' to his friend.[54] Adorno's later aversion to Brecht's concept of an interventionist politics of art was here applied, as it were in anticipation, to Benjamin.[55]

Adorno described the 'reconciliation of myth' as 'the theme of Benjamin's philosophy'.[56] His philosophical reading was based on existential categories such as 'reconciliation', 'rescue', 'hope' and 'despair', whose central value – we have only to consider his studies of Kafka – is undisputed; the political, the materialistic and to a great extent even the literary implications of Benjamin's writings take second place behind such categories. Adorno's main emphases were such that any traces of Benjamin's relations with Brecht could hardly be integrated in them: 'Hence the core of Benjamin's philosophy is the idea of the salvation of the dead as the restitution of distorted life through the consummation of its own reification down to the inorganic level.'[57]

Just as Scholem made Brecht quite simply responsible for any kind of mat-

---

* Adorno, *Mahagonny*, pp. 12–15. Benjamin's approval is supported by a letter of Siegfried Kracauer's: 'The day before yesterday I was with Benji. He is very taken with your essay on *Mahagonny*' (Kracauer to Adorno, 20 April 1930, in *Benjaminiana*, edited by Hans Putnies and Gary Smith, Gießen, 1991, p. 35).

† Benjamin/Adorno, 2–5 August 1935, p. 105; see also Adorno, 'Introduction to Benjamin's *Schriften*', in *Notes to Literature*, vol. 2, pp. 233–9; and Adorno, *Prisms*, p. 237: 'In its close contact with material which was close at hand, in its affinity to that which is, his thought, despite all its strangeness and acumen, was always accompanied by a characteristic unconscious element, by a moment of naïveté. This naïveté enabled him at times to sympathize with groups in power-politics which, as he well knew, would have liquidated his own substance, unregimented intellectual experience.'

erialism in Benjamin, Adorno blamed the crude, to his eyes faulty, application of such methodological principles on Brecht's influence.*

The distance between them had been expressed in a hesitant manner. Peter von Haselberg reported a statement by Adorno of around 1932 in which one can already discern scepticism, though not yet aggression: 'Under Brecht's influence Benjamin is doing only stupid things.'[58] The beginning of the open argument came in 1934: with an appeal to common ground, which is all the more striking because it is placed within parentheses, Adorno confronted Benjamin with the fact that, as he wrote in a letter, he could 'not suppress the most serious reservations about some of your publications (for the first time since we have been associated with each other)'. And he continued:

> I hope I will not be suspected of any unreasonable desire to interfere if I confess that the whole difficult problem is connected with the figure of Brecht and with the credence you are willing to give him; for this also touches on fundamental questions of principle with regard to materialist dialectics, like that concerning the concept of use value, the central role of which I can no more accept today than I could previously.[59]

Adorno's hope that with the 'tackling of the *Passagen*' (the *Arcades Project*) the difficulties would be cleared out of the way to an extent that Benjamin's work could take shape 'without qualms ... concerning any objections stemming from Brechtian atheism'[60] proved an illusion. Repeatedly, at a later stage too, Adorno expressed his reservations about 'Berta', a code-name for Brecht, 'and her collective'[61] in terms such as these:

> Just as I believe it would be a real misfortune if Brecht were to acquire any influence upon this work (I say this without prejudice to Brecht – but here, and precisely here, there is a limit) so too I would regard it as a misfortune if any concessions were to be made here to the Institute in this regard.†

That Adorno spoke about his fears to Max Horkheimer, the director of the Institute, is shown by the latter's communication:

> I have already had a discussion with Benjamin. He totally rejected the idea that the content of his treatise might have anything to do with Brecht. With regard to certain passages I made clear to him the correctness of my, and also your, objections. He will devote his attention to it once more in detail before the translation is begun.[62]

---

* Hannah Arendt formulated it as follows: 'Both Adorno and Scholem blamed Brecht's "disastrous influence" (Scholem) for Benjamin's clearly undialectic usage of Marxist categories' (Arendt, *Men in Dark Times*, p. 165).

† Adorno/Benjamin, 20 May 1935, p. 84; the text referred to by Adorno is the outline of the *Arcades Project*.

It was only after Benjamin's death, however, that Adorno expressed his un-concealed disapproval; first in an oral communication to his student, Rolf Tiedemann, which was to become the subject of violent dispute. He claimed that Benjamin had written the 'Work of Art' essay – according to his own statement to Adorno – 'to surpass Brecht, of whom he was afraid, in radicalism'.* In the *Frankfurter Rundschau* of 6 March 1968 Adorno confirmed his communication with Tiedemann, but only in one of his arguments: 'I clearly remember Benjamin's statement that with his 'Work of Art' essay he wanted to outdo Brecht in radicalism.'[63] Adorno did not say that Benjamin was afraid of Brecht.† And the story of the relationship in all its details provides eloquent testimony to the contrary: Benjamin's relationship with Brecht was free from fear. Adorno even went so far as to assert what was known not to be the case, shown for example by this statement on Benjamin: 'Those of his own works that did not directly refer to Brecht, as long as he was writing them, he did show to me, but not to Brecht – probably because he did not expect anything favourable as a result.'‡ Even where Adorno recognized the 'friendship', he still expressed distance:

> All the less is either arrogance or the need to dominate any longer
> visible in the mature Benjamin. He was characterized by an utter and
> extremely gracious politeness... In this he resembles Brecht; without
> that characteristic, the friendship between the two of them could hardly
> have lasted.[64]

Adorno's unequivocal statement about Brecht's importance to Benjamin is his silence: in the major works he devoted to Benjamin, Brecht's name hardly occurs. The omission is far from accidental, and cannot be explained by refer-ence to his philosophically accentuated interpretation of Benjamin. To Adorno, the conscientious editor and 'expert commentator on Benjamin's writings', the overall, appropriate interpretation of Benjamin's relationship with Brecht was denied, as it was to Scholem.

Siegfried Kracauer and Ernst Bloch voiced their opinions from a greater distance. Their maliciously mocking comments come from private letters, not

---

* Rolf Tiedemann, *Studien zur Philosophie Walter Benjamins*, Frankfurt, 1973, p. 112. Tiedemann's sentence continued with the statement, 'the relationship between Benja-min and Brecht should probably *also* be explained in biographical-psychological terms'.

† Hannah Arendt too considered such a statement by Adorno to be extremely dubious: 'It is improbable that Benjamin should have expressed fear of Brecht, and Adorno seems not to claim that he did' (*Men in Dark Times*, p. 165n).

‡ Adorno, 'Interimsbescheid', in *Über Walter Benjamin*, p. 94. Brecht's assessments of Benjamin's work confirm that Benjamin let Brecht know about texts he was still writing. Adorno's vehement distancing of himself from Brecht is evident in his language in a note on Benjamin of 1968: 'Possible that he concealed from BB and the latter's clique the par-ticularly *experimental* character of his Marxism – the player *must* always win' (ibid., p. 98.)

intended for publication. After a meeting between Bloch and Benjamin, at which the latter had described his relationship with Brecht, Bloch wrote to Kracauer (probably in the summer or early autumn of 1929):

> Benjamin, with whom I spent two hours yesterday, is his impossible self again. The [bad] weather did not last long. I got him to the point of formulating the spell cast over him by Brecht. He is completely in the dark about its causes, which are after all private, highly private. It has passed by like the spell of others, about which I know, and still it is Brecht (it used to be Klee).*

Around 1930, in connection with the *Krise und Kritik* journal project, in which he was involved, Bloch referred to the 'harmony between the Alexandrian genius of Benjamin and the unwashed genius of Brecht' as 'curious beyond measure'.[65] Years later, on 5 July 1934, Kracauer wrote to Bloch in a similar tone:

> Benjamin told me of his correspondence with you. He has left for Denmark to visit his god, and Hamlet would have had the opportunity to make a few remarks about the two of them. By the way, there is now a Verlag (publishing company) für Sexualpolitik in Copenhagen too.†

Before 1933, in Berlin, as he told Scholem in a letter in 1965, Kracauer had had a 'very violent argument' with Benjamin 'about his servile-masochistic attitude to Brecht'.[66] Kracauer's remarks alluded to the insinuation that Benjamin had been in a state of dependency on, even of submission to, Brecht – even one with homoerotic traits. This interpretation was close to the criticisms made by Scholem and Adorno. The psychologizing statements of Bloch and Kracauer seem to go well beyond the testimony of Adorno and Scholem. However, they should be evaluated in the context of the intimate circle of friendship for which they were intended. Adorno and Scholem made their views public from the mid nineteen sixties, and discussions on Benjamin and Brecht were for a long time influenced by their interpretations. Bloch and Kracauer, on the other hand, in the lifetimes of the two men, expressed themselves privately and their statements had much less effect. Moreover, less weight can be given to the malicious remarks that have become known posthumously from the letters of Kracauer and Bloch, than to the assertion of an intellectual dependence by the

---

* Bloch *Briefe 1903–1975*, edited by Karola Bloch et al, Frankfurt, 1985, vol. I, p. 316. The reference to Klee is to Klee's ink drawing 'Angelus Novus' (see Scholem, 'Walter Benjamin and his Angel', pp. 198–236). See also for this connection, Ernst Bloch to Peter Huchel, 10 June 1956: 'All Benjamin's letters to me have unfortunately got lost in the turmoil of the Thirty Years War. There were some quite interesting ones among them from a personal point of view, with discussions on the curve in Benjamin's sinful decline – from Hofmannsthal to Brecht' (Bloch, op. cit., vol. 2, p. 878).

† ibid, vol. I, p. 381ff. The Verlag für Sexualpolitik, Berlin, was run by Wilhelm Reich.

close friends – Scholem and Adorno – the effect of which was posthumously to discredit Benjamin while seeking to defend him.

Günther Anders, born Stern, Benjamin's second cousin and Hannah Arendt's first husband, was among the few male colleagues and contemporaries to have made discriminating and open-minded statements about the relationship. Anders, who had known Brecht from the late nineteen twenties, numbered Benjamin, along with Karl Korsch, Fritz Sternberg and Alfred Döblin, among his 'artistically or intellectually independent friends'.[67] In his memoir, *Bert Brecht*, in which he described Brecht as 'of exemplary courtesy', he recalled: 'And at times there were conversations (for example with Benjamin), even conversations with explosive content, from which uninitiated involuntary witnesses could only receive the impression that two gentlemen were conducting a Confucian ritual.'[68]

That Anders perceived this ceremonial behaviour not only as an expression of courtesy, but also of the distance between them based on their differences, is shown by a later description in which he observed the intimate contact between them with a certain puzzlement:

> I experienced the two of them, Brecht and Benjamin, together only a few times, in Berlin *before* 1933. After more than fifty-five years, I can't remember what was discussed, but I do remember that *Benjamin understood Brecht far better than Brecht understood Benjamin*. Benjamin was used to interpreting literature; Brecht, although bubbling over with enthusiasm, was not used to the complexities of the brooding WB. Their *'friendship'* was therefore probably, as one might say, *asymmetrical*; I couldn't really understand it. In addition, *Benjamin*'s interest had for decades been concentrated so much on France and French literature that in conversation – and I had many with him (he was my second cousin) – he was constantly slipping into the subject of 'Paris', even if the conversation had started on quite a different topic. – For *Brecht*, on the other hand, France and French culture played a very minor role – and in this he was an exceptional figure in postwar German literature. (Conversely, Anglo-Saxon literature, which had importance for Brecht, passed Benjamin by.) If I had not *known* that these two people, who followed *such* different directions and who were also so different in style and social background, were so closely associated with each other ... if this fact had been only a rumour, I would not have given it any credence.[69]

These statements by Günther Anders are revealing in many ways. They show on the one hand that Benjamin's close association with Brecht aroused bemusement and surprise even among individuals well disposed towards both. The characterization of the relationship as 'asymmetrical', on the other hand, challenges one to reflect on the distribution of weight within it, and to distinguish between active and reactive behaviour. Finally, Anders refers without any invective to significant differences between the two men – differences in character, mentality, style and literary orientation – which must be taken into account in an analysis of what united and divided them.

It is striking that it was above all women who showed understanding for the value of this relationship: Hannah Arendt, Asja Lacis, Margarete Steffin, Helene Weigel, Elisabeth Hauptmann, Ruth Berlau, the Dutch painter Anna Maria Blaupot ten Cate, and Dora Benjamin, Walter Benjamin's sister.* It is no coincidence that all of these, except Hannah Arendt and Blaupot ten Cate, were colleagues and partners of Brecht's. Women found it easier to judge this 'friendship between men'† without resentment, affirming their productive intellectual closeness. There were men who had a close relationship with Brecht, free from the jealousy of others – Karl Korsch, Hanns Eisler, Bernard von Brentano – but they have provided hardly any testimony of Brecht's contact with Benjamin, although they had had experience of seeing them together.‡

Hardly ever has the friendship between Benjamin and Brecht been assessed as positively, even euphorically, as by Hannah Arendt, who had met Brecht only occasionally, but had had a closer relationship with Benjamin. 'There is indeed no question but that his friendship with Brecht – unique in that here the greatest living German poet met the most important critic of the time, a fact both were fully aware of – was the second and incomparably more important stroke of good fortune in Benjamin's life.'§

* The significance of women as mediators in the context of literary work is discussed in Chryssoula Kambas: 'Walter Benjamin – Adressat literarischer Frauen', in *Weimarer Beiträge* (Vienna), vol. 39, no. 2, 1993, pp. 242–57. Walter Benjamin's divorced wife, Dora Sophie Benjamin, did not share the sympathy of the women named above for his relationship with Brecht. In a letter in which she demanded that he should change his accommodation in Paris, she wrote: 'I would consider that much better than the terribly expensive journey to the dreadful Brecht. But you must do as you think best' (Dora Sophie Benjamin to Benjamin, 5 December 1937, WBA 18/18).

† This was the term used by Hannah Arendt and Helmut Gollwitzer to denote the relationship between Benjamin and Scholem (see Arendt, *Walter Benjamin / Bertolt Brecht*, p. 13, and Helmut Gollwitzer to Gershom Scholem, 18–25 November 1975, in Scholem, *Briefe* III, op. cit., p. 365).

‡ This is particularly to be regretted in the cases of Korsch and Eisler, who retained intensive impressions of the summer weeks in Svendborg. In 1927 Eisler set two songs from a collection of Frankfurt children's rhymes about which Benjamin had written in the *Frankfurter Zeitung*.

§ Arendt, *Men in Dark Times*, p. 165. Benjamin's first 'pure piece of luck', according to Arendt, was the publication of his essay on Goethe's *Elective Affinities* by Hugo von Hofmannsthal in the mid twenties (ibid., p. 157).

Hannah Arendt's interpretation did not seek to conceal her bitterness about, as she saw it, the negligent way in which Adorno and the members of the Institute for Social Research had treated Benjamin's material and intellectual estate.* She was conscious of contradicting Adorno in her assessment of the relationship, but she too – from a different perspective from Adorno's – was critical of Benjamin's attitude to Marxism. Hannah Arendt saw Benjamin as a failure, an isolated figure, and she imputed to his thinking a resistance to any form of ideology which corresponded to her own anti-totalitarian concept rather than to his own political intentions.†

Asja Lacis, who was linked with Brecht through her theatrical work in Munich on Brecht's *Edward II*, and with Benjamin through their love affair since the summer of 1924 on Capri, wrote that 'a productive friendship'[70] had developed as the result of a meeting arranged by herself (see Chapter II below).

The correspondence between Margarete Steffin and Benjamin is permeated by her interest in his friendly working relationship with Brecht, which she encouraged wherever possible. She kept the contact going by writing letters for Brecht, who was irregular in this respect. Her function as mediator was based on the time spent together in Paris with Benjamin in the autumn of 1933, and is of decisive importance for the development of the relationship. Her letters are more than letters written to order; she approached Benjamin not only as a colleague and co-author of Brecht's, but also independently in her capacity as an author and translator. Brecht was informed about Benjamin's letters to Steffin, and he sent her requests and information for Benjamin.‡

* See Elisabeth Young-Bruehl, *Hannah Arendt – For Love of the World*, New Haven/London, 2004, pp. 167–8, and Arendt's letter to the editorial department of *Merkur*, 17 March 1968, in *Merkur*, Stuttgart, vol. 2, no. 4, 1968, p. 315. This issue prints the German version of 'The Pearl Fisher', part 3 of Arendt's Benjamin essay in *Men in Dark Times*, followed by a note by her stating that, although Benjamin always treated Adorno as a director of the Institute of Social Research, alongside Horkheimer, he did not hold this position – nor had he been merely a fellow contributor alongside Benjamin: 'Adorno decided what articles were published by Benjamin. Benjamin did not decide what articles were published by Adorno.'

† See Arendt, *Benjamin/Brecht*, especially pp. 8, 13, 18–20 and 44 and *Men in Dark Times*, passim. Jürgen Habermas thought similarly in 1972 when he wrote: 'Arendt wanted to protect the sometimes gullible, fragile private scholar and collector from the ideological claims of his Marxist and Zionist friends' (Jürgen Habermas, *Bewußtmachende oder rettende Kritik – die Aktualität Walter Benjamins*, pp. 175ff.).

‡ See Steffin to Benjamin, 22 April 1937, Steffin, *Briefe*, pp. 237ff.: 'Dear Dr Benjamin, I hear from Brecht that you have written me a letter. I am pleased, though I will probably never get to see it. I really have to think myself lucky on the few occasions when he even tells me that a letter has arrived for me. In my imagination, a mountain of interesting letters is growing in Skovsbostrand, all meant for me, and this mountain can never come

Elisabeth Hauptmann's correspondence with Benjamin shows, to the extent that Brecht occurs in it, that she was assuming a relationship between equals, with reciprocal stimuli between Benjamin and Brecht. She gave Benjamin hints for his work on Brecht, tried to place Benjamin's and Brecht's writings with publishers in the USA, and asked Benjamin to mediate when her relationship with Brecht ran into difficulties. The confidential tone of her letters to Benjamin is based on the fact that he was initiated into her relationship with Brecht.[71] And certainly Benjamin hoped for more from Hauptmann than a relationship motivated via Brecht.* She characterized her relationship with him in a letter of 22 May 1934 to her friend Otto Nathan in Jerusalem. The context makes it clear that Brecht and Eisler, previously mentioned, are included in the first person plural: 'We ourselves have been attached to Benjamin (now in Paris) in a long, robust literary friendship.'[72]

The situation was similar in the case of Helene Weigel, who had a cordial relationship with Benjamin based on meetings in Berlin and in the summer months in Svendborg. Benjamin admired her as an actress; she supported him by her hospitality and gifts, and she also filled gaps in communication between him and Brecht. She formulated her impression in 1966 in a letter to Benjamin's sister-in-law, Hilde Benjamin (widow of his brother Georg): 'We discussed Walter Benjamin once before and I told you that he had spent some time with us in Denmark and was a good friend of Brecht's and mine, whom we had already known well in Berlin before 1933.'†

Ruth Berlau's account unequivocally contradicts all insinuations that

---

to me. But since Brecht is also too correct to open them, I can't even find out what is in them. This is almost tragic, don't you think?' Or Steffin to Benjamin, 6 January 1938, Steffin, *Briefe*, p. 266: 'Please do write to me some time. I pass on all the latest news to Brecht, as ever.' On the significance of the Benjamin/Steffin correspondence, see Chryssoula Kambas, 'Walter Benjamin – Adressat literarischer Frauen', op. cit.

* This is supported above all by the comment in Benjamin's journal from Le Lavandou (*SW*, vol. 2, pp. 469ff, and see Chapter II, pp. 31ff. below). In his Will of 1932 Benjamin left her a Soviet Russian silver dagger.

† Helene Weigel to Hilde Benjamin, 26 May 1966, Academy of Arts (Berlin), no. 626. The letter quoted here, and another, were attempts by Helene Weigel to recruit an ally – Hilde Benjamin was then Minister of Justice in the German Democratic Republic (GDR) – in her plan to clarify the legal status of Benjamin's estate and to promote the publication of Benjamin's work in the GDR. Statements about Benjamin's estate in Rolf Tiedemann's *Studien zur Philosophie Walter Benjamins* (op. cit.) and the observation that 'the publication of his writings by Theodor W. Adorno was proceeding in a very hesitant manner and, as I always assumed, would not be comprehensive', had encouraged Weigel to turn to Hilde Benjamin: 'There is great interest in publishing Benjamin's writings here at home; among them are some which are being looked after by us, which are not in Frankfurt. Who has the rights? Whom do the publishing firms here contact? I confess

Benjamin was afraid of Brecht or dependent on him. In conversation with Hans Bunge she related: 'Whenever Benjamin and Brecht met in Denmark, an atmosphere of intimacy immediately grew between them ... Brecht was tremendously fond of Benjamin, he positively loved him. I think they understood each other without the need to speak.'[73]

Anna Maria Blaupot ten Cate, who had first met Benjamin in Ibiza in 1922, made the acquaintance of Brecht and Margarete Steffin in Paris in the autumn of 1933. In her description too there is no suggestion of fear of dependence or concern about a dangerous influence. She knew that the two men had worked together in Paris for several weeks.[74] In a letter to Walter Benjamin of spring 1934 she enquired:

> You speak of your journey to Denmark, which is now getting so close. I hope very much that you will enjoy it there and be able to work well. Having Brecht close to you will be pleasant and stimulating in any case, and I can understand your looking forward to seeing Steffin. By the way, how is her health? Please give my best regards to her, and also to Brecht, won't you?[75]

Dora Benjamin, who lived with her brother in Paris during her last years, wrote after his death in a letter to Karl Thieme:

> By the way, I have meanwhile seen *Galileo* ... I was particularly gripped and moved by his way of formulating things, and I believe – probably correctly – that I can detect in it the results of my brother's work with

---

that it is not without malice that I would like this matter to be investigated, and I have no way of my own of doing so.' The passage about the interest in editions of Benjamin in the GDR was expanded by Elisabeth Hauptmann, to whom Helene Weigel had given the draft of her letter for her comments. Hauptmann wrote to Weigel on 22 May 1966: 'As ever: despite Adorno's aversion to Brecht, reliable legal information must be obtained on this. He can hardly refuse or prevent this.' On 29 December 1966 Weigel reminded Hilde Benjamin that she was awaiting a reply to her inquiry: 'I would be very interested to know what you think of Benjamin's work. He is an astonishing writer, and it angers me that we have not published anything by him here.' As yet it is not clear whether the Minister of Justice ever took up the matter, since no response from Hilde Benjamin is recorded apart from a note of thanks for the books sent to her.

Weigel's attitude to the activities of the journal *alternative* is also characteristic. Hildegard Brenner had made an enquiry in connection with the second special issue devoted to Benjamin, asking for 'evidence of Benjamin's productive collaboration with Bertolt Brecht'. Helene Weigel replied on 6 November 1967: 'I am very much in favour, but I don't know whether we will find anything for you in the Brecht archives. I would very much like to be able to do battle with the Institute and in particular Adorno, but I ask you most sincerely to be as careful as possible. It must be done in a totally watertight and specific manner' (AdK, Berlin, Historisches Archiv, BBA files).

Brecht, which was – as you presumably know – very intensive for a number of years. During his time in Paris my brother spent several summers with Brecht in Denmark – the last was the summer of 38.[76]

Galileo could not have demonstrated direct 'results' of Benjamin's work with Brecht, since it was written during a period without any contact with Benjamin, but probably that was not what Dora Benjamin meant. Nevertheless, this suggestion, from an intimate observer, of the closeness and co-operation between the two friends is noteworthy.

II

The Story of the Relationship

First Meeting, A Literary Trial, Dispute over Trotsky, 1924–29

When in 1929 Benjamin, as we have seen, mentioned to Scholem his *'close* acquaintance with Brecht',[1] their first encounter had already taken place nearly five years earlier. It appears to have begun in November 1924. Asja Lacis had made the introduction in the Pension Voß in Berlin, where she herself lived, in an artists' *pensione* on one floor of 1 Meierottostrasse, not far from Brecht's studio apartment in Spichernstrasse.* Lacis described the meeting in her memoirs, *Revolutionär im Beruf* ('Revolutionary by Profession'):

> [Benjamin] asked me several times to introduce him to Brecht. Once I was going to a restaurant with Brecht. He said that I looked very smart in my new Parisian outfit, and in his rough clothes he would be totally out of place. Then I told him that Benjamin wanted to meet him. This time Brecht agreed. The meeting took place in the Pension Voß (opposite Spichernstrasse), where I was living at the time. Brecht was very reserved and they rarely met after that.[2]

She described the scene in more detail, with fuller dialogue, in the Russian edition of her memoirs, which was published in Riga in 1984 under the title *Krasnaya Gvozdika* ('Red Carnation'):

> In Berlin we met Brecht. Over lunch, I told him of my impressions and what an interesting person Benjamin was, and then I could no longer hold back: 'Look here, Bert, how can you refuse to meet Walter? This could end up looking like an insult!'
>
> This time Brecht was more compliant. But when they met next day, the conversation never got going, and the acquaintanceship petered out. I was confused. Was it possible that Brecht, such an intelligent person, could find nothing in common with Walter, a person of such intellectual curiosity and wide interests?
>
> It was not for a considerable time that Bertolt became interested in Benjamin and his work. During the fascist dictatorship, when both were living in exile, Brecht, who had settled in Denmark, invited Walter to come and see him. Later Elisabeth Hauptmann told me that they had finally become friends. But this happened several years later.[3]

---

* Lacis and Bernhard Reich had come from Paris to Berlin at the end of October 1924 (*Revolutionär im Beruf*, p. 48). Lacis mentioned in a conversation that the Pension Voß was in Meierottostraße (see Benno Slupianek et al, 'Gespräch mit Asja Lacis und Bernhard Reich über Brecht', in BBA Tape Collection, nr 582/3).

This first conversation between Benjamin and Brecht was not followed up. Brecht was indifferent, and Asja Lacis's enthusiasm was not infectious. No further encounter was arranged, which is hardly surprising considering the differences in their interests, temperaments, styles of writing and topics.

As early as the summer of 1924 in Capri, Benjamin had tried, via Lacis, to make contact with Brecht, who was staying in nearby Positano.[4] 'Now and then,' Lacis recalled, 'Reich would visit me in Capri, and Brecht would also come with Marianne [Zoff]. Benjamin asked me to introduce him to Brecht, but Brecht refused to get to know him.'[5] Asja Lacis also claimed to have aroused Benjamin's curiosity about Brecht: 'I kept telling Benjamin about Brecht.'[6] The exact course of events might be irrelevant, if the apparent discrepancy were not related to a particularly important phase in Benjamin's life. His interest in Brecht was not a result of his profound personal and political experiences during the years 1924–25, but expressed itself at the beginning of these life-changing developments. And even if their meetings did not bear fruit until May 1929, the first encounter between Brecht and Benjamin, and a few other occasions on which they met before they became more closely acquainted, deserve attention.*

The first occasion on which Benjamin and Brecht are known to have met between late Autumn 1924 and May 1929, in what might be called discrete, small discussion groups, was a meeting of 'Gruppe 1925' on 8 November 1926.

---

* Biographical sources on this as well as those devoted to Benjamin's work have been deficient in the secondary literature until now, because it was assumed that nothing could have happened before May 1929. Although the account of the first conversation between Benjamin and Brecht in Asja Lacis's memoirs, *Revolutionär im Beruf*, is placed immediately *after* the end of October 1929, the passage referring to Benjamin's communication of 6 June 1929, that he had become more closely acquainted with Brecht, is generally taken to refer to May 1929. However, there are no grounds for doubting the account by Lacis of this event, so momentous for her, and for attributing a 'lapse of memory' to her (as is done in *GS* II/3, p. 1363). The Russian edition of her memoirs, *Krasnaja gvozdika*, more precise in its chronology than the German, in general identifies leaps forward and backward in time, and relates the first meeting between Benjamin and Brecht as taking place *after* the journey by Lacis and Reich to Paris in the autumn of 1924, and *before* the story of her first acquaintance with Berlin, which Benjamin arranged at the end of October 1924, after the end of the stay in Paris (see *Krasnaja gvozdika*, op. cit., pp. 91ff, and Bernhard Reich, *Im Wettlauf mit der Zeit. Erinnerungen aus fünf Jahrzehnten deutscher Theatergeschichten*, Berlin, 1970, p. 279). A further argument for the meeting having taken place as early as 1924 could be the closeness, explicitly stressed by Asja Lacis, of the meeting place to Spichernstraße, where Brecht was living in 1924. In 1929 he was living in Hardenbergstraße. Elisabeth Hauptmann, who had been working for Brecht since 1926, also cast doubt on the dating of May 1929. In her private copy of Klaus Völker's *Brecht-Chronik* (Munich, 1984) she marked the relevant entry with a

Benjamin himself was not a member of this writers' society; a decision to admit him, which had been proposed in a letter by Ernst Bloch, had been deferred at the meeting of 15 February 1926.[7] However, he was able to attend the gathering of 8 November as a guest, and he reported back to Siegfried Kracauer in a letter of 16 November:

> In the last few days I have attended a rather curious private event: the writers' group 'Gruppe 1925' held a meeting where a debate took place on Becher's latest book *Levisite*, in the form of a public trial, with Döblin as prosecuting counsel and Kisch for the defence.[8]

Not only was Brecht among the members present, but he also presided over the 'trial'. Apart from Alfred Döblin and Egon Erwin Kisch, Klabund and Rudolf Leonhard also acted as lay judges. A total of only eight members took part in the session, including, apart from those already named, the author of the subject of the trial, Johannes R. Becher, as well as Leonhard Frank and Alfred Wolfenstein.[9]

To regard this 'legal case' as a mere curiosity would be to underestimate its aesthetic dimension and relation to literary history. The members were in agreement in defending Becher's anti-war novel, *(CH Cl = CH)$_3$ As (Levisite) oder Der einzig gerechte Krieg* ('The Only Just War') (Vienna, 1926) against political aspersions. In March 1926 protesters from Gruppe 1925 had attacked the seizure of the book as an 'attempt to restrict the discussion of themes of contemporary importance from party viewpoints'.[10] Their solidarity against censorship went without saying, but it by no means followed that differences in positions with regard to aesthetic politics or creativity should be glossed over, even if the 'verdict' on Becher's novel was ultimately characterized by a gesture of mediation. Döblin, according to the records of the trial, 'based his charges on the claim that Becher had misused the novel form in order to produce a party-political pamphlet'.[11] A letter by Rudolf Leonhard recorded Döblin's arguments:

> In his speech for the prosecution, and in numerous replies, Döblin supported a particular form of fiction, a novel that depicts the development of individuals and their destinies; he reproached Becher with not dealing with this human development, these destinies, but instead using

---

question mark: 'May (1929): Brecht meets Walter Benjamin through Asja Lazis [*sic*].' Lacis's note about the outcome of the meeting in the Pension Voß, that 'they rarely met after that' (Asja Lacis, *Revolutionär im Beruf*, p. 49), can only refer to the late autumn of 1924, and not to May 1929, when their contact developed rapidly and effectively. At this time Benjamin 'frequently met Brecht' (ibid., p. 59) and he wrote to Scholem about the 'very friendly relationship between me and Bert Brecht' (Scholem, *Benjamin*, p. 159).

scientific and political propaganda to assemble a book from seemingly unprocessed raw material, and above all without aesthetic design.[12]

The 'court' finally exonerated Becher, since he had not misused the novel form, but merely used it unskilfully. Brecht's attitude as chairman of this debate is not recorded; but he doubtless spoke out in favour of the condemnation of an author whose novel showed 'how (even aesthetically) excellent material can be damaged by the use of antiquated fictional forms, and above all through the writing style associated with them'.[13] The positions taken in this debate were to return as leitmotifs in later conversations between Benjamin and Brecht.

Brecht's appearance at the Gruppe 1925 'trial' could well have been the subject of conversation between Asja Lacis, Reich and Benjamin on 6 December 1926, immediately after Benjamin's arrival in Moscow. 'I filled her [Asja Lacis] in about Brecht,' Benjamin noted on the first page of his *Moscow Diary*, and it seems likely that Brecht's friends, Lacis and Reich, were interested in personal news about him, particularly since Benjamin could not have had much to say about Brecht's writings, which were scarcely known to him at that time.*

A further encounter between Benjamin and Brecht took place around 1927 at a dinner following a reading by the actor Ludwig Hardt. Those present were Hardt, Brecht, Klabund, Carola Neher, Benjamin – who had come with Klabund and Neher – and Soma Morgenstern, who described the encounter to Gershom Scholem in a letter in 1974. Morgenstern is not the most reliable of witnesses, but such matters as are described here can hardly be pure invention. The debate is revealing as evidence of the discussion of Stalin and Trotsky, and also as a document of changing political positions – above all in the case of Brecht. Morgenstern wrote:

> I have already told you that I had a further meeting with Walter Benjamin. It was in Berlin after a performance by Ludwig Hardt, whom of course you knew and properly appreciated. After the performance I went to dinner with him, and there were a few other people there, among them Brecht, Klabund, and his charming wife, Carola Neher, who a few years later was lured to Moscow and put to death there. I had

---

* Benjamin, *Moscow Diary*, p. 9. Two and a half years later, Benjamin had read only *The Threepenny Opera* and the *Ballads* (by which he undoubtedly meant *Devotions for the Home*) – texts to which he had no access at all at the time of his journey to Moscow (see Scholem, *Benjamin*, p. 159). As far as I know, only Peter Beicken has referred to the significance of the diary entry for the dating of the first meeting (see Peter Beicken, 'Kafkas "Prozeß" und seine Richter. Zur Debatte Brecht–Benjamin und Benjamin–Scholem', in Benjamin Bennett et al, *Probleme der Moderne*, Tübingen, 1983, p. 353). Gary Smith has also drawn attention to the entry, but nevertheless stuck to the dating of May 1929 (see Gary Smith, 'Afterword' in Benjamin, *Moscow Diary*, p. 139).

already made the acquaintance of Brecht, also, as it happened, through Ludwig Hardt. He was by no means famous at that time. He was to be met in Berlin in rich Jewish houses, where he performed his ballads, accompanying himself on his guitar. On one of these occasions I heard his 'Legend of the Dead Soldier', which he recited extremely well, if not nearly as well as Ludwig Hardt, who often performed it. I can't be quite sure of the year, but it was a time when the Trotsky affair was the subject of public attention. I know that at that time Trotsky was already living in exile in Turkey.*

In the course of the evening – and evenings with Ludwig Hardt were always very enjoyable – the conversation at the table took a new turn. This was caused by the mention of the name of Trotsky. Although you disagree, I am still convinced that Klabund was a communist. The party was split down the middle in the discussion on this affair. Brecht, with Klabund and his wife, were entirely on Stalin's side. Hardt and I hotly defended Trotsky. As for Benjamin, he joined us. This came about – and this is how I come to remember the whole thing – when I maintained that one thing proved by the affair was that the old Russian anti-semitism still played a part in Russia. Brecht became very vehement. And since I was not slow to respond to him, the debate became quite heated. Hardt, who at the time had greater admiration for Brecht than I, since I had read only his *Drums in the Night* – and that only thanks to Hardt himself – tried to conciliate us, but was clearly enjoying the raised temperature of the occasion, for no debate could be too fierce for him. Benjamin helped a little, but I had the impression that he was not very interested in the whole business. My weak point was that I allowed myself to be carried away into accusing Stalin of anti-semitism, for which at that time there was no evidence. Brecht was able to argue against this, and cited the Jewish Zinoviev as proof, since he too was against Trotsky. This was well known, and I had to admit it. But this was hardly a decisive factor in Stalin's victory. In Lenin's lifetime Stalin was a third-class man at best. That he had the force to oppose Trotsky – at that time the glory of the victorious Revolution – that Stalin, a cautious man, dared to do this, and that he succeeded, proves that the mood in the country by then was such that the Party placed itself behind him and that a Stalin could drive Trotsky out of Russia. With this argument I won the support of Benjamin and Hardt, but not the debate

---

* This is a lapse of memory on Morgenstern's part: Trotsky had indeed been banished to Siberia on 16 January 1928 – that is, before Klabund's death – but he did not arrive in Istanbul until 12 February 1929.

– because it was always Bertold [*sic*] Brecht who won debates, as I later found out in Hollywood, and he did it by starting to shout, and anything that didn't suit him was 'completely out of the question'.*

There was an indirect encounter between Benjamin and Brecht on 13 July 1928, which began in the pages of the *Literarische Welt*. This revealed a difference of attitude which could not be explained by their relative ages and degrees of experience. On the occasion of the sixtieth birthday of the poet Stefan George, the journal had asked writers what part George had played in their intellectual development. Benjamin confessed to the 'crucial upheaval in his work' that he had experienced alongside his friends – 'of whom none is still alive'. The force that had linked him with those friends, he said, was the same that had later caused him to become disenchanted with George's work.[14] In a letter to Willy Haas about George and in a note on him, Brecht reacted crudely to the survey; he remarked that 'he wouldn't for the world miss such a reactionary occasion', and expected that editors would come to the conclusion 'that this writer's influence on the younger generation is of no significance whatsoever'.[15] However, Benjamin and Brecht used the same image: Benjamin likened George's poems (compared to those of his boyhood friend, Friedrich Heinle), to an 'old forest of pillars',[16] while Brecht mockingly remarked that the pillar sought out by this particular saint had been selected with too much cunning, 'it stands in too populous a spot; it offers an excessively picturesque sight...'[17]

Further meetings between Benjamin and Brecht may have taken place as early as 1925, or later in the context of the 'Philosophical Group'. This group, 'one of the most significant discussion centres in Berlin',[18] had developed from the circle of the Jewish scholar Oskar Goldberg and met informally, under the chairmanship of Erich Unger, about every one or two weeks. As Werner Kraft recalled, 'the entire German and Jewish intelligentsia was represented: Scholem, Benjamin, Brecht, Döblin, Franz Blei and many others'. Other sources also mention Hans Reichenbach, Karl Korsch, Arthur Rosenberg, and Robert Musil.[19] Kraft's memory may be at fault, but in the public life of Berlin in the twenties it was inevitable that Benjamin and Brecht should meet. Their

---

* Soma Morgenstern to Scholem, 28 January 1974, in Scholem, *Briefe III*, Munich, 1999, p. 343 (see Morgenstern, *Kritiken, Berichte, Tagebücher*, edited by Ingolf Schulte, Lüneburg, 2001, pp. 547–9). In a further letter, Morgenstern commented on the dating of the evening: 'As for my debate with Brecht, I do believe it took place in 1927. For, at that time, Benjamin turned up for dinner not with Brecht, but with Klabund and Carola Neher' (Soma Morgenstern to Gershom Scholem, 25 March 1974, JNUL, Scholem Archive, Arc. 4° 1598/173, 135). Scholem erroneously dated the conversation to about 1930, but Klabund had already died in 1928 (see Scholem, *Benjamin*, p. 204).

circle of friends and acquaintances was already overlapping by May 1929. Apart from Asja Lacis and Bernhard Reich, it included Ernst Bloch, whom Benjamin had known since 1918 and Brecht since 1921, as well as Adorno, Ernst Schoen, Siegfried Kracauer, Bernard von Brentano, Peter Suhrkamp, Gustav Glück, Erich Unger, Alfred Döblin, Carola Neher, Klabund, Ludwig Hardt, Kurt Weill and others.

Stimulating Conversations, Plans for Periodicals, 'Marxist Club', 1929–33

After May 1929, the relationship between Benjamin and Brecht developed rapidly and intensively. It was based on an increasing concordance about aesthetics and politics, which was expressed in the commitment that Benjamin, as a critic, gave to Brecht's work (see especially Chapter IV). Moreover, it led to a series of projects in common, often coordinated protests against the restriction of those fields of activity with which artists and intellectuals were confronted towards the end of the Weimar Republic. Benjamin was hit harder by this than Brecht. In his diary of May–June 1931 he confessed to his 'exhaustion from my struggles on the economic front':

> This dissatisfaction involves a growing aversion to, as well as a lack of confidence in, the methods I see chosen by people of my kind and my situation to assert control over the hopeless situation of cultural politics in Germany. What torments me is the lack of clarity and precision of the groupings with which the few people close to me divide into factions. What disturbs my inner peace, which is also a peaceable attitude, is the disproportion between the bitterness with which they debate their differences of opinion in my presence – though they have long since ceased to do so among themselves – and the frequently very minimal differences in substance.[20]

Benjamin's attempt to extricate himself from this crisis was directly linked with his commitment to Brecht, to an aesthetic attitude that seemed to offer him a way out of this unproductive situation. Benjamin's reaction to Scholem's reproach (cited above p. 13), that his work 'in the spirit of dialectical materialism' was a 'singularly intensive kind of self-deception', was to utter a credo whose concept betrayed his own embattlement: Scholem's letter, he said, 'penetrates my own position'

> to land like a projectile squarely in the centre of the position currently occupied here by a small but most important avant-garde group. Much of what led me to ever greater solidarity with Brecht's production is

precisely what you bring up in your letter; but this refers to much inherent in that production itself and with which you are not yet familiar.*

How directly the elements of Benjamin's politics and methodology were linked to what Brecht represented for him emerges from his statement, sent to Scholem only a little later, that he was making Brecht's work his own, 'provisionally – ideologically – as testimony'.[21] Brecht's writings were 'the first – to be precise, of the poetic or literary essays' – for which he was standing up 'as a critic without (public) reservation', because part of his development in recent years had taken place in the context of his study of them, and because they, 'more rigorously than any others give an insight into the intellectual context in which the work of people like myself is conducted in this country'.[22]

By comparison, Brecht's first mention of Benjamin's name was restrained. For the editorial board of the journal *Krise und Kritik*, he wrote to Brentano at the end of October 1930, he was thinking of Ihering, Brentano, himself and Benjamin – 'whom Rowohlt wants and who would fully support us, from what I know of him'.[23] The twofold qualifier – the publisher would like to have him, and Benjamin would support them, *from what Brecht knew of him* – is characteristic of Brecht's pragmatic attitude to Benjamin, even if the sequence of names and the justification in the letter may have been formulated with Brentano in mind. Brecht saw in Benjamin an intelligent, useful interlocutor, an occasional colleague and adviser, and a respected critic on whose public solidarity he could rely.

From the start, there was a disparity in their feelings towards each other, although this did not imply one-sidedness. For Benjamin there was considerably more at stake; his relationship with Brecht was directly linked with his plans. From Brecht's point of view, his association with Benjamin may at first not have been free from accidental factors, which only the years of exile replaced by a committed interest. This constellation repeatedly took their relationship to its limits, which could be ascribed not only to divergent expectations, but also to differences in mentality and character. The differences – all the descriptions

---

* *Benjamin Correspondence*, 17 April 1931, p. 377. Benjamin complained in this connection that Scholem had not expressed any opinion on the 'highly significant essay about opera, from the *Versuche*, no. 1, I sent you some weeks ago' (ibid.). The *Versuche* were a total of seven grey, paperbound volumes of Brecht's 'work in progress', published between 1930 and 1932 by Kiepenheuer in Berlin (continued from 1949 by Aufbau and Suhrkamp in Berlin and Frankfurt). He undoubtedly meant the 'Notes to the Opera *The Rise and Fall of the City of Mahagonny*', in *Versuche*, no. 2, whose seminal theses, like the tabulated comparison of the dramatic and epic forms of theatre, Benjamin wanted to discuss, rather than the 'Notes to *The Threepenny Opera*' from issue 3, which was not distributed until January 1932 (for these texts see Brecht, *Collected Plays*, vol. 2, pp. 345ff. and 303ff.).

tend towards cliché – lie in the fact that Brecht, who was nearly six years younger, gave the impression of being more agile, belligerent, and self-confident than
Benjamin, whose nature was rather circumspect and contemplative – at times
depressive.*

Benjamin repeatedly mentioned problems in his communication with
Brecht, at first good humouredly: 'He has such a penetrating way of thinking
and speaking', was a remark by his own son, Stefan, which Benjamin reported
after Stefan had heard Brecht singing on a gramophone record. Stefan had said
this 'almost with respect', his father commented.† But in the same breath he
raised the question of his prospective colleagues' ability to work together on the
journal project. Furthermore, Benjamin reflected, there was 'the difficulty inherent in working with Brecht. I, of course, assume that I am the one who will be
able to deal with that if anyone can'.[24] This, to be sure, was to prove a life's work.

In June 1931 Benjamin met Brecht in Le Lavandou on the Côte d'Azur.
Brecht was staying there 'with a whole team of friends and with new projects'.
His circle included Elisabeth Hauptmann, Emil Hesse-Burri, Carola Neher,
Marie Grossmann, Margot and Bernard von Brentano, and Benjamin also put
him in contact with Wilhelm Speyer, an author of books for young people. One
of Brecht's projects was his work on the play *Saint Joan of the Stockyards*, in
which Benjamin was involved, although it was difficult to say precisely how far
his participation went: 'At the moment we are occupied in preliminary work on
a new play.'[25] Benjamin's diary contains a scene which casts light on the personal atmosphere of the relationship. In a tour de force of autobiographical
prose Benjamin describes a solitary walk, on which he picked a dog-rose and a
small bunch of peonies, and with these, full of memories and in a 'somewhat
unstable state of mind', he approached the Villa Mar Belo, where Brecht and
the others were staying.

---

* Werner Fuld has completely inappropriately tried to explain the attraction that Brecht
exercised over Benjamin by juxtaposing Brecht's 'sensually natural' and Benjamin's
'non-physical' charisma (see Werner Fuld, *Walter Benjamin. Zwischen den Stuhlen*,
Munich/Vienna, 1979, p. 128). Scholem contradicted the characterization by Jean Selz,
for whom Benjamin had been 'the perfect type of the exclusively intellectual person':
'Everyone who knew Benjamin personally can testify that he was a man with very intense
feelings; and this intensity, being the foundation of countless pages of his writings, is the
key to understanding them' (Scholem to Rudolf Hartung, 14 February 1967, in
Scholem, *A Life in Letters*, edited by Anthony D. Skinner, Cambridge (Mass.)/London,
2002, p. 421).

† Benjamin to Scholem, 3 October 1930, *GB* III, p. 542 (this letter is translated in
Benjamin Correspondence) (see note 24 below), but a paragraph in which Benjamin
reports his 'great pleasure' in reading Brecht's plays and listening to a gramophone
record of him singing, together with his son's remarks, is omitted.

I ... entered the hall. They had seen me coming, and at the door to the dining room Brecht came towards me. Despite my protestations, he refused to go back to the table, and took me into the next room. We stayed there and talked for about two hours, partly on our own and partly with others, mainly just with Frau Grossmann, until I felt it was time to go. As I picked up my book, the flowers peeked out of it, and when someone joked about them my embarrassment grew, since even before I had entered the house I had been wondering why I was arriving bearing flowers, and whether I shouldn't throw them away. But I hadn't done so, God knows why. Needless to say, I realized there would be no opportunity to give my rose to [Elisabeth] Hauptmann, so I decided I would at least hoist it like a flag. But this idea was a complete failure. In the face of Brecht's ironic jokes, I no less ironically presented him with the peony, keeping a firm grip on the dog-rose. Of course, Brecht refused to accept it. I ended up putting the peony unobtrusively into a large vase full of blue flowers next to me. The dog-rose, however, I threw in among the blue flowers from above. There it stuck, looking as if it were growing out of the blue flowers – a very botanical curiosity. And there it remained quite clearly. So the little bunch of flowers had hoisted my flag after all, and had to take the place of her for whom it was intended.[26]

This scene, which almost defies analysis, condenses motifs, images, attitudes, longings, success and failure.* Sympathy and trust are concealed under the cloak of ironic jokes and remarks. That Benjamin and Brecht always continued to use the polite 'Sie' form of address is no contradiction.† Benjamin's account reveals a conspiratorial rapport; they shared secrets, or at any rate Benjamin was privy to Brecht's complicated personal relationships. In Le Lavandou he observed how Elisabeth Hauptmann and Carola Neher succeeded each other as Brecht's lovers, while his wife Helene Weigel, who had stayed behind in Berlin,

---

* Rainer Nägele, 'Von der Ästhetik zur Poetik', in *Lesarten der Moderne*, Eggringen, 1998, p. 102: 'This enigmatic anecdote with its compressed erotic configurations, triumphs, defeats and strange shifts of meaning, in which the dog-rose and peony, as sliding signifiers, prepare or block the path, must for now, and perhaps for ever, remain enigmatic.'

† In his contacts with many of his good friends and colleagues such as Korsch and Feuchtwanger, Brecht maintained his use of the formal 'Sie'. And Scholem stated that Fritz Lieb had been the only person during the years of exile with whom Benjamin had used the familiar 'Du' (see Gershom Scholem, *Walter Benjamin*, p. 207). This, of course, applies only if we ignore older and closer relationships such as those with Gretel Karplus-Adorno, Asja Lacis, Alfred Cohn, Fritz Radt and Jula Cohn-Radt. It is noteworthy that in his letters to Gretel Karplus, Benjamin referred to Brecht familiarly as 'Berthold'.

was appeased by letters.* And in the autumn of 1933, in Paris, Benjamin became a confidant of the couple Brecht and Margarete Steffin. Brecht valued Benjamin's reserved and amicable courtesy: 'Here there are nothing but "females" far and wide (the German ones),' wrote Margarete Steffin to Benjamin in May 1934: 'B[recht] is "cock of the walk" at the coffee tables, and doesn't seem to enjoy the role very much. He keeps wishing you were here, and that not *only* for selfish reasons.'†

On the basis of this personal closeness, which also included a shared sense of humour, conversations about sexuality were possible. In the summer of 1931 Benjamin recorded a conversation about Romeo and Juliet, during which Brecht expressed the opinion that the 'epic' theme of the play was that the two characters cannot find common ground, and above all in a totally physiological sense: 'For just as "it is well known" that the sexual act does not work if the partners have only sexual intentions, so too the love of Romeo and Juliet failed because they were trying too hard, were too eager'.[27] Conversations of this kind seem to have taken place regularly in the years that followed. A note that Benjamin dated to 'presumably 1936' betrays stereotypical masculine attitudes. There was mention of 'social aims that exert an influence on eroticism', an idea that Brecht developed by means of examples: 'A man encumbers himself with a frigid woman, to show that he has been able to seduce someone unattainable; another is tempted to make a conquest of a career woman.' They both kept a record of a conversation in the summer of 1938 about the crisis of bourgeois sexuality:

* The succession of Brecht's partners can be reconstructed from Benjamin's journal. 'Brecht and the others' lived in the Villa Mar Belo (*SW*, vol. 2, p. 476). Brecht, however, wrote to Helene Weigel that he was staying with the Brentanos at the Hotel Provence, while Elisabeth Hauptmann was living in a private pension: 'I don't think there can be any such gossip' as a result (see Brecht to Helene Weigel, mid May 1931, Brecht, *Letters*, p. 128). Brentano's diary and his wife's statements reveal that the Brentanos, Brecht and Hauptmann arrived in Le Lavandou on 15 May 1931 and stayed together 'in a pretty villa'. On 27 May Hauptmann left the town, 'then Carola Neher arrived and took over Hauptmann's room' (Margot von Brentano, 'Bericht über unsere Reise mit Brecht und der Hauptmann', in BBA Z 8/43).

†Steffin, *Briefe*, p. 123. Certainly Benjamin's experience of Brecht's confusing private life and his own complicity was not free from tension. In the summer of 1934 he wrote from Skovsbostrand to Anna Maria Blaupot ten Cate, who had met Brecht and Steffin with Benjamin in Paris: 'That the closeness of Steffin sometimes makes the atmosphere in B's house oppressive, you will in any case easily be able to imagine. Besides, she is kept in such seclusion that days often go by without my seeing her' (Benjamin to Anna Maria Blaupot ten Cate, draft, 19 August 1934, *GB* IV, p. 481). In her letters to Benjamin, Steffin wrote of such difficulties, if at all, by means of allusions, or in recounting her dreams.

Benjamin maintains Freud thinks that sexuality will one day die out completely. Our bourgeoisie thinks it is mankind. When the heads of the aristocracy fell, at least their pricks remained erect. The bourgeoisie has contrived to ruin even sexuality.[28]

Benjamin's paraphrase is to be found among the notes on 'Prostitution, Gambling' in the *Arcades* text, where he laid stress on the exaggerated claims of the bourgeois class:

Apropos of Freud's conjecture that sexuality is a dwindling function 'of' the human being, Brecht remarked on how the bourgeoisie in decline differs from the feudal class at the time of its downfall: it feels itself to be in all things the quintessence of humankind in general, and hence can equate its own decline with the death of humanity. (This equation, moreover, can play a part in the unmistakable crisis of sexuality within the bourgeoisie.) The feudal class, by virtue of its privileges, felt itself to be a class apart, which corresponds to the reality. That enabled it, in its waning, to manifest some elegance and insouciance.*

Turning back to the summer of 1931, Benjamin's journal from Le Lavandou recorded a debate which, in its outlandish features, was equally characteristic of Brecht's conversational style. The starting point was the political news from Berlin, which had 'greatly exasperated' Brecht. From the example of collectives such as he had experienced in 1918 as a medical orderly in a military hospital in Augsburg, Brecht developed theories about the masses: 'The intelligence of the capitalists grows in proportion to their isolation; and that of the masses in proportion to their solidarity.' Brecht hoped that the critical situation in Germany would unite the German proletariat. Benjamin recorded:

He also gave very curious reasons in favour of such collective measures, in our discussion about the German situation. If he were sitting on the Berlin executive committee, he would devise a five-day plan, according to which at least 200,000 Berliners would be eliminated within that period. Simply because this would ensure that 'people get involved'. 'If this were done, I know that at least 50,000 proletarians would have been made to participate actively.'[29]

This macabre intellectual pastime is reminiscent of the themes of alienation, extinction and killing, as featured by Brecht in his *Reader For Those Who Live In Cities*, and in the 'Lehrstücke' *He Who Says Yes / He Who Says No*

---

* Benjamin, *Arcades*, p. 511. In his own index to his *Baudelaire* Benjamin added: 'Sexuality according to Freud a dying function (impotence)' (*GS* VII/2, p. 737).

and *The Measures Taken*. What in *A Reader For Those Who Live in Cities* appears as a dramatic provocation to betray, to kill and to behave irresponsibly, in *He Who Says Yes* as the approval of the fatal sacrifice of a young boy according to ancient custom, and in *The Measure Taken* as the shooting of a young comrade and the dissolution of his body in a lime-pit; all of this finds its perverse climax in the proposal to eliminate 'at least 200,000 Berliners, if only because this would "get people involved"'.

Who was actually initiating the provocation? In allusion to Brecht's formulation about Baal: 'He is antisocial, but in an antisocial society', one might say that Brecht was provocative in a society which was destroying the bases of social communication in a provocative and systematic manner. 'Communism is not radical. It is capitalism that is radical', was a saying of Brecht's that Benjamin had recorded.[30] Now Benjamin noted that the political news had shaken Brecht's conviction that 'Germany would have to wait years more for a revolutionary situation to arise'.[31] He reacted nervously to the political crisis in the Reich capital. The emergency decree of 5 June 1931 on the rehabilitation of Reich, *Land* and local authority finances had been greeted by disturbances – it was the sixth emergency decree under Chancellor Brüning in a year and a quarter. Salary cuts and cutbacks in social welfare benefits deepened the social crisis. The government crisis was accompanied by bloody clashes between demonstrators and the police, and renewed brawls between communists and Nazis. On 10 June 1931, the day before Brecht's statement, there was a confrontation in the Prussian Landtag (the state parliament), when the parliamentary faction of the KPD (German Communist Party) proposed a motion of no confidence in the regional government, because of its complicity in the 'brutal pauperization politics of the emergency decree'. A speech by a communist member of parliament culminated in a 'call to revolutionary action'.[32]

Brecht's statements put attitudes to the test, a procedure that corresponds to the idea of his 'Lehrstücke'. These were based, Brecht noted in 1937 in his text 'Zur Theorie des Lehrstücks', 'on the expectation that the actor can be socially influenced by the performance of certain kinds of behaviour, the adoption of certain attitudes, the rendition of certain speeches, etc.'[33] And Brecht continued: 'It is by no means a question only of the showing of behaviour and attitudes to be rated as socially positive; an educational effect can be expected even from the (possibly exemplary) showing of antisocial behaviour and attitudes.'

Brecht was counting on the 'educational effect' of intensified conflicts. In socially marginalized groups, conflicts clash. 'But Brecht's constant effort', wrote Benjamin, 'is to describe these asocial figures and hooligans as virtual revolutionaries.'* Brecht's calculation was that the proletarians who had to be drawn into the process of the 'elimination' of 200,000 Berliners would experience the brutality of a system in a shocking fashion and so be predestined to the overthrow of this social order.† The violence that Brecht was invoking was counter-violence. It was directed, in the summer of 1931, against a regime whose only instrument of government was emergency decrees. Brüning's Cabinet, in agreement with Hindenburg, cited Paragraph 48 of the Weimar constitution, which set aside basic civic rights in the event of a considerable disturbance of public safety and order, and permitted measures that were to be enforced 'where necessary with the help of the armed forces'. The state of emergency had become the rule.

Brecht's vision of terror contains anarchist elements. In an essay 'Defence of the Poet Gottfried Benn' in 1929, Brecht had attempted to describe the role of the intellectual in the revolution. His defined position coincided with that of Benjamin when Brecht wrote: 'The view they [the intellectuals] often air that it's necessary to submerge oneself in the proletariat, is counter-revolutionary', and: 'The revolutionary intellect differs from the reactionary intellect in that it is a dynamic and, politically speaking, a *liquidating* intellect.' 'In a non-revolutionary situation the revolutionary intellect appears as radicalism. Its effect on every party, even a radical one, is *anarchistic*, as long as it doesn't manage to found a party of its own, or is compelled to liquidate its own party'[34] (E.W.'s italics). Benjamin was no stranger to anarcho–syndicalist thinking. In his essay of 1921, 'Critique of Violence', he had, following Georges Sorel, stressed the proletarian general strike as a legitimate means of 'pure force'.[35] Brecht's reflections of 1931 went a step further intellectually. Benjamin, who noted them only from a timid distance, appeared open to such provocations. Brecht's radical ideas were a counterpoint against which Benjamin could test his own views.

This is reminiscent of Bernhard Reich's characterization of Brecht, that he expressed his views categorically, using paradoxical formulations, and did not enter into argument but 'swept away' contradictions.[36] Fritz Sternberg

---

* *SW*, vol. 2, p. 369. He was certainly aware of the difficulties into which he was led by this goal. Benjamin reports a reflection from the summer of 1934: 'It was completely impossible to import into the model of the proletarian fighter the gesture of the footloose vagabond who leaves his own concerns to chance and who turns his back on society' (ibid., p. 784).

† The possibility of learning through killing is also the inherent theme in 'The Report on the Death of a Comrade' from *The Mother*: 'But as he went to the wall where they intended to shoot him/ He went towards a wall which had been built by men of his own kind.../ Not even/ Those who were obliged to shoot him differed from him, or were forever incapable of learning' (Brecht, *Collected Plays*, vol. 3, p. 138).

described Brecht's tendency towards what Benjamin later called 'provocative tricks':

> Brecht demonstrated extraordinary skill during such discussions. Or perhaps one should say, developed his dramatic talent. In his earlier discussions with Döblin, Piscator, Feuchtwanger, George Grosz, and the director Engel, Brecht had already voiced a number of very pointed views, very sharp, aggressive aphorisms. On such occasions his manner of speaking was often very different from that in other conversations we had in private. When I asked Brecht about this, he maintained that what he said in a discussion of this kind, where between four and ten men were present, did not need to be his own opinion, any more than what he put in the mouth of a character in one of his plays. He said that he made some of these pointed remarks in order to provoke people, to draw them out, to make the situation more dramatic. And in fact he often succeeded in this. After such discussions we knew a great deal more about some people than before.[37]

Brecht himself described this 'ability' in a note made around 1930 as 'real thinking': 'He thought in the heads of others, and others also thought in his head.'[38] In 1932 Benjamin used the expression, which he had doubtless learnt in conversation, in a review of Kurt Hiller's volume of essays *Der Sprung ins Helle* ('The Leap into the Light'): what was decisive was 'not private thinking, but, as Brecht once put it, the art of thinking in the heads of others'.*

Another field of interest may serve as an example of the development of themes and internal correspondence between Brecht and Benjamin. In a conversation of 8 June 1931 they discussed different ways of *Wohnen* – living, in the sense of 'inhabiting'. The conversation is paralleled by an indirect dialogue in texts by Benjamin and Brecht, in which inhabiting and habitations (*Wohnungen*) play a part in social as well as aesthetic and creative terms.[39] The dimension of aesthetic politics in this dialogue consisted in its link with questions raised by the New Architecture, with advanced architectural theory and practice.† Benjamin had declared in his Hessel review in 1929 that

> the cult of 'inhabiting' in the old sense, with the idea of security at its core, has now received its death knell. Giedion, Mendelsohn, and Corbusier are converting human habitations into the transitional spaces of every imaginable force and wave of light and air.[40]

---

* *GS* III, p. 351. Rolf Tiedemann, extremely aptly, headed the Afterword to his second edition of Benjamin's writings on Brecht with this dictum: 'The art of living in other people's heads' (*Versuche über Brecht*, Frankfurt, 1978, pp. 175–208).

† In his study on Benjamin's *Berlin Childhood around 1900* Heinz Brüggemann pointed out connections between Benjamin's texts and the work of Siegfried Giedion.

In discussing his 'favourite topic', that of 'inhabiting' (*das Wohnen*)', Benjamin repeatedly refers to Brecht's saying in *A Reader For Those Who Live In Cities*: 'Erase the traces!' A note in Benjamin's journal of May 1931, which recorded a conversation with Egon Wissing, reads as follows: 'leaving traces is not just a habit (a *Gewohnheit*), but the primal phenomenon of all the habits (*Gewohnheiten*) that are involved in inhabiting (*Wohnen*) a place.'[41] This phrase recurs in Benjamin's sketch, 'To Live (*Wohnen*) without Leaving Traces' (from 'Short Shadows II') in the text 'Experience and Poverty'[42], and finally, modified, in his *Paris, Capital of the Nineteenth Century*: 'to inhabit (*Wohnen*) means to leave traces.'[43]

It is against a background of changing experiences, people's habits and ways of perception that one should look at Benjamin's and Brecht's mutual attempt to work out a typology of living or inhabiting, which identifies mutually complementary ways of behaving in 'habitations'. Benjamin recorded their arguments and criteria of classification in his diary of May–June 1931.[44]*

What is remarkable here is the playful formation of thoughts while speaking. What linked Benjamin and Brecht was their interest in people's social and practical habits and behaviour. Different ways of inhabiting can be models for the theatre: people's characteristics and attitudes can be studied through their psychological and social origins, and resultant ways of communication. The model has a dialectical character; the limits of classification are not rigid, but different attitudes can be found united in an individual. They engage with one another and are to some extent mutually conditional.

The meetings between Benjamin and Brecht up to 1933 are characterized by 'extended and extremely stimulating conversations'[45] and more and more new plans, the most interesting of which was the project for the journal *Krise und Kritik* (see Chapter III below). Benjamin attributed his interest in this collaboration to Brecht, whose writings were, he said, typical of the questions posed by the left-wing critical intelligentsia in general. To an increasing degree Benjamin spoke on his own behalf when trying to convince Gershom Scholem, in Jerusalem, of the status of Brecht's work and positions.

Apart from *Krise und Kritik*, a series of further significant and influential ramifications resulted from the encounter between Benjamin and Brecht in the years in Berlin from 1929 to 1932, their common denominator being an attempt to exert public influence. At the same time it is not always clear whether they were ever more than playful speculation. They will be documented here because they contribute to a more precise placing of the *Krise und Kritik* project in the context of intellectual and social history.

* The German original reproduces Brecht's fragmentary notes. However, their fragmentary, telegrammic nature precludes satisfactory translation.

1. The plan, in 1930, 'to annihilate Heidegger here in the summer in the context of a very close-knit circle of readers led by Brecht and me',[46] failed because of an illness of Brecht's, his later trip to Le Lavandou and his habitual summer holiday in Bavaria. The topic of Heidegger attracted Benjamin and Brecht. They wanted to get to grips with him in their putative journal as an example of a 'kind of leadership cult' and considered his philosophy a rival alternative to the practical thinking they themselves favoured. The plan might possibly have extended beyond the bounds of a 'reading group', as Günther Anders recalled in 1992:

> I can't tell you much about Brecht's various journal projects. I only remember that B. told me – this was probably in 1932 – that he and Benjamin were planning to start an anti-Heidegger journal. I recall also that I replied to him, somewhat bemused, that he had told me himself that he had neither read Heidegger nor heard him speak, and that the same went for Benjamin, and that I thought it was rash in these circumstances to found a journal with this aim. Nothing beyond this one conversation comes back to me.*

2. Another plan, strikingly close both intellectually and organizationally to the *Krise und Kritik* journal project, was for the foundation of a Society of Materialist Friends of the Hegelian Dialectic, which was being considered around 1931. The stimulus had come from a letter of Lenin's, dated 12 March 1922, to the Moscow periodical *Under the Banner of Marxism*, in which he proposed the formation of a society of that name.† Brecht may have known Lenin's letter from the German-language edition of *Under the Banner of Marxism*, where it was reprinted in 1925 and mentioned again in 1931.‡ And certainly Brecht knew that Karl Korsch, in *Marxism and Philosophy* (1923), and Georg Lukács, in *History and Class Consciousness* (1923), had referred by way of justification to the instructions prescribed by Lenin.§ In their studies, Korsch and Lukács had

---

* Günther Anders to the author, 17 March 1992 (postmark). See also Günther Anders, 'Bertolt Brecht', in *Merkur* (Stuttgart), vol. 33, no. 9, p. 890: 'His [Benjamin's] project to produce an anti-Heidegger pamphlet together with Brecht probably failed because Brecht – as I can report with certainty – never read as much as two pages of Heidegger's *Being and Time*. In any case, since he was lacking in all the qualifications in the history of philosophy which this would have demanded, he would not have been at all capable of understanding it.'

† Lenin's text had been published in German in 1922 in the periodical *Die Kommunistische Internationale*, of which Benjamin had been aware.

‡ Brecht possessed issues from 1925 to 1934, including the first issue from the first year of publication, 1925, in which Lenin's letter of 12 March 1922 had been reprinted.

§ Korsch used a quotation from Lenin's letter as the epigraph to his study: 'We must organize a systematic study of the Hegelian dialectic, from a materialistic standpoint' (Karl Korsch, *Marxism and Philosophy*, London, 1970, p. 29; the first edition appeared in

upheld the *philosophical* claims of Marxist theory and deplored the impoverishment of dialectics in the communist movement and in 'so-called "Marxism-Leninism"'.[47] The living Marxism of Korsch and Lukács was opposed to the idea of Marxism as a 'pure and unadulterated teaching'.[48]

How far the plans for the society progressed is not known; but Brecht certainly discussed them with Benjamin and Brentano. Benjamin noted the name 'International Society of Materialist Friends of the Hegelian Dialectic' as the subject of conversations with Brecht in late May and early June 1931 at Le Lavandou.[49] Outlines, a draft charter, and notes preserved among Brecht's papers in which the titles 'Organization of Dialecticians' and 'Society for (or 'of') Dialecticians' also exist, show that the plan was in many respects comparable to the attempt to create the journal *Krise und Kritik*.[50] The Society of Materialist Friends of the Hegelian Dialectic was envisaged as an organization for intellectuals and artists convinced of the need for proletarian revolution and whose preferred method was dialectical thought. As in the case of *Krise und Kritik*, 'interventionist thinking' was to be taught, 'inconsequential thought' avoided. A draft charter laid down that the members of the Society should take over the solution of specific theoretical tasks, and in doing so agree on uniform working principles, which were to be valid for all areas of art, politics, science, etc.[51] However, the aim was more radical: with *Krise und Kritik* all that was specified was the statement that the journal should be based on the class struggle; a party-political affiliation was explicitly excluded (see p. 188 below). The Society, on the other hand, aimed, on its own admission, at world revolution; the use of actual dialectic must, it was said, 'lead immediately and unswervingly to directly revolutionary actions and organizations', and the 'organizational union' with 'the communist workers' party' was considered to be the 'conclusion' of its work.[52] As a logical result, the instructions for the dialecticians had a conspiratorial character: the members of the Society would not be allowed to give up or endanger their bourgeois occupations and spheres of activity without the permission of the Society. With *Krise und Kritik*, specialists were to contribute articles for the journal; the Society adopted the tactic of practising one's profession and maintaining influential positions in the

---

1923); the quotation is taken from the copy in Brecht's library. Lukács quoted Lenin in the Preface to his collection of studies: '[The author] believes that today it is still of *practical* importance to return in this respect to the traditions of the Marx-interpretation by Engels (who regarded "the German workers' movement" as "the heir to German classical philosophy"), and by Plekhanov. He believes that all good Marxists should form – in Lenin's words – a kind of society of the materialist friends of the Hegelian dialectic' (Georg Lukács, *History and Class Consciousness*, London, 1971, p. xlv.).

interests of the world revolution, to some extent to use them as a bridgehead for the destruction of bourgeois society.

3. A paper in Brecht's literary remains, with the heading 'Marxist Club' – also in the Brecht Archive – seems to date from the same period, 1931.

> Marxist Club (name not yet fixed)
> The Club offers its members the chance to meet once a week in a specified place, convenient for discussions, meetings and conversation.
> The Club is a meeting place for left-wing elements who have decided to extend and deepen their studies of Marxism and use them in practice in their specialized fields. For this purpose the club regularly organizes
> a) short Marxist lectures on all possible topics,
> b) discussions with bourgeois scholars from all fields of study,
> c) the taking up of links with Soviet scientists.
> The effects of dialectical materialism on their specialist fields are to be communicated to members.
> For the time being the Club will not make itself known publicly.*

Whether the Marxist Club ever met has not been recorded, nor do we know how far the preparations progressed, or to what extent the people whose names turn up in the papers were involved in them. It is conceivable that the formation of the Marxist Club came about as a reaction to the measures taken by the Berlin city council in October 1931, which denied the Marxist Workers' School (Marxistische Arbeiterschule – MASCH) the right to use rooms in the city's schools. Following this ruling, a number of artists and intellectuals, including Brecht, Brentano, Eisler, Feuchtwanger, Heartfield, Helene Weigel and Kurt Weill, had made their apartments available to MASCH for their courses.† The rule that the club would not at first make itself known to the public would explain why there is no record of meetings, if any took place. The members of the board were, among others, Karl Wittfogel, Brecht, Brentano, Becher, Lukács and Feuchtwanger, as well as the physician Fritz Weiss and a Frau A. Harnack – this was probably Mildred Harnack, the American wife of Arvid

---

* BBA 1518/0. I am grateful to Michael Buckmiller and Michel Prat who drew my attention to the Marxist Club.

† See Silvia Schlenstedt, 'Auf der Suche nach Spuren: Brecht und die MASCH', in *Brecht 83. Brecht und Marxismus*, Berlin, 1983, pp. 25ff and 366. Klaus Völker reports that, parallel to Korsch's course of lectures on 'Marxism, Living and Dead', a study group had met in Brecht's apartment, in which Elisabeth Hauptmann, Slatan Dudow, Hans Richter, Hanna Kosterlitz, Paul Partos, Heinz Langerhans, as well as Brecht and Korsch had participated (see Klaus Völker, *Brecht: a Biography*, London, 1979, p. 166). Apart from those of Heartfield and Weill, the names appear in the documents of the Marxist Club.

Harnack, both of whom were later members of the 'Rote Kapelle' resistance group.[53] An overview of topics and list of members, or prospective members, are preserved in the Brecht Archive:

Topics

1. Hans Jaeger: Economics of fascism
2. Eisler, Vogel, (Scherchen?): On music
3. XY: The world view of modern bourgeois physics
4. Behaviourism (psychology)[54]

Members

Vogel / [Hanns] Eisler / [Heinz] Pol / [Hans] Sahl / Hiller / [Ernst?] Busch / Akermann / [Helene] Weigel / [Peter] Lorre / [Caspar] Neher / [Hermann] Scherchen / [Emil Julius] Gumbel / [Friedrich] Burschell / [Wilhelm] Wolfradt / [Ernst] Ottwalt / [Walter] Benjamin / [Heinrich] Mann / [Gustav] Kiepenheuer / [Ernst] Glaeser / [Franz Carl] Weiskopf / [Theodor] Plivier / [Wieland] Herzfelde / [Erwin] Piscator / [Elisabeth] Hauptmann / Paul Brauer / [E. A.] Reinhardt / Hans Jäger / [Kurt] Kersten / Durus [i.e. Alfred Kémény] / [Carl von] Ossietsky / [George] Gross [*sic*] / [J.] Schiff / [Manès] Sperber / [Bernhard(?)] Reich / [Alfred] Kurella / [Walter] Dubislav / [Siegfried] Kracauer / [Slatan] Dudow / Karl Lewin*

4. An unrealized journal project, probably dating from the same period, is recorded under the name *Signale*. Traces of the project are documented on three pages in Brecht's papers; Benjamin's name does not appear. The group of envisaged co-workers, the proposed themes and the method of working suggest contact with the plans in which Benjamin took part. A proposal for an editorial board in Brecht's handwriting survives: 'wittfogel / lucacs [*sic*] / günther stern / ihering / brentano / becher / brecht / gabor', as well as – presumably as contributors – 'kracauer / großmann / sternberg / dr schmal / schaxel / h pohl [*sic*] / musil / horkheimer'.† Among the topics to be covered by this journal on social theory and economics were: 'dying capitalism / socialism under con-

---

* BBA 1518/03. A version of the list of names and of part of the statute, varying only slightly from that given here, in the handwriting of Brentano and another, has been preserved (BBA 1518/01). The handwritten list has been used to add forenames or initials. Names not included in the typewritten list are [Kurt(?)] Sauerland, [Ernst] Bloch, T. H. Otto [?], [Ernst] Toller, as well as Armin Kesser and [Felix] Gasbarra as managers. In a conversation with the author on 13 October 1992, Hans Sahl did not remember such a circle, but considered its composition and political aims to be plausible.

† BBA 810/10ff. The name Schaxel could refer to Julius Schaxel, who had published an article in the periodical *Under the Banner of Marxism* in 1925.

struction / german ideology / marxist problems / ... "fascism" and "workers' movement".*

Benjamin's name is also missing in the project for a 'journal for the clarification of fascist arguments and counter-arguments', which can be dated to a period after 9 November 1931.[55] What was a side issue in the cases of *Krise und Kritik* and *Signale* here becomes the main focus of the work. With the aim expressed in the title, which was to be worked out systematically in groups, central themes of anti-fascist activity at the pre-totalitarian stage were to be covered, such as cultural politics and women's rights, economics, the leadership question, racial issues, as well as camouflaged class and economic issues, nationalism, etc. It is worth mentioning that the name of Harro Schulze-Boysen turns up among the actual or intended contributors – he was later also a member of the 'Red Orchestra' resistance group; he was to present a report on 'the national socialist state and nation'.

The projects for *Krise und Kritik* and Heidegger (respectively a journal and a reading-group), for a Society of Materialist Friends of the Hegelian Dialectic, the Marxist Club, *Signale*, and the 'journal for the clarification of fascist arguments and counter-arguments', all vary in respect of their protagonists, the political situation and their objectives. What they all have in common is the fact that intellectuals and artists felt the necessity to organize for the creation of an alternative public sphere. Their activities would largely depend on the professions of the participants, while dialectical materialism became to an increasing extent the driving force.

Exile, Detective Novel, Chess, 1933–40

With the beginning of exile, the conditions of communication changed. Relationships could be sustained only with difficulty; isolation, including linguistic

---

* BBA 810/09. The notes are in one of the notebooks with red cardboard covers and vellum paper that are difficult to date, because Brecht used them frequently. The notebook BBA 810 has been described and variously interpreted over a long period of time. Apart from drafts and notes on *The Mother*, it includes among other things similar notes on *Señora Carrar's Rifles*. Brecht's note on the inside cover, '*Brecht* / Svendborg / Skovsbostrand', provides no clue to the dating of the *Signale* project. Günther Anders, questioned about the *Signale* journal project, reacted as follows: 'I was highly surprised – I did not know – that I was included in Brecht's list of editorial board members; for he had a very ambivalent attitude to me. Being well read in philosophy, I was someone he regarded rather with suspicion; sometimes he didn't like me at all. So, as I have said, to find my name linked with the names of Brecht's closest friends, sixty years later, was a surprise for me, and I could hardly say whether it was a pleasant one' (Günther Anders to the author, 27 March 1992).

isolation, was one of the greatest dangers of exile.* Benjamin and Brecht lived most of the time in different countries; meetings needed to be precisely arranged. This meant an end to the casual contacts in Berlin, such as chance encounters, meetings fixed at short notice, telephone calls – with the disadvantage that intimate communication can be documented only in fragmentary fashion.†

Margarete Steffin kept Benjamin fully informed. The pressures of life forced the emigrants to adapt to the limited possibilities for work and income in the countries of their exile, and make their choice of residence dependent on the cost of living or the quality of working conditions (libraries, editors, publishers). Brecht and his family stayed in Denmark, where conditions were relatively favourable, for six years. Benjamin was highly reluctant to move far from the source of his studies at the Bibliothèque Nationale in Paris, to stay frugally for short periods with the Brechts, or with his divorced wife in San Remo. As long as it was still at all possible, attempts were made to salvage possessions and working materials left behind in Germany. It was of the greatest significance to Benjamin when, in the autumn of 1933, Brecht offered to look after his books at his own home in Skovsbostrand. This meant that from the spring of 1934 Benjamin knew that the more important half of his library was in a place of safety, and in addition he could make use of the books during his summer holidays there.[56]

Even exile did not offer total security. Opponents of Hitler were forced to flee from countries annexed or invaded by Germany, so as not to share the fate of the political prisoners about which 'horrifying rumours are circulating'.[57] Even in places of emigration that were not acutely endangered, there were threats from collaborators or secret police informers. Benjamin reported to Scholem on 7 December 1933 that 'someone who was a close acquaintance of both Brecht and myself in Berlin', who had been released by the Gestapo and reached Paris, might possibly have been denounced by 'a man in Paris we all know'.[58] It was

* Benjamin repeatedly complained of loneliness and isolation, even to correspondents who were not in his intimate circle, such as Alfred Kurella: 'I am only imperfectly informed about the conditions of exile. I am most grateful to you for any kind of information, and can only hope that the nonchalance with which so many people on whose news I had depended neglect the simplest form of communication is not symptomatic of the organization of our work' (Benjamin to Alfred Kurella, 2 May 1933, *GB* IV, p. 199).

† The years between 1933 and 1938 are particularly well documented; but in their correspondence Benjamin and Brecht to a great extent exercised restraint because of censorship, above all German censorship. It was feared that 'it is not impossible that letters from France to Denmark might travel through Germany' (Benjamin/Scholem, 2 June 1934, p. 115).

Elisabeth Hauptmann who had been interrogated in Berlin; but the identity of her betrayer is something we will probably never know.

Against the background of the difficult conditions of exile, a solid personal relationship grew between Benjamin and Brecht, whose intensity can partly be attributed to their physical proximity during the time they spent together in Paris and Skovsbostrand. In addition to the political and aesthetic interests they had in common, which were decisive for their work together between 1929 and 1933, practical questions of existence now came to the fore. Benjamin's attitude to Brecht was unchanged. In a description of his situation from the first year of his exile, he wrote unequivocally to Kitty Marx-Steinschneider in Jerusalem, on 20 October 1933: 'I will naturally not conceal the fact – if this must still be stated – that my approval of Brecht's production represents one of the most important and most defensible points of my entire position.'[59] At the same time he remarked, before his first journey to Denmark: 'As close as I am to Brecht, I do have reservations about having to rely solely on him once I am there.'* Benjamin overcame his reservations; he had no alternative. A stay in Skovsbostrand without Brecht would indeed have been quite unimaginable.† In the summer of 1936, in need of rest and relaxation, he considered travelling to Ibiza instead of Denmark, having 'more stimulation than strengthening to expect from a stay in Denmark', as he wrote to Alfred Cohn. But 'in the present situation' he could not 'endanger his relationship with Brecht'.‡

His fears were not without foundation, and 'stimulating' would have been a euphemistic description of many a conversation between Benjamin and Brecht. Writing to Werner Kraft when working on his own Kafka essay in November 1934, Benjamin says: 'I was struck by how accurately you guessed the opposition to the project that was to be expected from Brecht, although you can hardly have a notion of the intensity it occasionally reaches.'[60] At the height of the debate, Brecht reproached his friend with 'promoting Jewish fascism', and increasing the obscurity of Kafka rather than dispersing it, with this essay.[61] At

---

* ibid., 18 January 1934, ibid., p. 434. Almost the same formulation appears in an earlier letter to Scholem (30 December 1933) and in a letter to Gretel Karplus (30 December 1933). And when he was already in Skovsbostrand, Benjamin complained that because of his financial situation he was 'dependent upon B's hospitality to a degree that might some day turn out to be precarious' (ibid., 20 July 1934, ibid., p. 450).

† See *Benjamin Correspondence*, 9 August 1935, ibid., p. 504: 'The winter months in the remote Danish corner where Brecht lives would probably be all the more difficult to bear, since Brecht himself usually makes his Russian and English trips at that time.'

‡ Benjamin to Alfred Cohn, 4 July 1936, *GB* V, p. 326. The formulation, 'and my personal interest here coincides with a more general one', refers to the expressed hope that through Brecht he might find an opportunity to publish the German version of his 'Work of Art'' essay.

the end of this summer, Benjamin ruefully noted, in their conversations what Brecht himself called 'the inflammatory side of his thought' 'comes to the fore much more often than it did formerly'.[62] In the summer of 1938 there were differences over Baudelaire; Brecht mocked Benjamin's description of the concept of aura – without however, presumably, confronting its writer in conversation with his caustic comments: 'This is the way the materialist understanding of history is adapted! It is pretty abominable'.[63] And when, after Benjamin's death, he describes 'On the Concept of History' as 'clear and presents complex issues simply', this was not without the qualification, 'despite all its metaphors and Judaisms.'[64] However, the provocations also had their productive dimension: in the summer of 1936 Brecht received Benjamin's essay, 'The Work of Art in the Age of Its Technological Reproducibility' 'not without resistance, indeed collisions'. The revision of this work, undertaken in common, led to the extension of the text by a quarter. Benjamin referred to it as 'very productive', saying that it had, 'without affecting the core of the work in the least, led to a number of notable improvements'.[65] There were differences and difficulties, but also rapprochements and the solution of problems (see Chapter V below).

It is not known when Benjamin and Brecht last saw or spoke to each other before the Nazi takeover. Benjamin was informed as to the time and circumstances of Brecht's flight from Germany.* After this, the maintenance of the relationship seems to have been dependent on the mediation of third parties.† On a picture postcard from Sanary-sur-Mer, sent to Benjamin in San Antonio, Ibiza, by Eva Boy, Brecht and Arnold Zweig in late September 1933, Brecht asked: 'Are you coming to Paris?'‡ It was there that Benjamin and Brecht met for the first time in exile, in late October or early November 1933.§

---

* See Benjamin to Scholem, 20 March 1933, *Benjamin Correspondence*, p. 406: 'However, not too many of them [i.e. those close to Benjamin] were still in Germany at the time of my departure: Brecht, Kracauer, and Ernst Bloch left at the right time – Brecht one day before he was to be arrested.'

† Brentano passed on greetings from Benjamin to Brecht (see Bernard von Brentano to Bertolt Brecht, 4 April 1933, BBA 481/61ff.).

‡ Eva Boy van Hoboken, Bertolt Brecht and Arnold Zweig to Walter Benjamin, 29 September 1933 (postmarked Sanary-sur-Mer) (WBA 63/1). Eva Boy, whose married name was van Hoboken, a painter and writer, owned a studio in Prinzregentenstraße, in Berlin, where Benjamin had lived up to the time of his emigration. She wrote: 'We are thinking of you with affection, and wondering where you will be in the winter, do write to Brecht at the address above, we are now leaving for Holland, Germany and then Paris.'

§ Brecht and Margarete Steffin returned to Paris on 19 October (see Steffin's pocket diary, BBA 2112/40). On 8 November 1933 Benjamin, in a letter to Gretel Karplus, mentioned daily meetings with Brecht (*GB* IV, p. 309).

The seven weeks up to Brecht's departure on 19 December were marked by a lively exchange, so 'now that Brecht had gone', Benjamin felt that the city seemed 'dead'.[66] Benjamin, Brecht and Margarete Steffin lived in the same hotel in Paris, the Palace Hotel in the Rue du Four. There are records of encounters with other exiles: Klaus Mann, Hermann Kesten, Siegfried Kracauer, Lotte Lenya, Kurt Weill, Elisabeth Hauptmann (after her release), and with Eisler, to discuss the Brecht collection *Lieder Gedichte Chöre*.[67] Benjamin had come back from Ibiza with malaria; after his convalescence he searched for ways of 'earning something from bibliographical, library work'. He wrote reviews, planned an essay on Balthasar Gracián, and worked on his great study of Eduard Fuchs, with whom he made contact.[68] Margarete Steffin helped him to put together a manuscript of his book of letters, *Deutsche Menschen* (*German Men and Women*).* To Gretel Karplus, who, like Adorno, used the spelling 'Berthold' for Brecht, Benjamin wrote: 'Berthold, whom I see daily, often for long periods, is making efforts to put me in touch with publishers.'[69] Brecht worked with Steffin on *The Threepenny Novel*, the manuscript of which Benjamin read. Brecht also took part in editing the *Second Brown Book of Hitler Terror*.[70] And they joined forces on a project which Benjamin had already announced in the same letter to Gretel Karplus mentioned above: 'I am talking with Berthold about the theory of the crime novel, and perhaps at some time an experimental project will emerge from our discussions.'†

The intention of progressing from the theory of crime fiction to its practice had been discussed earlier. In June 1931 the 'idea for a crime drama' was among the topics touched upon by the group assembled in Le Lavandou. In May 1933 Benjamin mentioned the project for a crime novel, which he would, however, write only if he could assume that it would be a success: 'At present I can think of it only with great reservations, and all I can do for the time being is to make notes on small pieces of paper about scenes, motives, tricks, to be considered at a later time.'[71] Two of Benjamin's slips of paper contain sketches of material corresponding to a fragment of a crime novel in Brecht's papers.‡ Benjamin made notes for a division into chapters and key words for the plot,[72] while in Brecht's papers the first chapter, a plot outline and notes on figures, scenes and

---

* See Benjamin to Margarete Steffin, 4 November 1936, *GB* V, p. 413: 'You will certainly still remember how they worked together on the manuscript at the Palace Hotel two years ago.' For Benjamin's *German Men and Women*, see *SW*, vol. 3, pp. 167ff.

† Benjamin to Gretel Karplus, 8 November 1933, *GB* IV, p. 310. Benjamin's statement after Brecht's departure possibly also refers to this project: 'I had arranged a meeting with Kasper about the crime novel, but he unfortunately missed it' (Walter Benjamin to Bertolt Brecht, 23 December 1933, *GB* IV, p. 322). No further information has been discovered, nor the identity of Kasper.

‡ Lorenz Jäger was the first to pick up the traces of the joint experiment.

motifs have been preserved. The authorship is not precisely clarified; it could have been a genuinely joint enterprise. Benjamin might have contributed a general outline as well as some individual 'scenes, motives, tricks', and Brecht elements of material, such as the motif of blackmail, which corresponded to his interests.* To judge from the style and handwriting, the first completed chapter may have been dictated by Brecht.

The plot, which can be reconstructed from the various items of textual evidence, is fairly unspectacular: a retired judge gets on to the trail of a blackmailing small shareholder. The shareholder is also cheating on his wife, who finds him out when he is going about his business in a foreign city. He discovers her, tries to cover up by referring to his earlier activity as a sales representative, but she decides not to accuse him for fear of divorce. The blackmailer is killed by a secretary who is under pressure from him and who, when the opportunity presents itself, pushes him into an empty lift shaft. A series of motifs, topics and elements of plot are found in both Benjamin's and Brecht's papers (a suitcase of samples, an umbrella, a flower shop, a note reading 'Danger, leaving town', a camera, a hairdo, a corkscrew, a biscuit factory, a printing firm, a motiveless murder to cover up a murder with a motive). Some differences suggest changes made while dictating; for example, some names are similar or the same, but spelt differently (Seifert/Seiffert, Montana company/Mollison company).

These events, typical of the genre, are forced to the surface through the characterization of the judge and detective that emerges from a note among Brecht's papers, probably written by him. It reveals a view of justice and society which corresponds to the position and projects of Benjamin and Brecht. The judge is a 'sceptical man', 'who has no interest in any structures of law or ideology, and devotes the entire force of his intelligence to the observation of reality'. For him, in many cases, more disastrous than the malignity of the offender is the environment which caused the offence. His experience with the justice system has led him to 'recognize the consequences of a judgment as in many cases more harmful than the act for which the judgment has been made the penalty'. He 'has always been interested in what happens after the sentence is pronounced', and he does not want to assert the law at all costs, which leads to the fact that at the end only he and the reader know the result of his detective work. This suggests a new type of German detective for the period when the fragment came into being, one who is beginning to examine the laws of bourgeois society. Benjamin and Brecht, whose notes reveal their enjoyment of

* That Benjamin was the source of ideas is supported by a question by Margarete Steffin, who was an observer of the work: 'How is your novel coming along? You'd better hurry! Otherwise I'll start something of my own, but of course nothing might come of it' (Margarete Steffin to Benjamin, end of January 1934, Steffin, *Briefe*, p. 109).

the game of literary detective fiction, were also motivated by their interest in the exposure of the mechanisms of bourgeois society.

In the autumn of 1934 the two again collaborated on Brecht's literary texts, as with *Saint Joan of the Stockyards* in Le Lavandou in 1931 and with the crime novel. Benjamin reported to Anna Maria Blaupot ten Cate on a project that he was pursuing in Dragør with Brecht and Korsch: 'Secondly, there are three of us here occupying ourselves with some very interesting work; for a mutual acquaintance of ours is here. But I will tell you about the work itself when we meet.'* He was probably referring to the prose satire on Giacomo Ui, for which Brecht had asked Benjamin to send Machiavelli's *History of Florence* to him in Dragør.[73] It is also possible that he meant the *Tuiroman* or – precisely because Korsch was there – the 'idea of a philosophical "Lehrgedicht" [didactic poem]', in which various preoccupations of Brecht's 'at the time' converged, and in whose conception Benjamin participated by means of conversation.[74] The project is a prototype of one which he took up again after 1945 with Korsch, a 'didactic poem in the venerable metre of Lucretius's *De rerum natura* about, say, the unnatural nature of bourgeois society. The core of it is the (Communist) *Manifesto*'.[75]

A new factor in the relationship, thanks to the exile situation, was Benjamin's and Brecht's reciprocal support in plans for publications and performances. This encompassed the exchange of contacts, the passing on of information and manuscripts, and – as far as Benjamin's efforts on Brecht's behalf were concerned – at times amounted to the work of a literary agent. Brecht gave Benjamin *carte blanche* to conduct negotiations with publishers on his behalf and to pass on texts to editors and theatres. Benjamin's activities concerned the translation and printing of texts by Brecht by French publishers and periodicals; a performance of the *Threepenny Opera* at the Stedelijk Theatre in Amsterdam in 1934, which was discussed in conversation by Blaupot ten Cate[76]; the cover design for *Lieder Gedichte Chöre* – in connection with which he warned Brecht against 'a shade of brown as unpleasing as it is liable to be misunderstood';† and the promotion of

---

* Walter Benjamin to Anna Maria Blaupot ten Cate, draft, *c.* 26 September 1934, *GB* IV, p. 503. It is clear from Benjamin's handwritten plan for the structure of the letter that their mutual acquaintance could only be Korsch, whose name appears in it (see WBA 22).

† Benjamin to Brecht, *c.* 13 January 1934, *GB* IV, p. 335: 'Yesterday I saw the cover that has been designed for your volume of poems. It is a shade of brown as unpleasing as it is liable to be misunderstood. I hope it is still possible to intervene. Hauptmann will be speaking to (Otto) Katz again on Monday; perhaps I will go with her.' After the discussion of 15 January 1934, in which Benjamin took part, Elisabeth Hauptmann wrote to Brecht on 17 January 1934: 'would advise you to pass on corrections to Ka[t]z only through him [Benjamin]' (BBA 480/116–19).

Brecht's *Gesammelte Werke* (see Chapter V below). An apparently typical piece of evidence for this is to be found in a letter to Margarete Steffin:

> When you speak to Brecht, please tell him that I would like to have a letter of authority from him to deal with French periodicals in connection with the publication of some individual small things – above all the Keuner pieces. In any case I will be dealing in the next few days with a number of people who are influential in the editorial departments here, and perhaps could comparatively easily find space for certain things of Brecht's.*

It is also known that in 1939 Benjamin was instrumental in having an amateur performance of scenes from *Fear and Misery in the Third Reich* put on at the abbey of Pontigny in Burgundy, where combatants in the Spanish Civil War were being accommodated. The participants thought of the performance not as an act of cultural education, but as an act of resistance against Nazi terrorism. Benjamin informed Brecht via Margarete Steffin:

> Two dozen Spanish legionaries were quartered in the neighbourhood of the abbey. I had no contact with them, but Frau Stenbock-Fermor was holding courses with them. Since she was very interested in Brecht's work, after my return I sent her *Fear and Trembling* [*Furcht und Zittern*] (*sic*) for a few days, and she read out of it to the Spanish Brigade members (they were mostly Germans and Austrians). 'The greatest impression', she writes to me, 'was made on them by "The Chalk Cross", "Release", "Labour Service" and "Job Creation", and everything was genuinely and simply received.'[77]

Brecht was apparently not supposed to be told that it had not just been a question of a play reading, but also – on 3 June 1939 – a performance of individual scenes. Possibly Benjamin feared that Brecht would have been annoyed by an unauthorized performance of his work, but a reading would have been acceptable to him. At any rate, when passing on the information, Benjamin had

---

* Benjamin to Steffin, 4 March 1936, *GB* V, p. 255. See also Steffin's request to Benjamin to arrange the publication of Brecht's essay 'Alienation Effects in Chinese Acting' in France (Margarete Steffin to Walter Benjamin, 15 September 1935, Steffin, *Briefe*, p. 143) (this essay was first published as 'The Fourth Wall of China', in *Life and Letters*, xv, 6, London, 1936; it was not published in German until 1949). Another convincing example is a letter from Rudy Schröder to Brecht, 7 April 1937, BBA 398/18: 'Herr Benjamin has learnt, by means which he did not wish to disclose to me, that three of your poems will appear in French translation in the next issue of *Mesures*. He expressed his amazement at the fact that you were clearly as ignorant of this as he – nearly – might have remained.' Schröder, who had since 1935 been employed at the Paris office of the Institute for Social Research (see *GB* VI, p. 481), had occasionally translated poems by Brecht.

omitted the following details from the report from his source, Charlotte Stenbock-Fermor:

> So last Saturday we performed 'Two Bakers', 'The New Dress' and 'The Jewish Wife' in French. The last was really a stunning success! Gilbert and I did the translation together.
> I read a bigger selection in German to the Brigade members.*

Particularly time-consuming for Benjamin were his efforts, ultimately in vain, on behalf of the French translation of *The Threepenny Novel*, over which he negotiated for several months. He tried to get the designated translator, Charles Wolff, to speed up his work, but when this failed, he recommended his own translator, Pierre Klossowski. Finally Benjamin himself gave his attention to the quality of the translation; among his papers is a six-page typescript of excerpts of *The Threepenny Novel*, translated into French, with handwritten page numbers and minor corrections added by Benjamin.[78] How important this intervention was to Brecht is shown by his letter of 20 July 1936, sent from London to Éditions Sociales in Paris. After considering the choice of translator and a request to be informed before a decision was made, Brecht writes: 'I would prefer it if you would discuss the matter with my friend Dr Walter Benjamin, Paris XIV, 23 rue Benard.'[79]

Brecht's commitment to Benjamin was no less notable. During their first encounter in exile he was already, as mentioned earlier, attempting to obtain 'contacts with publishers' for Benjamin.[80] In June 1935 he asked Lisa Tetzner to offer the manuscript of Benjamin's *German Men and Women* to a Swiss publisher.[81] He repeatedly offered to pass on Benjamin's work to the periodical *Das Wort*, of which he was on the editorial board between June 1936 and March 1939 with Feuchtwanger and Bredel.† The offer was not restricted to

---

* Charlotte Stenbock-Fermor to Benjamin, 7 June 1939, WBA 120. There follows the sentence quoted by Benjamin. A letter from Rudy Schröder shows that the success of the performance was not unchallenged. As he wrote to Benjamin, he would decidedly refuse to take part in the performance of *Fear and Misery* in Pontigny: 'Mme St. will probably reserve the Jewish wife for herself. The lady is Aryan; how often will the Jewish wife "still weep at the play"' (Rudy Schröder to Benjamin, 27 May 1939, WBA 110/3).

† The first reference to *Das Wort* came from Margarete Steffin: 'I have given your address to the periodical "Das Wort", which is to be published from here monthly from June. Among the editors are Brecht, Feuchtwanger, Bredel, so I am not selling you off to just anyone. Perhaps you will send something in? They will look about the same as the new German papers. ... and finally a quite important piece of information: "Das Wort" will pay in foreign currency to where you are!!' (Steffin to Benjamin, 10 May 1936, in Steffin, *Briefe*, pp. 197ff.). The following statement by Steffin is further evidence of the intensive efforts made to publish Benjamin's work and ensure payment for it: 'If you come here at any time, you must have a look at the correspondence with *Das Wort*. There

Benjamin's essays on Brecht, and it was not restricted to *Das Wort*; Brecht and Steffin also tried to place Benjamin's contributions with other periodicals and publishers.* This was confirmation and support at the same time.

Benjamin discussed with Brecht how he should behave in situations requiring a decision. On the 'question of membership of the official Writers' Union', by which he meant the *Reichsschriftumskammer* (the Reich Chamber of Literature), Brecht wrote to him:

> Dear Benjamin,
>
> In my opinion you should always insist that you're a bibliographer, i.e. a scholar, and ask if there isn't some organization you can join. That way, you will at least gain time. The stupid part of it is that I don't know (do you?) whether your publishers in Germany would make it a rope to hang you with if you signed. It's possible, but it would be nothing less than Maulerism [i.e. behaviour of the most brutal kind, after the character Mauler in Brecht's *St Joan of the Stockyards*]. There is no real reason why you shouldn't join an obligatory organization; but the later you do it the more likely you are to be accepted (see *Pointed Heads*), that is, if you haven't broken off the connection.†

Benjamin thanked him and said he agreed: 'the later one registers, the better'. Whether he could succeed in keeping the connection going remained to be seen.[82]

It was an invaluable help to Benjamin to be able to visit Skovsbostrand in the thirties. He only occasionally stayed in Brecht's house, more often in a rented room in the neighbourhood, but as a rule he was invited to dinner by Helene Weigel, which significantly reduced his expenses. There was also no lack of help of other kinds: Helene Weigel gave him a suit, and Steffin regularly sent him tobacco and books from his library.[83] An application for financial assistance that Benjamin sent from Svendborg in the summer of 1934 to the Danish Committee for the Support of Intellectual Workers in Exile had been initiated or at

---

is really not one letter that does not mention your work, and from the other side too' (7 September 1937, ibid., p. 252).

* Before *Das Wort* came into being, Steffin had, for example, already opened negotiations for the essays 'Brecht's *Threepenny Novel*' and 'What is Epic Theatre?' and for stories Benjamin had completed in Svendborg in the summer of 1934 (see Steffin to Benjamin, 16 October 1935, in Steffin, *Briefe*, pp. 148–50).

† Brecht to Benjamin, middle of January 1934, GBA 28, p. 404. Theodor Adorno and Gretel Karplus urgently advised him to join the official Writers' Union, otherwise he would have difficulty with publishers. 'Finally it is very important for you to belong to the Writers' Union, which has no special regulations concerning Aryan descent' (see Adorno to Benjamin, 5 April 1934, Adorno/Benjamin, p. 27).

least supported by Brecht, as is shown by his letter to Benjamin from Dragør in mid September 1934: 'From what I hear, the committee is flourishing and has money.'[84] This solidarity was appreciated by friends of Benjamin's; Hannah Arendt's comment that Brecht had been 'the most important person in the last decade of his life, above all during his period of emigration to Paris', has already been quoted, as has that of Gretel Karplus, that Brecht was 'the friend who has given you most support in your present difficulties', and that she understood so well that Benjamin needed this contact in order to avoid the isolation that threatened all émigrés.[85]

Between 1933 and 1940, above all during Benjamin's extended summer stays in Denmark, he and Brecht spent a total of more than eleven months living and working in direct proximity to each other.* This is longer than either of them spent with anyone else in exile, with the exceptions of Benjamin's sister, Brecht's family and his lovers, Margarete Steffin and Ruth Berlau. In the late autumn of 1933 Brecht invited Benjamin to Denmark for the first time, and later he, Steffin and Weigel rarely omitted a similar invitation in their letters. As soon as he had arrived there from Paris, Brecht began to advertise the advantages of the island:

> It is pleasant here. Not cold at all, much warmer than in Paris. According-
> ing to Helli, you could get by here on 100 Kr (60 Reichsmark, 360
> francs) a month. Also, the Svendborg library will get *any* book for you.
> We have a radio, newspapers, playing cards, your books will be here
> soon; heating, small coffee houses, a very easy language and the world
> comes to an end more *quietly* here.†

Benjamin too appreciated the fact that the house on the sound seemed to have been removed from the field of battle. Of his second stay there, in the summer of 1936, he wrote: 'It is a very agreeable life and such a friendly one that we daily ask ourselves how long this existence can continue in the Europe of today.'[86] And two years later, with a clear reference to Brecht's formulation that the world was coming to an end more quietly there: 'Brecht's house is next door; there are two children there whom I like; the radio; supper; the kindest hospitality, and, after a meal, one or two lengthy games of chess. The newspapers arrive so late that you have to pluck up your courage to look at them.'[87]

* This is based on the following encounters: late autumn of 1933 (Paris): seven weeks; summer of 1934 (Skovsbostrand/Dragør): fifteen weeks; June 1935 (Paris): a week and a half; summer of 1936 (Skovsbostrand): about four and a half weeks; autumn of 1937 (Paris): about five and a half weeks; summer of 1938 (Skovsbostrand): fifteen weeks.
† Brecht to Benjamin, 22 December 1933, GBA 28, p. 395. Brecht 'would like me to follow him to Denmark. Life is supposed to be cheap there' (Benjamin/Scholem, 31 December 1933, p. 93).

Their time together in Skovsbostrand in the summer months of 1934, 1936 and 1938 was marked by an 'atmosphere of intimacy', to reiterate Ruth Berlau's description.[88] One of Benjamin's many reports provides some reasons for this – it dates from the first summer:

> Summer here has its bright and its dark sides. The latter includes the weather, as well as all things associated with the usual delights of summer, such as promenades, bathing opportunities, hikes. My hosts are even less attracted to these joys of nature than I, and the place where their farmhouse stands, pretty though it may be, cuts them – and me, as their neighbour – off completely from such pleasures. This is now slowly manifesting itself in my condition, which leaves something to be desired, not physically but doubtless mentally. And this, even though my rapport and dealings with the Bs have taken a pleasant form in every way.[89]

Among the activities that encouraged close contact were conversations, work in the garden, newspaper reading, and the news on the radio,* and occasional trips to nearby Svendborg. Extended conversations were concerned with the work of Brecht and his current guests – Korsch, Andersen Nexø and Karin Michaelis. In July and August 1934, Eisler was staying three minutes' distance away in the house of a fisherman's widow. His wife Lou reported:

> The rented piano from Svendborg took up almost the whole space of one room, despite which Eisler played and sang his compositions for *Roundheads and Pointed Heads*, as they became ready, to the Brechts, Grete Steffin, Karl Korsch and Walter Benjamin, who were just able to squeeze in, pressed closely together, with the door open, mostly by the light of smoking paraffin lamps, for there was no electric light in this shack.
>
> One evening, when Eisler was singing the 'Song of the Reviving Effect of Money', and had reached the verse, 'Look, the chimney is smoking', one of the two paraffin lamps fell through the open door into the small courtyard, where there were piles of newspapers which immediately caught fire. Benjamin, the first to go outside, cried out in terror: 'The straw roof has already caught fire, the chimney is smoking!' We ran out; the flames were quickly extinguished, but the chimney really was smoking. Frau Larsen, the fisherman's widow, was cooking her evening soup.[90]

Benjamin loved the Brecht–Weigel children, Barbara and Stefan, and they loved him – there was little, he said, that he missed as much since leaving

---

* See Benjamin to Cohn, 26 July 1934, *GB* IV, p. 470: 'I am busy with a Bachofen essay for the *Nouvelle Revue Française*. Apart from this of course – in a different sense – with the political events that are accessible to me by means of an excellent radio. The reception last night – following the murder of Dollfuss – was a sensation to be compared to the reception of Hitler's speech of 17 July.'

Germany as being with children.[91] Barbara remembers Benjamin's annoyance when it turned out that the tomcat, which had been named Benjamin, had suddenly become a mother.[92] The guests exchanged books, above all crime novels, and sent each other small birthday gifts and stamps and collectors' catalogues for their sons.

A gift made by Benjamin to Brecht, rich in associations, has been preserved. It is the Insel edition of 1931 of Balthasar Gracián's *The Art of Worldly Wisdom*, translated by Arthur Schopenhauer. Benjamin may have presented the little volume to Brecht on his first visit to Skovsbostrand, when he inspected his Berlin library, set up in his friend's house. The dedication has a particular significance. In an ironic phrase, Benjamin alluded to the character of the book as a vade-mecum, providing it with a quotation from Brecht's 'Song of the Insufficiency of Human Endeavour': 'For man is not clever enough for this life'. Brecht's interest in the thoughts of the Spanish Jesuit is apparent: Gracián's maxims, which he marked in various colours and annotated, corresponded to an astonishing degree with attitudes in his 'Lehrstücke' and his *Reader For Those Who Live In Cities*. One would have liked to witness what must have been a lively discussion: Benjamin had for years been contemplating the idea of writing an essay on Gracián, as Brecht may have learnt in Paris in the autumn of 1933. Thought, its effects and corruptibility, had been a topic discussed by Benjamin and Brecht at least since the *Krise und Kritik* journal project of 1930. Finally, a tendency towards aphoristic brevity, entirely comparable to the manner of Gracián, and producing much-quoted maxims and images, is common to the work of both.[93]

Brecht's old Ford was the object of endless jokes, such as Benjamin's request to Margarete Steffin before his first journey to Skovsbostrand: 'Give my regards to the neighbours, and my respects to the Ford.'[94] A note of about 1934 by Benjamin, concerning the vehicle, is probably ironic: 'The car. No journeys are to be undertaken in it except in an emergency.'[95] This can only mean that all journeys were considered to be emergency ones, as Brecht was known not to be fond of walking. 'How is the car?' Benjamin enquired of its owner in early 1935. 'If necessary, please lay a floral tribute on its cold engine on my behalf.'* And certainly Brecht was alluding to the car, a product of Henry Ford's Motor

* Benjamin to Brecht, 9 January 1935, *GB* V, p. 19. Steffin kept Benjamin informed about the state of the rather unreliable car: see among other references: 'Here the old Ford is finally being scrapped. It was really impossible, you cannot imagine what it cost the poor master in physical energy in the end. Now we have the choice of a not quite so old Chevrolet [*sic*]. One malicious person, aghast at the sight, said to Brecht: "How on earth do you manage to keep finding these old heaps?"' (Steffin to Benjamin, 22 June 1939, Steffin, *Briefe*, p. 203).

Company, when he invited Benjamin to Denmark with the following induce-
ments: 'Think of your books, of chess, the Führer's voice on the radio, the
paraffin lamps and the son of the great Henry!'[96]

The little community of exiles took with a passion to board and card games.
Chess was played most often, but also Monopoly,* which was patented in 1936,
table billiards, poker and 66 (a card game). 'Eisler is the uncrowned king of 66',
announced Steffin,[97] and Helene Weigel wrote to Benjamin:

> I would like to know how you are, and if you are able to play 66 with
> anyone, with all your unfriendly peculiarities, which I rather miss. I
> have begun to learn how to play chess, and so there would be an
> opportunity for you to annoy me to death. When would you like to do
> it?†

For his part, Benjamin noted Brecht's behaviour when playing poker.‡ Tournaments were organized and prizes offered – once they played chess for a
double whisky, Eisler losing 2:3; and on another occasion there was a bitter
poker battle for a piece of gingerbread, which Brecht would not give up.§ New
games were in demand: 'Are you familiar with Go?' Benjamin asked before his
first journey, 'a very ancient Chinese board game? It is at least as interesting as
chess – we should introduce it to Svendborg. You never move any pieces in Go,
but only place them on the board, which is empty at the start of the game.'[98]

To ward off boredom, Brecht proposed the invention of a new game. Benjamin recorded the suggestion, which Brecht developed after a game of chess on
12 July 1934:

* Barbara Brecht-Schall, in Joachim Lang and Jürgen Hillesheim (eds), *Denken heißt
verändern*, Augsburg, 1997, p. 18: 'I can only remember that Karl Korsch did not like
losing when he played Monopoly with us.'

† Helene Weigel to Walter Benjamin, 20 January 1935, in Stefan Mahlke (ed.), 'Wir sind
zu berühmt, um überall hinzugehen', in *Helene Weigel. Briefwechsel 1935–1971*, Berlin,
2000, p. 12. See his answer: 'To begin with the most important thing: I have no one with
whom to play 66. People here are much too cultured to play cards. This is a lesson for me:
people should not aspire to move beyond their own circles!' (Benjamin to Weigel, 3
February 1935, *Benjamin Correspondence*, p. 475).

‡ *GS* II/3, p. 1371. According to Adorno, 'some of the characteristics of the poker-
player, such as the way of speaking and thinking, were certainly not altogether foreign to
Benjamin' (Theodor W. Adorno, 'Erinnerungen', in *Über Walter Benjamin*, p. 81).

§ Steffin to Benjamin, 20 July 1936 and [January 1939], Steffin, *Briefe*, pp. 203 and 296.
In the first letter she said: 'I don't play chess any more, apparently I no longer play well
enough for Brecht, since he frequently beats Eisler.' And before Benjamin's first visit,
she had already written: 'Do you play chess, by the way? B. and I play a few games every
day. He plays better than I do, but carelessly, so that I often win. Now we are looking for
new partners, because we each know the other's moves so well' ([May 1834], ibid., p.
124). Benjamin was not present at these tournaments.

So, when [Karl] Korsch comes, we ought to work out a new game with him. A game where the positions don't always remain the same; where the function of the figures changes when they have stood in the same place for a while – then they would become either more effective, or perhaps weaker. As it is now, there is no development; it stays the same for too long.[99]

It is no coincidence that three out of four existing photographs show Benjamin and Brecht playing chess together. They played their daily game after eating, as Ruth Berlau recalled, without speaking, 'and when they stood up, they had had a conversation'.[100] The game provided a background for humour and friendly rivalry: 'I have had a beautiful chess set made here for ten kroner, finer and just as big as Benjamin's,' Brecht reported proudly to Margarete Steffin, and a little later: 'My chess pieces are as big as Benjamin's!'[101] And it became emblematic of the peaceful and intimate communication at Skovsbostrand that it should motivate Benjamin to undertake a 'trip to the northland. The chess board lies orphaned; every half hour a tremor of remembrance runs through it; that was when you made your moves.'[102] The games reflected Benjamin's mood, which for its part was dependent on the progress of his work: 'A game of chess or two which ought to introduce some variety into our lives, take on the colour and the monotony of the grey sound, for I seldom win.'[103]

And whenever a threat to this atmosphere became apparent, the chessboard duels were remembered: 'I doubt if we'll be able to play chess under the apple trees for many more summers.'[104] When the family had fled from Denmark, Benjamin deplored the loss in a letter to Lidingö: 'The chess games in the garden are now over too.'[105] Brecht's poem 'To Walter Benjamin Who Killed Himself Fleeing From Hitler', an epitaph for Benjamin, recalls a scene at the chess table 'in the pear-tree's shade'; the memory acquires its symbolic power from the significance of the games in the players' everyday life in exile (see pp. 181ff. below).

From the start of their exile Brecht and Benjamin took part in the development of projects whose aim was to combine forces against German fascism. In exile conditions, little could be achieved. Brecht's plan to form a Goncourt-like conversation circle in Paris in the winter of 1933, about which Wilhelm Speyer informed Benjamin, fell by the wayside.* And the project for a Diderot Society,

---

* See Wilhelm Speyer to Benjamin, 29 May 1933 (WBA 15/10). In Geret Luhr (ed.), 'was noch begraben lag', in *Zu Walter Benjamins Exil. Briefe und Dokumente*, Berlin, 2000, p. 64: 'We have decided to found a round table in Paris in the winter, like the Goncourts. I hope to see you again in Paris. Brecht is taking an apartment there. He has entirely sensible and quite dispassionate, but witty ideas about everything, and has no illusions about the Third International.'

which Brecht was pursuing in the spring of 1937, also failed to go beyond the planning stages. To Brecht's request for the advancement of the call for its foundation, and for an opinion,* Benjamin replied by return: 'The aims look excellent to me. But what about the readership here? Whether a man such as Moussinac can relate to them seems very questionable to me.'† The restrained nature of his reaction could be due to the fact that he was in demand only as a mediator. Benjamin's name did not appear among the envisaged contributors, who were mainly film directors and others in the film industry, and drama theorists. However, Brecht proposed Benjamin's essay 'The Work of Art in the Age of Its Technological Reproducibility' for publication by the Diderot Society in a collection of seminal writings – admittedly, without the author himself being informed about this (see Chapter V, pp. 151ff. below).

Benjamin's last stay in Skovsbostrand was from the second half of June to the middle of October 1938. He was working on his study *Paris of the Second Empire in Baudelaire*, and on the 'Commentaries to Poems by Brecht'. Brecht was working on his *Caesar* novel or reconsidering his existing concept, and occupying himself with the compiling of further volumes of his *Gesammelte Werke*. Benjamin's notes in his journal record conversations about the situation in the Soviet Union, Stalin and the purges, which both were following with the greatest concern, about experiences in the theatre, Goethe, Baudelaire, Soviet literature, about the struggle against Hitler and about the positions of communist émigrés in the Soviet Union (Becher, Gabor, Lukács, Kurella), whom Brecht called the 'Moscow Clique'. Benjamin, who had sight at Brecht's 'of writing that hews to the party line a bit more than what I see in Paris'[106], found in *Internationale Literatur* an attack by Alfred Kurella on his own piece on Goethe's *Elective Affinities*. In a review of a special edition of the *Cahiers du Sud*, which had published parts of Benjamin's book, Kurella interpreted Benjamin's essay as an attempt 'to interpret Goethe's basic attitude as Romantic and to declare that the "power of archaic instances", a metaphysical fear in Goethe's life, was the actual source of his greatness – an attempt that would do credit to Heidegger'.[107] This dig did not escape Brecht; he marked his copy of the journal with the note '*Kurella* / German Romanticism'. Kurella was evidently

---

* See Steffin to Benjamin, 14–22 March 1937, in Steffin, *Briefe*, pp. 231ff: Brecht 'asks you please if possible to forward the enclosed letter to Jean Renoir ... do read through the essays which are to go to Renoir and Moussinac. What do you think of them?'

† Benjamin to Steffin, 29 March 1937, *GB* V, p. 502. Benjamin seems not to have been able to discover Renoir's address; for the original letter to Renoir see Brecht to Jean Renoir, 17 March 1937, GBA 29, p. 23; in this letter Brecht tells Renoir that he is also approaching – among others – W. H. Auden, Christopher Isherwood and Rupert Doone (of Group Theatre) in England, Archibald MacLeish in the USA, and Eisenstein and Tretyakov in the USSR.

untouched by any considerations of loyalty. His attack was directed against a contributor to *Das Wort*, a well-known anti-fascist writer and scholar (i.e. Benjamin himself), who, by having his name linked with that of Heidegger, was indirectly being accused of Nazi ideology. 'This publication is quite wretched,' was Benjamin's comment on the attack.[108]

The closeness, indeed the affection, that had grown between Benjamin and Brecht was expressed in a great measure of agreement on questions concerning work, and in the remarkable frankness with which judgements were pronounced whose transmission to the 'outside world' was fraught with the utmost danger. At the same time, the participants in the conversations handled differences impressively; each knew the arguments of the other, and there was nothing that they had to prove to each other. What Kurt Krolop has written about the relationships of Karl Kraus with Liliencron, Altenberg, Wedekind, Loos and Schoenberg can be applied to Benjamin and Brecht: it was precisely the intellectual (and aesthetic) independence of each that became an enduring 'basis for a true alliance, through which both sides, in full awareness of what separated them, felt themselves to be all the more firmly bound to each other by what they had in common'.[109]

In a letter to Kitty Marx-Steinschneider Benjamin wrote that he had found 'the kindest hospitality'. He described his intellectual situation, four weeks after he had arrived in Skovsbostrand, as follows:

> I would give a lot for you to enter this room just once. I live here as if in a cell. It is not the furnishings that make it into that, but the circumstances under which I live in it. They impose a kind of test on me. In spite of my great friendship with Brecht, I take care to proceed with my project in strict solitude. It contains very specific moments that he is unable to assimilate. He has been a friend for a long enough time for me to know this and is perceptive enough to respect it. This way everything proceeds very nicely. But it is not always that easy to avoid talking about what preoccupies you day in and day out.[110]

In a letter to Gretel Adorno written on the same day, Benjamin complained that he had no one who understood him; on the other hand, he added, 'I feel that the understanding that Brecht shows for the necessity of my isolation is very beneficial.'[111] Benjamin certainly withheld the contents of his work on Baudelaire, but he still discussed the topic with Brecht; the latter's notes give an idea of the difference in their positions (see Chapter V, pp. 151ff.). On the other hand, Benjamin was restrained in the interest he expressed in Brecht's projected Caesar novel, in a manner which its author found disconcerting. One explanation for Benjamin's uncharacteristic restraint is to be found in his work situation: he had 'seen hardly anything at all' of the novel, he wrote to Adorno, because 'it was impossible for me to do anything at all while I was doing my own work'.[112] Brecht's impatience erupted after Benjamin's departure through Margarete Steffin, or more precisely, through her punctuation: 'It's a pity that you never told me in detail what you think of Caesar. Did you actually read it right to the end?????'[113]

Benjamin's approval failed to materialize. Perhaps it would have motivated Brecht to resume his work on the novel, which had been interrupted by *Galileo*. The project was both thematically and philosophically at a point of intersection of their interests, so that even Benjamin's restricted interest might have dismayed Brecht. The entry in his *Journal* of 26 February 1939 sounds irritated. Benjamin and Sternberg, 'very highly qualified intellectuals', had 'not understood [the novel] and made pressing recommendations for more human interest to be put in, more of the old novel!'*

At the end of his stay Benjamin drew up a résumé of his relationship with Brecht, which interpreted their differences and at the same time highlighted Brecht's situation in exile. It was addressed to Adorno, whose reserve towards Brecht could not have failed to influence the argument, and perhaps even gave it a tactical direction. A comparison with journal entries and letters to other recipients shows, however, that the description was genuine:

> The more natural and relaxed my contact with Brecht has been this past summer, the less equable I am about leaving him behind this time. For I can see an index of his growing isolation in our communication, which this time was much less problematical than what I had been used to. I do not want to exclude entirely a more banal explanation of the facts – that this isolation diminished his pleasure in certain provocative tactics that he was inclined to use in conversation; the more authentic explanation, however, is to recognize in his growing isolation the consequence of the loyalty to what we have in common. Given the conditions under which he currently lives, he will be challenged, head-on so to speak, by this isolation during a Svendborg winter.[114]

Brecht's isolation corresponded to that of Benjamin, whose relationship with the Institute for Social Research was put severely to the test during this summer and autumn; at first his proposals for the revision of his *Baudelaire* remained unanswered for weeks, and the study was then declined. With positive desperation – and ultimately in vain – Benjamin attempted to break through this constellation and to mediate between Brecht and the Institute. As in his letter to

---

* GBA 26, p. 331; Brecht, *Journals*, p. 24. The arguments of Benjamin and Sternberg reminded Brecht of his own reservations: 'The whole "Caesar" concept is inhuman,' he had noted on 25 July 1938. 'On the other hand, it is impossible to portray inhumanity without having some idea of humanity' (ibid., p. 10).

Adorno, he had already passed on to Gretel Adorno, and to Friedrich Pollock and Max Horkheimer, the leaders of the Institute, information designed to break down their mistrust of Brecht's political attitude. In his long letter to Gretel Adorno of 20 July 1938, for example, he writes:

> As for Brecht, he is trying his best to make sense of what is behind Russian cultural politics by speculating on what the politics of nationality in Russia requires. But this obviously does not prevent him from recognizing that the theoretical line being taken is as catastrophic for everything we have championed for twenty years. As you know, Tretyakov was his translator and friend. He is most probably no longer alive.[115]

The reference to 'everything we have championed for twenty years' is related to his formulation to Adorno that isolation was 'the consequence of the loyalty to what we have in common'. The period of time mentioned is not arbitrary. Benjamin was referring to the end of the First World War, to hopes which were set off by the October Revolution and to texts of those years, such as his own previously mentioned polemical treatise the 'Critique of Violence' (1920–21), in which he had criticized the parliamentary system and the general strike as revolutionary methods. The general experience of being pushed to the edge pointed to their common interests and motives, and allowed the significance of the friendship to grow.

Horkheimer, who had enquired about Brecht's political position, received precise information from Benjamin.

> Your question had often been mine in Paris – I do not need to tell you that. While I was to some extent certain in what sense my stay here would answer it for me, I was not certain to what extent this would be the case and with what degree of precision. It was clear to me that the difficulties encountered by our side in any debate with the Soviet Union would be particularly great for Brecht, whose audience included parts of the Moscow working class.

Benjamin made use of the notes in his journal in reporting on Brecht's position. He also informed Horkheimer that Sergei Tretyakov had probably been executed. One could still – and this was something that must link the Institute members, Benjamin and Brecht – 'regard the [Soviet] Union as a power whose foreign policy was not determined by imperialistic interests, and therefore as an anti–imperialistic one'.

> That we still do this, at any rate at present, and that therefore, if even with the most weighty reservations, we still see the Soviet Union as an agent of our interests in a future war as well as in the delaying of this one, could also accord with your way of thinking. That this agent is the most

costly imaginable, since we have to repay it with sacrifices which quite particularly diminish our own obvious interests as producers, is something which it would not enter Brecht's head to dispute, since he realizes that the present Russian regime is a personal one with all its terrors.*

In a letter of 1 May 1939 Gretel Adorno asked Benjamin about the rumour that both Eisler and Brecht had refused 'to sign an appeal that was only intended to serve the glorification of Stalin'.[116] What this was about is not known, but in any case Benjamin did not appear surprised by such a refusal. He replied from Pontigny: 'There was nothing surprising to me in your news about Brecht. I have been clear since last summer about what he thinks of Stalin.'†

In the moment of the greatest danger Benjamin invoked the common points that had arisen from practical considerations: aesthetic, political and philosophical necessities, not tactical or party-political calculations. The circle of these independent individuals, interested in aesthetic creation, had already emerged in the Weimar Republic – 'a small but most important avant-garde,' Benjamin had called it – and in the life-threatening splintering of exile it once again came together. Benjamin saw in this a challenge to the few to unite. In July 1938 he wrote to Friedrich Pollock that he would give Brecht the new issue of the *Zeitschrift für Sozialforschung* to read, since it impressed him as 'a particularly impressive manifestation of the work, standards and organization of the Institute'. 'I have the impression that the growing pressure of the reaction that he [Brecht], like all of us, senses from all parts of the world, decreases so considerably the scope of the truly irreducible intelligentsia that its union could one day be the consequence.'[117]

When after the Munich Agreement the political situation had become ever more threatening for the whole of Europe, the prospects of a meeting also receded for Brecht and Benjamin. Brecht's flight to Sweden from Denmark,

---

* Benjamin to Horkheimer, 3 August 1938, *GB* VI, p. 148. Horkheimer's reaction to the news about Brecht was one of satisfaction: 'The information that he actually has no friends over there [i.e. in Soviet Russia] makes one think. Isolation appears to be to an increasing extent the result and the sign of clarity and decency. It would be an undialectical idea that the truth which has once set the masses in motion should necessarily also develop with them there and then. The relationship between theory and practice is not that simple. Thus, for example, the circumstance that we believe we recognize a certain policy in some respects as the agent of our interests, by no means signifies that these interests are now safeguarded by the power that pursues it. As long as everything is not in order, theory cannot rely on any prestabilized harmony' (Horkheimer to Benjamin, 6 September 1938, in Max Horkheimer, *Gesammelte Schriften*, edited by Alfred Schmidt and Gunzelin Schmid Noerr, Vol. 16: Briefwechsel 1937–1940. Frankfurt, 1995, pp. 476ff.

† Benjamin to Gretel Adorno, 19 May 1939, *GB* VI, p. 284.

under threat as a neighbour to Germany, increased the distance between them. Helene Weigel invited Benjamin to Lidingö in Sweden, but he was unable to comply as the journey was too costly, and it was always dangerous to cross any border.[118] There are hardly any traces of communication to be found during the last year of Benjamin's life. In a letter of 16 August 1939, Bernard von Brentano reported to Brecht on an encounter in Paris: things were not going well for Benjamin and he had been unable to help him.* The non-aggression pact between Hitler and Stalin and the outbreak of war contributed to the lapse and total breakdown in their contact. A communication from Brecht to Benjamin via Martin Domke at the end of August 1939 has not survived.† If Benjamin ever replied, it was probably already from his internment, which he underwent on 4 September 1939. This may have been the last sign of life that Brecht received from him. In a conversation with Stephan Lackner, Benjamin said that he felt uneasy when thinking of Brecht.[119] These feelings were reciprocal: in June 1940 Brecht wrote on a postcard to the theologian Fritz Lieb that he had 'heard nothing from our friend Walter B. since last summer, do you know anything about him or does any common acquaintance of ours?'[120] The card did not arrive in Basel until September 1940. By the time Lieb passed on Brecht's concerned inquiry to Benjamin it was too late; on 17 October 1940 the Marseilles post office sent the message 'retour à l'envoyeur'. His 'On the Concept of History', which Benjamin wanted to send Brecht, never reached its destination.‡ Brecht did not receive it until after his arrival in America, from Günther Anders – together with the news of his friend's death (see Chapter V, pp. 180ff.).

Seven years later, the theologian Karl Thieme, who had had an intensive correspondence with Benjamin, sent Brecht, then living in Switzerland, his essay 'Gespräch mit dem Gottlosen?' ('Conversation with the Godless')§ In his letter of thanks, Brecht wrote that he had heard that Benjamin, while in the French camp where he had been last, had several times recited from memory Brecht's poem 'Legend of the Origin of the Book Tao-tê-Ching on Lao-Tzŭ's Road into Exile', which Thieme had quoted in his essay. 'So,' wrote Brecht, 'he himself found no frontier guard who would let him pass.'

---

* See BBA 911/06: 'In spite of his difficulties I found him as cheerful and witty as ever. What asses these worthy people are, not to make constant use of a brain such as his.'
† Martin Domke wrote to Brecht on 31 August 1939: 'I passed on your note to Benjamin straight away. I expect he will write to you direct' (BBA 911/58).
‡ Scholem, too, never received the copy sent to him (see Scholem, *Benjamin*, p. 221).
§ Thieme to Brecht, 8 April 1948, BBA E 73/249. The essay had appeared in the *Schweizer Rundschau*, vol. 46 (1946), April.

III
'Krise und Kritik'

Project for a Journal

From the autumn of 1930 to the spring of 1931, Benjamin and Brecht, with Bernard von Brentano and Herbert Ihering, and with the help of Ernst Bloch, Siegfried Kracauer, Alfred Kurella and Georg Lukács, were planning to bring out a periodical under the name of *Krise und Kritik* ('Crisis and Criticism'), to be published by Rowohlt in Berlin. They envisaged a journal

> in which the bourgeois intelligentsia can account for itself in regard to positions and challenges which uniquely – in current circumstances – permit it an active, interventionist role, with tangible consequences, as opposed to its usual ineffectual arbitrariness.[1]

Although not a single issue of the journal was ever published, the project deserves attention as a development in aesthetic politics typical of the years immediately before the Nazi dictatorship – especially since it characterizes more than just the relationship between Benjamin and Brecht. It seems paradoxical, but the evidence of the unrealized plan conveys more information about the aesthetic and political convictions of left-wing artists and intellectuals than many a document that did achieve publication.* *Krise und Kritik* should be seen in the context of other contemporary groups and journals which have already been documented. An analysis of the project will also help to avoid preconceptions in interpreting Benjamin. Benjamin's attitude in the discussions of the journal shows that, while politicized, and resolved to intervene in the battle of the day, he by no means forgot his early 'metaphysical' intentions. Rather are even his considerations of current issues founded on a rigorous fundamental philosophical position, arising from his immersion in themes and texts that were essential parts of his early work.

The plan for the journal concentrated the intentions of Benjamin and Brecht as with a burning-glass. In the context of the project, they developed positions in politics, aesthetic theory and aesthetic practice to which their discussions throughout the years 1931 to 1938 would be linked. Never before or since, however, was there so much reason for hope that these perspectives might be realized in practice.

The project seemed close to fulfilment just after the elections to the German

---

* The journal project has hitherto played only a subordinate role in the literature; see Bernd Witte, *Walter Benjamin: An Intellectual Biography*, Detroit, 1991, and Momme Brodersen, *Walter Benjamin – A Biography*, London/New York, 1996.

Reichstag of 14 September 1930 only a few weeks earlier. The Nazis' sensational gain in votes – from under a million in the May 1928 elections to nearly six and a half million in September 1930 – signalled more than a warning of National Socialist domination. Leo Löwenthal is said to have remarked on the day after the election to other members of the Institute for Social Research: 'We can't stay here any more, we must start preparing for emigration.'[2]

But the danger of the foundation of a fascist dictatorship was merely the extreme expression of a situation that was universally described as a 'crisis' – few other terms were used in such an inflated manner during those years. The political, economic and cultural tension of the situation gave every reason for this. The world economic crisis had reached its high point in Europe in Summer 1930; in Germany, the number of unemployed had risen within that year from barely two million to over four million. In the Spring, however, the Hermann Müller coalition government had fallen and the Reichstag had been dissolved; there were strikes, demonstrations, street-fighting, and a succession of emergency measures was announced. A decree against radicals enacted in January 1930 ensured that state employees deemed unreliable could not become civil servants. There was public talk of a wave of fascist indoctrination. Intellectuals and artists were affected by the crisis, and not only because of the high rate of academic unemployment. Theatrical performances were often prohibited and press censorship was intensified. The use of the word 'crisis' was characteristic of political debate. The ideologues of the growing National Socialist movement also made use of it when they saw the effects of a 'cultural crisis', which, 'properly considered, was in its nature a crisis of society'.[3]

These disturbing events in their society induced a group of authors to consider the founding of a journal, to be managed by themselves, to aid their mutual communication and to enhance their public influence. In *Krise und Kritik*, various threads came together; no one individual can be named as the originator of the idea. The stimulus came from discussions between Benjamin and Brecht after they had drawn closer in May 1929. In a notebook started during that month, Brecht made a note of the title *Kritische Blätter* (literally, 'Critical Leaves'), a title he also gave to the *Entwurf zu einer Zeitschrift* ('Draft for a Journal'), which was closely related to Benjamin's later outline for *Krise und Kritik*.[4] Brecht probably had these ideas in mind when he wrote to Bernard von Brentano, Berlin correspondent of the *Frankfurter Zeitung*, on 2 July 1929: 'We really must talk about a journal. I keep thinking up more contributors!'[5]

The progress of the project is recorded in letters Ernst Rowohlt wrote to his author, Bernard von Brentano, in 1930 and 1931.[6] The idea took shape within a few weeks in the summer of 1930. The publisher Rowohlt had been won over; he saw Herbert Ihering, a Berlin drama critic who was, like Benjamin and

Brentano, a Rowohlt author, as the leading figure. In his letter to Brentano of 25 July 1930, Ernst Rowohlt counselled restraint: 'Ihering's journal project will probably have to be postponed, for the times are too miserable for anything like that to be undertaken at the moment.' Even six weeks later, the publisher still saw 'the periodical thing' as 'in the bud, as it were', 'still very uncertain'. It needed to be 'discussed face to face and exhaustively'. But this did not stop him from noting down some quite precise ideas about the journal's character, content and contributors:

> It should have an extent of 32 pages, like the *Tage-Buch* in format, typeset quite simply and unpretentiously, almost like an academic journal; it should be concerned with literary questions, and perhaps include a few theatre and film reviews. The whole journal should be written by only five or six regular contributors. A so-called editor will hardly be necessary. In all probability Franz Hessel will simply undertake the production of the journal; editorial expenses, office or secretarial, will not be incurred, but each issue will be distributed more in the manner of a pamphlet; but of course subscriptions will also be accepted.
>
> The following, for a start, should be contributors: Benjamin, Brecht, Ihering and you [Brentano]...
>
> Benjamin, Ihering and Brecht at any rate are ready in principle to contribute. The main thing is that we should accept only those contributors whom we know to be strongly left-wing in their general outlook, so that all the essays in this journal will be written from this point of view.

Discussions between Benjamin, Brecht and Ihering about the official foundation of the project can be dated to about September 1930.* At the beginning of October, Benjamin reported to Scholem about the project, not without stressing his own and Brecht's participation:

> I cleared the way for the plan's acceptance by the publisher Rowohlt by appointing myself the representative responsible for the journal's organizational and practical aspects, which I have worked out in long conversations with Brecht. Its formal stance will be scholarly, even academic, rather than journalistic, and it will be called *Krise und Kritik*.[7]

---

* See Ernst Bloch to Karola Piotrkowska, 5 November 1930, in Anna Czajka, 'Rettung Brechts durch Bloch?', in *The Brecht Yearbook* (Madison), vol. 18, p. 122: 'During the summer, Benjamin, Brecht and Ihering worked out a plan for a journal that they want to bring out'. The earliest possible date for these discussions is September 1930; from 24 May Brecht was no longer in Berlin.

Only later does Brecht appear to have become involved in the process of realizing the ideas formulated during the Summer. 'As regards the journal,' he wrote to Brentano in late October 1930:

> I have no idea. I haven't discussed it with Rowohlt and all I know is what Ihering and Benjamin have told me... So far no agreement has been reached about the actual editorial board. I would suggest Ihering, Benjamin (whom Rowohlt wants and who would fully support us, from what I know of him), you and myself.[8]

In early November 'things', as Benjamin told Scholem, had 'progressed somewhat further along the road to a public announcement':

> In my next parcel, you will receive the announcement and bylaws of a new journal called *Krise und Kritik*, which is to be published bimonthly by Ihering through Rowohlt. My name appears on the title page as coeditor, along with Brecht's and two or three others...

'It will give you an ambiguous satisfaction,' Benjamin continued, 'to see my name given there as the only Jew among all the goyim [non-Jews].'[9] This was accurate with regard to the prospective list of editors – Bloch was, apart from Benjamin, the only one of Jewish origin involved to any great extent, but he had no official responsibility. But this was not the point. Benjamin's phrase, which conceals much more than it reveals, is a reaction to the mistrust with which Scholem was following Benjamin's presumed self-distancing from Jewish problems and contacts. The debate was to resume as early as Spring 1931, provoked by Benjamin's letter to Max Rychner of 7 March 1931 about theology and dialectical materialism.[10]

The documents mentioned – the programme and constitution for *Krise und Kritik* – and the informative records of editorial meetings have been preserved among the unpublished papers of Benjamin and Brecht. Apart from Benjamin, Brecht and Ihering, those taking part in the discussions of November 1930 included Bloch, Kracauer and Gustav Glück, as well as, probably, Brentano and Kurella. The extensive notes taken of the discussions give detailed information about the motives for founding the journal, its focal points and principles, and also proposals for topics which potential contributors were assigned to cover.*

> * The minutes of the sessions are documented below (pp. 190–203). A total of twenty-five sheets have been preserved in the Benjamin and Brecht archives, consisting of notes of five discussions or parts of discussions. Only two of these are dated, those of 21 and 26 November 1930. An earlier discussion, which is related to the dated ones, took place about the beginning of November 1930. The two parts of the discussions between Benjamin, Brecht and Ihering date, as has been mentioned, took place from September 1930.

At the editorial meetings, differences of opinion were already being expressed which intensified during the months that followed and contributed to the eventual abandonment of the project. External obstacles appeared in addition to the internal discord: the editorial board of the *Frankfurter Zeitung*, in the person of the arts editor Friedrich T. Gubler, were not prepared to allow their colleagues – above all Brentano and Kracauer – to participate in *Krise und Kritik*, as we learn from Benjamin's letter to Brentano of 18 November 1930:

> Dear Brentano,
> Your indignation is understandable. But I am not in the least to blame for these disagreements. It was not from me that Gubler heard about the project or your involvement in it. Rather, he knew about it even before I had seen him. And Kracauer, whom he would not allow to publish an essay in the *Weltbühne* and who, in the ensuing debate, referred to the journal project and the participation in it guaranteed by the circles of the *Frankfurter Zeitung*, did not get the information from me either. Brecht talked to him about the journal. But you can see from this what circuitous measures would have been needed to prevent Gubler, once he was in Berlin, from finding out immediately about the preparations. In any case I have been no less taken by surprise than you by his attitude, though in different circumstances.[11]

Nevertheless, Benjamin, who as early as December 1930 had already been considering withdrawing his name as a co–editor,[12] told Scholem in a letter of 5–6 February 1931 that things had 'taken more concrete shape in the last few days'.[13] The plan was to publish the first issue in April. However, Benjamin made the question as to whether his name would appear on the title page as a co-editor dependent on the content of the first issue.

On 10 February 1931, Ernst Rowohlt sent Brentano a contract which recorded the decisions agreed during 'various discussions' about the journal's title, fees, extent and production schedule. According to this, it would be a monthly journal of sixty-four pages and have the same small format as the *Tage-Buch* and the *Weltbühne*. The first issue was to be published at the end of March or, at the latest, the beginning of April. Rowohlt proposed an initial fee of 20 marks per page, with possible increases. He committed himself for a start to the publication of twelve issues; after the ninth issue, 'final discussions were to take place as to whether monthly publication should be continued or not'. A postscript read: 'The final title of the journal will be *Krise und Kritik*, edited by

Herbert Ihering, in collaboration with Walter Benjamin, Bert Brecht and Bernard von Brentano.'*

By the end of February 1931, three essays had been received for the first issue: 'The General Assault' by Brentano, 'The Kharkov Congress' by Kurella, and 'Idealism and Materialism' by Plekhanov.[14] They seemed to be leading the enterprise towards its realization, but in fact they brought it to an end. Benjamin withdrew his willingness to be responsible as a co-editor, because in his judgement none of the essays corresponded to the agreed principles, or could 'claim to have been written by an expert authority'. What he envisaged was something 'fundamentally new', which would be 'hard to reconcile with the demands of journalistic reality'. Otherwise, he feared that his co-editorship would 'be tantamount to signing a proclamation'.[15]

However, Benjamin's decision was not the last word in the matter, as has been assumed up to now. At least until the Summer of 1931 his comrades-in-arms held fast to their plans. In March 1931 Brecht announced at a press conference that he and Ihering wanted to publish a journal called *Krise und Kritik*, in which he would mainly enter into debate with the critics.[16] An agency report in the newspaper *Tempo* of 3 March 1931 stated: 'A new journal, *Krisis und Kritik*, will appear in Berlin from 1 April; edited by Herbert Ihering in collaboration with Bert Brecht and Bernhard [*sic*] von Brentano (published by Rowohlt).'[17]

To judge from Benjamin's entries in his private journal, by June 1931, when the three original co-editors – Benjamin, Brecht and Brentano – were staying at Le Lavandou in France, the project for *Krise und Kritik* seems no longer to have been discussed. In fact, however, even later than this Ernst Rowohlt still believed the launch of the journal to be possible, if Ihering, Brecht and Brentano 'stood together'. In the publisher's view the contract was theoretically still valid; however, in practice the plan would never be executed, because Ihering was no longer prepared to continue.[18] Ihering's withdrawal, the financial collapse of Rowohlt Verlag, involving legal proceedings, and an emergency press decree of 17 July 1931, all contributed to deal the death blow to the idea. 'The bourgeois organs are so intimidated by the present censorship

---

* I have standardized the title of the projected journal as *Krise und Kritik* in reference to this contract. Other titles were considered, but this seems to be the result of an agreement. The participants in the discussion were aware of the difference in meaning between the concepts *Krise* and *Krisis*. The latter, Greek version of the term, going back to Plato, was associated with its use in theology and philosophy – for example by Augustine, Rousseau, Schelling, Hegel, Feuerbach, Marx and Nietzsche, while the use of the more popular form *Krise* could be expected to be more effective in the context of day-to-day politics.

that from today we are all fair game,' wrote Brentano to Brecht. 'On the other hand there are now 200 reasons for us to have a journal.'*

But it did not come to that. The attempt by Brecht and Brentano to acquire Georg Lukács as a contributor to *Krise und Kritik* was already a fading echo of the ambitious project. It cannot have been undertaken earlier than the Summer of 1931, if exploratory talks in advance are not to be excluded. Lukács, who during this period had exchanged his exile in Moscow for exile in Berlin, saw the German intelligentsia as torn apart by a 'polarizing tendency'. As a literary functionary on behalf of the International Union of Revolutionary Writers, Lukács sought to contribute to the 'consolidation of the left-wing trend among the intelligentsia'.[19] In a draft letter to Lukács, Brecht regretted 'that work on the journal seems to be at a standstill'. Brecht criticized the 'propaganda *methods*' and the gesture of 'superiority' with which Lukács attempted to domineer the intellectuals in dogmatic terms: 'It is undoubtedly a mistake to believe that, because intellectuals have been jolted by the crisis, the slightest impact will send them toppling like ripe pears into the lap of Communism.'[20]

The activity of journal members increasingly departed from the journal itself, and those involved in the project found themselves fighting alongside each other on other fronts. After the 'President's Second Decree against Political Acts of Violence' of 17 July 1931, and the emergency press decree already mentioned, a 'Fighting Committee for the Freedom of Literature' was formed. It called for rallies 'against the suppression of intellectual freedom, against censorship and emergency decrees', at which Brecht, Brentano, Johannes R. Becher, Kurella, Wieland Herzfelde, Ernst Toller, Klaus Neukrantz and others spoke. After one rally, a newspaper article read:

> Bert *Brecht*, in a significant appeal, described the interests of creative intellectuals as *inseparably* linked with those of the proletariat...
>
> Since all the speakers were in agreement on the necessity of a close association, a 'working party for the freedom of intellectual work' was set up, in which all professional intellectual groups are represented.
>
> At the close of this successful rally, Bert Brecht's appeal was introduced as a resolution and unanimously accepted.[21]

---

* Benjamin wrote to Scholem on 20 July 1931: 'Rowohlt has gone bankrupt and hardly comes into consideration as a publisher for the foreseeable future' (*GB* IV, pp. 44–7). The Rowohlt financial crisis ended with its transformation from a limited partnership into a limited liability company (see Walter Kiaulehn, *Mein Freund der Verleger*, Reinbek, 1967, pp. 150ff.).

Contributors

The appointment of an editor was not a formal, legal affair, even if the publisher would like to have featured a prominent name. The editor, named as Herbert Ihering in all the documents, was granted wide-ranging rights. He was to have the casting vote in all editorial matters, he could reject committees, which were to be newly formed for each issue, in case of dispute, and he possessed sole authority over the journal's special rights.[22]

Benjamin, Brecht and Brentano were lined up as co-editors from the outset. Siegfried Giedion, the architectural historian and theorist, author of *Building in France*, *Building in Iron*, and *Building in Ferroconcrete*, is also named in one document as a co-editor; but after that his name does not appear again.* A further role as consultant and potential financial backer was played by Gustav Glück, a friend of both Benjamin and Brecht. Glück, whom Benjamin called 'a man in the banking profession, not without influence, sophisticated and first-rate',[23] was the director of the foreign section of the Reichskreditgesellschaft, in Berlin. His father, also Gustav Glück, was the director of the art gallery at Vienna's Kunsthistorisches Museum, and the author of books on Brueghel highly regarded by Brecht. Glück, the son, was a Marxist and very knowledgeable about art. He was in contact with Karl Kraus and is said to have introduced Kraus and Brecht to each other.[24] As Scholem testified, Benjamin 'thought highly of his reliability as a person'.[25] In 1931 he counted Glück among his closest acquaintances and said that Freud's text 'The Destructive Character' provided 'a kind of portrait sketch of him – *cum grano salis*'.[26] In 1932 Benjamin dedicated his 'Kraus' essay to Glück. For specialized questions of production, the publishers held out the prospect of the collaboration of an editorial secretary, and of the writer Franz Hessel, then working for Rowohlt.[27] It was clearly important to Brecht that Hessel should have only a subordinate role; at any rate, he stressed to Brentano that 'Hessel would of course be only a non-voting editor, a technician put in by the publisher to cut down editorial costs.'[28]

The contributors to the journal would have been writers and artists, critics and scholars. The lists that have survived show that proposals for contributors continued to be discussed and expanded. It is impossible to know which of the

---

* See *GS* VI, pp. 619ff., and WBA Ts 2468. The suggestion to involve Giedion may well have been made by Benjamin; he wrote an emphatic letter to Giedion on 15 February 1929 after reading *Building in France* (*GB* III, pp. 443ff.). On Benjamin and Giedion, see Heinz Brüggemann, 'Walter Benjamin und Siegfried Giedion oder Die Wege der Modernität', in Klaus Garber and Ludger Rehm (eds), *global benjamin*, Munich, 1992.

provisionally proposed authors were actually approached. Beyond the circle of those directly involved and already named, it is worth mentioning the writers Hermann Borchardt, Alfred Döblin, Albert Ehrenstein, Robert Musil, Hans Sahl* and Peter Suhrkamp, the theatrical producers and directors Slatan Dudow, Leo Lania, Erwin Piscator and Bernhard Reich, the composers and music theorists Adorno, Hanns Eisler,† Paul Hindemith, Heinrich Strobel and Kurt Weill, the theorists in art and architecture Adolf Behne, Siegfried Giedion and Hannes Meyer, as well as George Grosz,‡ the critics and essayists Erich Franzen, Armin Kesser, Ludwig Marcuse and Erik Reger, the sociologists Karl August Wittfogel and Fritz Sternberg, the historians Herman Kantorowicz and Arthur Rosenberg, the philosophers Karl Korsch and Hans Reichenbach, and the psychoanalyst Wilhelm Reich.

The above names are to be found in Benjamin's programmatic text on the journal (see pp. 188–9 below), in a letter from Rowohlt to Brentano of 8 September 1930, as well as in lists of contributors and topics among Brecht's unpublished papers:

1. In one of the two preserved typescripts of Benjamin's text on the journal, to which the editors have given the title 'Memorandum', handwritten additions have been made to the list of proposed contributors, possibly in the course of a discussion.[29] The notes on the sheet suggest that Eisler and Kracauer were to be included in the editorial team for *Krise und Kritik*. What also emerges from these notes is that one of the suggested topics was the music periodical *Musik und Gesellschaft*, with which Brecht, Eisler, Kracauer and Suhrkamp had personal links; at the same time, the initiators of *Krise und Kritik* may have felt a kinship with the position of *Musik und Gesellschaft* vis-à-vis politics and aesthetic theory.

2. In his letter of 8 September 1930 to Brentano, Rowohlt mentioned authors who came to his mind apart from the five or six regular contributors. It was important to him that they should be 'strongly left-wing in their general outlook':

> Musil – Erich Franzen – Albert Ehrenstein – Polgar – Alice Rühle-
> Gerstel – Ludwig Marcuse – Professor Arthur Rosenberg –
> Wiesengrund (i.e. Adorno) – Weill – Piscator, etc.

* Hans Sahl, in a conversation with the author on 13 October 1992, had no recollection of the *Krise und Kritik* journal project; it is conceivable that the proposal to involve him was never actually conveyed to him.

† The name Eißler (*sic*) in Benjamin's handwriting, is also on the back of one of the documents, but this could also refer to Hanns Eisler's father, the philosopher and lexicographer Rudolf Eisler.

‡ Undoubtedly the name written as 'Gross' refers to George Grosz (see *GS* VI, p. 620).

Even if the 'etc.' suggests a certain fortuitousness and inconclusiveness, Rowohlt's suggestions correspond closely to the preserved lists made by Benjamin and Brecht. It is conceivable that some of Rowohlt's suggestions were adopted in the list mentioned in Paragraph (1) above.

3. A list of authors from Brecht's papers should also be mentioned here, even if it is rather doubtful whether it belongs to the *Krise und Kritik* project. Among initiators and contributors to the project, such as Benjamin, Brecht, Bloch, Brentano and Döblin, it includes names of people actually suggested as contributors, such as Borchardt and Ehrenstein, but also names that were mentioned in the records of discussions as topics, or who are conceivable as topics, such as Remarque, Kästner and Mehring.[30]

Topics: Crisis, Criticism, Method, Role of Intellectuals

The title of the journal, if it had indeed been called *Krise und Kritik*, would have been integral to its programme. Among the focuses of discussion at the editorial meetings were the 'crisis' in theory, art and society, 'criticism' – both as a means of responding to the crisis, and as the object of debate – as well as 'basic methodological questions of intellectual and artistic activity', and the 'role of the intellectual'.

A fragmentary note by Brecht, part of the preliminary work for the journal, conveys an idea of the main use that was to be made of the concepts of 'criticism' and 'crisis':

> criticism is to be understood in the sense that politics is its continuation by other means
>
>   criticism does not by any means produce eternal laws by first setting up its main results beyond space and time (events in history and society) but rather ... the fact, accessible to all, that there are crises (in mathematics, medicine, foreign trade, marriage, etc.) does not necessarily lead straight to recognition of the great wide-ranging crisis of which these are often only momentary manifestations (emerging and disappearing again) apparently independent of each other, indeed this fact often even hinders such recognition.*

* BBA 332/49 (see on this Bernd Witte, 'Krise und Kritik. Zur Zusammenarbeit Benjamins mit Brecht in den Jahren 1929 bis 1933', in Peter Gebhardt et al (eds), *Walter Benjamin – Zeitgenosse der Moderne*, Kronberg, 1976, p. 35). On the concepts of *Kritik* and *Krise*, their original connection and change in meaning, see Reinhart Koselleck, *Kritik und Krise. Eine Studie zur Pathogenese der bürgerlichen Welt*, Frankfurt, 1973, pp. 196–9.

In his letter to Brecht of February 1931, already quoted, in which he withdrew from the editorial group, Benjamin describes the intended character of the project:

> The journal was planned as an organ in which experts from the bourgeois camp were to undertake to depict the crisis in science and art. This was meant to demonstrate to the bourgeois intelligentsia that the methods of dialectical materialism are dictated to it by its own most necessary characteristics – necessities of intellectual production, research, and existence. The journal was meant to contribute to the propaganda of dialectical materialism *by applying it to questions that the bourgeois intelligentsia is forced to acknowledge as those most particularly characteristic of itself* [italics in the original].[31]

Benjamin's dictum and its spectrum of decisive topics and problems give the impression that this would have been a journal which primarily dealt with political and philosophical questions. This is not a false impression, but there were artists and aesthetic theorists at work who had no intention of relegating discussions of aesthetics and creative theory to the background. It was above all the relationship between progress in society and in aesthetic technique that was being debated. As far as we know from Brecht's notes, *Krise und Kritik* would also have published literary texts, which would, so to speak, introduce work in progress. The journal would not present literary works 'as a finished product'; it should 'convey the image of a factory at work.'[32]

Crisis

Max Rychner reported a conversation between Benjamin and Bloch in Autumn 1931, in which Bloch stated that he could not understand 'how it could have come so quickly to a breakdown of German morale in all aspects of life, including politics'. Benjamin's reaction was one of amazement: 'what couldn't be understood? Inevitably, the serious economic crisis must produce manifestations of crisis in the superstructure.'[33] The 'crisis' in social life, with all its manifestations, was one of the motives for the founding of the journal, but also, as is to be gathered from a programmatic note, its object: 'The journal's field of activity is the present *crisis* in all areas of ideology, and it is the task of the journal to register this crisis or to bring it about, and this by means of criticism.'[34]

The intention was to be an authoritative source of decisive opinion – in accordance with the philosophical conceptual tradition in which 'crisis' is linked with functions of cognition such as distinguishing, deciding, judging, orientating. The view of the participants in the conversation went beyond the ideological crisis, as is seen in Brecht's note quoted above, in which the crises of individual areas and fields are perceived as forms of expression of a 'great wide-ranging crisis'.[35]

That the journal was supposed to help *bring about* the crisis shows that the word 'Krise' is not to be understood as meaning the end of something, but – as the term 'Krisis' is used in the course of an illness to describe the (dangerous) climacteric, when latent factors emerge, which is followed by recovery or death – rather as a decision that can be accelerated. The concept of 'ideology' was probably used predominantly in the pejorative sense of 'false consciousness'. To bring about the '*crisis* in all areas of ideology' would thus mean to 'dissolve' or 'demolish' ideology, as had been envisaged with Heidegger in Spring 1930 (see above, pp. 41ff.). The promotion of this process of dissolution might thus represent to the journal's initiators a precondition for genuine, praxis-based theory. It was their declared intention to work out a basic philosophical attitude which was to be substituted for 'false consciousness.'[36] This is the sense in which Brecht's utterance at the editorial meeting of 21 November 1930 is to be understood: he proposed a 'more "sensational" article' for the first issue under the title 'Die Begrüssung der Krise' ('Welcoming the Crisis').[37]

Criticism

Before the discussions on the journal *Krise und Kritik*, Benjamin and Brecht had, independently of each other, thought deeply, in complex and different ways, about the concept, content and function of criticism; their reflections are among the preconditions of the project.* Varying experiences had moved them both to get to grips with criticism, and it was different forms of criticism that they confronted. Benjamin and Brecht perceived and used criticism as an instrument of social theory, and Brecht was in addition interested in drama criticism – as a writer of reviews in Augsburg, as an observer of the theatrical scene, as well as being himself an object of criticism. He was intent on formulating critical principles. This grew out of his confrontation with a drama criticism whose basis seemed to be no more than the personal taste of the individual critic. As the object, indeed victim, of unfavourable reviews, Brecht was anxious to put 'non-objective' criticism in its place and organize a 'criticism of criticism'. As late as 1937, when he was entertaining the idea of founding a

---

* Benjamin's concept of criticism has been systematically examined; see Bernd Witte, *Walter Benjamin: An Intellectual Biography*, Detroit, 1991; Michael W. Jennings, *Dialectical Images. Walter Benjamin's Theory of Literary Criticism*, Ithaca/London, 1987. A fundamental text on the theme with relation to Brecht has still to appear (but see Ernst Schumacher, 'Brecht als Objekt und Subjekt der Kritik', in Schumacher, *Brecht – Theater und Gesellschaft im 20. Jahrhundert*, Berlin, 1981 and Steve Giles, *Bertolt Brecht and Critical Theory. Marxism, Modernism and 'The Threepenny Lawsuit'*, Bern, 1997).

Diderot Society, Brecht formulated as one of its tasks: 'Quotation from reviews and reviews of these.' In the twenties he had recognized that dramatic criticism could not be criticized and improved in isolation, and began to occupy himself more systematically with the philosophical and social bases of criticism.

In contrast to Brecht's need to use criticism to establish a foundation for his empirical experiences, Benjamin stressed the necessity to test theoretical considerations in terms of their practical application. Brecht's need for critical theory and Benjamin's reflective critical practice encountered each other and together formed a single strategy.

In his dissertation, *The Concept of Criticism in German Romanticism* (1919),[38] Benjamin had already examined the aesthetic and philosophical premisses and implications of the concept of criticism of the early German Romantics, together with that concept's origin in Kant and Fichte. He continued to be influenced by the evaluation of a reflective criticism worked out in this study. In his 'Announcement of the Journal *Angelus Novus*' (1921–22) he programmatically claimed a place for criticism on equal terms in the journal with that of literature and philosophy. It was imperative 'to restore criticism to its former strength'.[39] In his essay 'Goethe's *Elective Affinities*' (1921–22), which was to Benjamin 'just as important to me as an exemplary piece of criticism as it is as a prolegomenon to certain purely philosophical treatises',[40] he kept in mind the aim of formulating the task of a criticism worthy of the name. 'Critique seeks the truth content of a work of art; commentary, its material content.'[41] When the failure of his academic prospects forced Benjamin to apply his knowledge as an essayist and reviewer for newspapers and journals, he analysed his practical experiences and confronted them with what he encountered as criticism. A polemical expression of these experiences was the text 'The Critic's Technique in Thirteen Theses' from *One-Way Street* (1923–26): 'The critic is the strategist in the literary struggle.'[42] Around 1930, Benjamin contemplated the idea of formulating the programme of his critical work under the title 'The Task of the Critic'. This was to form the introduction to a collection of his critical essays planned by Rowohlt.*

Benjamin's and Brecht's views of the function of criticism converged, though the differences were not obscured.† They detected a deterioration in criticism, which in their opinion was caused by the lack of intelligible central ideas and critical standards. Subjective judgements based on individual taste

---

* A publisher's contract of 16 April 1930 is reproduced in Brodersen, *A Biography*, p. 183. (For 'The Task of a Critic', see *SW*, vol. 2, pp. 548–9.)

† See the relevant writings and notes on the status and significance of criticism for Brecht and Benjamin in *Brecht on Art and Politics*, pp. 90–1, and *GS* VI, pp. 161–80 and *GBA* 21, pp. 103, 250, 323–34.

had taken the place of reflective strategic programmes. They saw Alfred Kerr as the representative of the 'taste-based', 'culinary' school of criticism.* A draft by Brecht with the heading 'On New Criticism', which is assigned in a note to the journal project *Kritische Blätter*, is of interest. By the 'splitting-off of so-called "fine literature"', it states, criticism had dwindled into 'mere description'. Literature was being treated as autonomous, and the idea of its 'organic character, of course, nips any interventionist criticism in the bud'. Brecht proposed not only directing critical attention at 'fine literature', but also concentrating it on '*contemporary* works of other literary genres'.[43] Benjamin too, who in early 1929 was preparing an article entitled 'Tiefstand der literarischen Kritik in Deutschland' ('The Nadir of Literary Criticism in Germany'),[44] took exception to the idea that literature could not be analysed; in a note on 'False Criticism' he wrote that bourgeois criticism 'satisfies the need for character sketches, temperaments, originals, and personalities'.[45] According to Heinrich Kaulen, Benjamin had in mind

> nothing less than a re-establishment of criticism as a genre and, mediated by this, a secure basis, if for the time being only a fragmentary one, for a future aesthetic theory. It was imperative to ensure realization in a new way of the task and irreplaceable achievement of criticism, and to reclaim its lost public effectiveness – whether by means of polemic or by bold improvisation.[46]

The participants in the discussions considered devoting one issue of *Krise und Kritik* entirely to 'criticism' as a topic.[47] They had in mind both art criticism, whose low standard it was quite usual to complain about around 1930, and also – as Benjamin introduced it in conversation – criticism as a precondition and means of social cognition. Brecht suggested Herbert Ihering as author of a contribution on 'Contemporary Theatre Criticism',[48] and Benjamin thought a 'debate' was necessary on 'what has until now been brought to us from the materialist side about literary criticism (Franz Mehring, Merten [i.e. Lu Märten] etc.)'.† Criticism, the participants considered, should be 'a critical topic of the journal', and should be liberated from 'the dictates of taste and the individual'.[49] Brecht called for the development of standards and scientific principles, and for the feasability of systematic assessment for every critical activity. That

---

* See above all Brecht's polemic against 'culinary criticism' in his 'Notes to *Mahagonny*', and Benjamin's derogatory mention of Kerr in his fragment 'False Criticism' (*SW*, vol. 2, p. 406).

† Session of 26 November 1930 (pp. 190ff. below). Chryssoula Kambas has given reasons why the name 'Merten', written from dictation, must conceal Lu Märten, based on the reception of Märten during the 1920s (see Kambas, *Die Werkstatt als Utopie. Lu Märtens literarische Arbeit und Formästhetik seit 1900*, Tübingen, 1988, p. 189).

the situation in art criticism was only *one* viewpoint in the whole can, however, be gathered from a statement of Benjamin's of 26 November 1930:

> If we take the term 'criticism' in its widest sense, in fact as it is used by Kant, then we face a task that is simply insoluble without applying Kantian philosophy. I could write here about drama criticism or literary criticism – such terms are familiar – but if one should wish to express ideas about a critical attitude to events or to the world in general, that would be difficult (see p. 196 below).

Criticism, as envisaged by the participants in the discussions, was drastic, effective and consequential, a criticism which – in the words of Brecht's note, already quoted – would be perceived in such a way that 'politics is its continuation by other means'.* This claim could hardly be stated more baldly. The concepts 'crisis' and 'criticism' were aimed at the analysis and transformation of society.

Method

The whole social crisis, the necessity to replace inadequate critical practice with a philosophically based criticism which could react to the crisis – this positively enforced consideration of the 'methodological foundations' of thinking. Clearly, this problem was one that particularly preoccupied Brecht; after all, he had also demanded scientific criteria for criticism. But he went even further:

> I imagine that a Russian scholar from such-and-such a university is commissioned to write a short cultural-historical survey of the role of thinking in history. And that he's been given this task in order to collect together any possible methodological guidelines, aids or tricks, by which thinking solved any problems so far, and if so, which ones.[50]

Brecht's proposal, made in all seriousness, is an expression of the search for usable methods and tried and trusted means. Brecht, who, in the examination of social phenomena, felt the lack of a 'scientific approach', an interest in experiment, argued in favour of 'introducing a certain empiricism in critical behaviour, finding a scientific foundation, remote from matters of taste and individualism', so that criticism should be 'always open to scrutiny'. Such positions are near equivalents to the Vienna School of logical positivism or logical empiricism, centred on Hans Reichenbach, Otto Neurath, Rudolf

---

* BBA 332/49. See Günter Hartung's definition of the concept of criticism as 'the art of separation, which totally penetrates its subject, to separate what is true in it from the false and artificial (Hartung, 'Literaturwissenschaft und Friedensforschung', in *Zeitschrift für Germanistik* (Leipzig), vol. 10, no. 5, 1989, p. 597).

Carnap, Moritz Schlick and Walter Dubislav, with whose theories Brecht intensively engaged.* Brecht was really searching for an answer to the question: 'How do we actually think scientifically?'† He had himself followed with interest the posing of such questions, including findings in the natural sciences.‡ A later expression of this topic is the plan for a satirical book, developed with Benjamin around 1936:

> All the things one doesn't know, what no one tells you, how poorly equipped one is for life. People always tell you what they know. That is unreliable and often uninteresting. If they told you what they didn't know, that would be reliable and mostly interesting.[51]

Brecht's approach is at first pragmatic: 'one must destroy every mode of thinking but that which is socially realizable', was his formulation in a conversation with Benjamin.§ Benjamin's contribution to the conversation which follows is significant: it is one of those fragments that conceal more in themselves than is contained in many a fully developed system of thought:

> There have always been movements, formerly predominantly religious ones, which, as Marx did, start out with radical iconoclasm.
>   Two methodologies: i) theology; ii) materialist dialectic.||

---

* I am grateful for this insight to Hans-Joachim Dahms.

† Session of 26 November 1930 (pp. 190ff. below). I have referred elsewhere to Ernst Bloch's laconic reply 'that scientists think differently in the different sciences' (see Erdmut Wizisla, 'Ernst Bloch und Bertolt Brecht', in *Bloch-Almanach*, Baden-Baden, 1990).

‡ See Brecht's suggestion in the Session of 21 November 1930: 'Is there perhaps a chance of having a detailed essay on "Measuring Human Intelligence"'? (see p, 192 below). This suggestion of Brecht's was stimulated by the Gestalt psychologist Wolfgang Köhler (author of *The Mentality of Apes*) and by an essay, which Brecht underlined in his copy, by L. S. Vygotsky (author of *Thought and Language*) in the journal *Unter dem Banner des Marxismus*. Benjamin also quotes from Köhler and Vygotsky in 1934 in his essay, admired by Brecht, entitled 'Problems in the Sociology of Language: An Overview'. And Brecht also mentions Köhler's experiments in a later letter to Benjamin: 'My work makes me think of Köhler's intelligence tests for anthropoid apes, in which the animals can reach certain fruits only if they swivel away from the barred window, turn their backs to the fruit for a moment, and choose the door' (Brecht, *Letters*, p. 230, writing from London in Spring 1936; in the same letter Brecht praised Benjamin's essay).

§ BBA 217/06. This sentence, too, can be related to Moritz Schlick (see Lutz Danneberg and Hans-Harald Müller, 'Wissenschaftliche Philosophie und literarischer Realismus', in *Exil* (Maintal), 1987, p. 53).

|| BBA 217/06. Bernd Witte was the first to point out the significance of this conversation (see Witte, *Krise und Kritik*, p. 23).

Benjamin understood theological and materialistic methods as complementary, because to him the criterion for judging a statement was not its tradition or ideology, but its 'usefulness'. Thus Benjamin might, for example, find philological potency in historically based theological research that he found lacking in the *Geisteswissenschaften* (the humanities). Processes such as textual criticism, and the study of literature and form, without which any interpretation forgoes its openness to examination, would also have appeared to him as useful for his disciplines. Benjamin had to rein in his tendency to determine the social context of a piece of writing, its 'position in life'. His proposal to identify works of art as part of the era in which they were created, so as to make the era in which they were being observed identifiable, owed its motivations to research into historical criticism, even if there is no proof of a direct link. Benjamin preferred the 'clumsy and rough-and-ready analyses of a Franz Mehring' to the 'most profound circumlocutions of the realm of ideas emanating today from the Heidegger school',[52] because the former seemed to him methodologically better suited to solve the problems of aesthetics, indeed, of philosophical-critical thought in general. The reference to materialist dialectic he considered to be absolutely necessary when it was a question of the relationship of works of art to reality: 'Do you see any possibility other than dialectical materialism for investigating works of art in their reality?'[53] Above all, however, he was interested in the methodology and claims of theological thought, because it takes account of totality, while every other kind of observation proceeds from facts. His open-mindedness to apparently contradictory positions resulted from an attempt to break up long-established ways of posing problems, and to confront social reality in radical terms. Dialectical materialism is given pride of place in the programmatic documents – a position which is, however, misunderstood if the basic direction is reduced to 'propaganda journal for dialectical materialism'.* A dogmatic concentration on specific methodological principles was explicitly excluded.

The encounter between theology and materialist dialectic, between Messianism and Marxism, in Benjamin's thought is certainly not to be reduced to questions of methodology. Theology had for him, as Adorno said of Benjamin's Marxism, an 'experimental character'.[54] Benjamin's interest in directing his thinking 'to those subjects into which truth appears to have been most densely packed at this time'[55] led to an original fusion of apparently contradictory traditions of thought. At the time of *Krise und Kritik* the range is expressed in his programmatic letter to Max Rychner of March 1931, in which he asked Rychner to see in him not

---

* As it is in Michael Rumpf, 'Radikale Theologie. Benjamins Beziehung zu Carl Schmitt', in Peter Gebhardt et al (eds), op. cit., p. 39.

a representative of dialectical materialism as a dogma, but a scholar to whom the *stance* of the materialist seems scientifically and humanely more productive in everything that moves us than does that of the idealist. If I might express it briefly: I have never been able to research and think in any sense other than, if you will, a theological one – namely, in accord with the talmudic teaching about the forty-nine levels of meaning in every passage of the Torah.[56]

Almost a decade later, this unusual confrontation of philosophical models was to find its authentic expression in Benjamin's theses 'On the Concept of History'.

The participants in the project discussed whether philosophical or scientific thought and creative work must be, in Brecht's words, 'realizable in a society'. The historical situation seemed to leave no place for inconsequential artistic and intellectual activity. Thinking should not be developed in isolation from action. Thinking was, as Brecht noted at about this time, '*social* behaviour'.[57] The programmatic documents also established that the journal was to teach 'interventionist thinking', and would take account of the insights which permit the intelligentsia 'an active, interventionist [*eingreifend*], consequential role with tangible consequences, as opposed to its usual ineffectual arbitrariness' (see below, p. 188).

The concept of 'interventionist thinking' comes from conversations between Benjamin and Brecht. It is found in written form for the first time in a notebook of Brecht's begun in May 1929. Even before the note on the journal headed 'Critical Leaves', it contains the statement: the thinking of the individual is 'disinterested [*interesselos*]' and 'almost always worthless'. 'What is valuable, i.e. interventionist, is when a number of people create "committed" [*interessierte*] arguments'. The word '*eingreifend* (interventionist)' has at this point been revised to the wider concept of 'interventionist thinking'.*

Role of Intellectuals

The fact that intellectuals wanted to discuss and change the possibilities and limits of their work, their dependence on institutions, and their relationship

* BBA 363/30. Brecht wrote the words 'about interventionist thinking' below the note. In his own writings, Benjamin used the term only in an altered form, as 'interventionist' or 'interventionist ... criticism' (*SW*, vol. 2, p. 309 [*eingreifend* is translated here as 'radical' in the Harvard edition]). In the notes 'On Thinking as Behaviour', written about 1930, Brecht refers to the close connection between the behaviour of the thinker and the subject: 'Interventionist thinking. Pragmatic definitions: such definitions as permit getting to grips with the defined field. The behaviour of the defining person always appears among the determining factors' (GBA 21, p. 422).

with political forces, had already been the object of public attention for some decades. Since 1898, when Emile Zola and the Dreyfusards, with their *manifeste des intellectuels*, as it was later called, had achieved the rehabilitation of the unjustly accused Captain Dreyfus, the concept of the 'intellectual' had been as familiar as it was controversial. The term has never been able to free itself from the conflicting connotations attached to it during its public circulation in the course of the Dreyfus scandal. While Zola and kindred spirits waged their crusade on grounds of conscience and on a democratic and rational basis, their opponents accused them as intellectuals of being over-rational, unpatriotic, Jewish, decadent and unqualified. In Germany, constant denigration of intellectuals meant that the negative interpretation of the word was dominant. The public debate about the role, social position and function of intellectuals intensified in the nineteen twenties.*

Walter Benjamin, who as a student had already studied social science, was familiar with texts of that period such as Viktor Hueber's pamphlet *Die Organisierung der Intelligenz*, with an introduction by Ernst Mach (1910), Max Weber's *Science as Calling* (1919), Hugo Ball's *Zur Kritik der deutschen Intelligenz* (1919) and Alfred Weber's *Die Not der geistigen Arbeiter* ('The Crisis of the Intellectual Worker') (1923).† Benjamin's writings are inspired by the view 'that the time when neutral, "objective" research could produce far-reaching results had irretrievably passed'.[58] Benjamin's publications during those years presuppose the literature on the situation of the intellectual and are themselves part of it, since they take the 'crisis of the intelligentsia'‡ as their theme. This became clear in his review of Siegfried Kracauer's book *The Salaried Masses*, entitled 'An Outsider Makes His Mark'.[59] Benjamin's text, given the heading 'Politicization of the Intelligence' by the editors, was the final article in a debate on Karl Mannheim's book *Ideology and Utopia* (1929) in which, among others, Hans Speier, Herbert Marcuse, Hannah Arendt and Paul Tillich had taken part.[60] In his review of Kracauer, Benjamin argued that the author should be seen as an individual, as a 'malcontent, not a leader'. In conscious opposition to intellectuals of bourgeois origin such as Johannes R. Becher, who had placed their work at the service of the Party, Benjamin for-

---

* See the 'survey into the social situation of intellectual workers' conducted by Bernard von Brentano for the *Literarische Welt*, Berlin, vol. 8 (1932), nos 11, 22 and 23.

† This concept was widespread. As early as 1920, Benjamin told Scholem he had drafted an 'essay with the charming title "There are no intellectual workers"' (*Benjamin Correspondence*, 13 February 1920, p. 160).

‡ This phrase is referred to at the beginning of the 'Surrealism' essay (*SW*, vol. 2, pp. 207ff.), which is among the writings by Benjamin that deal directly with the theme. The essay's subtitle in English is 'The Last Snapshot of the European Intelligentsia'.

mulated the statement that 'the proletarianization of the intellectual hardly ever turns him into a proletarian'.[61] The 'politicization of one's own class' rather took place indirectly, and this 'indirect impact' was 'the only one a revolutionary writer from the bourgeoisie can aim at today'.[62] Brecht went a step further when rejecting the demands of the Association of Proletarian Revolutionary Writers (BPRS): he described the 'view they [the intellectuals] often air, that it's necessary to submerge oneself in the proletariat', as 'counter-revolutionary'.*

The discussions on the plan for founding a journal were a direct response to Mannheim's theories, which were fraught with consequences to an unusual degree in the debate on the intelligentsia. They thus form an independent contribution to the 'Debate about the Sociology of Knowledge'.† In a conversation before 21 November 1930, Brecht had introduced a proposal of the theme 'The Historic Role of Intellectual Leadership' as follows:

> The intelligentsia floats freely above everything else, can't decide
> anything for itself, takes up a 'third' position, is influenced by no one,
> but still wishes to exert influence, and attempts to reconcile differences.
> This gives it a claim to power on account of its supposed impartiality.[63]

The course of the discussion shows that in these remarks Brecht was commenting critically on Mannheim, even though he would have liked to claim the intellectual's freedom for himself. In the talks, Mannheim, first and foremost, provided the cue where there was disagreement on the role of the intelligentsia. He had taken up and popularized the concept, already used by Alfred Weber, of the 'socially unattached intelligentsia'. Mannheim characterized the active forces of intellectual activity as 'a social stratum which is to a large degree unattached to any social class',[64] who were entitled to possible leadership tasks on account of their potential political insight. Brecht and Benjamin differed over this. Brecht insisted: 'You need a leadership position to perform a function.'‡ Benjamin, however, rejected this, for example in his review of Kracauer: 'An intellectual today should not step up to the platform and make a

---

* In his uncompleted 1929 article entitled 'Defence of the Lyric Poet Gottfried Benn' in *Brecht on Art and Politics*, p. 85. See also Brecht's harsh judgement on the inaugural congress of the BPRS: 'They are just enemies of bourgeois writers and they hope with the help of their congress to corner the proletarian market for themselves' (Brecht to Brentano, September/October 1928, in Bertolt Brecht, *Letters*, p. 119.)

† Benjamin's interest had certainly also been nourished by his friendly encounter with Karl Mannheim in Heidelberg in 1921/22 (see Scholem, *Benjamin*, p. 111).

‡ In his 'Defence of the Poet Gottfried Benn', Brecht had described the leadership function of intellectuals around 1929 as 'quite indispensable' and 'of the utmost importance' (*Brecht on Art and Politics*, p. 84).

claim, but should work under public supervision, not lead.'* Benjamin and Brecht agreed that the free-floating condition defined by Mannheim was a petty-bourgeois position, which could not contribute to the overcoming of the crisis. Benjamin, who had already detected the 'decline of the "free" intelligentsia' in 1929,[65] now asked, in the course of the discussions: 'How are intellectuals to be brought into the class struggle?'† He was assuming a 'situation before the seizure of power by the proletariat'.[66] Accordingly, the leadership role fell to the proletariat. The intelligentsia renounced the position of leader; according to Benjamin's surprising proposal of Summer 1930, on the seizure of power, the intelligentsia should go into the factories and there fulfil 'servile' functions, 'those allotted to it'.[67] When making this proposal he was certainly thinking of the type of the 'operative' writer defined and incorporated by Sergei Tretyakov: 'Send the writers to the collective farms!' In 1934, in his essay 'The Author as Producer', Benjamin was to describe the concept as 'interventionist'.‡ Benjamin shared the incorrect assessment that proletarian revolution was imminent with many of his comrades-in-arms, but only briefly with Brecht. The discussion of the problem of the intelligentsia, which led to a series of concrete proposals,§ was seen not as an abstract topic but as an existential one.

In retrospect, Brecht tackled the attitude of the intellectuals ironically. His *Buch der Wendungen* ('Book of Twists and Changes'), but above all his so-called *Tui* novel, assume an experience by which the discussions on *Krise und Kritik*

---

* See *GS* IV/1, p. 480: in the same vein, Benjamin stressed the lack of any 'leadership attitude' in Valéry.

† See *GS* III, p. 175, 'Bücher, die übersetzt werden sollten' ('Books which should be translated'), in which Benjamin rejected classlessness in intellectuals as a luxury.

‡ See *SW*, vol. 2, p. 770. Although Tretyakov had been in Germany only since December 1930, his work was already well known in Brecht's circle (through Meyerhold's performances in April and May 1930) – see Brecht's reaction to the bourgeois reviews, GBA 21, pp. 374; and through Asja Lacis, Bernhard Reich, and Leo Lania who had translated Tretyakov's *Roar, China!* in 1929.

§ On 21 November 1930 a topic was proposed 'for Brentano with the cooption of Korsch and Kurella': '"Current Varieties of Intellectual Leadership". " The professor" (Mannheim)/ "the politician" (Hellpach)/ "the journalist" (Kerr)/ "the freelance writer" (Tucholsky)' (see p. 194 below). At the 26 November Session Kracauer proposed modifications to the study plan: Heidegger was to be examined rather than Mannheim, and by Adorno; instead of Willy Hellpach, the former state president of Baden, the Social Democrats Rudolf Breitscheid, Rudolf Hilferding and Otto Braun were suggested; and the successful Romanian writer Valeriu Marcu was proposed instead of Kurt Tucholsky. The topics of 'politician' and 'freelance writer' were to be offered to Brentano. The idea was probably for each contributor to characterize in critical terms a type of intellectual as he presented himself in public (see p. 202 below).

were still unaffected. Walter Benjamin described it in a letter to Klaus Mann of 9 May 1934 as 'the defeat of the German intelligentsia'.[68]

A number of topics are only proposed, but not examined, in the discussions, so that no outlines of the content are recognizable. In the dialogue that took place about the beginning of November 1930, 'proposals for future issues' were being collected, to each of which, like the debate about the intelligentsia, a whole issue was to be devoted, and the main focuses were named: fascism, anarchism, Judaism, critique of the judiciary, public education. Brentano was to prepare a special issue on 'newspapers' (see p. 192 below). On 21 November, Benjamin suggested a topic on which he had published an article in the *Frankfurter Zeitung* five days earlier: 'Critique of publishing firms (not of the books published by them), but the political tendency of publishers.'[69] Contributions on philosophy were planned. Kracauer was to write 'on the major trends in philosophy of the last ten years', a proposal that he rejected 'giving detailed reasons'.[70] Ernst Bloch suggested the idea of an essay 'on class thinking'. 'How deeply does class consciousness penetrate?' Bloch asked, and he considered a review of Lukács's essay collection *History and Class Consciousness*, to be '*very important*' (emphasis in the original, see p. 201 below). That *Krise und Kritik* would not have shied away from tackling the ever-intensifying practice of censorship is shown by the proposal on 'censorship and the intelligentsia' made by Brecht.[71]

Two lists preserved among Brecht's papers contain proposals for topics which go beyond those summarized so far. These lists belong to the intellectual milieu of the project, even if the way they are organized is not entirely clear:

[1] Difficulty of reading Marxist texts   Wittfogel
Defence of Marxism   Döblin
Overcoming of prejudice (by novelists) with reference
     to problems of how human destinies are played out in
     Wang-lun + Wallenstein   Döblin
On quality   Benjamin
Film censorship – Kesser – Brentano – Ihering
Ihering responsible for topics
Individual contributors take responsibility for implementation.*

[2] 1) Nazi programme and Nazi practice (in Thuringia) – socialist side
     The revolutionary side of the petit-bourgeois revolt

---

* *Wang-lun* is the best-selling novel by Alfred Döblin, called *Die Drei Sprünge des Wang-lun* (1915); *Wallenstein* refers to a two-volume novel by the same author, published in 1920.

If bought, then bought off the peg without being tried on.
When did they become commodities? What do they demand
from capitalism? For whom? What have they achieved? Has
the National Socialist movement already won a victory?

2) The soil   Tretyakov
3) Para 218 in Thuringia (see footnote below)   Lania?
4) The new guest (does Benn deliver ideology?)   Benjamin
5) Heidegger   Bloch
6) The ideological struggle of the Nazis against Marxism
   (egalitarianism Jewish international class struggle racial
   conflict)   Wittfogel
7) on 'HockeDöblin'*

The working instructions in the first list refer to the procedure proposed by
Benjamin for *Krise und Kritik*. The reference to the statement that Ihering
should be 'responsible for topics' suggests the association of the list of topics
with the journal project. The names Wittfogel and Kesser shown here were
subsequently completed in Benjamin's list of contributors.[72] The second list
contains a proposal that Benjamin presumably also brought up at the editorial
meetings: '*Döblin*: diary entries.' This refers to Döblin's correspondence with
the student Gustav René Hocke, which had appeared in the *Tage-Buch* and was
published in February 1931 as a book under the title *Wissen und Verändern* ('To
Know and to Change'). 'One would however have to wait until the book was
published,' reads an addendum.[73] In his essay 'The Author as Producer',
Benjamin would deal critically with Döblin's positions.

The two lists of proposals loosely to be assigned to the *Krise und Kritik*
project correspond to the records of discussions about such topics as the
problem of the intelligentsia (Döblin/Hocke), writing technique (Döblin),
censorship,† ideology or typology of 'characters', and representatives of the
intelligentsia (Heidegger/Benn). At the same time, the proposals show that the
project's participants judged the political situation with great clarity. While
there were, as mentioned, isolated illusions about an imminent victory of the
proletariat, the conviction that the social crisis which had arisen out of the
world economic crisis would lead to a new era grew from a realistic view of the
situation. This applies also to Benjamin's fear, expressed in Summer 1931, that

---

* For Gustav René Hocke, see immediately below.
† Brecht himself was affected by censorship through the ban on *The Threepenny Opera*
film. The note 'Para 218 in Thuringia' refers to the ban on abortion and therefore of films
such as *Cyankali* and *Frauen in Not*, which had already been imposed by the Nazi-head-
ed Thuringian government (with Wilhelm Frick as Minister of the Interior) by the end
of 1930 (see Hildegard Brenner, *Die Kunstpolitik des Nationalsozialismus*, op. cit., p. 32).

it was 'very doubtful that we will have to wait longer than fall for the start of civil war'.[74] Finally, the intention of analysing the National Socialist movement, against the background of the Nazi Party's success in the state parliament election in Thuringia on 8 December 1930, shows that the extent of the danger represented by the National Socialists had been clearly recognized. That it was not just a question of whether 'the National Socialist movement [had] already won a victory' – that is, politically, but also philosophically and ideologically – emerges from the key phrase, 'the ideological struggle of the Nazis against Marxism'. While others were still dismissing with 'mockery and disbelief' the measures of the National Socialist regional government in Thuringia, which was exerting power over all public areas by means of decrees and prohibitions, the *Krise und Kritik* team observed the early signs of a development it was essential to resist. Brecht's notes 'On Thought as Behaviour', set down around 1930, point out that fascism totally invalidates progressive thought. He identified the 'necessity of establishing a *critique of fascism* via different responses based on *interventionist thinking*'.[75]

Ambition and Failure

The contents of the planned issues would, as far as could be predicted, have been as topical as is possible for a monthly or bi-monthly journal, which – unlike the daily press – must rely on continuity and thoroughness. The intention was to conduct a critical debate and make public statements on the problems of intellectuals. Apart from the Döblin correspondence with Hocke, which had been severely criticized in *Linkskurve*, mention was also made of a speech by Thomas Mann attacking the Nazis – his 'Deutsche Ansprache ('German Address – An Appeal to Reason') of 17 October 1930. Lack of topicality, or insufficient consistency of content, could not have been arguments against the project. So why did *Krise und Kritik* never get beyond the planning stage? A whole range of explanations for its failure have been named: financial difficulties* and the unstable legal position of Rowohlt, resistance by the *Frankfurter Zeitung*, Ihering's withdrawal. Another factor in the foundering of the

---

* Margot von Brentano recalled that 'from the beginning there was a lack of money for the journal' (letter to the author, 16 March 1989). Similarly, Michael Jennings concluded that *Krise und Kritik* 'foundered on the lack of financial support' (see Jennings, *Dialectical Images*, op. cit., p. 3). Jennings continues, 'although the tensions that characterized every stage of Benjamin's relationship to Brecht undoubtedly exacerbated the material difficulties'. However, there is absolutely no evidence for this. My account is based on the contrary assessment that precisely at this time the relationship between Benjamin and Brecht was characterized by elements of agreement.

project may have been that at the beginning of 1931 too few contributors were available equal to the task – at least, fewer than had originally been envisaged.

Ernst Bloch, for example, expressed himself cautiously in a letter of 5 November 1930 to his later wife, Karola Piotrkowska. Bloch's sense of distance from the project also emerges from his comparatively untypical restraint during the discussions. The letter casts light upon Bloch's envisaged prospects for the undertaking and on how he assessed Benjamin's talent for organization:

> During the summer, Benjamin, Brecht and Ihering worked out a plan for a journal they want to bring out. Tomorrow Benjamin is going to tell me about the 'guidelines' (some things are not quite right). Through Benjamin and Brecht the thing has – apart from its obvious importance – something unnecessarily offbeat, even cliquey... Besides, the alliance of the pure man of genius, Benjamin, with the unwashed genius Brecht is exceedingly curious.
>
> And whatever Benjamin touches as far as organization goes, he gets wrong. He makes elephants out of mosquitoes and then tries to thread them through the eye of a needle. He is so eccentric and, at the same time, so unhuman [*unmenschlich*] and such an outsider to the common cause. Not in my sector of the front, even if he is at the front and in the same detachment. I probably won't take part in the first few issues. (For this is something different from a 'trial issue', as I don't care in the least where that is published; even in the *Literarische Welt* as far as I am concerned.)[76]

Two months later even Siegfried Kracauer – apparently a prospective co-editor – expressed himself with similar scepticism. His letter to Adorno of 12 January 1931 contains a double negative, which makes his attitude somewhat opaque. Be that as it may, his impression of one of the editorial discussions – probably that of 26 November 1930, in which he took part – is revealing:

> The journal planned by Brecht, etc. will, as I believe and hear, not come into being at all. I was actively present at a decisive meeting which, despite the presence of two secretaries who took everything down in shorthand, was so amateurishly conducted that I would not care at all if it did not come out.[77]

It becomes clear that the idea of allowing creative, independent spirits to sail under one flag was here approaching its limits. *Krise und Kritik* was planned as an authors' journal, shaped by a group rather than by a lone editor who commissions articles, reaches agreements and makes decisions. By setting up a succession of editorial committees, and with the collective responsibility of the contributors, the group could have demonstrated in exemplary fashion how intellectual work could be effectively organized. Kracauer, an experienced journalist, considered agreement as to methods and language to be important: 'A uniform way of dealing with everything must be found' (see p. 202 below). A basic working rule must be that it was not the singling out of individuals and the communication of individual positions that would be of benefit, but the working out of common principles. Benjamin proposed that supplementary issues of the journal should 'establish a collection of theses which can serve as guidelines for contributors to future volumes of the journal' (see below, p. 189). Although this was not a dogmatic working instruction, some leading authors, like Bloch, concerned about their reputations, seemed to have understood such proposals as a restriction of and threat to their independence. The collective to which the group aspired remained a pipe dream.

However, what was crucial to the failure of the project were the differences between the participating authors, which went deeper than Bloch's scepticism. These were personal tensions, representing fundamentally divergent political and aesthetic positions. The editors were in agreement that society and, therefore, culture, was determined by class struggle, and that the materialistic dialectic was one way, or perhaps the *only* way, of confronting the resulting conflicts. Authors who did not share this view were immediately excluded from the shortlist.

The idea of 'interventionist thinking' was taken up by all potential contributors as a dominant concept, but opinions on how it should operate, or how reality should influence thought, diverged considerably. The general ideological framework should not obscure the fact that, among the authors envisaged for *Krise und Kritik*, there opened exactly the same abysses that divided other left-wing intellectuals at the close of the Weimar Republic. The ability to compromise was limited. It totally failed when individual interests broke up intended alliances with such vehemence that one wonders if the participants realized the significance of the political force-field in which they were operating.

The divergences are evident from a glance at the contributions planned for the first issue. The only article to be preserved, in Brecht's papers, is by the Russian Marxist Georgi Plekhanov, who had died in 1918, a 37-page typescript entitled 'Idealist and Materialist World Views'.[78] This text, whose origin and date are unknown, seeks to answer the 'task of philosophy' by means of a choice, going back to Feuerbach, for materialism as a basis for cognition. Benjamin considered Plekhanov's argumentation to be outdated. Of the prospective contributions he wrote to Brecht: 'Not one, whatever value they may have, can lay claim to expert authority. Plekhanov's could have done so at one time, but that was 25 years ago.'[79] The rejection of the text 'The General Assault' by Brentano, who at that time was holding fast to the Communist Party line, was perhaps the result of the same weariness with which Benjamin reacted a few months later in Le Lavandou to Brentano's contribution to a discussion: 'Brentano was in the midst of one of his blustering speeches about the revolutionizing of intellectual workers, the situation of the intelligentsia, and so forth, when Brecht interrupted rather fiercely.'[80]

Alfred Kurella's essay on the Kharkov Congress, which was also rejected, hardly differed from reports he had already published in *Linkskurve* and the *Roter Aufbau* on the Second World Congress of Revolutionary Literature in Kharkhov in October 1930, where he represented the German proletarian-revolutionary delegation.* There was considerable dissension between Kurella and Benjamin, and it is probably not by chance that when Kurella mentioned the journal project in a conversation in 1975, he recalled Brecht, Brentano, and Ihering, but not Benjamin.† Benjamin must have regarded the attempt to launch a semi-official report on the Congress in the first issue as something of a betrayal. In fact, Kurella and Brecht were merely supposed to *suggest* an author for the first topic, 'The Role and Idea of Intellectual Leadership in History'. Kurella was to take on the essay on Karl Mannheim, and Ihering the one on Frank Thiess and Kurt Tucholsky, while the 'organization of the essay on Thomas Mann' was entrusted to Benjamin.[81] A preliminary decision had probably already been made when, at the undated meeting which took place about the beginning of November, it was established that the working committee for the first issue should consist of Ihering, Brecht and Kurella.

The Kharkov line, which Kurella propagated on behalf of the Comintern, was politically in opposition to what Benjamin wanted to see represented in *Krise und Kritik*. Furthermore, Benjamin could not be anything but dismissive about its fixation on the politics of the German Communist Party, consistent with the theory – also put forward at Kharkov – of social fascism, involving the rejection of 'supporters' or 'sympathizers', and the struggle now for and now against left-wing bourgeois writers, and the demand of the Association of Proletarian Revolutionary Writers (BPRS) that intellectuals should become 'part of the army of the proletarian struggle'.‡

The Kharkov propagandists and those close to both Benjamin and Brecht

---

* For the Kharkov Conference and the debate about Plekhanov, see Edward J. Brown, *The Proletarian Episode in Russian Literature, 1928–1932*, New York, 1953, pp. 186–7.

† See Helmut Baierl and Ulrich Dietzel, 'Gespräch mit Alfred Kurella', in *Sinn und Form* (Berlin), vol. 27, no. 2, 1975; on *Krise und Kritik*, see p. 233: 'We were often together, Brecht, Brentano (the eldest of the brothers, who was a very clever man and a member of our party), and Ihering. We even wanted to bring out a new journal, *Krise und Kritik*. I went on my Italian journey with my business card as editor of this journal. Apart from my passport, it was the only document I had.'

‡ On the theses of the Kharkov Conference, only briefly mentioned here, see Edward J. Brown, ibid.

also diverged over aesthetic principles. The proposal to publish a translation of Plekhanov in the first issue of *Krise und Kritik* was in response to a request from the German group in Kharkov for the publication of Plekhanov's works in German.* It constituted support for Wittfogel's preferred line – the tradition of Hegel, Marx, Engels and Plekhanov, over that of Kant, Schiller, Lassalle and Mehring.† Benjamin's 'deviation' was evident. In the editorial discussions he had explicitly referred to Kant and Mehring (who had fallen into disrepute), and made no secret of his rejection of Plekhanov.‡ The points of difference presented to Benjamin also applied, *mutatis mutandis*, to Brecht. In Brecht's case they were expressed in his controversy with Lukács, about the latter's 'propaganda methods' and about the readiness of intellectuals to embrace communism. Brecht's relationship with Kurella was equally tense, since Kurella had only three weeks earlier written a harsh review of his *The Measures Taken*. Kurella attributed the growing distance between himself and Brecht to Brecht's closer contacts with Korsch and Sternberg, who were looked on critically by the Communist Party.§

Alfred Kurella's intentions were obvious. If the editorial group had followed the proposals put forward by him and his Communist Party adherents (among whom Brentano was also to be counted for a time),‖ *Krise und Kritik* would

---

* Plekhanov's text, including its topic, corresponded to one of the Kharkov demands: 'The proletariat is carrying out a reorganization of the whole of literary history, by confronting its various '-isms' with the two great currents which also battle against each other in philosophy: materialism and idealism.'

† See Karl August Wittfogel's series on Marxist aesthetics in *Die Linkskurve* (Berlin), vol. 2 (1930), nos. 5–11. See also Helga Gallas, *Marxistische Literaturtheorie*, Neuwied/Berlin, 1971.

‡ See also the reference to Mehring in Benjamin's letter to Max Rychner, quoted earlier, of 7 March 1931, *Benjamin Correspondence*, p. 372; he also made critical and comments on Plekhanov to Asja Lacis (see *Revolutionär im Beruf*, pp. 6off.).

§ See Bertolt Brecht to Georg Lukács, draft, *c.* summer 1931 (Brecht, *Letters*, London, pp. 127–8). Lukács, who wanted to 'work seriously in the German party' and who also had to carry through the basic direction of Kharkov, at that time considered Brecht to be a deviationist (see Lukács, *Record of a Life*, London, 1983, pp. 91–2). Kurella remembered the beginning of the tensions; see Helmut Baierl and Ulrich Dietzel, 'Gespräch mit Alfred Kurella', op. cit., p. 233.

‖ Brentano, according to Alfred Kantorowicz, was among the 'most fervent propagandists' of the Association of Revolutionary Writers (see Ulrike Hessler, *Ber- nard von Brentano – ein deutscher Schriftsteller ohne Deutschland*, Frankfurt, 1984, p. 20). That Brentano was a member of the German Communist Party, as Kurella recalled, is confirmed by his letter to Brecht (*c.* April or May 1934), in which he writes: 'In Germany I went into the organization and noticed how bad the flag was, how stupidly the articles for Teddy [i.e. Ernst Thälmann, the German communist leader] were written, but like all the others I just believed in the whole thing, in the proletariat, etc.' (BBA 481/26).

have looked like a party organ. It would have become the homogeneous voice of an originally heterogeneous left-wing circle, which encompassed Rowohlt authors and writers for the *Literarische Welt* and the *Frankfurter Zeitung*, as well as intellectuals from Brecht's milieu, writers from the journal *Musik und Gesellschaft*, and members of the Association of Revolutionary Writers. This attempt by Communist Party literary functionaries to infiltrate the project dogmatically and ideologically, to take it over and exploit it for propaganda purposes, failed.

Behind the differences over political questions and aesthetic tradition lay considerably diverging ideas about progress in artistic technique. Benjamin and Brecht refused to make the quality of a work of art dependent on its content. As is well known, they paid great attention to the development of new aesthetic techniques and forms, since these seemed to them both dependent on the development of society in general and also ahead of it in anticipation. This attention found expression in the talks about the foundation of the proposed journal in the course of discussion of the topic, 'Is there a technical element, implying a technical standard in literature?'[82] The records noted:

> *Brecht* speaks again on the general topic 'Crisis and Criticism'. In purely bourgeois literature, for example in belles-lettres, we have, after all, enormously progressive consequences, perhaps even an improvement in the literary means of production. We should definitely look into this. I mean the change of viewpoint rather than the methodological improvements (James Joyce and Döblin in contrast to Mann and Wassermann). What would be of personal interest to me would be, for example, evidence that James Joyce and Döblin are to be linked to certain other improvements of creative construction. Thought as a productive force. Then I would want to produce evidence that this improvement of productive forces, as implemented by these literati, by these leaders of belles-lettres, has counterparts in other fields, in which productive forces would also be improved.[83]

Brecht assessed the improvement of literary technique by Joyce and Döblin as 'creations of the crisis', or as he also called it 'the crisis in belles-lettres', but these phenomena were 'in a certain sense attempts to emerge from the crisis'.*

---

* See pp. 197ff.below. It has justifiably been objected that Benjamin expressed himself on questions of writing style in a substantially less well-informed, indeed partly more orthodox, manner than Brecht. When Brecht pointed out that the changing point of view in authors such as Joyce and Döblin should be related to certain other improvements of creative construction, Benjamin replied: 'This interests me more than you could possibly have wished, from a depth of ignorance, I don't know Joyce, have only heard about him and have formed a certain very inadequate impression of him that doesn't immediately coincide with what you are saying. I would be very interested to learn more' (see p. 197 below).

The decisive factor in the moulding of new technical or constructive means in literature and art was their relationship to reality. Brecht criticized the closed world-view of authors such as Thomas Mann and Jakob Wassermann. The 'apparent totality' which they assumed as an expression of their personality restricted the context of their writing. The 'Joyce' and 'Döblin' type, on the other hand, established interchangeable 'apparatuses'. Such thinking methods were separated from private personality; they were something 'transferable'.[84] There was a 'technical element'. The journal would represent

> the viewpoint that literary inventions and discoveries exist that are bound to alter the methods of all writers, just as all scientific and technical disciplines at all times have a technical standard which each individual employed in them must have reached.*

These and other reflections on technical aesthetic problems would have found ready listeners among avant-garde theorists such as Siegfried Giedion and Adolf Behne, the writer on art from the *Werkbund* circle, and Hannes Meyer, the recently dismissed Marxist director of the Bauhaus. The circumstance that Behne and Meyer had been envisaged as authors, Giedion for a time even as a co-editor, acquires its real importance only in the context of a subsequent conversation with Ernst Bloch, who, even if in retrospect he named the wrong year, was undoubtedly remembering a meeting of the editorial team of *Krise und Kritik*:

> One evening, probably in about '27, the following people met in an apartment: the theatre critic Ihering, who was on Brecht's side against Kerr; the arts correspondent of the *Frankfurter Zeitung*, Siegfried Kracauer; the essayist and philosopher Walter Benjamin; the playwright Bertolt Brecht, and the essayist and philosopher Ernst Bloch. Together these individuals came up with a plan to form a committee for publishing a new journal. It was to be called *Journal for Cultural Bolshevism*. The term 'cultural bolshevism' at the time suggested the Bauhaus, Gropius and everything that was good and fine and strange and unusual and astonishing – everything denounced as 'cultural bolshevism'.[85]

Bloch's recollection introduces a notable aspect into the presentation of the journal. It is actually conceivable that *Krise und Kritik* was a direct response to the Nazi Kampfbund ('Militant Association') für deutsche Kultur, an offshoot of the National Socialist Association for German Culture, founded at the end of

---

* GBA 21, p. 331 ('Draft for the journal *Kritische Blätter*'). See Brecht's text 'On New Criticism', in which he criticizes the fact that the writer need not admit in 'his own subject area that there is "progress"', i.e., new methods of representation, ignorance of which makes all further writing "old-fashioned"' (*Brecht on Art and Politics*, pp. 90–1).

1928 by Alfred Rosenberg, Heinrich Himmler and Gregor Strasser. Among the Kampfbund's tasks were the battle against the 'cultural bolshevism' of the artistic avant-garde, which was denounced as the 'driving force of the proletarian world revolution'; one of its propagandists, the architectural writer Alexander von Senger, wrote polemics against Le Corbusier and the Bauhaus, and called the new style in architecture 'a purely bolshevist affair'.[86] At this time, as Fritz Sternberg recalled, Brecht had contacts with idealistic young Nazi students and 'with various right-wing circles'.[87] An indication that the Kampfbund für deutsche Kultur, whose public activity was increased in 1931, was under discussion by the participants in the planning phase of *Krise und Kritik*, emerges from the following sentence in a letter from Benjamin to Brentano:

> The planned meeting has still not taken place; on the other hand a
> recent session with the National Socialist opposition, the Strasser
> group, which started out on an alcoholic basis in the morning hours,
> ended in a rather fine, partly fascinating debate, at which I could have
> wished you to be present.*

Bloch's reference to the Bauhaus was also relevant to the group's modus operandi. Independence and intellectual authority, as well as a creative attitude based on thorough knowledge of artistic production processes, were considered prerequisites for a readiness to work together. What Walter Gropius wrote about his concept of the Bauhaus idea could have been the standard for *Krise und Kritik*:

> I realized that a whole staff of employees and assistants were needed,
> men who did not work like members of an orchestra, under a con-
> ductor's baton, but independently, even though working closely
> together, in the service of the common cause.[88]

This decisiveness, tangible in Bloch's words, with which the leading representatives of *Krise und Kritik* had made the dimension of art in terms of technical construction into a component of their own aesthetic, makes the tensions in the group vis-à-vis Kurella and Lukács, who were politically partisan and rather traditional in their argumentation on aesthetic theory, quite comprehensible.

The interest shown by Brecht, Benjamin and the others in problems of content and the aesthetics of production, may have seemed to the supporters of

---

* Walter Benjamin to Bernard von Brentano, 23 October 1930, *GB* II, pp. 546ff. The 'planned meeting' concerned the journal project. In Benjamin's letter to Brentano of 11 October 1930 he added: 'The journal projects have not moved forward an inch. The reasons for this are only external, however; there is to be a definitive discussion next week, and I will let you know of the outcome immediately' (*GB* III, p. 545).

the movement for a proletarian revolution, intent on political agitation, like a dangerous, bourgeois aesthetic game. The latter demanded of art that it should directly serve the proletarian struggle for liberation, while the former believed experiments in art, which made the destruction of closed reality and the testing of new, open forms into aesthetically and thus socially effective principles, to be indispensable.

Benjamin, Bloch, Brecht and their comrades-in-arms, however, by no means wanted to exclude political effectiveness, but strove after a synthesis of the technical-constructive and social dimensions of art, which sought to link high artistic standards indissolubly with politically advanced ones.*

The attempt to connect art and politics in such a way as to do justice to both sides moves the project, even though it could not be realized, into a highly significant space in the intellectual and cultural life of the Weimar Republic. Its failure was rooted in the disagreements between left-wing intellectuals. It had turned out that the reply to the question posed by Benjamin at an early stage of the project had to be in the negative: 'Now the great question will arise as to whether it is still possible to unite people who have something to say in a project that is organized and above all subject to scrutiny.'[89] Such an unsuccessful attempt was at the same time an anticipation of the uncompromising debates on aesthetic politics of the years of exile. It is true to say that none of the numerous journals actually published around 1930 fulfilled a programme comparable to the ambitions of *Krise und Kritik*.† And yet for a short moment in history, *Krise und Kritik* seems to have laid down conditions under which a journal project could have been realized. The intention of artists and scientists to intervene with their own work in the issues of the day, without at the same time losing their standards or their competence to make judgements, remained unfulfilled. Its failure does not, however, prove that the ambitions of *Krise und Kritik* were illusory.

* In the words of Walter Benjamin in his 1934 speech 'The Author as Producer': 'I would like to show you that the tendency of a literary work can be politically correct only if it is literarily correct' (*SW*, vol. 2, p. 769).
† In 1931 the total number of German literary journals reached its highest point since 1910.

IV
Benjamin on Brecht

Agreement

In a letter to Gershom Scholem of 26 July 1932 Walter Benjamin – 'with a grimness verging on hopelessness' – spoke of a series of unexecuted, untouched plans, which formed 'the real site of ruin or catastrophe' of his work. Among the 'large-scale defeats' offset by 'small-scale victories' was, even though he does not explicitly mention it, his plan for a book on Bertolt Brecht.[1] In 1939, under the heading 'Material for a discourse on Brecht', Benjamin made a list of his essays on and records of conversations with him. Its scope and thematic diversity are considerable.* Benjamin completed eleven pieces of work exclusively or substantially concerned with Brecht, but during his lifetime only five of these were published (and of one other text only a part).† The majority of Benjamin's reviews, talks and essays arose from performances and publications, but beyond the occasions for their creation, they together form a complex and varied study. Out of Benjamin's preoccupation there emerged a monograph on Brecht devoted to different factors in his work and activity. It is incomplete but not disparate.‡

---

* Four of the total of twenty listed dated journal entries have not been preserved. The list was created for a conversation intended for publication with Ferdinand Lion, the editor of *Maß und Wert* (see the account of the writing of 'What is the Epic Theatre? (2)'), pp. 140ff. below.

† The following specific texts are listed:
  1 'Commentary on Poems by Brecht' (1930)
  2 'Bert Brecht' (1930)
  3 'Studies for a Theory of Epic Theatre' (1931)
  4 'What is Epic Theatre? (1)' (1931)
  5 'Family Drama in the Epic Theatre' (1932)
  6 'Theatre and Radio' (1932)
  7 'Brecht *Threepenny Novel*' (1934–35)
  8 '*The Threepenny Opera*' (1937)
  9 'The Country where it is Forbidden to Mention the Proletariat' (1938)
  10 'Commentary on Poems by Brecht' (1938–39)
  11 'What is the Epic Theatre? (2)' (1939)

The texts published during the author's lifetime were nos 1, 2 (as a radio broadcast), 5, 6, 9, and one of the interpretations from no. 10. With the exception of texts 3, 4 and 8, these articles are included in *SW*.

‡ See Rolf Tiedemann: 'Even the earliest of the texts, with its title "*From* the Brecht Commentary", seems to indicate the plan for a more comprehensive representation of the writer as literary phenomenon, and the actual connection between the texts, without

Benjamin's examination of Brecht extended over ten years; the texts were published between 1930 and 1939. His first public references were to Brecht as a poet. Brecht was 'the best chansonnier since Wedekind', he wrote as early as June 1929 in a review of poetry by the cabaret-writer, Walter Mehring. In Brecht, wrote Benjamin,

> the *chanson* emancipated itself from the *Brettl* (cabaret); decadence was beginning to become historical. His hooligan is the mould into which the image of classless people would eventually be poured with better, fuller material. This gave the genre its sharp, topical definition.[2]

Mehring, Benjamin wrote, was alien to the 'irrational, the bitter, the despised and to the homesickness and *amor fati* of the disreputable'. 'Someone like Brecht can be as nasty as he likes; we will always have pleasure in the sensitive way he does it.'[3] The 'task of all political lyricism', he added a few years later in distancing himself from Erich Kästner, was today 'most strictly fulfilled in Brecht's poems'.*

The initial stimulus for a comprehensive discussion of Brecht's work came from the first issue of *Versuche*, published in April 1930.† In a conversation with Siegfried Kracauer on 18 April, Benjamin developed some of the arguments of his Brecht commentary. Kracauer quoted Benjamin, paraphrasing the commentary to *Lindbergh's Flight*, as maintaining that 'Brecht champions the saying that in a classless society the individual should be poor, the whole rich'.

---

exception written as occasional pieces, is evident. It is by no means exhausted by the fact that many formulations are repeated verbatim, or more often in modified form. What Benjamin's commentaries on Brecht have in common is, for a start, their political and literary-political tendency. This allows us to read the individual pieces as fragments of a larger whole, at least as a preliminary to one, even if Benjamin had at some point given up such a project' ('Afterword', 'Die Kunst, in anderer Leute Köpfe zu denken' ('The Art of Thinking in Other People's Heads'), in *Versuche über Brecht*, Frankfurt, 1978, p. 175.) However, Benjamin's commentaries on Brecht are more than prolegomena.

* *SW*, vol. 2, p. 426. As early as 21 April 1929 Benjamin had written in a review of *Deutsche Lyrik* by Franz Heyden in the *Literarische Welt* that the writer 'should have explored the new, post-Stefan George poetry', like Brecht and Ringelnatz (*GS* III, p. 164).

† See Kracauer to Adorno, 20 April 1930, in Hans Puttnies and Gary Smith (eds), *Benjaminiana*, Gießen, 1991, p. 35: Benjamin wanted to comment on Brecht's 'recently published *Versuche*'. 'So far I have merely glanced briefly inside the book.' This seems to discredit the publication date of mid June, which has become widespread in the literature. Benjamin declared himself 'very taken' with Adorno's essay on Brecht and Weill's *Mahagonny*, which had been published in April, and asks whether Adorno has read the first part of Benjamin's 'Paris Diary' in the 17 April issue of the *Literarische Welt*. There can therefore be no doubt about the dating of the letter.

To my question as to who should represent the whole and look after the money, Benji replied that Brecht would presumably refuse to answer this question... Benji also said that Brecht was the only one who applied his talents in the right area.[4]

Brecht's work seemed to Benjamin to point the way out of a cul-de-sac which he was to describe in 1932 as 'the crass confrontation of conventional writing [*Schriftstellerei*] and literary or creative writing [*Dichtung*]'. No great creative writing could be understood without the factor of technique, which is literary.[5] The old polarity, which contrasted the 'real' *Dichter* (creative writer) and his imaginative works, not to be grasped rationally, with the *Schriftsteller* or *Literat* (conventional writer) and his mundane, inartistic communications, appeared questionable to Benjamin and – in view of the intensification of the capitalist system and the threat of war, which required political commitment in art – no longer at all plausible. Brecht too, with regard to the journal project, opposed 'the splitting-off of so-called fine literature, and its separate treatment as "true literature"', which had 'turned literary history into a stomping ground of tastes'.[6]

The 'Notes to *The Threepenny Opera*', in the third issue of *Versuche*, published in early 1932, are to be seen in this context. Here Brecht had referred to the screens on which the titles of scenes had been projected as a 'primitive attempt' at 'literarizing the theatre'. 'This literarizing of the theatre needs to be developed to the utmost degree, as in general does the literarizing of all public occasions.'[7] Benjamin quoted these reflections approvingly in 'What is Epic Theatre? (1)'.[8] 'Literarizing entails punctuating "representation" with "formulation",' Brecht clarified. 'The orthodox playwright's objection to the titles is that the dramatist ought to say everything that has to be said in the action, that the text must express everything within its own confines. The corresponding attitude of the spectator is that he should not think about a subject, but within the confines of a subject.'*

* *Brecht on Theatre*, p. 44. Brecht had already used the term 'literarizing' earlier, for example in 1930: 'literary people have the task of literarizing the people' (GBA 21, p. 407), and, elsewhere, the demand could be made 'that *the spectator (as mass) should be literarized*' (GBA 21, p. 441). The far-reaching consequences associated with this by Brecht are recognizable from his contribution to the debate (for *Krise und Kritik*): the active, enumerative style of writing corresponded to a stage of social life attainable only through revolution: 'the fully literarized life' (BBA 217/07 [see Chapter III, pp. 89ff.]). This corresponds to the emphatic judgement expressed by Brecht as late as May 1935 in Moscow, in an interview in the *Deutsche Zentral-Zeitung*: 'I was particularly struck by the power of the word to move the masses, and how it has penetrated their consciousness by means of slogans, quotations, books, newspapers, public meetings. I would like to call it the "literarizing of the conditions of living". But it is not just a question of words, for

During the debate on realism, some eight years later, Brecht returned to the relationship between action and representation when he identified the breach between the ideological and political and its representation as a basic creative problem. The problem had been that theses and arguments were 'mostly written in a very "uncreative" way'.

> In practice there were two possibilities for coping with this. The thesis or argument could be subsumed into the action or the action into the argument, and this could be presented creatively. On the other hand, one could also present the action creatively and the argument creatively (which would then of course lose its character as a thesis or argument), and preserve the leap from one idiom to another and present this creatively as well.*

Benjamin, who with few exceptions worked as an ordinary writer – that is, wrote his texts without the invention of plot and character, and without poetic devices such as rhyme schemes – saw something original in the link between political intention and creative presentation to which Brecht aspired. Brecht, he wrote in 1931, 'embodied the most important characteristic of contemporary literature: the intimate fusion of great creative achievement with that of the writer'.† The decisive criterion for judging literary texts was language. In this conviction Benjamin and Brecht showed themselves to be greatly influenced by Karl Kraus, whose work was dominated by the critique of language and who

---

they are constantly followed by insights, by action' (Werner Hecht, *Brecht Chronik – 1898–1956*, Frankfurt, 1997, p. 443). Benjamin made use of the term in the form, 'literarizing of all the conditions of life', for the first time in September and October 1931 in the *Literarische Welt* in his 'Little History of Photography' (*SW*, vol. 2, p. 527). (Here incidentally he was quoting from Brecht's 'The *Threepenny Opera* Lawsuit', then still only in proof.) In 1934 he used the same formulation in his article 'The Newspaper' (*SW*, vol. 2, p. 742), which he then quoted in 'The Author as Producer' (ibid., p. 772).

* *GS* III, p. 302. Jean Selz, when writing about Benjamin, focused on this longing to combine writing and poetry.

† GBA 22/1, pp. 443ff. Similar thoughts are expressed in the much-quoted earlier remarks in 'The *Threepenny Opera* Lawsuit' (1931): 'The situation has become so complicated because the simple "reproduction of reality" says less than ever about that reality. A photograph of the Krupp works or the AEG reveals almost nothing about these institutions. Reality as such has slipped into the domain of the functional. The reification of human relationships in the factory, for example, no longer discloses those relations. So there is indeed something to "construct", something "artificial", "invented". Hence, there is in fact a need for art' (in *Brecht on Film and Radio*, pp. 164–5) Benjamin refers to this passage in 'A Berlin Chronicle' (see *SW*, vol. 2, p. 599).

had repeatedly pointed out that language is not only statement but also expression.* Benjamin's interpretations of Brecht reflected Brecht's quest for a language that should be at the same time artistic and appropriate to reality. People like Brecht, he wrote as early as September 1929 with reference to Marieluise Fleisser's *Pioniere in Ingolstadt*, were today in search of 'an unliterary, but by no means naturalistic language'.† This is shown even more clearly by a note relating to Benjamin's 1933 texts 'Doctrine of the Similar' and 'On the Mimetic Faculty':

> Development line of language: the distinction between the magical and the mundane functions of speech is eliminated in favour of the latter. The sacred is closer to the mundane than to the magical. Tendency towards a language purified of all magical elements: Scheerbart, Brecht.[9]

This purification from all that was magical was linked with the question of the value of a non-auratic art. Brecht and Benjamin posed this question to each other from closely corresponding positions with regard to aesthetic theory; whether one of them was influenced by the other may remain an unresolved issue. In 'The *Threepenny Opera* Lawsuit' – written in the spring and summer of 1931, proof-read in the autumn of that year and published in January 1932 – Brecht expressed the hope that film would exercise an influence over literature, because new 'apparatuses can be used better than almost anything else to supersede the traditional untechnical, anti-technical "transcendent" art associated with religion'.[10] Benjamin's technical analysis of perception in 'Little History of Photography', published in September and October 1931, arrived at a similar conclusion, even if he was restrained in his condemnation of the auratic:

* See, for example, *Die Fackel* (Vienna), vol. 26, nos. 649–56, June 1924. In the interpretations of Kraus by Benjamin and Brecht, central positions are taken up by the question of the meaning of language for Kraus: Benjamin coined the phrase 'a contribution to the linguistic rules of court' to describe Kraus's 'theory of language' (*SW*, vol. 2, p. 443). Brecht wrote that Kraus was interested in the 'critical examination of the language' (GBA 22/I, p. 35) and urged him to write down his 'theory of language'. Both expressed opinions on Kraus's technique of quotation, which Benjamin called 'Kraus's basic polemical procedure' (*SW*, vol. 2, pp. 455ff. and see Chapter V below). The two interpretations of Kraus show further similarities with respect to the significance of courts of law. For Brecht, Kraus operated in a 'frame in which everything becomes a legal process' (GBA22/I, p. 34) while Benjamin placed him 'on the threshold of the Last Judgement' (*SW*, vol. 2, p. 443); for Kraus, everything – language and object – took place 'within the realm of law' (*SW*, vol. 2, p. 194).

† *GS* III, p. 190 ('Echt Ingolstädter Originalnovellen'): 'Her *Pioniere in Ingolstadt* has shown how happily she has succeeded in creating the unliterary, but by no means naturalistic, language that people like Brecht seek today, in imitation of the equally non-naturalistic vernacular.'

The peeling away of the object's shell, the destruction of the aura, is the signature of a perception whose sense for the sameness of things has grown to the point where even the singular, the unique, is divested of its uniqueness – by means of its reproduction.[11]

Brecht's work, as Günter Hartung has observed, was for Benjamin the unexpected phenomenon of a great modern non-auratic art, and in the German language to boot – to the extent that even the powerful effect on Benjamin of surrealist texts paled by comparison.[12]

That Benjamin was not straying from the main path in his work on Brecht is shown by its close interlinking with the Kafka essay, the *Arcades Project*, the essays on 'The Author as Producer' and 'The Work of Art in the Age of Its Technological Reproducibility', and the theses 'On the Concept of History'. Thoughts and motifs developed in the Brecht essays were taken up in other works of the nineteen thirties, and the same process took place in the opposite direction.* Brecht, like Baudelaire and Kafka, was one of the authors with whom Benjamin primarily concerned himself after the failure of his plans to qualify as a university lecturer. Before this, among German poets Goethe, Hölderlin, the early Romantics and Hofmannsthal had held this position. But his interest as a critic and translator had always been in French writers: Balzac, Baudelaire, Proust, Gide, Jouhandeau, Valéry. In France, Benjamin wrote in 1927 to Hugo von Hofmannsthal, 'individual phenomena are engaged in something that also engages me – among authors, Giraudoux and Aragon; among movements, surrealism'. In Germany, on the other hand, he felt 'completely isolated'[13] among the people of his generation. As his relationship with Brecht grew more intense, he saw a chance of overcoming this isolation.

Benjamin's cognitive interests were reflected in his choice of subject. Even if his commentaries on Brecht did not attain the central significance of his *Arcades Project*, they did provide a remarkable continuity in his critical and philosophical work. But it was more than this: Benjamin perceived Brecht, as Hannah Arendt said, 'as the poet who was most at home in this century'.[14] A sentence from Benjamin's essay 'Experience and Poverty' of 1933, referring to the 'best minds', clarifies this formulation: 'A total absence of illusion about the age and at the same time an unlimited commitment to it – this is the hallmark.'[15] Here Benjamin agreed with Karl Kraus, who saw Brecht as 'the only German writer worth considering today' because he gave valid form to the post-war 'consciousness of the time' and tried to progress 'linguistically beyond the banality of described life'.[16] It was not by chance that Benjamin, in a note on his Kraus

* The connections which emerge above all between concepts such as gesture, surprise, shock, interruption, caesura, dialectics at a standstill, quotation, montage, structure, reduction, commentary, etc., are taken up at various points in Benjamin's work.

essay of 1931, had named Brecht as one of 'the most progressive of German artists'.* Unlike Kraus, however, Benjamin also agreed with Brecht's position on dramatic theory and politics.[17] In the planning discussions for *Krise und Kritik*, he referred to the objectives of Brecht's writings as a standard for the contributions to be expected, which 'represent something fundamentally new within German literature'. 'The journal,' he wrote, 'was meant to contribute to the propaganda of dialectical materialism by applying it to questions that the bourgeois intelligentsia is forced to acknowledge as those most particularly characteristic of itself. I also told you how obvious to me this tendency is in your works'.[18] What was essential to Benjamin was the combination, evident in Brecht's concept around 1930, of advanced aesthetic technique and political commitment. In a note on the typescript of his 'Studies for a Theory of Epic Theatre' Benjamin expressed the synthesis of aesthetic content and aesthetic technique in diagrammatic form:

high standard	–	bad technique	classics
low standard	–	good technique	popular media
—	– —		Brecht[19]

Although the characterization of Brecht has not been completed, one can conclude that Brecht's work signified for Benjamin the attempt at a synthesis of high standards and good technique. This criterion was finally to be an essential element in connection with Benjamin's essay 'The Author as Producer':

> I would like to show you that the tendency of a creative work can be politically correct only if it is also literarily correct. That is to say, the politically correct tendency includes a literary tendency. And I would add straight away: this literary tendency, which is implicitly or explicitly contained in every *correct* political tendency of a work, alone constitutes the quality of that work. The correct political tendency of a work thus includes its literary quality *because* it includes its literary *tendency*.[20]

For Benjamin, Brecht was 'always starting afresh'.[21] Among the great creative spirits there have always been those 'who begin by clearing a tabula rasa', as he wrote in the essay 'Experience and Poverty' (1933): 'They need a drawing table; they were constructors.'† The interest in design in Benjamin's interpretation of Brecht is striking. It corresponded with formulations such as that in the

---

* Names mentioned here other than Brecht's are those of Paul Klee, Adolf Loos, Paul Scheerbart, Joachim Ringelnatz and Salomon Friedländer (see *GS* II/3, p. 1112).

† *SW*, vol. 2, p. 732. Benjamin picked up the concept of 'construction' in the 'Little History of Photography'; he pointed out the value of photographs as documents of 'exposure' and 'construction', quoting the passage already mentioned about a 'photograph of the Krupp factory' from Brecht's '*Threepenny Opera* Lawsuit' (ibid., p. 526).

introductory text to *One-Way Street* (1928), that the 'construction of life is at present in the power far more of facts than of convictions', and it prefigured the theses 'On the Concept of History', in which Benjamin wrote that materialist historiography was 'based on a construction principle'.[22] Epic theatre, he wrote in 1931, 'corresponds to the highest level of technology';[23] like an engineer* drilling for oil in the desert, Brecht began his activity 'at precisely calculated places';[24] 'what he writes' was for him 'not a "work", but an apparatus, an instrument'.[25] Benjamin spoke of simplifications 'which are not agitational but constructive'[26] – and in a working note on the 'Work of Art' essay he commented that, from a historical point of view, perhaps the most important aspect of Brecht's work was that it allowed theatre 'to take on its most sober and unassuming, even its most reduced, form – to get it, as it were, through the winter in this way'.[27] As a result of this reduction to essentials, of impoverishment, of renunciation of ornament, as demanded by Adolf Loos, new working possibilities emerged: 'theory of poverty' was a keyword in the plan for Benjamin's radio talk 'Bert Brecht'.[28] And Benjamin noted: 'technique is economy, organization is poverty'; 'new maxims', which celebrated 'the invalidation of our oldest experience': 'The thinking man does not use one light too many, one piece of bread too many, one thought too many.'†

Benjamin named Brecht in the same breath as renewers of aesthetic means such as Paul Klee, Adolf Loos, Paul Scheerbart. He developed 'a new, positive concept of barbarism'.[29] Brecht demonstrated that the activity of 'constructors' involved necessarily destructive energies. In Benjamin's character study of 1931 dedicated to Gustav Glück, 'The Destructive Character', only the initiated were able to discover parallels to Brecht.‡ But what Benjamin

---

* See the dedication of *One-Way Street*: 'This street is named/ Asja Lacis Street/ after her who/ as an engineer/ cut it through the author.' (*SW*, vol. 1, p. 444).

† *GS* II/3, p. 1105 (supplement to the Kraus essay). The second maxim is the Keuner story 'Organisation' (*Stories of Mr Keuner*, translated by Martin Chalmers, San Francisco, 2001, p. 2). In another variant Benjamin takes up this thought: 'With Bert Brecht one certainly has to understand the poverty of Herr Keuner – "The thinking man does not use one idea too many" ... in order to understand how the ship that carries these emigrants from humanist Europe into the promised land of man-eating has set its sails... Scheerbart and Ringelnatz, Loos and Klee, Brecht and S. Friedländer – they all set off from the old shores, the lavish temples full of noble human images ceremonially hung with sacrificial offerings, to turn towards their naked contemporary who lies screaming like a newborn infant in the dirty nappies of this era' (*GS* II/3, p. 1112).

‡ *SW*, vol. 2, pp. 541–2. Echoes of Brecht are found in formulations such as 'the destructive character obliterates even the traces of destruction' (ibid., p. 542), And 'Some people pass things down to posterity, by making them untouchable and thus conserving them); others pass on situations by making them practicable and thus liquidating them. The latter are called destructive' (ibid.).

said of the 'destructive character' could to a great extent be applied to Brecht. This was confirmed by a note of the Summer of 1938, in which he wrote that 'Brecht's destructive character' 'always calls into question what he's just accomplished'.[30] While here the stress was placed on creative doubt, the character study of 1931 had ranged further afield. Brecht could rather have felt identified by being categorized as a destructive character and one who 'stands in the front line of traditionalists': he was not among the artists who transmitted things 'by making them untouchable and thus conserving them', but among those who transmitted situations 'by making them practicable and thus liquidating them',[31] that is, those artists with a negative, 'destructive' approach to tradition.

A specific form of Brecht's approach to tradition was his use of old literary texts, which he wished to be understood as documents. For this reason the violent accusations of plagiarism levelled against him since May 1929 made little impression on his concept of literature and of himself as an author. Benjamin, with Karl Kraus, was among the few who aggressively took Brecht under their protection:[32] the quotability of canonical literature was based on a 'theory of plagiarism that will speedily reduce the quips to silence'.[33] Benjamin identified quotation as a basic element of Brecht's style of writing. Keuner's style, Brecht had written about 1929, 'should be quotable', and in the foreword to his *Versuche* volume he wrote: 'The second piece, "Stories of Herr Keuner", represents an attempt to make gestures quotable'.[34] Benjamin applied the turn of phrase to the theatre: '"making gestures quotable" is one of the signal achievements of the epic theatre'.*

In the totally altered conditions of exile, Brecht's exemplary significance for Benjamin remained constant, as is seen in the plan for lectures on 'Les courants politiques dans la littérature allemande', which Benjamin proposed to hold at the house in Saint-Germain of the Parisian physician Jean Dalsace in April 1934. He informed Brecht:

> I am announcing a lecture series, 'L'avantgarde allemand', in the
> French circles accessible to me and some other ones as well. A series of
> five lectures – people will have to subscribe to the whole series. I will
> select only one figure from the various areas of literary activity in whom
> the current situation is authoritatively revealed.

---

* 'What is Epic Theatre? (1) and (2)' (*SW*, vol. 4, p. 305). In a variant of his own essay, 'Problems in the Sociology of Language', Benjamin was later to pick up this statement in a sentence about Kraus: 'His technique consists in illuminating the gestus of the journalist and the masses of readers whom he serves by means of quotation' (*GS* III, p. 675).

1) le roman (Kafka)
2) l'essay [*sic*] (Bloch)
3) théâtre (Brecht)
4) journalisme (Kraus)

There will be an introductory lecture to precede these, called 'Le public allemand'.*

For the purposes of his talks, Benjamin created a group which actually did not exist. Since only keywords have been preserved, Detlev Schöttker reconstructed the context as a contribution to a 'theory of literary constructivism'. Benjamin's statements on Kraus, Kafka, Bloch and Brecht have in common an interest in structure and aesthetic techniques, in spareness of style and reduction to essentials, as they are bundled up in the concept of 'poverty of experience' in the Kraus essay.[35]

In an outline entitled 'Refunctioning (from the point of view of production)' developed for this purpose, Benjamin succinctly summed up the criteria of Brecht's art: 'refunctioning (from the point of view of production)' was represented by its theorists Brecht and Tretyakov, and its elements were defined by Benjamin as 'resolution of the character of the work by collective work, didactic transparency, inclusion of criticism, variants'. Under the aspect of 'refunctioning (from the point of view of consumption)' Benjamin made further definitions: 'The reader is not convinced but instructed, perceived not as public but as class, less excited than amused, changed less in his consciousness than in his behaviour.'[36]

'Laboratory of Versatility'

'Commentary on Poems by Brecht' and 'Bert Brecht'

The first public statements by Walter Benjamin on Brecht, the essay 'Commentary on Poems by Brecht' and the broadcast talk 'Bert Brecht', were more than occasional works. Against the background of a changing concept of literature, Benjamin presented the author Brecht to his audience as a *total*

---

* Benjamin to Brecht, 5 March 1934, *Benjamin Correspondence*, p. 438. The title 'Les courants politiques dans la littérature allemande' is on a printed invitation card for 13 April 1934. The host, Jean Dalsace, was a French gynaecologist who was consulted by Lotte Lenya in 1935 (see the letters of Kurt Weill and Lotte Lenya, *Speak Low When You Speak of Love*, edited by Lys Symonette and Kim H, Kowalke, Berkeley/Los Angeles, 1996, pp. 151 passim). However, the series of lectures did not take place, because Dalsace became seriously ill (see Adorno/Benjamin, 9 April 1934, p. 41).

phenomenon. His discussion of concepts such as 'gestus',* 'attitude', 'strategy' and 'function', with regard to Brecht's work, clarified the latter's rejection of a view of literature that acquired its standards from categories such as 'empathy', 'creative inspiration' and 'freedom from purpose'. Benjamin had repeatedly polemicized in theory against the type of research that sought to divide literature 'into sacred groves containing temples of timeless worth'.† Brecht is introduced as a new literary type, who was breaking with traditional aesthetics and indicating a 'change of function' for the institutions and elements of literary life. 'The texts of the epic theatre are not written with the intention of supplying the bourgeois theatre. They are written with the intention of reshaping it'. The literary product would change: from work to laboratory, to 'innovations'. The most convincing phrase found by Benjamin for Brecht was 'laboratory of versatility'; it is found in an unpublished draft for the broadcast talk 'Bert Brecht' of June 1930.[37]

> Literature here no longer expects anything from a feeling on the part of the author, other than one in which the will to change this world has allied itself to sobriety. It is fully aware that its only chance is to become a by-product in a highly ramified process designed to change the world. That is what it is here. An invaluable by-product. The principal product, however, is a new attitude.‡

---

* An example of Benjamin's use of the concept with reference to Brecht in the forms 'Gestisches' and 'Geste' is found in his note on Marieluise Fleißer's play *Pioniere von Ingolstadt*, premièred on 1 April 1929. The note therefore dates from the time before his closer acquaintanceship with Brecht, about whom Benjamin also speaks in his notes: 'Fleißer's words are extraordinarily meaningful. They convey the gestural in the language of the people – a creative power, composed equally of a decidedly expressive impulse and of faults and errors, similar to the speech of an eccentric' (*GS* IV/2, p. 1028).

† *SW*, vol. 2, p. 463. The quotation comes from the review 'Literary History and the Study of Literature', published in 1931, in which Benjamin expressed his reservations most succinctly. See also these formulations: 'In this quagmire, the hydra of scholastic aesthetics is at home with its seven heads: creativity, empathy, freedom from time, imitation, sympathetic understanding, illusion and aesthetic enjoyment' (ibid., p. 461).

‡ *SW*, vol. 2, p. 366. Benjamin's writings implicitly argue not only against depoliticizing readings, but equally against attempts to exploit Brecht and his work for party-political purposes, as was repeatedly done by communist critics in the *Linkskurve* and the *Neue Bücherschau*. Typical of this appropriation is a polemical piece by Otto Biha against the construction of an 'ideological contrast between [Brecht] and the writers representing the proletarian revolution, Johannes R. Becher and Friedrich Wolf'. Biha criticized Brecht's 'principles of the epic form of theatre in contrast to the dramatic', which 'are by no means to be approved from the standpoint of Marxism. They are relics of the development from creative writer to proletariat – a problem yet to be resolved' (Otto

It is well known that Benjamin influenced the development of Brecht's theory of drama beyond his critical accompaniment of it: the concept of the 'untragic hero' from *The Origin of German Tragic Drama* can be applied to figures on the epic stage. Benjamin pointed out that Baroque tragedy and epic theatre were linked by a related anti-Aristotelian aesthetic; in both dramatic forms it was rather a question 'of the social sphere of the interaction' than 'of individual characters'.* The article 'Revue oder Theater', which Benjamin and Bernhard Reich wrote in 1925 for the *Querschnitt* in imitation of Hofmannsthal's 'Lord Chandos Letter', linked observations on Baroque drama with the revue theatre of the nineteen twenties. With clear reference to Brecht's theatre work, in which Reich was involved, the writers pleaded in favour of revue: 'It is an advantage of this loose form that one comes and goes as one wishes, without losing the connection.' 'Present-day theatre' was 'not equal to the demands of an age', but had 'become useless when the masses began to make their entrance into the big cities'.† This article showed that Benjamin was at that time already familiar with Brecht's views on the theatre.

There are clear further parallels – for example, in the emphasis on gesture – between 'A Programme for a Proletarian Children's Theatre', which Benjamin had written with Asja Lacis in 1928–29, and Brecht's theory. This article, in its collective theory of education based on imagination, represents a link between performances by Soviet children's agitprop troupes, which Benjamin knew from Asja Lacis's reports, and Brecht's later operas for performance in schools and his 'Lehrstück' practice.‡

Biha, 'Der gefälschte Brecht', in *Arbeitersender* (Berlin), vol. 5, no. 7, 1932, p. 4). A curious circumstance in this connection: Biha was polemicizing against the participants in a radio discussion, whose unreliability was evident from their arbitrary perception of Brecht. One of these radio critics was the German scholar from Breslau, Werner Milch who, as has already been mentioned, had adversely reviewed Benjamin's *One-Way Street* and the *Tragedy* book in 1928 (see Chapter I, p. 3 above).

* See *Understanding Brecht* ('What is Epic Theatre? (1)', and *GS* I/1, p. 234 and *The Origin of German Tragic Drama* (the criticism of 'empathy'). With reference to a conversation with Brecht on the epic theatre on 29 June 1938, Benjamin recalls a performance of *El Cid* in Geneva, which had occurred to him again while he was writing the *Tragic Drama* book (see *SW*, vol. 3, p. 336).

† *GS* IV/2, pp. 799 and 802. The final sentence recalls Brecht's enthusiasm for sport; it refers to the theatre they aspire to as 'the Wembley of theatrical art'.

‡ *SW*, vol. 2, pp. 201–6. That Brecht had these connections in mind is shown by a passage from Benjamin's journal of 29 June 1938: 'Brecht speaks of the epic theatre: he mentions children's theatre, in which errors in representation, functioning as alienation effects, can impart to a performance the qualities of an epic theatre' (*SW*, vol. 3, p. 336).

In the theatre, the processes of transformation in the relationship between author and audience were verifiable. Benjamin himself pointed out the connection between the theory of epic theatre as interpreted by himself and the programmatic study written in exile, 'The Author as Producer'. That essay 'represents an attempt to supply a companion piece on literary writing to the analysis I undertook for the stage in the piece on "Epic theatre"'.[38]

The bourgeois criticism of the nineteen twenties had seen Brecht as something unusual and had tried to construct an opposition between his political statements and the aesthetic qualities of his works. Critics like Herbert Ihering conceded original aesthetic value to his drama, while expressing a sense of its unfamiliarity. It was only in Brecht's immediate circle – for example, in the cases of Erwin Piscator and the young Adorno – that positions were expressed which proved equal in theory to Brecht's new attempts, which were supported by Benjamin.* In this respect Benjamin's writings on Brecht take up a unique position in his contemporary reception. They are the first evidence of a theoretical discussion of Brecht's work that did not use its political content as an excuse to reject its whole direction, which did not exhaust itself in description or in judgements related to taste, but worked towards the recognition of its inner laws.

In his commentary on the text *Fatzer, Komm* (in 'Commentary on Poems by Brecht'), Benjamin treated Brecht's text as a document that must be read and interpreted.† He intensified his definition of the 'purpose of commentary': it was a question of promoting the 'pedagogical effect' of the words 'as much as possible and to retard the poetic one'.[39] The educative purposes of his commentaries corresponded to the aim of epic productions, which he outlined in

---

* Piscator enters the discussion at the same point as Benjamin, with his reflections on the 'elimination of the boundaries between stage and auditorium'. See Erwin Piscator, *Schriften* 2, p. 37, and the beginning of Benjamin's 'What is Epic Theatre? (1)'. Adorno's essay on *Mahagonny* in Hannes Küpper's journal *Der Scheinwerfer* also shows a remarkable affinity with Benjamin's analysis of aesthetic characteristics; the epic performance of *Mahagonny*, Adorno wrote, served 'the intention to represent, instead of closed bourgeois totality, that totality's fragmented series of ruins; to take possession of the fairy story secreted within the hollows of that ruin; and to be an intimate destructive force, precisely as a result of its own infantile mania for digging for gold'. Adorno, like Benjamin, stressed the elements of the 'intermittent', the character of the work of art as montage and the effect of 'shock elements' (Adorno, 'Mahagonny', in *Der Scheinwerfer* (Essen), vol. 3, no. 14, April 1930, pp. 12–15).

† See Judith Wilke, *Brechts 'Fatzer'-Fragment*, Bielefeld, 1998, p. 48. Judith Wilke points out that the typesetting in columns in accordance with the print layout of the newspaper opens up 'associations with the appearance of old Bibles and devotional books'.

the 'Studies for a Theory of Epic Theatre': 'All the recognitions achieved by epic theatre have a directly educative effect; at the same time the educative effect of epic theatre is immediately translated into recognitions...'[40]

The figure of Herr Keuner was for Benjamin representative of the meaning and intention of Brecht's work. Keuner's attitude, he wrote, was quotable and thus related to the gestural principle in epic theatre.* 'Where the name comes from, we need not speculate', observed Benjamin, but he himself proposed several interpretations of it. Lion Feuchtwanger, he said, discovered in the name 'the Greek root *koinos* (κοινος) – the universal, that which concerns all, belongs to all. And in fact, Herr Keuner is the man who concerns all, belongs to all, for he is the leader'.[41]

In 'What is Epic Theatre? (1)' Benjamin expanded on this. Keuner was known as a stranger, 'a Swabian *outis*', a counterpart to the Greek Odysseus as 'Nobody'. That these derivations of the name, in which interpretations are concealed, were discussed with Brecht is shown by Benjamin's note 'Origin of Herr Keuner', a record of a conversation with Brecht, in which both explanations of the name are integrated. Brecht recalled a teacher:

> This man regularly interchanged the 'eu' and 'ei' sounds in his speech...
> According to this way of speaking, 'Keiner' (nobody) – because *outis*
> (ουτισ) ('nobody') is Brecht's original name for the thinking person –
> becomes Keuner. Now this name sounds curiously close to the Greek
> *koine* – and that is as it should be, for thinking is what they have in
> common.[42]

Herr Keuner is the thinking person – so Benjamin takes up Brecht's description. If he ever came on the scene, if he were introduced, 'for the thinking person does not inconvenience himself', he would follow events in silence, or not follow them, for it was 'typical of so many situations today that the thinking person cannot follow them at all'. Concealing his true face behind Chinese courtesy, he pursued his goal, as it were, unconsciously, but soberly and realistically. 'This goal is the new state.'[43]

---

* See 'The Quotable Gesture' (*SW*, vol. 4, p. 305). Günther Anders, in a talk of about 1930 (not preserved) on Frankfurt radio, on 'Bertolt Brecht as Thinker', had also stressed the correspondence between the author Brecht and his figure Herr Keuner. His article published fifty years later contains astonishing correspondences with Benjamin's interpretation of Brecht. Anders writes of Brecht 'the experimenter', saying that 'the changeability of man and the world' was the basic thesis of Brecht's life, stressing the didactic elements of his work and rejecting the accusation of plagiarism made against him (see Günther Anders, 'Bertolt Brecht, *Geschichte von Hern Keuner*', in *Merkur* (Stuttgart), vol. 33, no. 6, September 1979, pp. 882–92).

'What is Epic Theatre? (1)'

In his 'study on Brecht', 'What is Epic Theatre? (1)', Benjamin was reacting to a dispute about Brecht's theatre which had flared up on the occasion of the Berlin production of *Man is Man*. The significance in theatre history of this production, whose première was on 6 February 1931 at the Schauspielhaus am Gendarmenmarkt, is based above all on the fact that a few weeks earlier Brecht had for the first time expressed his thoughts on a theory of epic theatre. These were published in the second issue of *Versuche* with the title 'Notes on the opera *Rise and Fall of the City of Mahagonny*'. The production, in which Brecht himself was involved, thus became a model case. Critics such as Alfred Kerr and Bernhard Diebold compared performance and theory, and found both inadequate, but Herbert Ihering too considered the epic style to be wrongly applied to this material.[44] In the *Berliner Börsen-Courier* of 8 March 1931 Brecht confronted the attacks by clarifying the function of epic acting, using the example of the actor Peter Lorre.[45] In Benjamin, who had attended the première of *Man is Man*,* he found one of his most determined advocates.

A year and a half earlier, Benjamin had already expressed himself on the political significance of military plays, on the occasion of the première of Marieluise Fleißer's play *Pioniere in Ingolstadt*, on which Brecht had collaborated. Fleißer's play, he wrote, was among the first attempts 'to show the collective powers that are created in the uniform masses and which are counted on by clients of the military'. Benjamin polemicized against the critic Hans Kafka, who wanted 'to see in the theatre the one person who throws away his weapon'. The 'defeatist heroic drama' was, however, 'the ethical chimera of keeping oneself "pure from the war", "one's hands clean of blood"'. There was, though, 'no *purity* in these things beyond the expedient procedure of *purification*, the armed revolt'. 'Whether the theatre can do anything towards this, is very much the question.'†

Brecht's theatre, Benjamin now argued in 'What is Epic Theatre? (1)', changed the function of theatre from entertainment to knowledge, whereby the political thesis-play was also superseded. This change exploded at a stroke the 'functional relationship between stage and public, text and performance, director and actor'.[46] The change could be more precisely determined with reference to the stage than to the drama itself: 'It concerns the filling-in of the orchestra

---

* See *Understanding Brecht*, p. 3: 'The public found Brecht's comedy perfectly accessible – once the sultry atmosphere of the first night had been cleared – without help from any professional criticism.'

† *GS* IV/1, pp. 461–3. Benjamin's reply to Hans Kafka was published on 10 May 1929, precisely at the time of his closer relationship with Brecht.

pit.' The abyss that separates the actors from the audience had lost its function.[47] Benjamin saw the production of *Man is Man* as 'a model of epic theatre', 'the only one so far', and he commented on the dissent by other reviewers: 'What prevented the professional critics from recognizing this will be seen in due course.'[48] Benjamin argued, in the same vein as in the journal discussions, that the epic theatre threatened 'the privileges of the critics', since the critic needed today was no longer 'ahead of the masses, but actually finds himself far behind them'.[49] The reasons why they had difficulty in recognizing the epic theatre lay, according to Benjamin, solely in a performance practice 'which has nothing to do with our existence', while Brecht's theory was an expression of 'closeness to life'.[50]

It was unfortunate for the general reception of Brecht that Benjamin's committed and lucid judgement was not made public at the time. Brecht's opponents in the editorial offices were too powerful. Benjamin reported to Scholem:

> Precisely at the present time, things are once again getting particularly complicated, because the *Frankfurter Zeitung* is trying to avoid the obligation it had accepted to publish my essay on Brecht's drama. Its reasons are partly blatantly political, partly to do with office politics – both equally worthless. I am forced to defend myself against these people in this case, because otherwise their shamelessness would be unbounded.[51]

The galley proofs of the essay commissioned by the *Frankfurter Zeitung* had already been produced, Benjamin reported later to Gretel Adorno; they were still in his possession. They had been withdrawn by the arts editor Friedrich T. Gubler, following an ultimatum by Bernhard Diebold.[52] This despite the fact that Benjamin had readily acceded to requests for changes that had been made to him via Kracauer, weeks after the submission of the essay.* Diebold, who presumably had already put paid to Benjamin's intention to review Brecht's *Devotions for the Home* in the *Frankfurter Zeitung*,† was at first clearly still prepared to allow Benjamin's essay to be published with a reply from himself.‡ His later veto is the attitude of a renegade: Diebold had at first welcomed Brecht's theatre, but the course of the years brought to light a rejection on his part, at

---

* See Benjamin to Kracauer, *c.* end of May 1931, *GB* IV, p. 32: 'There were no difficulties in Frankfurt. Gubler will print the article, in which the alterations discussed with you have meanwhile been incorporated.'

† Diebold himself undertook the review (see Bernhard Diebold, 'Baal dichtet. Zu Bertolt Brecht "Hauspostille"', in *Frankfurter Zeitung*, 30 April 1927).

‡ See Benjamin to Kracauer, *c.* end of May 1931, *GB* IV, p. 32: 'He [Gubler] has also taken notice of my urgent request not by any means to let Diebold reply in the same issue.'

first careful and ironic, but later unconcealed, of Brecht's work.* Diebold called Brecht's *Man is Man* a 'chaotic piece', using the word 'epic' only within quotation marks. Brecht, he said, was presenting his own version, the equalization of mankind, of the Communist ideal. 'This notion of equality can also be served by fascist methods. Into battle, torero – against individuality! Away with the soul. Man is man. The Nazis would put on the play – if it were not too woolly even for their own interests.'†

Kracauer too, who had meanwhile become Berlin correspondent for the *Frankfurter Zeitung*, and whose assessment of Brecht was becoming increasingly negative, was involved in the rejection of Benjamin's essay. In a letter to Ernst Bloch of 29 May 1932, he opposed the accusation that a decision he had made, which was said to be about 'Benjamin's Brecht essay', was 'to be traced back to a kind of private hatred of Brecht'.[53]

Further attempts at publication also failed. A note by Brecht – '*Frankfurter* essay to MORT / *with name!*' – invites the conclusion that Benjamin's essay was to be forwarded to the International Association of Workers' Theatres (MORT), with which Brecht had contact through Bernhard Reich.‡ The copy of the study made by Margarete Steffin for Benjamin in the autumn of 1935 could have been prepared for this purpose.§

---

* See Bernhard Diebold, 'Dreierlei Dynamik', in *Die Premiere* (Berlin), vol. 25, October 1925, pp. 4ff., and *Baal dichtet*. Bernard von Brentano also reported that Diebold had little time for Brecht (see Bernard von Brentano, *Du Land der Liebe. Bericht von Abschied und Heimkehr eines Deutschen*, Tübingen/Stuttgart, 1952, p. 47).

† Bernhard Diebold: 'Militärstück von Brecht', op. cit., p. 10. At the beginning of the Nazi regime Diebold was to speak out against Brecht, Kraus and Tucholsky as 'unscrupulous rabble-rousers' (see Kurt Krolop, *Sprachsatire als Zeitsatire bei Karl Kraus*, op. cit., p. 720). Kraus knew how to defend himself against Diebold's attacks. When Benjamin had read the text 'Der Fall Diebold' in *Die Fackel*, he believed he knew the real reason for Diebold's negative attitude to his own essay on Kraus: 'If my essays had only contained Diebold's name somewhere, however inconspicuously, and had alluded, however indirectly, to his denigration of Kraus, he would have overwhelmed the work with compliments' (*SW*, vol. 2, p. 503). Now, in 1933, Diebold's denunciation of the above-named people showed, as Karl Kraus said, 'an unparalleled negative prescience' (Karl Kraus, *Die Dritte Walpurgisnacht*, Munich, 1952, p. 39, on Diebold pp. 21–40).

‡ BBA 1284/20. That Brecht's note refers to the first version of 'What is the Epic Theatre?' emerges from the keyword before it, in which Benjamin is named, while the description 'Frankfurt essay' refers to the place where the piece was to be published.

§ Steffin to Benjamin, July 1935, Steffin, *Briefe*, p. 138: 'I have only just received the manuscript from you. There was so much other stuff to be dealt with. I will start on it today and I am very happy to do it, you can be sure. First, it is by you, and secondly, on the epic theatre. I would never be unwilling to copy something like this. Are two carbon copies enough for you there?'

'Theatre and Radio'

In July 1932 the Leipzig periodical *Blätter des Hessischen Landestheaters Darmstadts* ran a special issue on the topic of 'Theatre and Radio'.[54] It included Benjamin's contribution 'Theatre and Radio' as well as extracts from Brecht's essay, 'The Radio as an Apparatus of Communication', and also extracts from a conversation headed 'Radio and Theatre' between Ernst Schoen and Kurt Hirschfeld. The connection with the periodical had probably been set up by Ernst Schoen, the artistic director of the Südwestdeutsche Rundfunk in Frankfurt and a contributor to the *Blätter*. He had engaged Brecht to read and Benjamin to lecture and had repeatedly made contacts between radio and theatre, for example with the Hessisches Landestheater in Darmstadt – his programming concept led to his being described in Frankfurt as a 'radio avant-gardist'.[55]

By means of radio talks and plays, radio features and experimental radio productions Benjamin and Brecht sought in their different ways to make radio useful to themselves: *'the radio not to be served but to be changed'*.[56] Brecht had suggested making radio – as well as film and theatre – into a 'really democratic thing', and transforming the broadcasting medium 'from an instrument of distribution into an instrument of communication'.[57] Benjamin also saw the possibility that broadcasting would 'satisfy the expectations of an audience that is contemporary with this technology'.[58] The extent of Brecht's and Benjamin's collaboration when discussing the democratization of art is shown by the basic notion they share in common that production and reception should no longer be separated. In a dispute over censorship with the directors of *Neue Musik* about *The Measures Taken* in 1930, Brecht and Eisler proposed:

> We are cutting these important performances clear of all kinds of dependence, and allowing them to be realized by those they are meant for, who alone have a use for them: workers' choruses, amateur dramatic groups, school choruses and orchestras, in other words those people who neither can pay for art nor are paid for art, but just want to take part in it.[59]

In a journal entry for 16 August 1931, which deals with the dialectic of the theses of 'art for the people' versus 'art for the connoisseur', Benjamin analysed a tendency in literature according to which 'the separation between the author and public ... starts to be overcome in an admirable way'.[60] Benjamin's essays on aesthetic theory from his time in exile, 'The Author as Producer' and 'The Work of Art in the Age of Its Technological Reproducibility', again take up his reflections on the democratization of the media.*

---

* On both texts, see primarily Chryssoula Kambas, *Walter Benjamin im Exil. Zum Verhältnis von Literarpolitik und Aesthetik*, Tübingen, 1983.

'*Brecht's* Threepenny Novel'

Benjamin's review of Brecht's *Threepenny Novel* is, like his essay 'What is Epic Theatre? (1)', closely linked with discussions of literary politics during the years of exile, and it is not only the result of the restricted opportunities for publication of the time that this text, too, remained unpublished during its author's lifetime.

Benjamin read the novel in the summer of 1934 in Skovsbostrand, while Brecht was still working on it.* He had already become familiar with passages from the book in Paris during the previous Autumn.† The book was published in October 1934 and he noted that he had read the printed version in his 'Verzeichnis der gelesenen Schriften' ('List of Texts Read').[61] While working on his review, he enquired about friends' opinions and asked Brecht, Helene Weigel and Klaus Mann for copies of any reviews already published. In a letter to Werner Kraft from San Remo of 9 January 1935, Benjamin wrote:

> Why don't you write more to me about *The Threepenny Novel*? In my, perhaps fashionably central, but literarily remote corner I have no idea of the reception that the book has had all around. Since I am working on a review of it myself at the moment, I have asked Brecht to give me an insight into the press reactions.‡

The essay 'Brecht's *Threepenny Novel*' was written between December 1934 and the beginning of February 1935.§ It was a commissioned piece‖ for the periodical *Die Sammlung*, whose editor Klaus Mann, however, declined to publish Benjamin's manuscript. The conflict had a previous history. Mann noted an encounter in Paris on 16 November 1933 in his journal with the comment: 'A kind of reconciliation.'[62] It was of short duration; in the spring of 1934 there had been a controversy about the publication of Benjamin's talk 'The Author as

---

* See Benjamin to Kracauer, end of July/beginning of August 1934, *GB* IV, p. 474: 'In the next few days *The Threepenny Novel*, whose completion I have been following with great interest, is to be printed.'

† See Steffin to Benjamin, May 1934, Steffin, *Briefe*, p. 124: 'B. would like to show you the novel, it is greatly changed and we are really no longer "cool observers" at the umpteenth reading.' The wording indicates that Benjamin was familiar with parts of earlier versions of the novel.

‡ *Benjamin Correspondence*, p. 474. There were also earlier enquiries and requests for press reports in letters from Benjamin to Werner Kraft, Adorno and Kracauer.

§ On 26 December 1934, Benjamin told Scholem that he was dealing with the review; according to a letter to Brecht of 5 March 1935, Klaus Mann had received the manuscript of the review as early as the first half of February.

‖ See Benjamin's formulation that it was a question of 'honouring a commission given to me' (Walter Benjamin to Klaus Mann, c. beginning of April 1935, *GB* V, p. 72).

1. Emil Hesse-Burri, Benjamin, Brecht, Bernard von Brentano and Margot
   von Brentano, Le Lavandou, June 1931
2. Brecht and Bernard von Brentano, Hotel Provence, Le Lavandou,
   June 1931 (photo by Margot von Brentano)

3. Brecht in 1931

4. Benjamin, unknown woman, Carola Neher, Gustav Glück, Valentina Kurella, Bianca Minotti (later Margaret Mynatt), Alfred Kurella and Elisabeth Hauptmann, in Berlin (Berliner Strasse 45), Christmas 1931

5. The same, without Kurella and with Bernard von Brentano

6.   Brecht, Weigel, Brentano and Stefan Brecht, Berlin, 1932

7. Helene Weigel, Moscow, 1933
8. Helene Weigel with Barbara and Stefan in Skovsbostrand, Denmark, August 1935
9. Elisabeth Hauptmann, Berlin, 1932
10. Asja Lacis, Berlin, around 1929 (photo Joël-Heinzelmann)

11. Gretel Adorno, Berlin, March 1931 (photo Joël-Heinzelmann)
12. Theodor W. Adorno, Los Angeles, 1946
13. Margarete Steffin, 1940
14. Hannah Arendt, 1933

15. Benjamin in front of the Brechts' house, Skovsbostrand, Summer 1938 (photo by Stefan Brecht)

16. Benjamin and Brecht, Skovsbostrand, Summer 1934

Producer'. Mann described Benjamin's account as 'fascinating in its dialectical forcefulness'; but Benjamin's 'uncompromising judgement' was characterized 'by an extraordinary radicalism', and it was directed against several authors who

> in the present struggle are the most indispensable comrades and who are also closely linked with the circle of my periodical and the publisher – for example, Heinrich Mann. To speak bluntly, he, like Döblin and all the others, is counted among the reactionaries; the one and only exception is Berthold [*sic*] Brecht.[63]

In Klaus Mann's journal this impression is formulated in an undiplomatic manner: 'Read Benjamin's essay on the author as producer. Extremely annoying, despite all his intelligence. The most dogged materialism applied to literature, always embarrassing. Practically speaking, Bert Brecht, the *only* one left out; everything else "reactionary".'[64]

He returned the manuscript to Benjamin, who stepped in and expressed his willingness to omit the name of Heinrich Mann, who together with André Gide and Aldous Huxley was one of the patrons of the periodical. Benjamin pointed out:

> It is a question of fundamental explanations, which I cannot adjust in any way...
>
> Should it not be very convenient for Heinrich Mann – or one of the other influential persons affected – to deal with a question that as a result of the downfall of the German intelligentsia has become more pressing than ever? Do I deceive myself, or would such a controversy – which, God knows, has after all nothing to do with a quarrel between literary men – not be positively welcome to you and your periodical?[65]

Klaus Mann expressed his willingness to submit the essay to his uncle for a decision.[66] Heinrich Mann's reply, which has not previously been considered in connection with Benjamin's text, was a negative one. It is interesting not only as a document of the misunderstanding of Benjamin's essay, but also as evidence of the failure of attempts at alliance in exile:

> Dear Klaus,
>
> You must make the decision yourself as to whether to accept the article, and the mention of my name, however dismissively it is intended, should not deter you. On the other hand: I myself am not deterred by this mention from saying no. The impertinence of the Communist literati is actually increasing since their party was eradicated. Failure has not caused them to consider whether everything, even thinking, is really a component of the economic process, 'as we know'. They know it, and this determines their revolutionary convictions. They believe in power – and

only want to transfer it from one 'beloved leader' to another 'beloved leader'. The authority of creative achievement does not exist for them, and it is very convenient for these little people that it does not exist. In reality, they have the same cast of mind as the Nazis, and that is deeply to be regretted, because it prevents their, probably correct, economic theory from progressing. – Let us move away from these generalities. I would consider the pages on Brecht to be readable. These, expanded and stripped of the attacks on those of different opinions, would make an article. But if you publish the whole article as it is, then I would urgently recommend another from different points of view for the next issue. The literature of exile should not, particularly with the help of *Die Sammlung*, look as though it consisted entirely of the remains – or the vanguard – of one party.[67]

Klaus Mann decided against publishing the essay 'The Author as Producer' or any other manuscripts by Benjamin.

The dispute over the review of *The Threepenny Novel* flared up over the question of the fee. Benjamin considered Mann's offer of 150 French francs for a twelve-page manuscript to be an 'impertinence'. He demanded 250 francs, which he still described as an 'exceptionally modest sum', and refused to allow the periodical to publish the review for less. Thereupon his text was returned to him, although it had already been typeset.* Klaus Mann's reply has not been preserved, but can be deduced from Benjamin's last statement on this matter, which exists only as a draft:

> Dear Herr Mann,
>
> I can indeed be 'obstinate' when it comes to respect for literary work. This respect, which has so clearly been set aside in your proposed fee for an essay commissioned by you, is just as important a subject as all those that have been written under the banner of *Die Sammlung*.
>
> You suggest that your assessment of a fee for a book review is defensible. That it would be sufficient for an essay is something that, happily, you do not even defend yourself. But as far as that categorization is concerned, I will restrict myself to the observation that in the present case it may correspond to journalistic routine as practised at Ullstein, but is not appropriate in this case.
>
> Readiness to make sacrifices, which you assure me is present on your part, originates in my case from comradeship, such as arises in the course of working together and as I have experienced it from the editors

---

* On this, see Benjamin's descriptions in letters to Werner Kraft, 3 April 1935, Bertolt Brecht, 20 May 1935, and Gershom Scholem, 20 May 1935, *GB* V, pp. 68ff., and *Benjamin Correspondence*, pp. 481ff.

of the few periodicals on which I have worked regularly. With such a comradeship I take everything for granted: the private question of the byline and the economic one of the fee. Your proposal of a fee and, even more, its retrospective justification, shows me that it is not to be expected from you. As a result, I have lost interest in collaboration with you.*

Later Benjamin regretted his uncompromising stand; as he told Brecht, he would of course have swallowed 'Mann's impertinence' if he had anticipated the outcome.† The conflict of interests that had arisen allowed no simple solution satisfactory to both sides. Like most exile periodicals, *Die Sammlung* was in a financially wretched situation. Its publishers, Querido in Amsterdam, were trying to drop it. Mann worked for a long time without any payment, and Querido's director, Fritz Landshoff, was having to invest the scanty proceeds of book sales in the journal. Nevertheless, attempts were made to ensure that particularly needy contributors were paid regularly.[68] On the other hand, 150 French francs, or about 25 marks, for an exiled writer in serious difficulties, was really little more than a 'pourboire'.[69] Benjamin's demand is not to be explained by a disproportionate estimation of his own work, nor is the editor's decision to be simply explained by a poor opinion of the submitted article or for its author in general, as Landshoff too observed:

> Difficulties over the fee for *The Threepenny Novel* review:
> These are very well known to me. It is a sad fact that a literary journal produced in exile must be a hopeless and costly undertaking. Herzfelde, as well as ourselves and *Maß und Wert* [in Zurich], have experienced this and the result has been failure. The authors' fees, though punctually paid, were indeed low. This was a disappointment to Benjamin. But it would have been unfair to pay Benjamin a higher fee than Heinrich Mann, Döblin, or any other contributor. Even today, I can see no lack of 'respect' for literary work in the unfortunate situation in which not only the contributors but also the journal found themselves.‡

* Benjamin to Klaus Mann, draft, *c.* beginning of April 1935, *GB* V, p. 72. There is no fair copy of the draft letter in the Klaus Mann archive of the Munich City Library. Since the archive of the Querido publishing firm was destroyed by fire on the day of the German entry into Amsterdam, it is an open question whether Benjamin's letter was ever actually sent.

† See Benjamin to Brecht, 20 May 1935, *GB* V, p. 80: 'I have proved not to be clever enough for this life, and at a point when cleverness would have been very valuable to me.'

‡ Fritz Landshoff in a letter to the author of 12 October 1987. This differs from the laconic verdict of Werner Kraft, who, as an outsider, advised Benjamin: 'May you learn from this in future always to be in agreement beforehand with the lower sum, since even the higher one is so low that the difference hardly comes into question as far as earning one's crust is concerned. Objectively it is of course the case that a periodical such as this

Benjamin commented laconically on the dispute: 'This is how some fellows find opportunities for pranks even in very late puberty.'[70] This is reminiscent of Brecht's polemic against Thomas and Klaus Mann, which had been published in 1926 in the *Tage-Buch*. Klaus Mann undoubtedly saw in Benjamin a person of like mind to Brecht, and with his rejection of 'The Author as Producer', 'Brecht's *Threepenny Novel*' and other work by Benjamin, he contributed to the revival of old reciprocal aversions. However, the context of literary politics had changed, and the editor of *Die Sammlung* was bound to realize that avoiding debate would have serious consequences.*

Immediately after Mann's rejection of his review, Benjamin tried to place it elsewhere, but without success.† He sent it to Moscow, where, however, as Margarete Steffin wrote to him, 'reviews of the novel have been published everywhere'. She regretted 'that the piece was not being used; I like it very much'.[71] Later the manuscript reached the editorial office of *Das Wort*; two years later Fritz Erpenbeck sent it back on the grounds that too much time had passed since the publication of the book, which by this time was of course the case.‡ In May 1935 Benjamin had given the review to the editors of *Neue Deutsche Blätter*, where in the meantime an essay by Alexander Moritz Frey had already appeared in the January issue.[72] In France, England and the US, plans to publish Benjamin's review on the occasion of the publication of Brecht's novel also fell through.§ Brecht supported these plans, as a note records: 'Give

---

on the one hand has very little income, but on the other hand, with a healthy class instinct, holds its authors to ransom' (Werner Kraft to Walter Benjamin, 4 May 1935, *GB* V, p. 92).

* For Brecht's polemic against Thomas and Klaus Mann, see *Brecht on Art and Politics*, pp. 41–3.

† See Benjamin to Kraft, 3 April 1935, *GB* V, p. 69: 'I would gladly have made the review of *The Threepenny Novel* available to you. But now the two or three available manuscripts must again embark on their wanderings.'

‡ See Fritz Erpenbeck to Benjamin, 3 July 1937, RGALI Moscow, Fond 631, Opis 12, nos 141–79. See also Benjamin to Wieland Herzfelde, 5 May 1936, *GB* V, p. 284: Benjamin asks 'if my review of *The Threepenny Novel* is of interest to you for *Das Wort*'.

§ See Slatan Dudow to Brecht, 30 September 1935, BBA 478/49: 'I am trying to help Benjamin to get his essay on you published in some French periodical before the novel comes out.' Benjamin to Steffin, 26 April 1937, *GB* V, p. 521. 'There remains the question as to whether the review can be published. Is there no possibility of translating it into English, since there is after all great interest in this book in England?' Brecht to Benjamin, 6 February 1935, Brecht, *Letters*, p. 200: '[Elisabeth] Hauptmann is waiting for your article for America.' (The novel was first published in English as *A Penny for the Poor*, translated by Desmond Vesey, verse translation by Christopher Isherwood, London, 1937.)

Benjamin's essay to a Czech translator. Which one? Name needed! 50% to him. He is to place it.'*

The Threepenny Novel was among the works of Brecht to which Benjamin gave unqualified approval; he considered it 'a consummate success'.[73] As he wrote to its author, he had read the printed book 'with continually renewed enjoyment'. 'The book seems to me very durable. I also hear from G. that he considers it a total success.'† To Asja Lacis, Benjamin laid stress on the universal status of the novel: 'I think it will take its place in world literature next to Swift.'‡

Benjamin's position becomes clearer when compared with other reviews, to which, in the case of those published before the beginning of February, he reacted indirectly.§ He pursued various objectives with his text. He compared the novel with *The Threepenny Opera*, considering particularly the development of the main figures; he assessed the quality of the book as an analysis of society, and examined the text from the point of view of genre and stylistic history: as a crime novel and as a satire. The comparison with the dramatic version was an obvious one, undertaken by all the reviewers of the first edition. Benjamin examined the changes, bearing in mind that the period between the opera and the novel had been 'politically decisive years'[74], which had given the new work its character – an unmistakable statement on the allusions to the fascist German present day of the nineteen thirties.‖ Some, mostly communist,

---

* BBA 1284/20. On this, see Steffin to Benjamin, 15 September 1935, Steffin, *Briefe*, p. 144: 'I can't write anything to you yet about your essay (because of Czech translation). De Lange has not replied, despite being asked four times about a translator or publisher. But now Brecht has a new man there, so with him it may work out all right.' In a later letter Steffin writes: 'I sent your essay on *The Threepenny Novel* to Svetova Romanova Soutez, the secretariat for Czechoslovakia... they have not replied yet' (Steffin to Benjamin, 16 October 1935, Steffin, *Briefe*, pp. 148ff.).

† Benjamin to Brecht, 9 January 1935, *GB* V, p. 19. 'G.' is Gustav Glück, whom Benjamin met from time to time in the first half of the nineteen thirties in Paris.

‡ Benjamin to Asja Lacis, *c*. end of February 1935, *GB* V, p. 55. It does no harm to Benjamin's emphatic comparison that he himself at that time did not know Swift's work at all and wanted to use the novel as a stimulus to studying it (see Benjamin to Brecht, 5 March 1935, *GB* V, p. 58).

§ Before finishing his review, Benjamin had seen at least those by Alexander Moritz Frey, ([Basel] *National-Zeitung*, 25 November 1934) and Leo Lania (*Pariser Tageblatt*, 2 December 1934), and an anonymous one (*Deutsche Freiheit*, 29 November 1934) which Helene Weigel had copied for him (see Weigel to Benjamin, 6 February 1935. In Stefan Mahlke (ed.), 'Wir sind zu berühmt, um überall hinzugehen', in *Helene Weigel. Briefwechsel 1935–1971*, Berlin, 2000, p. 13.

‖ See Benjamin's unmistakable reference to Macheath as 'a born leader' (*Führernatur*) (*SW*, vol. 3, p. 6).

reviewers saw Brecht's novel as a successful, because Marxist, examination of the economic and social form determined by exploitation and profit, with the character of a textbook; with its help, young socialists in the future would be able to study history and national economics, sociology and psychology.[75]

Benjamin was more restrained, although in his view, too, Marx was present in the background of the book. The striving of the ruling powers to use force to preserve the property relationship, indeed even to urge the dispossessed themselves to exercise it, was, as the article argued, a basic feature of capitalism. In his description of the function of *The Threepenny Novel* as an instrument of social analysis, Benjamin went noticeably further than his fellow reviewers. In clear connection with his and Brecht's joint project of writing a crime novel together, he evoked Brecht's *paradoxes* of capitalism, based on the 'laws of exploitation':[76] '*This* crime novel depicts the actual relations between bourgeois legality and crime. The latter is shown to be a special case of exploitation sanctioned by the former.'[77]

Benjamin's theses on the political/economic content of *The Threepenny Novel* deem the exposure of capitalist power mechanisms an essential component of a work of art. This relegated the aesthetic dimension of the novel to the background. From the point of view of cultural politics, however, Benjamin's account of this novel was taking up a definite position in the new debate on realism among exiled writers. With his view that satire, 'which had always been a materialistic art', had with Brecht 'now become a dialectical one',[78] Benjamin was rejecting Alfred Kantorowicz's reproach that *The Threepenny Novel* was an idealistic book.[79] Although there is no evidence of explicit agreement – indeed, no such agreement was necessary – Benjamin was arguing in the spirit of Brecht, who had protested to Becher in January 1935 about the attack by Kantorowicz: both cited the realistic satirists Cervantes and Swift.*

Benjamin also identified the satiric quality of the novel in the freedoms that Brecht took in dealing with real people and settings: 'Such displacements are part of the optic of satire'.[80] Reality, however, was much more unlikely than something invented in the mind. In the textual comments set in italic, Benja-

---

* See Brecht to Johannes R. Becher, early or mid January 1935, Brecht, *Letters*, p. 192, and *SW*, vol. 3, p. 9. Leo Lania had also referred to Cervantes and Swift: 'The novel is as unreal as Gulliver and Don Quichote, and just as realistic' (*Pariser Tageblatt*, Paris, vol. 2, no. 355 [2 December 1934], p. 3). Benjamin's response to Kantorowicz might seem rather moderate, because Kantorowicz's view had had a decidedly mixed reception. The communist critics Max Schroeder and Otto Katz distanced themselves from it. The review was 'just about the most stupid thing that could have been written about your book', Katz wrote to Brecht on 17 December 1934. 'I think *The Threepenny Novel* is splendid, the model of a political novel. I wish we had many more of such books and fewer Kantorowiczes' (BBA 367/09).

min discovered an 'invitation to the reader now and again to forgo illusion. Nothing is more appropriate to a satirical novel.'* These passages interrupted the text, like illustrations; in this respect they were like the songs in the plays, which created a distance and took away from the spectator the possibility of empathizing totally with the presented plot. In his recognition of satire and the montage technique as realistic methods, Benjamin was implicitly arguing against the concept of Lukács, who, in the debate on realism, particularly invokes the validity of such categories of the bourgeois novel as totality and unity of representation.

In terms of genre theory, Benjamin placed *The Threepenny Novel* in close proximity to the crime novel; he knew what he was speaking about: 'The crime novel, which in its early days, in the hands of Dostoyevsky, did much for psychology, has at the height of its development put itself at the disposal of social criticism.'[81]

Brecht in fact exploited the genre more exhaustively than Dostoyevsky because, unlike him, he was not concerned with psychology, but with politics.† Brecht 'makes visible the element of crime hidden in every business enterprise'.[82] With proof that the bourgeois legal system and crime – in opposition to each other according to the rules of the game of the traditional crime novel – were actually in close correspondence with each other, Brecht, said Benjamin, dismissed the rules; he retained only the highly developed technique of the crime novel.

It may remain an undecided question whether it was only after a hint from Elisabeth Hauptmann that Benjamin undertook the comparison with the crime novel. She had drawn his attention to Brecht's essays on crime novels and added: 'But I am afraid that apart from you, no one understands the meaning and the tricks of this novel. There are many things that will cause objections.'‡

Part of the background of Benjamin's 'Brecht's *Threepenny Novel*' is an extract prepared by Benjamin from G. K. Chesterton's book *Dickens*, which, as

---

* *SW*, vol. 3, p. 7. In the very first paragraph of the review 'Brecht's *Threepenny Novel*, entitled 'Eight years', Benjamin took up the subject of the modes of action of satire and the attitude of the satirist.

† It was not without acrimony that Benjamin had hit upon the idea of placing Dostoyevsky's novels as ancestors of *The Threepenny Novel*. In the autumn of 1934 Brecht had assigned the chief blame for Benjamin's illness to his reading of Dostoyevsky, and attributed to him, who was not to be compared with Hašek, 'particularly dire effects on health' (see *SW*, vol. 2, p. 789).

‡ Hauptmann to Benjamin, 5 January 1935 (WBA 57/52). See in addition Hauptmann to Brecht, 12 January 1935: 'I have drawn Benjamin's attention to your present essay on crime novels, in connection with people who leave traces behind. Is he aware of this? It would be good for him.'

he declared to Steffin, 'says the best things about *The Threepenny Novel* that it is possible to say'. His intention was to incorporate the passage into his review of the novel.[83] Benjamin saw parallels between Brecht's satirical way of writing in *The Threepenny Novel* and the impetuous satirical power of Dickens and Rabelais, which rested on moderate thinking:

> His [Dickens's] books were in some ways the wildest on the face of the world. Rabelais did not introduce into Paphlagonia or the Kingdom of the Coqcigrues satiric figures more frantic and misshapen than Dickens made to walk about the Strand and Lincoln's Inn. But for all that, you come, in the core of him, on a sudden quietude and good sense. Such, I think, was the core of Rabelais, such were all the far-stretching and violent satirists. This is a point essential to Dickens, though very little comprehended in our current tone of thought. Dickens was an immoderate jester, but a moderate thinker. What we moderns call the wildness of his imagination was actually created by what we moderns call the tameness of his thought. I mean that he felt the full insanity of all extreme tendencies, because he was himself so sane; he felt eccentricities, because he was in the centre. We are always, in these days, asking our violent prophets to write violent satires; but violent prophets can never possibly write violent satires. In order to write satire like that of Rabelais – satire that juggles with the stars and kicks the world about like a football – it is necessary to be one's self temperate, and even mild. A modern man like Nietzsche, a modern man like Gorky, a modern man like d'Annunzio, could not possibly write real and riotous satire. They are themselves too much on the borderlands. They could not be a success as caricaturists, for they are already a great success as caricatures.*

'The Country Where it is Forbidden to Mention the Proletariat'

Brecht's 'Spanish play', *Señora Carrar's Rifles*, was premièred in Paris on 16 and 17 October 1937, directed by the author. Benjamin called it a play of a new kind – for Brecht.

For the first time Brecht approaches a realistic mode of representation. He does this, in *Señora Carrar's Rifles*, without sacrificing any of his mastery. [Helene] Weigel came here to play the leading role. She had not set foot on a stage for four years and yet her acting perhaps surpassed her

---

* G. K. Chesterton, *Dickens*, London, 1925 (first published, 1906), pp. 158–9. Benjamin quoted an excerpt from the French translation, for which he gave the reference: 'G K Chesterton: Dickens, Traduit par Laurent et Martin-Dupont, Paris, 1927, pp. 155–6'.

greatest performances from the Berlin days... If one looks today at the French theatre – which I have been able to do for the first time for years with Brecht here – one is convinced not only of the enormous distance that Brecht's experiments (*Versuche*), even the realistic ones, maintain from the avant-garde, but probably also of the solid basis of the prognoses made on the theatre by my article on reproducibility.[84]

Brecht's opinion agrees with Benjamin's: Weigel was 'better than ever', she had sacrificed nothing as a result of her break from the theatre; her acting had been, as he wrote to Karl Korsch, 'the best and purest that has been seen in the epic theatre anywhere'. And, he added, 'it was interesting to see how she was able to negate the usual contradiction between a realistic and a cultivated style of acting'.[85] The première of scenes from *Fear and Misery of the Third Reich*, half a year later, faced the same aesthetic and performance conditions; again, all depended on the acting of Helene Weigel.

Benjamin, who had already written a short text* for the Paris production of

---

* The original of Benjamin's text on *The Threepenny Opera* (*GS* VII/1, pp. 347–9) is headed with the French title *L'Opéra de Quat' Sous* (BBA 1503/05–07). Benjamin attended rehearsals of the production, as Stephan Lackner reported: '*The Threepenny Opera* was staged in Paris in the autumn of 1937, and Benjamin took me to the rehearsals a couple of times' (see Stephan Lackner, 'Von einer langen, schwierigen Irrfahrt', unpublished Benjamin letters in *Neue Deutsche Hefte*, vol. 26, no. 1, 1979, p. 55). The text was probably to be published in the periodical *Europa*, but for unknown reasons this did not take place. A letter to Benjamin from the editor-in-chief, Jean Cassou, of 6 October 1937 points to Benjamin having offered him a review of the production: 'Cher Monsieur Benjamin, J'ai été ravi d'avoir de vos nouvelles et de voir l'Opéra de quatre sous. Oui, voulez-vous me faire une petite note de deux pages sur cette représentation?' (WBA 144/3). The text was not written before 16 September 1937; on the back of a letter to Margarete Steffin of that date are some key phrases which precede the writing of the essay. These are notes on characteristics, features and typical quotations referring to people in the play, introduced as 'main characters' by Benjamin in his essay, though without exhausting his notes: 'Mackie// Anything but a cynic/ position of congratulation/ knife and trout/ "With other people/ on such a day as this/ something does take place"/ Castor and Pollux/ ... //Tiger-Brown/ grown up/ in the spirit of the combines/ Mackie himself introduces him/ Something of the schoolboy on/ the last bench// Peachum/ all catastrophes lie behind him/ the worst of all possible worlds/ "Because no one believes his own misery" / knows his Bible well/ knows the gesture of the world/ his hat// Polly/ moves naturally/ between the worlds/ wool merchant/ connection with the gang/ "Before he goes to/ such ladies"/ blackmail of P's/ parents' (WBA 118/17^v).

Apart from the carbon copy of the text of *The Threepenny Opera* in the Bertolt Brecht archive there is a sheet of paper with key phrases for the essay written on both sides. It contains data on the life and career of John Gay and other notes which are given here for the sake of completeness:

'*2... 1688† 1732/ cloth dealer /secretary to the Duchess of Monmouth 1712/ Beggars' Opera 1728 French by A Hallam Londres 1750/ Polly 1729, not performed/

The Threepenny Opera, staged on 28 September 1937 at the Théâtre de l'Étoile with Yvette Guilbert as Mrs Peachum, now reviewed the first performance of eight scenes of the total series on 21 and 22 May at the Salle d'Iéna, under the title *99%*. The review was written as a favour to Brecht, who had stayed in Svendborg. Margarete Steffin had passed on Brecht's request: 'Brecht would so much like you to write something to him about the latest performance, so that he will have an expert opinion, as he says. Couldn't you do that?'[86]

There were obstacles at first: Benjamin was not allowed to attend the rehearsals, although Helene had taken over several roles. Slatan Dudow demanded 'categorically', she wrote to Svendborg, 'that no one be allowed into the rehearsals, not Piscator and not Benjamin'.[87] Benjamin's account of the performance, which was published by *Die neue Weltbühne* on 30 June 1938 under the title, given by the journal, 'Brechts Oneacters', opened out the topic beyond that of the occasion to the theatre of exile.

Benjamin's reflections centre on the potential of art in exile conditions: 'The cycle represents a political and artistic opportunity for the German émigré theatre, and also makes clear for the first time the necessity of such a theatre. In these works, both elements – the political and the artistic – are one.'[88]

If one carefully examines Benjamin's arguments, it becomes evident that his review of *99%* does not establish the unity of political and aesthetic factors, but invokes it, because he found it lacking in the performance. The opportunity offered by Brecht's one-act plays to the German exile theatre was seen by Benjamin as being exclusively political.

In his review of the performance Benjamin referred to his own earlier observations on epic theatre. He detected an altered relationship between drama and stage. The audience at the Paris première 'experienced itself as a drama audience for the first time'.[89] The reviewer explained the beginnings of the epic theatre as 'non-Aristotelian', doing without cathartic effects, without 'the discharging of affects through empathy with the emotional fate of the hero'.[90] Once again Benjamin stressed the principle of interruption: epic theatre

---

friend of Pope/ Peachum/ Trivia ou l'art de se promener dans les rues de Londres/ Poetic Works 2 volumes/ ~~London~~ 1812 1772/ 'Ses moeurs étaient simples et/ douces, aussi est il de nombreux amis'/ 1750 Yk 1830/ 1767 Yk 1920/ L'imagination de Gay/ dépendait aussi de la/ situation de fortune/ où il se trouvait: elle/ prenait de l'essor quand / il était heureux; elle/ baissait quand la fortune/ cessait de lui servir.// laid, ignoble, manque de l'élévation/ pensée morale/ annobli [sic] la caricature par la morale/ / epitaph, by Pope: / Of manners gentle) of/ affections mild,/ In wit a man, simplicity a child./ Towns Eclogues// Four Seasons/ Epuisé after the fashion / life of a debauchee/ life of a courtesan/ Industrie et Paresse/ Elections/ Comédies ambulantes/ Scènes de cruauté.' (BBA 1503/03ff.).

proceeded 'in bursts', its basic form was that of the shock. Songs, subtexts and gestures divided the sequence of scenes by intervals, which restricted the illusion of the audience, and thus created space for consideration and the formation of critical opinion.* Benjamin admittedly assumed that the 'standard of Brechtian theatre', as it had taken shape since the beginning of 1933, could not be preserved in exile in all respects. 'The epic theatre was not yet established solidly enough, and had not trained enough people, to be able to reconstruct itself in exile.'[91] This realization corresponds to the demand expressed at the start of the review, that the theatre of exile should start afresh. The claim of aesthetic technique is not reduced, but its fulfilment, according to Benjamin, proves to be a problem in the conditions of exile.

In the first performance of scenes from *Fear and Misery of the Third Reich* Benjamin detected elements of the bourgeois theatre. These one-act plays were 'constructed according to traditional dramatic principles'.[92] A dramatic element sometimes flared up unexpectedly at the end of a scene; intrigue – an integral component of the theatre of illusion – sometimes comes into its own; the scenes represented opposition in social relationships 'through dramatic tension'. Benjamin spelled out the difference between Brecht's claim to theatre-theory, which Benjamin regarded as the only correct one for the particular historical situation, and actual performance. This difference was unmistakably shown by the fact that the audience followed the plays 'with passionate interest'. Such an effect thwarted the author's intention; it was reminiscent of the movement of the wave which sweeps the audience away with itself in the Aristotelian theatre.

In his review, Benjamin distinguished Helene Weigel's performance from that of the other actors, in order to mention that 'despite everything' a tradition of Brechtian theatre had endured from the early days until now. 'She succeeded in upholding the traditional European standard of acting.'[93] The introductory sentence of the review 'The Country where it is Forbidden to Mention the Proletariat' is therefore also to be read as a limitation: 'The émigré theatre must focus exclusively on political drama.'[94] Beyond the common feature of political experience, Benjamin found political content in the 'decisive thesis' of the series of scenes, which he defined in Kafka's phrase: 'The lie is made into a universal system.'[95] If the lie, as shown by the one-act plays from Hitler's Germany, becomes the moving force of society, the confrontation with truth becomes a declaration of war against the 'reign of terror now swaggering before nations as the Third Reich'.[96] Here the moral claim is an unmistakably political

* See *SW*, vol. 2, p. 560 and vol. 4, pp. 305–6. In 'On the Concept of History' Benjamin used the term 'Chok' (shock) in connection with the 'standstill' of thoughts (Thesis XVII, *SW*, vol. 3, p. 396).

one: truth, Benjamin says, is 'no more than a weak spark', but like a purifying fire it will one day 'consume this state and its system'.

Many reviewers, like Benjamin, sensed a difference between the high quality of Brecht's series of scenes and the routine quality of the Paris production. Brecht's expectations of the play were not fulfilled either. While working on the text he had expressed his hopes of the production: 'There could be no better way of developing the epic style of acting.'[97] And he urged Dudow to preserve the standard attained with the performance of *Carrar*: 'In this case, weakness resulting from insufficient artistic talent will translate into political weakness. What authority can we have in exile other than that of quality?'[98]

Later Brecht conceded that in the series of scenes, the epic theatre could show 'that both "intérieurs" and almost naturalistic elements are within its range'.[99] Here is a recurrence, though expressed a little more positively, of Brecht's old fears from the beginning of the project, as Margarete Steffin had recounted them to Benjamin; Brecht was not at all clear whether the one-act plays 'worked', they were '"to some extent" (that is, entirely) naturalistic'.[100]

'Commentary on Poems by Brecht'

Since the publication of the *Devotions for the Home* in the spring of 1927 Benjamin had been planning an examination of Brecht's poetry, the genre of Brecht's that had first interested him.* He frequently referred to poems by Brecht, for example in the reviews of Mehring and Kästner already mentioned, and in a conversation about anti-war literature between Benjamin, Joseph Roth, Friedrich T. Gubler and Soma Morgenstern in the autumn of 1932 in Frankfurt. Benjamin, who had already declared at the beginning of the controversial discussion that the effect of anti-war novels was over-estimated, finally named Brecht's 'Legend of the Dead Soldier' as an example for his theory that a poem against the war had a greater impact than a long novel.†

* See Benjamin to Kracauer (at the *Frankfurter Zeitung*, 13 April 1927), *GB* III, p. 248: 'On this occasion – but on another matter: can I review his new volume of poems, *Devotions for the Home*, in the arts section? All in all, I consider it the best thing he has ever done (from my knowledge of individual pieces – I have not yet seen the whole book).' As has been mentioned, it was Diebold who wrote the review for the *Frankfurter Zeitung*; it proved to be a negative one.

† See Soma Morgenstern to Gershom Scholem, 6 November 1973, in Gershom Scholem, *Briefe III*, pp. 343ff. (see Soma Morgenstern, *Kritiken, Berichte, Tagebücher*, Lüneburg, 2001, pp. 532–7). Benjamin knew that the poem would later serve as justification for depriving Brecht of his citizenship: 'In the document depriving him of citizenship, Brecht is said to have dragged the soldiers of the world war in the dirt' (*GS* VII/2, p. 659).

The 'Commentary on Poems by Brecht', which he wrote more than a decade later, offered Benjamin the opportunity to organize his thoughts. Apart from *Devotions for the Home*, he was particularly concerned with the *Reader For Those Who Live In Cities*, poems from *Mahagonny*, the series of sonnets he called *Studien*, and the *Svendborg Poems*. The 'Commentary on the volume of poems'[101] was produced on the occasion of the publication by Malik Verlag of the two-volume 'complete edition' of Brecht's works, that is, as a commentary on the poetry written by Brecht up to that point, to be contained in the third volume of the edition (which was never published). Benjamin's commentary was commissioned by the journal *Das Wort*, and written as early as the Summer and Autumn of 1938 in Skovsbostrand, where Brecht read it. Some individual passages were written even earlier.*

It was Brecht who had arranged the commission for *Das Wort*, in Summer 1938.† Despite all the disruptions in the correspondence between Benjamin and Fritz Erpenbeck, the editor of the journal, the publication of the 'Commentary' seems to have been definitely planned:

> Erpenbeck is asking us in amazement why your article has not come, and why he has heard absolutely nothing from you. Perhaps you will now get in touch with him directly? It would mean so much to Brecht if the piece could be published soon.‡

But this project too failed: Benjamin's manuscript did not reach the journal's editorial office. When he sent the article to Steffin on 20 March for Brecht to

---

* Margarete Steffin, in a letter to Benjamin (mid May 1939), Steffin, *Briefe*, p. 300, mentions Brecht's reading it 'already in Svendborg'. There are annotations to poems, copied by Margarete Steffin, which go back to the Summer or Autumn of 1938. There is a commentary by Brecht on the poem 'The Child Who Didn't Want to Wash', which is not part of Benjamin's Commentary, but is also preserved in Benjamin's handwriting, with minor differences. There exists, too, a section of Brecht's commentary on the poem 'Against Temptation', which is also incorporated in Benjamin's manuscript with a minor variation. That the first of Benjamin's Commentaries already existed months *before* the summer of 1938, whether written down or not, emerges from a letter from Alfred Cohn to Benjamin, 3 February 1938 (WBA 37/29); Cohn mentions Brecht's sonnet sequence *Studies*, which Benjamin had read aloud; they had been 'good', and Benjamin's Commentary was 'plausible'.

† See Steffin to Benjamin, [January 1939], Steffin, *Briefe*, p. 297: 'Today I read the letter of 28.7. (!), in which Br. called upon Erpenbeck to confirm the commission to you. The whole thing could almost be more than just sloppiness.'

‡ Steffin to Benjamin, 12 December 1938, Steffin, *Briefe*, p. 289. See Benjamin to Steffin, 20 March 1939, *GB* VI, p. 244: 'If Erpenbeck claims not to have received a reply from me, this is one of his editorial lies. My last letter, which remained unanswered, contained a request for a date for payment to be fixed, not dependent on the date of going to press.'

look through and forward to the journal, *Das Wort* had already ceased publication; the final issue had appeared that month.* Margarete Steffin expressed her regret: 'As far as your manuscript is concerned: unfortunately it came too late for *Das Wort*, which had already peacefully passed away.'[102] Apart from the interpretation of the Lao-Tzû poem, which Fritz Lieb placed with the *Schweizer Zeitung am Sonntag* (see p. xxii above), the 'Commentary on Poems by Brecht' remained unpublished during its author's lifetime.

Benjamin regarded his studies of Brecht's poems as 'incomplete'. A series of amendments and variants were not incorporated in the final version of the 'Commentary';† or they were formulated only orally, like Benjamin's critique of the symbolism of the poem 'Germany' from *Lieder Gedichte Chöre* ('Songs, Poetry and Choruses'), which Werner Kraft recorded in his journal on 10 May 1934:

> 'Deutschland' ('O Germany, pale mother'), the last poem and the greatest linguistically in the volume... Benjamin finds the passage that says that whoever sees Germany, the pale mother, reaches for a knife as at the approach of a robber, disturbing, because the identity of the person is here unmasked: this robber cannot be thought of as the same woman who has been dishonoured by her sons. A justified objection.[103]

Despite this, the interpretations are consistent and clear-sighted analyses of Brecht's poetic oeuvre. Benjamin was well aware of this. Without false modesty about his own or Brecht's work, he outlined the status of the Commentary in an introduction whose programmatic gestus is reminiscent of the introductory sentences of his essay on *Elective Affinities*:

> A commentary, as we know, is different from an assessment. The assessment evaluates its subject, sorting out light from obscurity. The commentary takes for granted the classical status of the work under discussion and thus, in a sense, begins with a prejudgement. It also differs from the assessment in that it concerns itself only with the beauty and positive content of the text. So the situation becomes highly dialectical when the commentary, a form that is both archaic and authoritarian, is applied to a body of poetry that not only has nothing archaic about it but defies what is recognized as authority today.[104]

---

* See Benjamin to Steffin, 20 March 1939, *GB* VI, p. 244, and 7 June 1939, *GB* VI, p. 293: 'I have not sent a manuscript to Erpenbeck but only to you.'

† See Benjamin to Steffin, 20 March 1939, *GB* VI, p. 244. Not included in the last version were draft commentaries on the poems 'On the Drowned Girl' and 'The Crane-Song' as well as on the 'Chronicles' from the *Svendborg Poems*.

In Benjamin's attempt to historicize Brecht's poetry up to that time, for which he referred to Brecht's own self-interpretations, the dialectical treatment of the authoritarian commentary form becomes meaningful. Benjamin identified both the 'development' from the *Devotions for the Home* (of 1922–27) to the *Svendborg Poems* (of 1937–39), that is, the difference between them, and also 'what the two collections of poems have in common'. He considered 'a closer reading of a collection of poems such as Brecht's' to be calculated to 'surprise people for whom Communism seems to bear the stigma of one-sidedness'. 'Whereas the attitude in the *Devotions for the Home* is asocial, in the *Svendborg Poems* it becomes socially responsible'.[105]

The astonishing affinity between the arguments of Benjamin and Brecht is explained by the fact that in his introduction to the 'Commentary' Benjamin made use of notes he had made during a conversation with Brecht. They are headed 'Commentary by Brecht' and at the same time form a remarkable variant on the final passage of the introduction:

> Commentary by Brecht
> People to whom Communism seems to bear the stigma of one-sidedness may be surprised when reading a collection of poems such as Brecht's. This surprise is lost, by the way, if you lay excessive stress on the development of Brecht's poetry from the early forms of his *Devotions for the Home* to those of his Svendborg poetry, and accept only the last of the cycles as important for Communism. The 'asocial' attitude of *Devotions for the Home* becomes a social attitude in the *Svendborg Poems*. But this is not exactly a conversion. There is no burning of what was originally venerated. Rather, the collection offers a great dialogue between the nihilist of *Devotions for the Home* and the Communist of the *Svendborg Poems*. Everything depends on the reader's attempt to hear, as far as possible, both voices at once. The enjoyment and instruction to be found in the collection is increased when one carefully follows the rich communications and diverse hints that it contains, its genuine contradictions.*

Benjamin's implicit elimination of the characterizations 'nihilist' of *Devotions for the Home* and 'communist' of the *Svendborg Poems* is significant. They may have meant for him a renunciation of the 'genuine contradictions' contained in the *Svendborg Poems*. That Benjamin's judgement was as close as it could possibly be to Brecht's self-assessment is shown by Brecht's introductory remarks to a reading in Moscow in 1935: he explained how, setting out on a literary

---

* BN Paris, Walter Benjamin Archive (now WBA 269/05ᵛ). This note is not yet included in Benjamin's published writings.

career, 'he had not got beyond a rather nihilistic critique of bourgeois society'.*
In a journal note on the same topic, written during Benjamin's stay in Skovsbostrand, Brecht used, instead of 'asocial' or 'nihilistic', the term 'decadent'.
He refused to describe the relationship between the two collections of poems as
'withdrawal' or 'advance', which corresponds to Benjamin's warning that the
development should not be overstressed. Brecht's journal entry had been
motivated by attacks 'by journals published by Marxists' against him, such as
that by Georg Lukács in 'Marx and the Problem of Ideological Decay' in the
July 1938 issue of the journal *Internationale Literatur*.

> My first book of poems, the *Devotions for the Home*, is undoubtedly
> branded with the decadence of the bourgeois class. Under its wealth of
> feeling lies a confusion of feeling. Under its originality of expression lie
> aspects of collapse. Under the richness of its subject matter there is an
> element of aimlessness. The powerful language is slack. etc., etc. Seen
> in this light the subsequent *Svendborg Poems* represent both a with-
> drawal and an advance. From the bourgeois point of view there has been
> a staggering impoverishment. Isn't it all a great deal more one-sided,
> less 'organic', cooler, 'more self-conscious' (in a bad sense)? Let's hope
> my comrades-in-arms will not let that go by default. They will say the
> *Svendborg Poems* are less decadent than *Devotions for the Home*.
> However I think it is important that they should realise what the
> advance, such as it is, has cost. ... Withdrawal and advance are not
> separated according to dates in the calendar. They are threads which
> run through individuals and works.[106]

Benjamin's 'Commentary' follows such threads in the person and work of
Brecht, and does so without prejudice, which also means that it is unimpressed
by a bias towards the classic nature of the texts and has an eye for the relevance
of the poems. Benjamin changed his perspective and the focus of his analysis
according to the text. He identified poetic traditions of which the poet had
made use, for example that of the big-city poem in Baudelaire, Verhaeren,
Dehmel and Heym; he investigated themes such as the 'drowned corpse' in the
poems of Rimbaud and Heym; and he referred to the traditions of philosophy
and intellectual history taken up or rejected in Brecht's poetry: biblical,
platonic, the medieval lamentation, the early socialist tradition of Fourier, art

---

* GBA 22/1, p. 138. A variant on this statement, which was later cut, is even more
clearly connected with Benjamin's note: 'There were after all, in a book of poems
[*Devotions for the Home*] that I had published by a large German publishing firm and
which contained 150 pages of nihilism, some poems with an attitude to society, including
an anti-war poem, "The Ballad of the Dead Soldier", written in the war year 1917, which
you will hear.'

nouveau).[107] With his overlapping analysis of the history of form, subject matter, theme and tradition in the 'Commentary', Benjamin created a new standard in the interpretation of Brecht's work.*

Even before the commentary on the poems, Benjamin had made a significant statement on the traditions of Brecht's poetry. This was provoked by a statement by Werner Kraft that there were poems of Heinrich Heine's 'which one could almost publish under Brecht's name without the reader who does not know Heine noticing the slightest thing'. With all the differences – for example Brecht's indisputable theoretical strength – the problem was posed

> as to whether a poet is capable at all of creating without or against any tradition. As yet I have no adequate answer to this. Perhaps you have! It was very revealing to me that Trotsky in particular, in his important text *Literature and Revolution*, takes for granted the right connection between revolution and tradition.[108]

Benjamin's reply of 30 January 1936 shows that he himself had in mind traditions other than those mentioned in his 'Commentary':

> I was interested in what you wrote about Heine and Brecht. There seems to me to be much truth in what you say even if I am unable to think of any verses by Heine that might be specifically reminiscent of Brecht. This is understandable, given my limited knowledge of Heine. I am less able to follow you when, with your reference to Brecht, you treat the question whether a poet can create ouside tradition. Tradition is surely present in Brecht's work. It is just that we must look for it where we have not often looked before: I am thinking primarily of Bavarian folk poetry, not to mention manifest characteristics that can be traced back to the didactic and parabolic sermon of the south German baroque.[109]

In Brecht's poems Benjamin found human experience described in all its beauty and vulnerability. In the line, 'Who now in flight lie alongside each other' from the 'Crane Song' (from *The Rise and Fall of the City of Mahagonny*), he discovered the 'bliss of love' and 'the primeval erotic experience: the deep peace of mutual interfusion and pleasure'. 'Friendliness' and 'courtesy of the heart' are wrested from 'inhumanity', there is a warning against 'seduction'. One would look in vain in Brecht's collections of poems for an 'unpolitical, non-social' attitude. It was Benjamin's avowed intention in his interpretations 'to

---

* Scholem's judgement, that Benjamin's Commentaries 'display a rare and pathetic helplessness – disconcerting in a mind of Benjamin's sovereign power', misses the substance and form of the work in an unfortunate manner; it can probably be explained only by Scholem's negative view of Brecht (see Scholem, 'Walter Benjamin, p. 196).

demonstrate the political content of the very passages that are purely lyrical in tone'.[110] This didn't mean that in his eyes the political events of the nineteen thirties dominated the poems' interpretation; but detailed, unmistakable references to the growth of Nazi rule, emigration, the expulsion of the Jews, the turmoil of Hitler's opponents, and the Hitler–Stalin pact nevertheless made that poetry topical. Benjamin found the political core of Brecht's poems in their anti-fascist stance. Thus Brecht's work was a poetry that, as Benjamin's introduction says, 'not only has nothing archaic about it, but defies what is recognized as authority today'.[111] Benjamin's orientation had something far-sighted about it. The 'courage of despair' was to be gained from the reflection 'that tomorrow could bring destruction on such a scale that yesterday's texts and creations might seem as distant from us as centuries-old artefacts'.[112]

In commenting on poems in the *Reader For Those Who Live In Cities*, Benjamin showed that texts could acquire unexpected topicality years after their creation:

> Arnold Zweig has remarked that this sequence of poems has taken on new meaning in the past few years. It depicts the city as it is experienced by the émigré in a foreign country. This is correct. But we should not forget that he who fights for the exploited class is an emigrant in his own country. For Brecht, a Communist aware of his situation, the last five years of his political work in the Weimar Republic amounted to a crypto-emigration.[113]

Benjamin was referring to a letter in which Zweig had described his experience of the alienating perspective of exile:

> By the way, when my left eye was still working, I several times read the poems from the *Reader For Those Who Live In Cities* in public, with altered titles, that is with titles that referred to the experiences of people in exile. I can assure you that the effect on the bourgeois audiences was stunning. They had never suspected that a poet could construct the reality of bourgeois life before they themselves had experienced it. My dear Brecht, you should persuade our friend Herzfelde to reprint these poems in the *NDB* [*Neue Deutsche Blätter*, an exile periodical] under the title 'Bertolt Brecht describes exile before exile'; you yourself should invent new titles and in each case cite the year of publication of issue 2 of the *Versuche*.[114]

How powerfully the experience of emigration transformed the point of view becomes clear in Benjamin's note on a conversation with Heinrich Blücher, subsequently Hannah Arendt's husband, probably written after the completion of the manuscript. Blücher, a politically independent man, may well have made a highly provocative contribution to the discussion. He was a Spartacist and later member of the German Communist Party faction headed by Heinrich Brandler, of which Karl Korsch was also a member, and a co-founder of the left opposition to the Communist Party. In exile, Blücher was famous for an independent critique of the Stalinization of the communist movement.*

Benjamin saw Brecht's *Reader For Those Who Live In Cities* as a kind of summation of the era: 'The ABC says they will finish you off.' The topicality of this line from the eighth part of this sequence lay in the failed politics of the popular front, in the imminent internment of the exiles in France and Britain, and in the extreme perversion of Soviet politics: while Hitler attempted to conquer the world, Stalin was massacring his opponents within his own ranks – the difference between the two seemed to have shrunk to a nuance.

The fatal affinity between the Nazis and those communist functionaries whose 'unscrupulous' politics had done such harm to the movement was a topic of the conversations between Benjamin and Blücher. Blücher drew Benjamin's attention to a reading of Brecht's poems which in an important respect contradicted the commentary written during the preceding months. Hitler, Benjamin had written, in his driving out of the Jews had made an originally revolutionary process – the expulsion of the exploiters by the oppressed class – into a distorted image. Blücher objected that the sadistic element had not been first introduced by Hitler, but was 'already implicit in the

---

* There is hardly a statement that better illustrates Heinrich Blücher's astonishing independence than his reaction to Benjamin's theses, 'On the Concept of History'. When, in August 1941, shortly after her arrival in America, Hannah Arendt discovered that the Institute for Social Research did not initially intend to publish the last work of her deceased friend, her fury knew no bounds. She abused Horkheimer, Adorno and the others as 'blockheads' (*Hornochsen*); it was lucky in the circumstances that she had at least saved one copy of the manuscript. 'We'll hardly be able to lecture them on loyalty to dead friends,' she said. Arendt and Blücher considered that they had a particular duty towards this work, because it included the results of conversations in which they had taken part. Blücher, boiling with rage, comforted his wife: 'But you see, it's really only a squabble among clerics, and they're only seeking revenge on the dead pope because he has handed down to their guild a humiliating edict which demands that they canonize him while at the same time the guild knows full well that the saint is mocking them. Benji initially dimly felt that he and all the clerics had been driven out of paradise, basically stripped of the paradisal status they had occupied for centuries, the purpose of which was to prevent mankind from reaching the full awareness that it has really and truly been banished from paradise. But now we have reached the time when humankind has begun suspecting this, and is prepared fully to grasp the idea. Humankind is still now launching its final insane attempt to realize paradise within its realm in the form of a bloodbath, and when humankind is satiated, then one must begin to talk sensibly to it' (Blücher to Arendt, 4 August 1941, in *Within Four Walls, The Correspondence between Hannah Arendt and Heinrich Blücher 1936–1968*, edited by Lotte Kohler, New York/London, 2000, pp. 72–3, translation emended).

"expropriation of the expropriators" as described by Brecht'. In the poems from the *Reader* Blücher discovered 'the procedures in which the worst elements of the Communist Party resonate with the most unscrupulous ones of National Socialism'. According to this, certain passages in the *Reader* were no more than formulations of the methods of the GPU (Russian secret police).*

Let us look more carefully at the final sentences of Benjamin's record of the conversation. Its gestus is unprecedented in Benjamin's interpretation of Brecht up to that point:

> It is possible that contact with revolutionary workers could have prevented Brecht from poetically transfiguring the dangerous and momentous errors into which GPU practices had led the workers' movement. At any rate, the commentary, in the form I gave it, is a pious falsification which obscures the extent to which Brecht is implicated in the development in question.†

Prompted by Blücher, Benjamin developed objections to Brecht's political and literary practice, which implied more than was evident up to that time. The precarious thing about the note is that it contains an allusion to a term that Ruth Fischer was later to use of Brecht: in her book *Stalin and German Communism* she referred to Brecht as 'the minstrel of the GPU'.[115] Benjamin's perspective differed from that of the anti-communist Ruth Fischer, but in his struggle to understand the contradictions, his own position somewhat changed: Brecht's share of the responsibility for political development consisted for Benjamin in texts which, like some of the poems in *A Reader For Those Who Live Cities*, represented the brutal depersonalization and extinction of people, in the voice of an invented character who only recorded and did not condemn the brutality. He analysed Brecht's relationship with the workers and did not omit his own interpretative and political errors. Benjamin's note shows that the political dialogue between Benjamin and Brecht, if it had not been broken off, would have included a reconsideration of their attitudes.

For Benjamin, Brecht's poetry was so closely bound up with the politics of Communism and the Soviet Union that the meteoric loss of confidence in these politics could not fail to affect his solidarity with Brecht's political attitude. How strongly political convictions influenced his literary assessment of Brecht became evident in a situation experienced by Werner Kraft in Paris in 1936. In a

* As Brecht had already seen earlier with Kafka (see *SW*, vol. 2, p. 785).

† See *SW*, vol. 4, p. 159. Certainly this note, as Rolf Tiedemann has said, is hardly a document of Benjamin's 'basic turning away' from Brecht, 'but a basic rejection of coping with the Communist Party as a result of the Moscow trials' (see Rolf Tiedemann, *Dialektik im Stillstand*, Frankfurt, 1983, p. 70).

conversation between Benjamin and a communist, the subject of Brecht came up. 'Suddenly this communist interrupted him with the abrupt question: "Don't you think that when we say Brecht is a great writer, we do so only because it is in our interests to say he is a great writer?' Benjamin replied: "Of course.""*

Gisèle Freund remembered meetings with Benjamin in Paris: 'On one occasion he read me poems that Bertolt Brecht had sent him, and commented: "We can see from these verses that Brecht is slowly distancing himself from communism.""† It is difficult to imagine texts for which this reading would be appropriate – it was certainly not in the spirit of Brecht, but in combination with the Blücher note this evidence gains in probability.

Its anti-fascist dimension places Benjamin's commentary on the poems alongside his political reflections. It expresses an opposition to fascism whose clarity corresponds to the theses 'On the Concept of History'. In a conversation on 29 July 1938, one of the most intensive testimonies to their relationship, Benjamin and Brecht discussed the exile situation and the constraints they had experienced through being forced into emigration. The occasion was Brecht's question as to whether the 'Kinderlieder' ('Children's Songs') should be included in the *Svendborg Poems*. Benjamin noted:

> I was against it, because I thought that the contrast between the political and the private poems conveyed the experience of exile especially clearly; this contrast must not be diminished by a disparate series...
> Soon afterwards, something else emerged – yet another justification for incorporating the 'Children's Songs' into the 'Poems from Exile'. Brecht, standing before me in the grass, spoke with rare forcefulness: 'In the struggle against them, it is vital that nothing be overlooked. They don't think small. They plan thirty thousand years ahead. Horrendous things. Horrendous crimes. They will stop at nothing. They will attack anything. Every cell convulses under their blows. So we mustn't forget a single one. They distort the child in the womb. We can under no circumstances forget the children.' While he was talking, I felt moved by a power that was the equal of that of fascism – one that

---

* Werner Kraft, 'Gedanken über Brecht', in *Neue Zürcher Zeitung*, 16 October 1965. Kraft described the incident in a slightly altered form in Siegfried Unseld (ed.), *Zur Aktualität Walter Benjamins*, Frankfurt, 1972, p. 68.

† Gisèle Freund, *Photographien*, Munich, 1985, p. 64. Asked about this sentence, Gisèle Freund wrote: 'I remember precisely that W.B. showed me a letter from Brecht and read me a paragraph of a poem, and made that remark which I have never forgotten, although I can remember neither the year (1936–9) nor the verse' (Gisèle Freund to the author, 31 March 1989).

is no less deeply rooted in the depths of history than fascism's power. It was a very strange feeling, wholly new to me.*

Benjamin's response to the unexpected energy with which Brecht wanted to resist the opposing forces is his commentary on Brecht's poem 'Legend of the Origin of the Book *Tao-Tê-Ching* on Lao-Tzû's Road into Exile'. Benjamin made it his business to lend his text a hopeful and friendly tone. He writes of the 'minimal programme for humanness', encountered again in the phrase 'You understand, what is hard must yield'. The poem, in Benjamin's formulation, 'has been written at a time when this statement rang in the human ear like a promise nothing short of messianic'.[116] Benjamin's commentary on this poem – the only one published in his lifetime – had a direct impact, originating, as we shall see, from the French internment camps.

Benjamin had already read the poem in April or May 1938 in Paris, when Helene Weigel brought it to the rehearsals for *99%*; he was 'enthusiastic'.[117] The circumstances of its publication were explosive. Brecht's poem, which had been rejected by *Maß und Wert*,† was published in the *Schweizer Zeitung am Sonntag* on 23 April 1939, with Benjamin's commentary. This Swiss Sunday newspaper followed an openly anti-fascist line, directed against the politics of appeasement, and from neutral ground called for armed resistance. The Swiss theologian and Karl Barth scholar, Fritz Lieb, who had arranged for the poem's publication, published an article in the same issue called 'Why We Must Shoot'. The concept of early resistance met with Benjamin's explicit agreement; he called the proposal of a preventive people's army, which a Swiss called Hans Schwarz had put forward in an article three weeks earlier, 'excellent', and he added: 'If only you would get it done!'[118]

It was with impatience that Benjamin awaited the issue of the newspaper that contained the poem and commentary. He himself contributed to its diffusion; his request for copies has a conspiratorial undertone: 'Now I am very keen to have specimen copies. Please let me have 10 or 15 if at all possible. One of the main purposes of such a publication lies in being able to get it into the hands of the right people; this is my intention.'[119]

---

* *SW*, vol. 3, pp. 340–1. Brecht's outburst corresponds with the entry in his *Journal*, quoted earlier, about the difference between *Devotions for the Home* and *Svendborg Poems*. The note, written only a short time after the conversation, on 10 September 1938 in Denmark, also deals with the question as to 'what the advance, such as it is, has cost us. Capitalism has forced us to take up arms. It has laid waste our surroundings. I no longer go off "to commune with nature in the woods", but accompanied by two policemen. There is still richness, a rich choice of battlefields. There is originality, originality of problems' (*Journals*, p. 17).

† See Brecht to Fredrik Martner, June 1939, Brecht, *Letters*, p. 315. The first edition of the poem was in the January issue of *Internationale Literatur*.

Benjamin's commentary and Brecht's poem moved even those close to Benjamin whose interest in Brecht's writing had noticeably waned or who had always expressed scepticism towards Brecht, such as Brentano, Scholem and Karl Thieme.* But it was in the French internment camps that the newspaper cutting had its real effect. When the internments began in September 1939, Heinrich Blücher treated Brecht's poem 'like a talisman with magical powers': 'Those of his fellow inmates who, when they read it, understood it were known to be potential friends.'[120] Hannah Arendt remembered its tremendous effect: 'Walter Benjamin had brought it back to Paris from a visit to Brecht in Denmark, and speedily, like a rumour of good tidings, it travelled by word of mouth – a source of consolation and patience and endurance – where such wisdom was most needed.'[121]

Benjamin had similar experiences to Blücher's. When he was in the Nevers camp in the Autumn of 1939 he circulated Brecht's poem, and most probably also his commentary, among the internees.† This is also documented by a later letter of Brecht's to Karl Thieme, in which he writes: 'I hear that in the French camp where Benjamin was most recently interned, he recited several times, from memory, the Lao-tzû poem you quoted.'[122] Brecht owed this information to Hans Sahl, who had given him a report on the camp during a conversation in New York in 1945. Brecht noted:

> B[enjamin] explains Lao-tzû poem to French officers in the camp –
> B disconnects telephone when Sahl asks after Brecht's well-being
> – in Paris B wants to sit on a café terrace and twiddle his thumbs.[123]

The lesson of the victory of water over stone which exile had brought to Lao-tzû now encouraged the exiles and – through Benjamin's mediation – their

---

* See the relevant reactions:

Bernard von Brentano to Benjamin, 21 July (1939), WBA 28/6: 'Brecht sent me his *Svendborg Poems*, and I confess to you, I am somewhat embarrassed; the only one I liked is the ballad of Lao-tzû – which however is quite excellent; beautiful in form – the curious baroque metre, for example – clear, profound – a pleasure, like your essay.'

Scholem to Benjamin, 30 June 1939, Benjamin/Scholem, no. 123: Scholem mentions 'the beautiful package of your commentary on Brecht's Lao-tzû poem, which had all the qualities suitable for loosening the tongue of someone like me'.

Karl Thieme to Benjamin, 3 May 1939 (WBA 121/31): 'And then, sincere congratulations on having been able to find such a worthy object of your commentary as this poem; quite frankly I would not have believed the author capable of something like this...'

† Former fellow prisoners, in a card of 21 November 1939, reacted with relief to the news of Benjamin's release, mentioning at the same time that they had benefited from the 'lecture reconfortante de la légende de Laotse' (see *GB* VI, pp. 370ff., and Chryssoula Kambas, 'Bulletin de Vernuches. Neue Quellen zur Internierung Walter Benjamins', in *Exil* (Maintal), vol. 10, no. 2, 1990, pp. 15ff.).

guards as well.* Brecht, too, must have felt encouraged by this evidence of the mediating role of probably his most important commentator.†

'What is the epic theatre? (2)'

Benjamin told Gretel Adorno[124] that he had placed his second essay on 'What is Epic Theatre?' with *Maß und Wert*, 'with slight changes'. This is as inaccurate a description of the difference as a note by him which states that it is 'much rather a question of two different texts, of which the second merely puts individual formulations from the older one into a new context'. Benjamin made use of extensive passages from his first essay, but also of his review of 99%.[125] For publication in *Maß und Wert*, the essay of 1931 was reduced in length by almost half, was restructured and divided up by sub-headings, and significant sections were reformulated. The difference in content shows a new insight in Brecht's dramatic theory: the term 'Verfremdung' (alienation) appears in the second essay, and there is a whole section on the 'Lehrstück', which is referred to only once as a concept in the first. But in the 1939 text, the elements that bring Benjamin's interpretation of epic theatre close to his own philosophy of history have increased.

The editors of *Maß und Wert* referred to Benjamin's essay 'What is the Epic Theatre? (2)', which was published anonymously, as a contribution to a debate: 'We are calling upon a yes-sayer and a no-sayer to speak, or rather a strict supporter of his theory and one who carefully weighs the pros and cons of his works.' The unconcealed sympathy for the 'no-sayer' is easily explained. Ferdinand Lion, the editor of the journal, had – true to his motto, 'L'état, c'est moi' – himself allowed it to be known that he was the author of the essay

---

* See Chryssoula Kambas, 'Bulletin de Vernuches...', op. cit., p. 16: 'According to a note, Benjamin passed on the poem not only as a consolation for the hopeless victims, but he commented on it, as it were, with his face turned towards France, and this must be rated as a step towards redrawing, in an active sense, the boundaries between humanity and inhumanity. Apart from the political aspect, it was a step in linguistic communication; inevitably, some sort of rough translation into French must have been created.'

† Benjamin's reference to the café terrace, which Sahl used in his novel *Die Wenigen und die Vielen* ('The Few and the Many') is also found in his journal, although with an ironic twist which is certainly not unconnected with Sahl's tense relationship with Brecht: 'One day Benjamin said to me: "If I should come out of here alive, all I would ask would be to sit on a café terrace – in the sun – and twiddle my thumbs!" A short time after that, Benjamin was released from the camp. When I visited him a few months later in Paris, he was just dictating a manuscript to his sister. I heard him say the last words: "...The basic principles of Marxism are not contradicted by the latest events. The proletarian class-consciousness ... etc. etc." I asked: "Do you call that twiddling your thumbs?"' (DLA Marbach, Hans Sahl estate).

'Grenzen des Brecht-Theaters' ('Limits of Brecht's Theatre'), which followed Benjamin's article.*

The original idea had been to publish, instead of these essays, a dialogue between Benjamin and Lion. Such a dialogue on Brecht did in fact take place in Paris at the end of April or beginning of May 1939, which was recorded in shorthand. For this purpose, Benjamin prepared the summary 'Material zu einem Diskurs über Brecht'.† But immediately after the 'attempt at a dialogue', as Lion called it, Lion and Benjamin rejected this format and decided to publish accounts of their positions as separate texts. This prehistory of the Brecht debate, which is important for the understanding of the essays, emerges from a letter from Lion to Benjamin of 14 June 1939, in which the former asks for a more equitable payment method,[126] Benjamin was accommodating towards Lion, as the draft of a reply, dated 16 June 1939, shows:

> I understand your reflections very well. I am glad that you have written to me quite plainly, instead of allowing a 'misunderstanding' to be created, adding a further division to those existing between Germans living in exile. I would prefer two pages, which you are able 'most amicably' to set aside for me, to five which would allow you to see our discussion in an unfavourable light.‡

* *Maß und Wert*, Zürich, vol. 2 (1938–9), no. 6 (July–August 1939): to follow the texts by Benjamin and Lion, the scene 'Sermon on the Mount' from *Fear and Misery in the Third Reich* was published. The editor's credo is quoted in Walter Benjamin to Max Horkheimer, 6 December 1937, *GB* V, p. 617. In the literature it has so far only been presumed that Lion was the author of 'Grenzen des Brecht-Theaters'; but this emerges unmistakably from his letter to Benjamin dated 14 May (actually June) 1939 (WBA 153/9): 'The issue, splendidly Brechtian ['brechtig–prächtig'], will be out the day after tomorrow... From what I saw of the page proofs, I believe your direct contribution takes up five pages, mine the same number.'

† See *GS* II/3, pp. 1372ff. On 10 May Benjamin told Karl Thieme that in the days before his departure for Pontigny, that is, about the end of April, he had had 'discussions with Lion', including a 'conversation about Brecht, when I was again able to refer to your essay, under whose influence I was at the time' (see Benjamin to Karl Thieme, 10 May 1939, *GB* VI, p. 276). Benjamin's summary begins with Thieme's essay 'Des Teufels Gebetbuch?', in *Hochland* (Munich/Kempten), vol. 29, no. 5, February 1932.

‡ Benjamin to Lion, draft, 16 June 1939, *GB* VI, p. 302. For the dialogue, Benjamin was originally to get the modest fee of a total of about 80 Swiss francs, not counting the writing costs. After he himself had written an essay, Lion asked Benjamin to content himself with the fee for his five pages and an additional donation from Lion corresponding to the fee for two pages. It seemed to Lion 'pure imposition' if he were to obtain absolutely nothing for his work, which had been '*extremely* laborious'. Nevertheless he would have been willing to keep to the original agreement: 'But you must clearly understand that in that case you will never hear from me again, either in an editorial or a personal context' (Lion to Benjamin, 14 May [actually June] 1939, WBA 153/9).

It is not surprising that the attempt at a dialogue on Brecht between Benjamin and Lion proved in vain, for their positions could hardly be more opposed; Lion had been the editor at *Maß und Wert* who had rejected Brecht's 'Legend of the Origin of the *Tao-tê-Ching*'. With his essay on Brecht, Lion resumed his stocktaking exercise in 'Über vergangenes und zukünftiges Theater' ('On Theatre in the Past and Future'), which he had published in the previous issue, and in which he had declared European theatre to be in danger.[127] Now he asked whether Brecht's dramatic work embodied the end of European theatre, the only theatre appropriate to contemporary conditions, or the primitive core of a future theatre. Lion was disturbed by the epic theatre whose mechanisms Benjamin's essay had laid bare. Brecht, in his opinion, had moved away from his 'original temperament' towards a form of expression which was 'meagre, dry, taut, mechanical, purposeful, decisive'. He concluded that the rejection of empathy in Brecht's theatre accounted for the lack of feeling on the stage in general. This was why all the figures were similar to each other, without character or differentiation. Lion denounced the political implications of Brecht's aesthetic: 'If the Nazis or the Fascists had created a theatre of their own, it would have looked exactly like Brecht's.'[128] Lion's comparison is reminiscent of Diebold's statement that the Nazis would have performed *Man is Man* if it had not been too woolly for them, but – eight years later, and in view of the despotic regime that had then spread throughout Europe – it is more drastic. In the previous year Lion had demanded that a Benjamin essay on the Institute for Social Research should '*not* be communist'.[129] Benjamin had been warned and had retreated politically in comparison with the first version of 'What is Epic Theatre?', but he was not prepared for such a denunciation, which revealed how Lion was going against the programmatic motto of *Maß und Wert* – solidarity, composure, unanimity, unity. This too is an expression of the fragmentation of literature in exile, to which this contribution by Benjamin did not fall victim, as did the 'Author as Producer' essay, but which gave little cause for hopes of coordinated action by opponents of Hitler.

Benjamin, who knew Lion's attitude from their conversations, even though the latter might have formulated his arguments more moderately in that context, reacted in his essay to his adversary's points. Lion had assumed that Brecht, in apathetic dependence, had subjugated himself to the 'fourth estate' and become an ambassador for Russia. Benjamin, on the other hand, emphasized the political will that was asserting itself in Brecht's dealings with the audience. Lion's comment that Brecht's dramas were neither tragedies nor comedies, and that his characters were passionless, stood in opposition to Benjamin's reference to the 'non-tragic hero'. For their opposing interpretations both authors invoked Shakespeare.* In Brecht's rejection of audience empathy, which Lion violently criticized, Benjamin recognized considerable scope for a different relationship between the audience and the performance. Only a relaxed attitude of attention facilitates astonishment about conditions from which something can be learned. The 'Lehrstück', which, according to Lion, presented 'teaching for the sake of teaching', was defined by Benjamin as simply the opportunity to free the audience from its passive role. What to Lion was propaganda, Benjamin understood as a new theatrical means, because it freed itself from the close connection between theatre and propaganda, which Lion took for granted. Benjamin had in mind above all the alteration of the conventions of bourgeois theatre, and the multifarious functions at which epic theatre, with all its experimentalizing, aimed. Lion's assessment missed the point of Brecht's theatre, because he saw the structure of relationships as unalterable.

---

* With regard to Brecht's characters, Lion wrote: 'All Shakespearean passions cease to exist.' Benjamin, on the other hand, placed Brecht's dramas on a road of 'Western secular drama' in which Shakespeare's 'scenes are its roadside monuments' (SW, vol. 4, p. 304).

Brecht on Benjamin

'Expert Opinions'

Brecht followed Benjamin's work attentively and with a sympathy undimmed by differences over content. His opinions are pointed, sometimes polemical, and always committed to Benjamin's topics. Admittedly, they do not provide a counterpart to Benjamin's essays on him, but they reciprocate the critic's interest and show that the relationship was a mutual one. Brecht's statements on the texts 'Problems in the Sociology of Language', 'Eduard Fuchs, Collector and Historian' and 'On the Concept of History' are among the few perceptive contemporary reactions to Benjamin's work. In Benjamin, Brecht saw above all an advocate, a critic who strategically supported him, and he valued him as a partner in discussions, whose knowledge and opinions were of benefit to him. How enduringly he was affected by Benjamin's fate is shown by four poems in which he made creative use of the news of his friend's death.

Brecht's interest in Benjamin the critic, who made no secret of his approval, without doubt had self-serving features. For a start it corresponded to his strategy of influencing the reception of his own works and dramatic productions, but it did not end there. An entry by Benjamin in a notebook of 1929 is like a reflection of Brecht's attitude to the public: 'Ad vocem Brecht/ We are, God knows, too isolated to allow ourselves to make enemies of our opponents.'* If the reference is to a spoken aphorism of Brecht's, this would recall his quarrelsomeness, but also his efforts to disarm presumed or actual opponents by making a pact with them.

Brecht involved Benjamin in his work, as he did many of his friends and acquaintances, making manuscripts available to him with requests for criticism, and sending him textual variants asking him for his preference. He expected 'expert opinions' from his friend.† From 1933 Margarete Steffin acted as go-between, and her letters also reflect Brecht's interest in his critic. In the spring of 1934, for example, when Brecht and Eisler were working on the first version of *Roundheads and Pointed Heads*, they needed 'someone who is not so deep inside the material and could therefore take a more objective view of how things are going'. Steffin asked whether Benjamin would not like to be that

---

* *GS* II/3, p. 1370. I consider it unlikely that this entry refers to Benjamin's own relationship to Brecht.

† See Steffin to Walter Benjamin, 30 May 1938, Steffin, *Briefe*, p. 286: 'Brecht would so much like you to write something to him about the latest performance [of 99%], so that he can hear an expert opinion, as he says.'

someone.* Similarly, in the case of *The Threepenny Novel*, whose creation Benjamin had followed in the autumn of 1933 in Paris, Steffin wrote that Brecht would gladly send him the revised version of the novel, as they were 'no longer "cool observers" by the umpteenth reading'.[1]

A particular sign of Brecht's confidence in Benjamin was his request to the latter to accompany the publication of his *Gesammelte Werke* by Malik Verlag with one or two major essays on Brecht's work. As early as the planning stage, in the autumn of 1935, Margarete Steffin had asked Benjamin:

> I have a little project in mind: sayings from Brecht's works. I'm sure such a little volume would be useful and would also mean a great deal to him. It occurred to me that – if [Wieland] Herzfelde were to publish it, which is not out of the question – you might write a preface to it. What do you think?
>
> As you know, Wieland is publishing B's works. I propose a blurb (you will smile at the term 'blurb' when you learn that it will take up 6–8 pages) for publicity purposes, including short essays on B. by you, [Arnold] Zweig, Bern[h]ard Reich, perhaps others, but I can't think of any others. What is your opinion?[2]

In November 1937, referring to the total of three planned volumes of plays, she renewed her request, linking it with detailed proposals for topics and pointing out that it was Brecht's own wish:

> Brecht's works are being published by Herzfelde, Prague, as you know! And the first two volumes (plays) are coming out at Christmas. On the occasion of this joyful event, Brecht would like to have an essay from you, no, two, one about
>
> the major characters in Brecht's plays (from Kragler to Galy Gay and Peachum and so on up to Callas etc.) and a second
>
> the major plots in Brecht's plays.
>
> Would you like to do it? It would be urgent! If so Brecht would ask *Das Wort* to write to you about it.[3]

In November 1937 Brecht passed on the proposal to the editorial staff of *Das Wort*, who hastened to confirm the commission to Benjamin.† The latter

---

* ibid., 15 March 1934, p. 119. Further requests were added in the weeks that followed: 'Br. would be pleased if you could quickly glance through it and write to us what struck you?' (ibid., p. 121). And: 'Have you received the Roundheads? Read it? Given to E[isler]? How do you like it?' (p. 123).

† See Erpenbeck to Benjamin, 9 December 1937, RGALI Moscow, Fond 631, Opis 12, no. 141/70. This letter contains a request that Benjamin should review Brecht's *Gesammelte Werke*. Erpenbeck was quoting from a letter of Brecht's in which he had proposed to the journal that they should entrust the task to Benjamin.

agreed on condition that the fee-paying process was speeded up and that he should immediately receive the still outstanding payment for his second 'Paris Letter'.* He received this on 1 February 1938,† but Benjamin still did not write the essay or essays that had been requested of him, although Brecht arranged in March for Herzfelde to send him the first two volumes of the edition,‡ and although Brecht and Steffin persistently urged him to do so.§ Benjamin's own projects were making too heavy demands on him; in the spring of 1938 he was preoccupied with reorganizing his notes on Baudelaire. But Benjamin's subtle method of refusing a request which had almost developed into a demand, and in addition allowed him very little scope because of the way the topics had been fixed in advance, is unambiguous. Nevertheless, Benjamin fulfilled Brecht's wish with his 'Commentary on the Poems of Brecht' – belatedly, but at least with free choice of subject.

Brecht made use of Benjamin's critical judgement; he asked the 'Much-Knowing One' ('Vieles wissende'), as he called Benjamin in the poem 'Die

---

* See Steffin to Benjamin, 29 December 1937, Steffin, *Briefe*, pp. 263ff., and Benjamin to Erpenbeck, 22 December 1937, *GB* V, pp. 635ff. In the latter Benjamin refused to respond to Erpenbeck's letter to him until the fee was paid.

† See ibid., 1 February 1938, p. 267: 'We are glad you have finally received the fee from *Das Wort*.' Steffin specified Brecht's ideas about the material that Benjamin should base himself on: 'Perhaps the characters first? Br. was thinking of Macheath, Polly, Peachum; Galy Gay; Pelagea Wlassowa... Iberin, Callas, Nanna Callas; Mauler, Johanna; and would you like to add Frau Carrar? Of the fables, (perhaps) *Roundheads*; *Saint Joan*; *Mother*; *Threepenny Opera*; *Man is Man*.'

‡ See Brecht to Wieland Herzfelde, 2 March 1938, GBA 29, p. 77: 'Walter Benjamin (Paris XV, 10 rue Dombasle) is going to write a major essay for *Das Wort* about the drama volumes, so do please send him the volumes as quickly as possible, as review copies of this kind are worth having.' Herzfelde promised to send both Benjamin and Brecht in advance the first volume, which had just come out (Herzfelde to Brecht, 6 March 1938, BBA Z 47/11).

§ See the following letters from Steffin to Benjamin:

February 1938, Steffin, *Briefe*, p. 270: 'Brecht would really like to know if and when you will be able to write the essay about the drama volumes, which are just coming onto the market now, and he would particularly like them to be reviewed very soon in *Das Wort* (among other things, because he says – but I write this to you only, as it were, in confidence – who knows how long the journal will go on being published, or for how long it will go on publishing this sort of thing).'

Beginning of March 1938, ibid., p. 271: 'it is very important for Brecht.'

12 March 1937 (*sic*, actually 1938), ibid., p. 277: 'Brecht asks you once again, as soon as you receive the volumes, to give priority to this essay, as *Das Wort* will not publish it if it arrives too late.'

April 1938, ibid., p. 284: 'As far as the piece on Brecht is concerned, it will be rather late if you have to wait until you are here. The editorial office has already been *pressing* for it.'

Verlustliste' ('Casualty List'), for information, literary references and advice on decisions to be taken. In his journal of the Summer of 1938 Benjamin noted conversations of this kind, for example on whether Brecht should publish his 'polemical discussions with Lukács', or whether 'part of the lyric cycle "Children's Songs" should be included in the new volume of poems'.* Margarete Steffin – both on her own initiative and at Brecht's request – often brought variants of the text or plot to Benjamin; the experience of working together on the text, as in the case of the *Saint Joan* play, or the crime novel, aroused hopes of a useful response. Her letter of 25 September 1935 is typical of many:

> Now I am going to send you something new straight away, in fact today, by 'printed matter' post, the 'Lehrstück' *The Horatians and the Curiatians*. B. would very much like you to read through it as soon as you have time. I have probably told you already that Wieland Herzfelde is publishing an edition of Brecht, and this little play, which he completed in quite a short time, is going to be in it. On page 15 there is a disputed point, we have two versions of this passage. Won't you write and tell us which you prefer? I will send them both.†

When Margarete Steffin sent Benjamin two scenes from *Fear and Misery*, she urged him to reply promptly: Brecht did not know 'whether they "work" or not', he was still in the middle of writing the play and would very much like Benjamin's opinion about it.[4] This was no empty phrase. If Benjamin's reply was unduly delayed, Steffin pressed him for it. If Benjamin's verdict was anything other than positive, she questioned it:

> Couldn't you write – at least give a hint of – why you can't make anything of 'The Chalk Cross'? I am sure you know that this is to be a little series of five plays, and you can imagine that any criticism is only too welcome, since there will hardly be a possibility of putting the play on again soon.‡

---

* *SW*, vol. 3, p. 339. This attitude of Brecht's is reflected in his requests, for example that of 1931 that Benjamin should prepare synopses for publication of Calderon's dramas *The Great Zenobia* and *The Greatest Monster, Jealousy* (see *SW*, vol. 2, p. 483).

† Steffin expressed her pleasure at the fact that he liked the 'Lehrstück', 'but particularly the inserted version of the dubious passage' (ibid., p. 138). See the following letters:

5–8 April 1938, ibid., p. 282: 'What do you think of the title "Fear and Misery of the Third Reich" for it? Do you like it better than "Germany – a Horror Story"? Please write to us about this!'

30 May 1938, ibid., p. 286: 'And how do you like the beautiful Lao-tzû poem? Which line in the doubtful verse do you prefer?'

‡ ibid., 27 October 1937, p. 260. Her reaction was similar when Benjamin asked about a verse from the 'Ballad of the "Jewish Whore" Marie Sanders': 'Brecht is rather sad that you did not understand "Marie Sanders" straight away. It is "about" a pogrom ("God in

Whatever Benjamin wrote about him, Brecht almost always approved; it coincided with his intentions and contributed to their public expression. His reaction must, however, often be inferred, as hardly any direct statements are preserved. An approving echo of the essay on 'Brecht's *Threepenny Novel*', for example, is preserved only by Margarete Steffin: 'It is a pity that the piece has not been used; I like it very much.'[5] Brecht's encouragement to have the text completed immediately, and his repeated efforts to get it published, suggest that he shared Steffin's opinion.* A comparable assessment emerges from his efforts on behalf of 'What is Epic Theatre? (1)'. Brecht was also sympathetic to the 'Commentary on the Poems of Brecht', even if Benjamin himself was not at first certain about this, as is shown by his question to Steffin: 'In your letter I did not find any news, however incidental, about Brecht's reception of the Commentary. Should I take it that no news is good news?'[6]

Steffin was able to reassure him: her reply referred to Brecht's approval of the previous Summer, without clarifying it further. Brecht had erroneously assumed that Benjamin's Commentary would be published by *Maß und Wert*:

> Brecht is still in a state of confusion because of the exertions of moving house and the awful general disorder, but apart from this he has little to add to what he had already said to you in Svendborg about your splendid Commentary. He is extremely pleased that the things are going to be published. He was also pleased about the little reprint in Lieb's newspaper.[7]

Exceptions – misunderstandings about Brecht's reactions, or withheld approval – are rare. After *Das Wort* ceased publication, which meant that the Commentary would not appear, Benjamin had hopes that Brecht would use his influence with *Internationale Literatur* on behalf of his work. Brecht, after all, presented himself to this journal, which had absorbed *Das Wort*, as a former co-editor of the latter. Benjamin wrote to Steffin:

> As far as the 'Commentaries' are concerned, it is naturally very important for them to be published. I would be very pleased if Brecht would take the initiative and do me the favour of sending them direct to

---

heaven... tonight")' (ibid., 9 April 1937, p. 235). Brecht's touchiness when his work did not meet with approval was also vouched for by Hermann Greid, who had reacted coolly to drafts of *Ui* when in exile in Sweden, and after that was never given another scene of the play to read; in such cases, Brecht sealed himself off hermetically (see Greid, *Der Mensch Brecht wie ich ihn erlebt habe*, Stockholm, 1974, p. 4).

* See Brecht to Benjamin, 6 February 1935, Brecht, *Letters*, p. 200: 'Hauptmann is waiting for your article for America and it would be a good idea for you to write chop-chop ... because *Die Sammlung* may not be appearing for ever...'

Internationale Literatur. I do not so much have in mind that he should do so as the author of the poems treated in the Commentary, but rather in the name of the editorial board of *Das Wort*, since my essay is one of the manuscripts that had been submitted to them (I am speaking figuratively, for I did not send a manuscript to Erpenbeck but just to you). Be that as it may, Brecht is in touch with *Internationale Literatur*, and I have no contact with it. I think it will be easy for Brecht to inquire whether such Commentaries are of interest to these people. But if he does not want to submit them himself, he can surely request that the editorial board ask me to submit them. If the poetry volume [*Svendborg Poems*] appears now, this will make everything easier, whereas it would be very difficult for me to approach *Internationale Literatur* on my own. Please write me about this.[8]

Benjamin's hopes were not fulfilled. Brecht's influence was weak; at *Das Wort* his suggestions and objections had often been disregarded. With *Internationale Literatur*, which unlike *Das Wort* made no concessions to popular front tactics and was severely kept to the party line by Becher, Lukács, Kurella and others, Brecht was unable to make any headway.

And the *I.L.*: Brecht has written to the people there that he is prepared to work with them, but he thinks that exiled writers should be paid their fees in the currency of the country where they are forced to live, and on that subject he only received the answer that negotiations are in progress about this. But from the way that he was treated when *Das Wort* was closed down, along with Feuchtwanger, who complained a great deal about it, he does not think it a particularly happy idea for him to write in on your behalf. He is certainly prepared to do so, but you understand: Erpenbeck is continuing to conduct the correspondence. And since Brecht was unable to get anywhere even with 'his own' periodical ... don't you also think that it would be better for you to write to these people direct? Brecht smiled wearily when he heard that you expected anything to come from his recommendation.[9]

There were notes of discord when 'What is the Epic Theatre? (2)' had been published in July 1939. Brecht withheld his usual approval from this piece, as a letter of Margarete Steffin's makes clear:

You ask why I didn't write to you about the essay in *Maß und Wert*. I can tell you, although Br. didn't want me to. To be *honest*, I didn't like it. Neither did some friends of mine. But I *cannot* write anything more precise about it now (Helli promised to do so), since I don't have the essay here any more. Just one thing: why do you persist so obstinately (I did ask you about this last time) in calling the play *Fear and Trembling*?

Don't you yourself think this is a bad title? (But I will write just once more that it is called *Fear and Misery in the Third Reich*.)[10]

This unambiguous rejection, not even supported by any reasons, is striking in the correspondence between Benjamin and Margarete Steffin, which is marked by a high degree of reciprocal sympathy. Her hint that the essay was not liked by her friends either, and the announcement of a letter from Helene Weigel, leave no doubt that Brecht, whose name was cautiously given only in abbreviated form, shared her view, which indeed may actually have emanated from him. Margarete Steffin had made a copy of 'What is Epic Theatre? (1)' for Benjamin. This was four years earlier, admittedly, but at the time she had expressed explicit approval. The essay now published under the same title may have lost some of its political content, but it had gained in argumentative power and substance. Apart from the trivial matter of the confusion over the play title, it contains nothing that could have caused annoyance to Brecht or his circle. Had the confrontation with Ferdinand Lion's contemptible attacks aroused Brecht's displeasure to such an extent that it caused conflict with Benjamin, who after all had stood up for him? Benjamin reacted with irritation; he could not imagine any reason for this rejection.

> Dear Grete,
> We are not to have any luck with each other this summer. I had to reject your tobacco just as you have done my essay. As regards the tobacco, the reason is easily stated: 15 francs in duty. As regards the essay, I am repentant on the title of Brecht's play (there was an unforgivable collision with Kierkegaard's *Furcht und Sitte* [*sic*]). As far as the rest of the essay is concerned, I am prepared to be instructed.[11]

Benjamin's further confusion over the title of Kierkegaard's *Fear and Trembling* (in German, *Furcht und Zittern*) was more a Freudian slip than an error caused by a typist's mishearing; the reprimand from Brecht's circle had clearly rattled him.* This letter is the last in the extant correspondence between Benjamin and Steffin. His annoyance was patent, but there were other circumstances that led to the breaking-off of the correspondence: Benjamin's internment, Steffin's illness, and the ever-increasing difficulties in communication between France on the one hand and Sweden and Finland on the other.

There is one further utterance of Brecht's that would have disappointed Benjamin if it had come to his ears. When, in June 1940, Brecht asked the Swedish librarian and author Arnold Ljungdal for an article on his 'recent production', he wrote:

---

* The editors of Benjamin's letters assume that a mishearing took place here during dictation (see *GB* VI, p. 327).

There is nothing decent that has been written on my recent work, and nothing about the older work apart from an essay by a Jesuit priest [Karl Thieme] in the periodical *Hochland*. Without practising dialectics one can of course produce only culinary writing. All these idiocies (for example that an appeal to reason must mean a turning away from emotion, or that the epic and the dramatic are irreconcilable opposites, or that sociologically constituted characters can have no biographies) should finally be wiped out of literary history.[12]

It was exactly these 'idiocies' that Benjamin's studies had energetically challenged, and Brecht was aware of this. It must therefore have been more than thoughtlessness that moved him to refer to Karl Thieme's essay 'Des Teufels Gebetbuch?', but not to mention Benjamin's writings of the last ten years. He knew that Benjamin was not only closer to him, but also superior to Thieme in matters of both aesthetic theory and politics. Unlike Thieme's essay, however, Benjamin's – with the exception of the rejected essay 'What is the Epic Theatre? (2)' – were comparatively or totally inaccessible, since they had been published in newspapers or broadcast, or remained unpublished. Brecht himself was only able to supply an incomplete selection of material to Ljungdal.*

The final conclusion is not affected by the exceptions described. Benjamin was Brecht's first systematic critic with a claim to theory, and he was the first to identify Brecht's originality and his role in contemporary writing. According to Hannah Arendt, Brecht knew that in Benjamin he had encountered 'the most important critic of the time'.[13] This was confirmed by a note by Adorno, certainly in this case an incorruptible source, and certainly free from suspicion of having represented the relationship between Benjamin and Brecht as closer than it was: 'Story that BB, when I saw him again for the first time since 1932, in exile in the autumn of 1941, spoke of WB as his best critic.'[14]

'Useful to Read'

Brecht's attitude to writings by Benjamin that were not devoted to his work was not restricted to his high opinion of the 'Fuchs' essay and the theses 'On the Concept of History' on the one hand, and his rejection of the 'Kafka' essay and the study on 'The Work of Art in the Age of Its Technological Reproducibility'

---

* Similarly striking is the omission of Benjamin's name in a list of 'Friends, collaborators' prepared by Brecht for Gerhard Nellhaus in which he included Piscator, Grosz, Weill, Eisler, Hindemith, Dudow, Feuchtwanger and Viertel, and even Kraus, Döblin and Kaiser (see Brecht to Nellhaus, October 1942, GBA R, p. 744).

on the other.* In fact, his judgements were far more complex. Records here, admittedly, are sketchy: unlike Benjamin, who commented in essays and letters on almost every piece of work by Brecht, we have only isolated explicit statements by the latter on the work of Benjamin. This despite the fact that Brecht was fully informed about his friend's projects – not least as a result of the time spent together in Paris in 1933 and in the summer months of 1934, 1936 and 1938 in Skovsbostrand. Conversations were, however, recorded only in the form of excerpts; printed documents, typescripts sent by Benjamin to Brecht, and letters including Brecht's opinions are missing. There is, for example, no record of Brecht's view of *One-Way Street*, which he unquestionably knew. Neither have any opinions of his on the *Arcades Project* been preserved; Brecht's opinions are restricted to parts of this, such as the 'Baudelaire' or the history theses. However, they did discuss it: Benjamin wrote to Brecht that his book – 'the long one I once told you about' – was much closer to being realized as a text than he had thought; he had written a detailed précis of it. [15]

Brecht took an interest in Benjamin's work and he arranged commissions for him; the motivating influence of his interest should not be underestimated. This applies, for example, to the essay Benjamin planned on Baron Haussmann. Brecht and Benjamin were interested in the revolutionary strategy of Haussmann's innovative urban planning – the boulevards of Paris were to cut through the narrow old quarters like corridors, to make the erection of barricades more difficult – and thus also in the tension between advanced technology and regressive politics. Benjamin discovered in Haussmann's urbanistic ideal the 'tendency, encountered over and over again in the nineteenth century, to ennoble technological necessities through artistic ends'.† In the closing scenes of Brecht's *Days of the Commune* we find an echo of conversations with Benjamin, when a bourgeois gentleman with an eyeglass praises the boulevards:

> Now we appreciate the genius of Haussmann in providing Paris with boulevards. There was some discussion as to whether they contribute to the beautifying of the capital. But there can be no doubt now that at the very least they have contributed to its pacification! [16]

---

* See statements by Tiedemann (et al.) that the relationships at least bordered on 'a relationship of one-sided solidarity' (*GS* II/3, p. 1368, also in *Versuche über Brecht* [1978], p. 181), and that Brecht 'took a very distanced attitude to Benjamin's writings and, apart from the essay on "Eduard Fuchs, Collector and Historian" and the theses "On the Concept of History", hardly gave his approval to any of them' (*Marbacher Magazin*, 55/1990, p. 193).

† *SW*, vol. 3, p. 41. On Brecht's interest in the project, see Benjamin to Gretel Karplus, after 4 January 1934, *GB* IV, p. 330: 'secondly, Berthold thinks particularly highly of the topic'. Benjamin kept Brecht informed about the project, which finally failed.

As an editor of the journal *Das Wort*, Brecht had commissioned Benjamin to write the 'Pariser Briefe' ['Paris Letters']. The first of these, 'André Gide und sein neuer Gegner' ('André Gide and His New Adversary'), had at its centrepoint the depiction of a current conflict: Gide, said Benjamin, had had the fascists to deal with as soon as he had made communism his business. Benjamin directed his attention to the analysis of fascist art as an art of propaganda, which was intended to 'stand in the way of any alteration to the class situation of the proletariat'; he called the text 'an essay on fascist theories of art'.[17] The publication of the first letter was already linked with his thoughts on a series of letters, as Benjamin informed the editorial staff:

> As far as the report on French literature is concerned, it is Brecht's particular wish that the general title of 'Pariser Briefe' should be retained. He had already told me when giving me the commission that the classic literary report form of the 'letter' particularly suited him. He has now confirmed this, but has no objection to a subtitle.[18]

Brecht's postscript to Benjamin's letter clarified the choice of genre and reinforced the idea of continuity:

> Dear Comrade Bredel,
>   The Paris essay is written simply as a *letter* – that is, fairly loosely structured. I think it is a good idea for the journal too to have *regular* letters such as this one.[19]

Even more than the first one, the second 'Paris Letter', which begins in the manner of a literary article, corresponds to this notion of a loose composition. Brecht had suggested to Benjamin a discussion of the orthodox Social Democrat 1937 anthology, *A la lumière du marxisme*.* Brecht promptly passed the manuscript on to the editors,† but unlike the first letter, it was not published. Only after insistent urging by Brecht – after three enquiries with no response he had written 'an incredibly nasty letter', in which he demanded the fee for the contribution, whether or not it was published – did the editors deign to send a rejection.[20] According to Steffin, who reported their reaction, they would pay the fee for the second 'Paris Letter', but could not publish it, as it was

---

* See Benjamin to Bredel, 19 September 1936, *GB* V, p. 384. However, Benjamin did not deal with the anthology.

† See Steffin to Benjamin, 11 February 1937, Steffin, Briefe, p. 226: 'Your second letter from Paris arrived in Svendborg, and Brecht immediately forwarded it to *Das Wort*. About 10 days ago I complained, but have not yet received a reply. Brecht is now on rather severe terms with these people; please, if you have still had no reply from them, write to me immediately, and I will complain again straight away' (Benjamin's second 'Paris Letter' entitled 'Painting and Photography' is in *SW*, vol. 3, pp, 236–43).

'outdated'.[21] Their reasoning was flimsy. Benjamin's essay on the relationship between painting and photography, which corresponded to his 'Work of Art' essay, again took current debates as its starting point, for example, the Nazi politics of art; but the text was far too profound to become outdated so quickly. It is impossible to see what objections the editors could have had to it. The reasons given for rejection were not based on anything actually found in the text. Benjamin's remark that the contents of the 'Letter' 'nowhere conflict with current slogans'[22] is striking: the first 'Paris Letter' had turned overnight into a political faux pas. Immediately after its publication, Gide had published his report *Return from the USSR*, which 'was interpreted by Communist Party reviewers as the report of a renegade, although it expressed only a sense of disappointment, not rejection'.[23] Gide himself, until then still its embodiment, was now considered a traitor to the Popular Front. Ernst Bloch had foreseen the conflict: 'I read your essay in *Das Wort*; it will probably turn out to have been the last one there on Gide.'[24] It was not only the last essay on Gide in *Das Wort*, but also Benjamin's last essay published in that journal.*

Benjamin's 'Paris Letters' were the only contributions that corresponded to notes Brecht drew up on the idea of 'literary letters' for *Das Wort*. They were not orientated to new publications, but to literary life, dealing with debates on literature and art as social events. They were to examine works and positions on the basis of what ideas they represented or challenged, Benjamin's attention being given to the dispute with the Nazi politics of art. And finally, they were dedicated to the innovation of describing works of art in terms of technological practice, rather than as 'forms of creative expression'.[25]

Ignoring the rejections, Brecht and Steffin repeatedly tried to acquire Benjamin as a contributor to *Das Wort*. When Benjamin mentioned that he had come across the early nineteenth-century German writer, and exile in France, Carl Gustav Jochmann,[26] Margarete Steffin beseeched him in a letter of 9 April 1937:

> But as far as Carl Gustav Jochmann is concerned, Brecht thinks that he would not like to let him escape by any means from *Das Wort*, under the famous rubric 'cultural heritage'. He will of course understand if, after the wretched experience you have had with the editors, you are not inclined to send anything else, but perhaps just this once you might turn a blind eye? Brecht is also very worried lest you identify him with

---

* Chryssoula Kambas has pointed out that the 'unhappy' point in time when the first 'Paris Letter' was published probably had its effect on the rejection of the 'Work of Art' essay (see Kambas, *Walter Benjamin im Exil. Zum Verhältnis von Literaturpolitik und Aesthetik*, Tübingen, 1983, pp. 172ff.).

their sloppiness, but I really must tell you that Brecht hardly sends off a letter to Bredel or his secretary without an admonition to reply to you, to publish your work, to send your fee...
Where else would you publish Jochmann? Can't you at least send a carbon copy?*

Benjamin did not respond to the encouragement to send his Jochmann introduction to *Das Wort*. On the one hand, this was certainly because of annoyance over the dilatory and negative treatment of his manuscripts by the editors, but on the other hand because his proposal had immediately fallen on fruitful ground with Horkheimer.

Benjamin received several further similar offers of mediation from Brecht. Benjamin's review of Anna Seghers's novel *Die Rettung* ('The Rescue'), 'Eine Chronik der deutschen Arbeitslosen' ('A Chronicle of the German Unemployed'), was published in the *Neue Weltbühne* on 12 May 1938. Margarete Steffin and Brecht had already known about this review:

> What is the situation with the *Weltbühne* and your piece on Seghers's novel? Brecht is asking if this would not after all be something for *Das Wort*? But probably it is too long for that? I hope the *Weltbühne* will publish it. Do they actually pay a fee?[27]

Brecht's judgement of the articles 'The Present Social Situation of the French Writer', 'Problems in the Sociology of Language' and 'Eduard Fuchs, Collector and Historian' was unconditionally positive. He acknowledged the succinctness, clarity and authority of Benjamin's style and method of argumentation, and gave him credit for sound knowledge. Benjamin had sent the first of these essays from the *Zeitschrift für Sozialforschung* (No. 1, 1934) in the hope that Brecht would champion its publication in the French edition of *Internationale Literatur*.† It is not known whether Brecht did make an attempt to do so, but when Margarete Steffin received the publication, Brecht immediately took possession of it and showed himself impressed by it:

---

* A shortened version of Benjamin's essay on Jochmann's 'The Regression of Poetry' was published by Horkheimer and Adorno in the *Zeitschrift für Sozialforschung* in 1940 (see *SW*, vol. 4, pp. 356–76 for Benjamin's and Jochmann's texts).

† Benjamin to Brecht (beginning of 1934): 'Hauptmann has recently read the essay 'The Present Social Situation of the French Writer' (in *SW*, vol. 2, pp. 744–63). 'She thinks the piece would be of great interest to *Littérature et Révolution* – the official journal, which of course also appears in French. She insisted that I should ask you if you would not like to bring it to the attention of Kolzov, so that he can submit it to the editorial department.' In a postscript Benjamin corrects the title of the journal to *Littérature Internationale*.

Dear Benjamin,
Many thanks for the essay. It reads splendidly well and says more than a good 400-page book.*

Benjamin's essay reflected discussions on the function of the intellectual – once again in France, where the term had been created, and above all debates on intellectual attitudes to politics. He challenged Julien Benda, who had written on the 'treason of the intellectuals'. 'The decline of the independent intelligentsia,' Benjamin argued, 'is determined crucially, if not exclusively, by economic factors.' Benda, he said, 'understands as little of the economic basis of their crisis as he does of the crisis in the sciences, the undermining of the dogma of objective research' free from preconceptions.[28] This not only continued the conversations on *Krise und Kritik*, but also directly coincided with interests of Brecht's. This is undoubtedly true of the reflections on literary technique in his article, which Benjamin illustrated by using the example of Paul Valéry: among contemporary French writers, Valéry 'possesses the greatest technical expertise'; his special position was sufficiently designated by the statement that 'he has reflected on the nature of technique in writing like no one else'. With the comment that writing in this context 'includes poetry',[29] Benjamin resumed the discussion on the relationship between the conventional and the creative writer (see above, p. 100).

Brecht went even further in his concurrence with Benjamin in the case of the latter's multiple review, 'Problems in the Sociology of Language', which had been published in the second issue of 1935 of the *Zeitschrift für Sozialforschung*. Brecht reacted in April 1936:

Dear Benjamin,
Alerted to your article on linguistic research by Korsch, who spoke very favourably of it, I read it and was also very impressed. It is written in an excellent style, allows a wide overall view of the material, and demonstrates the restraint appropriate to contemporary research. A new encyclopedia could well be written in this manner.
I would like to have a copy, otherwise I would have to steal Korsch's copy, and that would be nasty.[30]

One must bear in mind Brecht's high regard for the importance of the encyclopedic project, to comprehend in all its far-reaching significance his recognition of Benjamin's text as the model for a 'new encyclopedia'. Brecht had been pursuing such a project for more than six years and discussed it with

---

* Brecht, *Letters*, p. 173, 4 May 1934. In a letter written in March or April, in which Steffin thanked Benjamin for the volume of the *Zeitschrift*, she also complained that Brecht had taken it away from her (Steffin, *Briefe*, p. 120).

156

Benjamin.* The keyword occurs for the first time in the run-up to the *Krise und Kritik* journal project. At the end of his programmatic 'Outline for a periodical, *Kritische Blätter*' of 1929, Brecht noted:

> Sequence of results
> Recapitulation, consolidation, correction. Value judgements allowed because of so little importance here. Encyclopedic technique.

The characteristics of a 'new encyclopedia', specified here and later, include: the ability to objectivize knowledge, the analysis of linguistic, social and ideological criticism, the rejection or disregard of value judgements, continuity, precision and authoritative command of the material. It was qualities such as these that Brecht attributed to Benjamin's essay, which gave a critical overview of the disciplines and tendencies of linguistic research. Benjamin was sympathetic towards positions that examined linguistic development in the light of 'special economic, environmental and social conditions' or that, like the works of Nikolai Marr, sought 'to invalidate the concept of race, and indeed of peoples, in favour of a history of languages based on the movements of classes'.[31] His review thus fulfilled the expectations formulated by Brecht for his encyclopedia project. He considered it a technique that could be learnt; the decisive factor for Brecht was that such a project should be structured out of radical ideas, including their consequences, as is shown by a list drawn up around 1930:

> *Proposition for entries in a new encyclopedia*
> 1. For whom is the proposition beneficial?
> 2. For whom does it claim to be beneficial?
> 3. What does it invite one to do?
> 4. *What practice corresponds to it?*
> 5. What propositions result from it? What propositions support it?
> 6. *In what situation is it all expressed?* By whom? [Brecht's italics]

In the conditions of exile, with a growing need for discussion and reflection, Brecht pursued the idea more intensively. In mid-1933, as he wrote to Otto Neurath, he wanted to 'start from a small association, whose members, working closely together, will try to draw up a *Catalogue of operative phrases*'. This 'association I'm speaking of, which is to bear the name (which you will not, I hope, find too distressing) of *Association for Dialectical Materialism*, will attempt to derive certain insights and potential insights from social transformations while helping as it were to bring these transformations about'.[32] He would, as he

---

* Benjamin, who must have been familiar with the concept of a 'new encyclopedia' from the days of *Krise und Kritik*, explicitly mentioned it in a record of a conversation of 27 September 1934 (*SW*, vol. 2, p. 788).

wrote to Johannes R. Becher at the end of December 1934, prefer a congress to discuss a specific common project to 'get-togethers for the sake of being together'. And he sketched out a plan for a 'new encyclopedia', a literary work that might come out in serial form, 'a sort of reference work, a compendium of the opinions of anti-fascists'.[33] In 1935 Brecht formulated his thesis under the slogan '*Kämpferischer Realismus*' (Militant Realism), in which he wrote:

> The attempt to create, for example, a new kind of encyclopedia of a semi-scientific kind, an encyclopedia written by writers, could today count on a high degree of participation. Such an encyclopedia could of course not have a definitively scientific and political character; it would not obviate the publication of an urgently necessary communist encyclopedia, but it might make a decisive contribution to the clarification and self-understanding of anti-fascist writers.[34]

In the spring of 1937, Brecht attempted with the foundation of the 'Diderot Society' to bring together the various initial strands. What was needed were the 'little, carefree, candid reports on some attempts, some emergent problems, partial attempts, partial problems, a brief proposal for a new *terminus technicus*', etc.; 'the scientific nature of a science does in fact always begin with division into branches, with the specific'. It is no accident that he recommended 'The Work of Art in the Age of Its Technological Reproducibility' as a piece which could be included in a collection of numbered writings by the Diderot Society, 'for the sake of some continuity'.[35] The essay on 'Problems in the Sociology of Language' seemed to him to fulfil the demands for a 'new encyclopedia'; Benjamin's text fitted into the continuum of informative discussion circles which Brecht never tired of promoting. Their closeness is borne out by the fact that Benjamin was aware of the significance of Brecht's support. As he wrote to Alfred Cohn, he had had 'a surprising amount of success' with his piece on linguistics: 'Brecht, for example, though it is not in his nature, has written enthusiastically to me about it.'[36]

When Benjamin was working on the essay 'Eduard Fuchs, Collector and Historian', Margarete Steffin offered to send the piece to *Internationale Literatur*.[37] In this case, Benjamin was not dependent on such support. The study was a commissioned piece, and was published in the *Zeitschrift für Sozialforschung* (No. 2, 1937). Brecht, who would have been familiar with the manuscript in the summer of 1936 in Skovsbostrand, when Benjamin was writing it, reacted enthusiastically on rereading it:

> Dear Benjamin,
> I have reread your essay on Fuchs and this time I liked it even better. You will learn this with a certain nonchalance; but I think that it is

precisely the moderate temperature of your interest in the subject of your piece that has helped you to achieve this economy. There is not a trace of decoration, but everything is delicate (in the good old meaning of the word) and the spiral is never prolonged by means of a mirror. You always stay with the topic, or the topic stays with you.[38]

Brecht's letter, which exists only as an unfinished draft and presumably did not reach its intended recipient, added to the specific virtues of Benjamin's work a further one, which Brecht called 'economy'. It was based on the fact that the author had a distance from his theme, which enabled him to deal with his material in a composed manner. The paradox was that Benjamin had taken a great deal of trouble over this very essay, as Brecht well knew. His tribute thus implied that this effort was not visible in the result, but it was also reminiscent of the attitudes of epic theatre: the author Benjamin had behaved like the ideal Brechtian actor by not empathizing with his subject, but keeping his distance and presenting his conclusions without pressure. Distance does not mean a lack of connection. The writer and the subject bear a close relation to each other: 'You always stay with the topic, or the topic stays with you.' With the pairs of concepts 'decoration' and 'delicate' (*Zierat* and *zierlich*) and 'mirror' and 'spiral', Brecht was also illustrating qualities of Benjamin's study: '[*zierlich*] (in the good old meaning of the word)' refers to the Old High German word *Zier* (ornament or decoration) and means 'fine, splendid, precious'; what is meant is a perfection in composition, a form without ornamentation, without decorative, superfluous accessories.* The image of the spiral stresses the dynamic manner of presentation. That the spiral is never prolonged by a mirror means that the writer has not restricted himself to the creation of images of reality, to reflection as in a mirror, but has sought to get to the root of connections. Brecht betrayed his defensiveness against the mirror as an instrument in a comment from the 'Notes on the Realist Mode of Writing' around 1940: 'In literature, you cannot use the same mirror to reflect different periods in the way that you can use one and the same mirror to reflect various heads, and even tables and clouds.'[39]

Brecht certainly knew Benjamin's collection *German Men and Women: A Sequence of Letters* from the publication of the individual pieces in the *Frankfurter Zeitung*. We have only a reaction from Margarete Steffin to the book version. On 7 November 1936 she expressed thanks for 'letter and letters' – undoubtedly she meant Benjamin's latest letter and a copy, enclosed with this, of his collection of letters, to whose publication Steffin had contributed in the

---

* Benjamin would have been pleased by this characterization, for it coincided with Adolf Loos's verdict on ornament. He had expressed his sympathy with Loos in the essays 'Karl Kraus' and 'Experience and Poverty' (see *SW*, vol. 2, pp. 434 and 733).

autumn of 1933 with her secretarial work:* 'I have already begun to read them with real pleasure and the few that I already know, I greet as old acquaintances – acquaintances whom one is glad to see again.'⁴⁰

Brecht had tried to place Benjamin's manuscript with a Zurich publisher via Lisa Tetzner. The gesture in itself implies recognition of the project, but in addition Brecht commented on the significance and possible effects of Benjamin's selection:

> Dear Tetznerin,
>
> Here is a request: Walter Benjamin some time ago put together a collection of German Letters for the *Frankfurter Zeitung*, a very flattering collection for Germany. Now he thinks that a Swiss publisher might perhaps be interested in it; because a Swiss would take responsibility for it and it would probably sell well over there (it could even appear anonymously). Would you now perhaps pass the manuscript (12 of what would be about 40 letters) to a publisher in Zurich? This would of course be better than trying to do anything from Paris. You would not have to do much after that, perhaps make one telephone call. Otherwise we have no one.†

In the case of the essay 'The Work of Art in the Age of Its Technological Reproducibility' Brecht's mediation was unsuccessful. After the typescript of the first German version had gone via Margarete Steffin to Asja Lacis, Bernhard Reich and Sergei Tretyakov, Brecht submitted the second version to the editorial department of *Das Wort*.‡ The latter justified its rejection of the

---

* See Benjamin to Steffin, 4 November 1936, *GB* V, p. 413: 'I am sure you will remember working on the manuscript at the Palace Hotel two years ago.'

† Brecht to Lisa Tetzner, (June 1935), in *Autographen aus allen Gebieten*, Catalogue 672, Berlin, 1999, p. 19. Heinrich Blücher's hitherto unpublished comment about Benjamin's collection is of interest here. In a letter of February 1937, Blücher writes that he thoroughly enjoyed this anthology: 'For it is good, after the screaming of overheated stupidity, to hear once again the calm and therefore more convincing voice of reason, which will not cease to engage in argument, while barbarians gesticulate. Commentaries such as the second one on Goethe's letter are probably among the best things that German literary history has produced and need not fear comparison with some of Schopenhauer's masterpieces. In short: I am happy, in the noisy throng that has gathered around our fathers' inheritance, where the fascists strive to destroy it and the communists cannot possess it yet, because they do not yet understand how to take possession of it, to find someone who knows how to administer it' (WBA 25) (for *German Men and Women*, see *SW*, vol. 3, pp. 167–220).

‡ See *SW*, vol. 3, pp. 101–22 [second version]; ibid., vol. 4, pp. 252–70 [third version]. See Benjamin to Alfred Cohn, 10 August 1936, *GB* V, p. 349: 'Brecht wants to publish the German version in the journal *Das Wort*.' See also Benjamin to Steffin, 4 March 1936, *GB* V, pp. 254ff., and Brecht to Benjamin, beginning of December 1936, GBA 28,

essay for two separate reasons: the text was too long, and a contribution had already been received from another author on a similar topic.* The extent of the text alone does not explain the rejection; Benjamin's theses might have met with hostility in Moscow, such as had already been expressed by Reich; Benjamin's essay had aroused 'violent repulsion' in him, Reich wrote to him, and the manner of proceeding was foreign to him. He did not understand that 'the destruction of the aura [appeared] as an advantage', and he was prepared to bet 'that the highly personal relationship with the work of art and the expression of the highly personal in it would be maintained even in Socialism, and develop even more strongly'.† The Gide case and also the Moscow trials played their part in preventing publication.

As much as the editorial staff of *Das Wort* exerted themselves to conceal the true reasons for the rejection of Benjamin's essay, the more certain it is that Brecht had no part in the failure of the intention to get it published.‡ On the contrary, he would not have taken the part of Benjamin's essay so vehemently if he had not valued it. How else but approvingly could the description be intended that Brecht prepared for the already mentioned recommendation of the 'Work of Art' theses as a product of the Diderot Society? Brecht wrote to Gorelik that he would get hold of a piece by Reich on Shakespeare and also 'an essay, 'The Effect of Technical Reproducibility on the Arts', by Benjamin, in which he shows the revolutionary effect that the possibility of mass reproduction (photography, cinema, etc.) has had on art and attitudes towards art'.[41]

A decisive indication of Brecht's positive attitude to Benjamin's study must

---

p. 568: 'I haven't been told when your long article, 'The Work of Art in the Age of Its Technological Reproducibility', is to appear' (Brecht, *Letters*, pp. 237–8). Brecht abbreviates the title of the piece: 'd K i Z s t R' ('Das Kunstwerk im Zeitalter seiner technischen Reproduzierbarkeit') (WBA 26/9) – a token of his familiarity with it and his correspondent. On the difference between the various versions of the 'Work of Art' essay, see Steve Giles, *Bertolt Brecht and Critical Theory. Marxism, Modernism and 'The Threepenny Lawsuit'*, Bern, 1997, pp. 113–31.

* See *Das Wort* to Benjamin, 27 May 1937 (RGALI Moscow, Fond 631, Opis 12, nos 141/80). Benjamin had already known a month earlier that it had been refused on grounds of space (see Benjamin to Steffin, 26 April 1937, *GB* V, p. 521).

† See Bernhard Reich to Benjamin, 19 February 1936 (WBA 150/2–3). Benjamin called Reich's letter 'negative, and in an unproductive way'; the letter was 'not a basis for discussion' (Benjamin to Steffin, 4 March 1936, *GB* V, p. 254).

‡ The editors of the current Suhrkamp *GS* 'Collected Works' repeatedly stated in reproachful terms that the dilatory treatment of the intention to publish, and the rejection of Benjamin's essay, derived from Brecht's critique of it; however, this argument was based on a passage of 25 July 1938 in Brecht's *Journals*, which refers not only to the 'Work of Art' theses, but to the 'Baudelaire' studies.

be the joint editorial work which was undertaken in a critical but productive atmosphere in Skovsbostrand in August 1936. Benjamin reported:

> The mornings were devoted to a detailed discussion of my essay, best known to you in its French version. Its acceptance by Brecht was achieved not without resistance, even clashes. But it was all very rewarding and led to a number of notable improvements, without affecting the core of the work in the slightest. Its extent has probably increased by a quarter.[42]

Brecht was predestined for this debate. Benjamin's analyses of the theory of perception were closely bound to the ideas of texts such as Brecht's '*Threepenny Opera* Lawsuit', which for its part had again referred back to Benjamin's *Little History of Photography*.[43] It was thus an unmistakable gesture when Brecht associated himself with the essay in a postscript to a letter by Benjamin to Willi Bredel:

> Dear Comrade Bredel,
> The editing of the essay 'The Work of Art in the Age of Its Technological Reproducibility', in which I was involved, took up some time, so that Benjamin now needs a few more days [for the first 'Paris Letter']. Please keep the space free for it!
> Regards,
> Brecht[44]

This was more than friendly protection; Brecht attached importance to the text in terms of literary politics. Indirect approval is also recognizable in Brecht's echoing of Benjamin's comparison: 'Such is the aestheticizing of politics, as practised by fascism. Communism replies to it by politicizing art.'[45] In his poem 'Prohibition of Theatre Criticism' from the cycle *German Satires* of 1939 Brecht wrote: 'The regime/ Dearly loves the theatre. Its accomplishments/ Are mainly on the theatrical plane.'[46] And in Brecht's notes 'On the Theatricality of Fascism' of 1939 we find: 'Let us consider the theatricality of the way in which the fascists present themselves.'[47] This is referred to in the *Journal* entry for 6 December 1940: 'We ought to study the theatrical elements in customs and traditions. I have already done some work on the application of theatrical techniques to politics in fascism.'[48]

More specifically, Brecht occasionally picked up texts by Benjamin, quoting them in a cryptic manner or – as will be seen in the example of the philosophy of history – developing ways of thinking related to them. These are forms of appropriation which demonstrate his familiarity with his friend's work and approval of his themes and ideas. The following, from about 1929, is from one of the 'Keuner Stories':

Some philosophers, Herr Keuner related, put forward the question as to what sort of life would always be guided in a decisive situation by the latest hit-song. If we were conducting good lives, we would actually need neither weighty motives nor very wise advice, and the whole businesss of choosing would stop, said Herr Keuner, quite wise to this question.[49]

Brecht owed the stimulus for this text to Benjamin's 'Surrealism' essay of 1928, in which Benjamin wrote: 'What form do you suppose a life would take that was determined at a decisive moment by the street song last on everyone's lips?'[50]

The philosopher Chuang Tzu from the Keuner story 'Originality', also written in 1929, is reminiscent of Benjamin's treatment of quotations, which was to become methodically constitutive above all in the *Arcades* text:

When he was already in the prime of life, the Chinese philosopher Chuang Tzu composed a book of one hundred thousand words, nine-tenths of which consisted of quotations. Such books can no longer be written here and now, because the wit is lacking. As a result, ideas are only produced in one's own workshop, and anyone who does not manage enough of them thinks himself lazy.[51]

It was out of quotations that Benjamin had wanted to compose his magnum opus, the *Arcades Project*. When Brecht wrote the story quoted above, Benjamin had only just begun work on that project. But it was already true of the *Tragic Drama* book that 'what I have written consists, as it were, almost entirely of quotations'.[52] It would be safe to assume that he reached agreement with Brecht about the theory and practice of quoting – the link was too obvious, between quotation and avant-garde art forms such as montage and construction technique; in addition, both discussed the connection between quotation and plagiarism, while they had a shared interest in Karl Kraus's technique of polemic-by-quotation.* There is also a similarity between an aphorism from *One-Way Street* – 'Quotations in my work are like wayside robbers, who leap out, armed, and relieve the idle stroller of his conviction'[53] – and a passage from Brecht's *Buch der Wendungen* ('Book of Changes'):

* 'Quotation without comment' is 'the least imitable of forms', wrote Brecht about Kraus (GBA 22/1, p. 34). Benjamin called quotation 'Kraus's basic polemical procedure'; a quotation 'summons the word by its name, wrenches it destructively from its context, but precisely thereby calls it back to its origin' (*SW*, vol. 2, pp. 453–4). In a variant to his essay 'Problems in the Sociology of Language' of Autumn 1934, written in 1935, we find the following: 'KK is now conducting in *Die Fackel*, with masterly polemic, the political critique of language which academic scholarship has for transparent reasons failed to do.' In defending Brecht against the charge of plagiarism, Benjamin also took up Kraus's position (see Chapter IV, pp. 98ff. above).

Philosophers generally become very angry when their sentences are torn out of context. Me-ti recommended it. He said: Sentences that are part of systems hang together like the members of criminal gangs. Singly, they can easily be overpowered. So they must be separated from each other. One must confront them one at a time with reality, so that they can be revealed.[54]

Brecht's poem fragment 'The Doubter' of 1938 corresponds with passages from Benjamin's radio broadcast 'Bert Brecht' of 1930. Brecht may have been remembering an image that had been used by Benjamin:

It will turn out to be a whole bundle of assumptions that will fall apart once you have loosened the string that binds them together. The string of fixed opinion: somewhere or other, people are certainly thinking – we can rely on this.[55]

'And with this the knot is untied,' Benjamin said about the public who asked whether thinking corresponded to particular interests. When the knotted string was untied, the 'bundle of assumptions' falls apart, 'transforming itself into sheer question marks. Is thinking worthwhile? Should it be of use? And to whom? – Blunt questions all of them, no doubt'.[56] Brecht transforms these expressions into a poetic model in which the closeness in choice of words and tone is astonishing:

Whenever we seemed
To have found the answer to a question
One of us untied the string of the old rolled-up
Chinese scroll on the wall, so that it fell down and
Revealed to us the man on the bench who
Doubted so much.
I, he said to us
Am the doubter. I am doubtful whether
The work was well done that devoured your days...
Are you truly in the stream of happening? In agreement with
All that develops? Are *you* developing? Who are you? To whom
do you speak? Who finds what you say useful?[57]

What had Benjamin said? 'Blunt questions all of them, no doubt. But we, or so says Herr Keuner, have nothing to fear from blunt questions, have our most refined answers ready to hand for those blunt questions.'[58]

Among Benjamin's works criticized by Brecht are the lecture 'The Author as Producer', the essay 'Franz Kafka' and the essay 'The Paris of the Second Empire in Baudelaire'. Brecht's assessment of the 'Author as Producer' essay, which Benjamin recorded after a conversation in the hospital at Svendborg on 3

July 1934, is a discriminating critique of Benjamin's theses, which for their part had come into being in debate with Brecht. Benjamin noted the objections thus:

> I develop the theory that a decisive criterion of a revolutionary function of literature lies in the extent to which technical advances lead to a transformation of artistic forms and hence of intellectual means of production. Brecht was willing to concede the validity of this thesis only for a single type – namely, the upper-middle-class writer, a type he thought included himself.[59]

The upper-middle-class writer 'experiences the interests of the proletariat at a single point: the issue of the development of his means of production'. As producer he was proletarianized by this, and this made him united in 'a solidarity [with the proletariat] all along the line'.[60] Brecht's opposition aimed at a more precise formulation of Benjamin's theses. His lively interest was based on a fundamental agreement which allowed for differences in specific points of view. Even the observation that Benjamin's 'criticism of proletarian writers of the Becher type' was 'too abstract'[61] can be understood as a continuation of the debate.

The case of the 'Franz Kafka' essay was a different one. Benjamin had written this for the *Jüdische Rundschau* and completed it before his journey to Denmark in June 1934. Kafka had been a topic of discussion since the summer of 1931. Brecht had 'seemed to devour' the posthumous volume, *The Great Wall of China*; Benjamin had been surprised by Brecht's 'thoroughly positive attitude to Kafka's work'.[62] He was entitled to expect receptiveness on Brecht's part. But his journal entries of August 1934 betray disappointment – at first over the fact that Brecht did not react at all for more than three weeks, and then at the latter's violent criticism:

> Three weeks ago I gave Brecht my essay on Kafka to read. He had doubtless read it, but did not allude to it of his own accord; and on the two occasions when I brought the subject up, he responded evasively. Finally, I took the manuscript back, without comment. Yesterday, he suddenly referred to the essay again. With a somewhat abrupt and forced transition in the conversation, he remarked that I, too, could not totally escape the charge of writing in diary form, in the style of Nietzsche. My Kafka essay, for example. It was interested in Kafka only as a phenomenon; looked on the work as if it – and likewise the author – were a product of nature and isolated it from every possible context, even the author's life. I was always interested exclusively in the question of *essence*.[63]

This objection makes Brecht's long silence understandable. The very casualness of his critical remark must also have offended Benjamin. It went to the core of the essay and found its high point in the 'long, heated debate' of 29

August 1934, whose 'basis' was Brecht's 'accusation' that the essay 'promoted Jewish fascism'.* Brecht's reproach, in its form and substance, broke through the boundaries of friendly communication and aimed directly at those very elements of Benjamin's thinking which Brecht was unable to assimilate'.†

The study of Kafka took up arguments of Brecht's from the discussions of the summer of 1931 and elements of Benjamin's reading of Brecht. Benjamin interpreted Kafka's work as a sign of the distortions and alienations of existence, he took up Brecht's comparison between Josef K. and Schweyk, and recalled Brecht's characterization of Kafka's theme as being that of astonishment.‡ Benjamin's observations on the significance of gesture and gestus in Kafka as well as on the 'Nature Theatre of Oklahoma' (in Kafka's *America*), which led back to the Chinese theatre and – as with Kafka – was 'the logical place for such groupings', are direct references to Brecht's theatre.[64] In a conscious parallel in the politics of literature, Benjamin situated Kafka's work, like that of Brecht, in the region of the avant-garde, as had been shown in the planned Paris lecture series of the Spring.§ In agreement with Brecht, he had made observations relating to narrative technique on Kafka's break with 'a purely narrative prose',

---

* *SW*, vol. 2, p. 787. The term 'Jewish fascism' had been current since the late nineteen twenties as a negative synonym associated with 'Zionism', analogous perhaps to the concept of 'social fascism' (see Arendt, *Men in Dark Times*, p. 185). The term 'fascism' here did not refer to the ideology of Italian or German fascists, but to the related attitude of fanatical supporters of a Zionist state. The use of the concept becomes clear in the essay 'Nationalismus und Judentum' of 1933, in which Lion Feuchtwanger turned against Zionist political ideologists, 'a kind of Jewish Hitlerism', to which he opposed his concept of 'true Jewish nationalism'. 'Nothing could be more pointless,' wrote Feuchtwanger, 'than to oppose the fascism of others, whether German, Polish or whatever they be, with a Jewish fascism.' The use made by Brecht of the concept has a political element that polemicizes against an apparent rejection of social categories; it becomes blurred if one interprets Brecht's use of the concept as 'Jewish tradition' or 'Jewish mysticism'.

† See Benjamin to Marx-Steinschneider, 20 July 1938 (*Benjamin Correspondence*, p. 569). Scholem pointed out that reading Benjamin's essay 'rightly turned the stomach of the Marxist Brecht' (Scholem to Pierre Missac, 27 October 1969. In Scholem, *Briefe II*, p. 223). Likewise: 'Of course Brecht had a thoroughly healthy instinct and smelt the intolerable mystic in Benjamin' (Scholem to Siegfried Unseld, 15 May 1973, in Scholem, *Briefe III*, Munich, 1999, p. 77).

‡ See Benjamin's journal note from Le Lavandou of 6 June 1931 (*SW*, vol. 2, pp. 477–9) and his adoption of the motifs in 'Franz Kafka' (ibid., pp. 814–15). There is an unidentified echo here of Benjamin's concept of allegory: everything Kafka described 'makes statements about something other than itself' (ibid., p. 478).

§ Siegfried Kracauer commented mockingly on Benjamin's attempt to bring Kafka and Brecht together: 'Kafka would certainly be astonished if he learned that he entertained such a neighbourly relationship with Brecht and communism' (Kracauer to Ernst Bloch, 5 July 1934, Bloch, *Briefe I*, p. 382).

on his allegorical and parabolic way of writing.[65] Brecht's view of Kafka's 'prophetic', 'visionary', even 'authentic Bolshevist' qualities[66] is therefore to be understood not only as a political one, but also as one based on aesthetic theory. Brecht's original brusque dismissal of Benjamin was aimed at the latter's attempt to merge insights which stemmed from precise, historical, materialist viewpoints which linked him with Brecht, and motifs that went back to discussions on the tradition of Jewish scriptural interpretation. The theme of Benjamin's conversations with Scholem on Kafka was the law, and Benjamin adopted from Jewish theology concepts such as doctrine and scripture, and the comparison of Halacha and Haggadah and, in a comparison with the Hebrew prose writer Samuel Joseph Agnon, 'developing in his own way the category of deferment'.* Brecht held it against him that instead of examining Kafka's work for its utility value,† he attempted to penetrate 'into the depths' – this was no way to go forward, depth 'is simply a dimension; it is just depth – in which nothing can be seen'.[67] Brecht refused to recognize that Benjamin's procedure was not so very different from his own. He too was working on the exposure of social structures – admittedly without the radically pragmatic gesture of the creative writer.‡

For Benjamin, in the context of the discussions on Kafka, the weeks in Svendborg in the summer of 1934 meant 'an agonizing acid test'.[68] In this debate, strangeness and closeness meshed together in occasional dramatic friction. Nevertheless it would be wrong to call it unproductive. Benjamin carefully noted Brecht's objections, in order to be able to formulate a counter-position for his planned 'revision' of the essay.§ These objections broke into a force field whose dynamics disappear with the maintenance of an irreconcilable opposition.‖ The discussion on Kafka showed that Benjamin, as Lorenz Jäger has described it, 'during this Spring brought central but divergent motifs of his

---

* Scholem, *Walter Benjamin*, p. 145. Scholem's influence on Benjamin can be gauged from his letter of 1 August 1931 (see ibid., pp. 169–74).

† See 'Fitting Comment on Kafka' (*c.* 1926) in *Brecht on Art and Politics*, p. 40. In conversation with Benjamin, Brecht remarked that one would 'find a number of very useful things' in Kafka's writings, 'the real task was to shed light on Kafka, and that meant formulating the practical proposals that could be distilled from his stories' (*SW*, vol. 2, pp. 786–7).

‡ See for example Benjamin's formulation that Kafka was concerned with the 'question of how life and work are organized in human society' (ibid., p. 803).

§ See Benjamin to Werner Kraft, 12 November 1934. Benjamin's notes 'Zur "Kafka"-Revision' contain wide-ranging 'pleas' of Brecht's, chiefly excerpts from the transcripts of conversation, but also drafts of the revision in which Brecht's proposals are taken into account.

‖ Such a rigid confrontation of positions was rather the problem of his interpreters.

thinking to a new heightening, a new intensity'.[69] For Benjamin, despite the harsh rejection he encountered from Brecht, it made sense to confront his own searching procedure with Brecht's pointed interpretation.* In any case, Benjamin appeared to be less dismayed than were his disciples. The time after the dispute over the Kafka essay – after all, he stayed in Denmark until the Autumn – does not seem to have been clouded by it. If he had retrospectively felt wounded, he would hardly have vigorously devoted himself after the dispute to a review of *The Threepenny Novel*. Furthermore, it is certainly not going too far to recognize traces of the discussion with Benjamin even in the greater complexity of Brecht's later assessment of Kafka.†

* Scholarship has treated this debate as one of the significant discussions within German exile literature. See Hans Mayer, 'Walter Benjamin and Franz Kafka. Report on a Constellation', in *On Walter Benjamin*, pp. 185–209. See also Werner Mittenzwei, 'Brecht und Kafka', in *Sinn und Form* (Berlin), vol. 15, no. 4, pp. 618–25; Klaus Hermsdorf, 'Anfänge der Kafka-Rezeption in der sozialistischen deutschen Literatur', in *Weimarer Beiträge* (Berlin/Weimar), vol. 24, no. 9, pp. 4–69; Peter Beicken, *Kafkas 'Prozeß' und seine Richter*, op. cit.; Stéphane Moses, 'Brecht und Benjamin als Kafka Interpreten', in Stéphane Moses/Albrecht Schöne (eds), *Juden in der deutschen Literatur*, Frankfurt, 1986, pp. 237–56; Lorenz Jäger, 'Primat des Gestus', op. cit.; Alexander Honold, *Der Leser Walter Benjamin. Bruchstücke einer deutschen Literaturgeschichte*, Berlin, 2000, pp. 277–413. Heiner Müller has also understood Benjamin's Svendborg interpretation of Kafka as a question about Brecht's own work: 'Between the lines of Benjamin's text lies the question as to whether parable in Kafka is not more spacious, can accept more reality (and deliver more) than in Brecht. And this not despite the fact that, but because it describes gestures without a frame of reference, not orientated to a movement (practice), not to be reduced to a meaning – strange rather than estranging, without a moral. The rockfalls of recent history (Müller was writing in 1980) have inflicted less damage on the model of the penal colony than on the ideal dialectical construction of Brecht's "Lehrstücke"' (Müller, 'Keuner +Fatzer', in Reinhold Grimm and Jost Hermand (eds), *Brecht Jahrbuch*, Frankfurt, 1980, p. 15). The following reading by Müller is also notable for its understanding of the relationship between Benjamin and Brecht: 'It is clear that in his discussions on Kafka Brecht always insisted on sticking to his position. He never managed to loosen or even occasionally question his position. Whereas, for Benjamin, the discussion on Kafka was a matter of putting in question Brecht's position, of trying to break something down. That is what I believed. Brecht tried to reduce Kafka to a moralist who wrote parables' (Erdmut Wizisla, 'Über Brecht. Gespräch mit Heiner Müller', in *Sinn und Form* (Berlin), vol. 48, no. 2, 1996, p. 237).

† See Brecht's essay about contemporary Czech literature (GBA 22/1, pp. 37ff.). What is striking here is, for example, the different reading of the 'dark' (*Dunkel*): Brecht had criticized Benjamin's interpretation because it 'increased and spread confusion (*das Dunkel*) about him, instead of dissipating it' (*SW*, vol. 2, p. 787). Brecht writes: 'Often writers serve us with obscure, dark and inaccessible works, which must be read with great skill and expertise, as though they were illegal letters, obscure for fear of the police' (GBA 22/1, p. 38).

It remains an open question whether Brecht read the manuscript of Benjamin's study 'The Paris of the Second Empire in Baudelaire', or was told about it in conversation. He reacted to it with displeasure; his objections overruled the 'good' that he found in it. Unlike his criticism of the Kafka essay, Brecht seems to have kept his views on 'Baudelaire' largely to himself. At least, there is no evidence that he would have expressed himself as bluntly to its author as he did in his journal on 25 July 1938:

> Benjamin is here. He is writing an essay on Baudelaire. There is good stuff there, he shows how the project of an age without history distorted literature after [18]48. The Versailles victory of the bourgeoisie over the Commune was discounted in advance. They came to terms with evil. It took the form of a flower. This is useful to read. Oddly enough it is spleen that enables Benjamin to write this. He uses as his point of departure something he calls the *aura*, which is connected with dreaming (daydreams), he says: if you feel a gaze directed at you, even at your back, you return it (!) The expectation that what you look at will look back at you creates the aura. This is supposed to be in a decline of late, along with the cult element of life. Benjamin has discovered this while analysing films, where the aura is decomposed by the reproducibility of the art-work. A load of mysticism, although his attitude is against mysticism. This is the way the materialist understanding of history is adapted. It is abominable.[70]

Between Benjamin's texts ('The Paris of the Second Empire in Baudelaire' and 'Central Park') and Brecht's comments ('Die Schönheit in den Gedichten des Baudelaire', 'Beauty in the Poetry of Baudelaire'), there developed a dialogue, which took place largely on paper, as a reaction from Brecht, without direct confrontation. Their differences of opinion concerned Baudelaire's political attitude, his topicality and the poetic quality of his writing. Benjamin saw Baudelaire as a representative of his time: 'In the historical action which the proletariat brings against the bourgeois class, Baudelaire is a witness.'[71] He wanted to show 'Baudelaire as he is embedded in the nineteenth century'.[72] Brecht 'replied': 'In no way does [Baudelaire] express his epoch, not even ten years of it.'[73] For Benjamin, 'in this poetry nothing is yet outdated',[74] whereas Brecht wrote: 'He will not be understood for long; already too much commentary is necessary.'[75]

Both saw Baudelaire as representative of the petty bourgeoisie – but with different value judgements. Benjamin understood Baudelaire's social status as a camouflage; for him Baudelaire was a 'secret agent' – an 'agent of the secret discontent of his class with its own rule'.[76] He attempted to trace the revolutionary dimension of Baudelaire's writing in its affinity with the political concept of Auguste Blanqui: 'To put Baudelaire side by side with Blanqui is to rescue him'. The *Fleurs du Mal* became in his reading 'the poetic counterpart to Blanqui's revolt': 'Blanqui's action was the sister of Baudelaire's dream.'[77] Brecht violently disagreed, naming reactionary and parasitic features: 'Baudelaire is the poet of the French petty bourgeoisie in an age when it was already certain that the lackey services it had rendered the upper-middle class in the bloody suppression of the working class would not be rewarded.'[78] The divergence of Benjamin and Brecht over Baudelaire's political position led to aphoristic confrontation: Brecht reacted to Benjamin's judgement that 'Blanqui's action was the sister of Baudelaire's dream' with the mocking remark: 'Baudelaire is the stab in Blanqui's back. Blanqui's defeat is his Pyrrhic victory.'* While Benjamin praised the aesthetic value of Baudelaire's poetry and its novelty value,† Brecht discerned only empty ballast, affectation and clichés, only reluctantly conceding 'a certain beauty'.‡

The controversy over Kafka had flared up over Benjamin's efforts to merge varying traditions; in Brecht's divergent views on Baudelaire, however, there was no fundamentally different methodological basis. Benjamin defended a 'sociocritical interpretation of the poet'.[79] Brecht had attacked as 'abominable' the 'remains' of non-materialist, mystical thought, among which he included Benjamin's concept of 'aura', the cultic, the experience of the response to a gaze, which indeed is not free from mystical characteristics (see p. 169 above). In a note to his *Arcades* Project, Benjamin himself spoke of the '"metaphysical" determination of *Spleen*'.[80] Brecht was referring to observations such as the following from 'On Some Motifs in Baudelaire':

> What was inevitably felt to be inhuman – one might even say deadly – in daguerreotype was the (prolonged) looking into the camera, since the camera records our likeness without returning our gaze. Inherent in the gaze, however, is the expectation that it will be returned by that on which it is bestowed. Where this expectation is met (which, in the case of thought processes, can apply equally to an intentional gaze of awareness and to a glance pure and simple), there is an experience [*Erfahrung*] of the aura in all its fullness.[81]

---

* GBA 22/1, p. 452. See also, on the confrontation of Blanqui and Baudelaire, note J 84a, *Arcades*, p. 375.

† See 'Baudelaire's production is masterly and assured from the beginning' (*Arcades*, p. 243) and '*Les Fleurs du Mal* is the first book of poetry to use not only words of ordinary provenance but words of urban origin as well' (*SW*, vol. 4, p. 62).

‡ GBA 22/1, pp. 450–3: 'His words are used like worn-out clothes, "as good as new" again. His images seem framed, and everything is overstuffed. What should be sublime is only affected.'

It was not only 'elements' like these, which could not be assimilated, as far as Brecht was concerned; Baudelaire's representative position in history also became a contentious issue. The Baudelaire debate, however, went beyond the confrontation of their views. Benjamin picked up Brecht's objections and suggestions when he revised his Baudelaire study. Brecht was subsequently able to relate to Baudelaire in a way that was free from his brusque rejection of 1938.* Brecht, the poet, unmistakably cast doubt on his own verdict when, probably prompted by Benjamin's work, he began to adapt some poems of Baudelaire's.† His translation of the third section of 'Les Petites Vieilles' has been called 'a striking and paradoxical approach to the style of the French original': 'Brecht proves how different, that is, how much less "poetic", less precious, less emotional a German Baudelaire could have appeared, who was not prefigured by the great but unbalanced achievement of [Stefan] George.'[82] Perhaps the actual benefit of this exemplary dispute lay in productive interpretation through adaptation. How little, moreover, Brecht's lack of understanding was capable of overshadowing his friendship with Benjamin can be gauged from the statement by the latter already quoted, that 'communication' during that summer had been 'more natural' and 'relaxed', 'much less problematical ... than I had been used to'.[83]

On Brecht's mistrust, expressed in his reproach that Benjamin's adaptation of the materialist conception of history was 'abominable', Gershom Scholem remarked:

> Benjamin's painstaking alertness and his emphasis on the identity of views could not conceal the fact that something had to be excluded. Brecht was visibly disturbed by the theological element in Benjamin. Benjamin was not unaware of the fact, nor did he conceal it from me.[84]

Scholem's view of Brecht's feelings about the theological element in Benjamin is relevant to a comment by Hans Mayer, who circulated a later statement of Brecht's to Bloch. When the conversation turned to Benjamin and his 'social stance', Brecht said: 'I know my Benjamins...'[85] This sounds inoffensive, even

---

* Rosemarie Heise has pointed out traces of Brecht's reception of Baudelaire in his work. In *The Good Person of Setzuan* and in *The Days of the Commune* there is an echo of the closing verses of Baudelaire's poem 'La Crépuscule du Matin' (see Heise's foreword to her edition of Benjamin, *Das Paris des Second Empire bei Baudelaire*, Berlin/Weimar, 1971, p. 19). Lorenz Jäger has drawn my attention to a further parallel: the meeting-places of the conspirators, the wine-merchants' bars with their wine-fumes, also appear in Brecht's *Caesar* novel. In fact, Benjamin and Brecht, as we know from a note in 'Central Park', did talk about the *odeur de futailles* ('the reek of wine-casks') in 'Le Vin des Chiffoniers' (*SW*, vol. 4, p. 177).

† A reference to a further attempt at translation is in *Arcades*, p. 354: Benjamin quotes a half-line from Baudelaire's poem 'Bohémiens en voyage' in Brecht's version.

if Brecht's allusion to the Pappenheimer quotation (a quotation from Schiller's play *Wallenstein's Death*, 'Those are my Pappenheimers all right') recalls not the appreciative tone of Schiller's General Wallenstein, but rather the derogatory one of colloquial language. Nevertheless, the impression that the differences between them could hardly be more basic should be seen in context. These were discussions between like-minded people; quarrels were part of lively discussion and were based on a closeness, intimacy and accord that could accommodate conflicts. Neither did differences of opinion of this kind lead to a renunciation of practical solidarity. Brecht had criticized Benjamin's Baudelaire study, but he did not totally reject the essay. He repeatedly enquired about news of its publication, for example in December via Margarete Steffin: 'Why aren't they publishing your Baudelaire? Brecht would be very interested to know the reasons. He would like you to write about this in rather more detail.'[86]

In February 1939, Brecht reacted to the difficulties Benjamin's text was experiencing with the Institute for Social Research by offering to publish the piece he had criticized in *Das Wort*: 'Br. also asks if part of "Baudelaire" would not be suitable for *Das Wort*, perhaps you could get it ready when you have finished with the "Commentary"? That would really be good, and interesting.'[87] Benjamin thanked Brecht 'for his invitation to think of *Das Wort* in connection with the Baudelaire', and informed him that he was working on a new version of the rejected text, which would be published in the *Zeitschrift für Sozialforschung*.*

From the period after Benjamin's death, there are few records of Brecht's views on Benjamin, but these at least show that he maintained his high opinion of his friend's work. What became particularly clear was Brecht's immediate reaction to the theses on the philosophy of history. Benjamin had intended to send Brecht a copy of 'On the Concept of History'.† Retrospectively, Brecht's positive attitude confirms that Benjamin was right to envisage him as one of the

---

* Benjamin to Steffin, 20 March 1939, *GB* VI, pp. 243ff. In mid May 1939, Steffin inquired about the piece: 'What is happening with Baudelaire? Has the American journal published part of it?' (ibid., p. 301). Benjamin replied in letters to Steffin, reporting (in early June 1939) that he was working on the revision of the text demanded by Adorno (*Benjamin Correspondence*, p. 608), and (on 6 August) that he had completed it: 'Now I'm awaiting the storm clouds that will break over my head over *this* text' (*GB* IV, p. 327).

† This emerges from a letter from Benjamin's sister Dora to Karl Thieme of 20 September 1943, in Geret Luhr (ed.), 'was noch begraben lag', in *Zu Walter Benjamins Exil – Briefe und Dokumente*, Berlin, 2000, p. 278: 'I hasten to reply to you, because I would like to draw your attention to an essay of my brother's which was presumably his last completed work. He finished it in February or March 1940 and I myself helped him to prepare a version of his manuscript in such a way that he could get it past the censors to other countries. At the time, he intended to send a copy of the essay to Brecht and one or more to Switzerland (to Professor Lieb?).'

first readers of the theses: 'In short, the little treatise is clear and presents complex issues simply (despite its metaphors and its Judaisms), and it is frightening to think how few people there are who are prepared even at least to misunderstand such a piece.'[88]

These theses provide an insight into the productive communication between Brecht and Benjamin on questions about the philosophy of history. What is of interest here is not who first hit upon a thought and who then adopted it, nor should the discussion be taken out of the context of the contemporary discourse of exile. Rather does the development of their, in part, astonishing closeness throw interesting light on the reciprocal influences of their individual stances and respective approaches.

Benjamin and Brecht rejected the optimism of belief in progress. In a note of about 1931 Brecht criticized the Socialists' 'very dynamic concept of progress' which had had 'detrimental consequences for the concept of dialectic'.[89] In the theses 'On the Concept of History' Benjamin dismissed the Social Democrats' 'conception of progress'.* With their automatic rejection of the idea of progress, and fearing that fascism might be victorious – that progress and catastrophe would become synonymous – they were both in opposition to the communist movement's certainty of victory.†

Doubts about a world-view dependent on the 'infinite perfectibility of humanity'[90] allowed categories such as interruption, destruction and discontinuity to appear in a new light. 'What characterizes revolutionary classes at the moment of action is the awareness that they are about to make the continuum of history explode.,' Benjamin wrote in his Thesis XV.[91] In connection with his work on Baudelaire, Benjamin had noted a remark made by Brecht in conversation, probably in the summer of 1938:

> Observation by Brecht: the proletariat lives at a slower rate than the bourgeoisie. The examples set by its fighters, the realizations of its leaders, do not go out of date. At any rate, they date more slowly than the eras and the great figures of the bourgeoisie. The waves of fashion

---

* See Theses XI and XIII (*SW*, vol. 4, pp. 393–5), and also Brecht's notes on *Galileo* (in Brecht, *Collected Plays*, vol. 5, pp. 189–233).

† See Thesis X (*SW*, vol. 4, p. 393) and Brecht's statement in conversation with Benjamin that he believed the inception of an era without history to be more likely than victory over fascism (op. cit., vol. 3, p. 340), and also a note reading: 'The catastrophe is progress, progress is the catastrophe.' 'Like Gramsci they [Brecht and Benjamin] were distinguished from the official Communist movement of the thirties by a deep historical pessimism into which, according to Romain Rolland's formula, "Pessimism of the Intellect, Optimism of the Will", they planted seedlings of hope, and upon which they grounded a dialectical understanding of past and future' (Stanley Mitchell, Introduction to *Understanding Brecht*, p. ix).

break on the *rochers de bronze* of the proletariat. On the other hand, after their victory, the movements of the bourgeoisie always have a fashionable element.[92]

This statement, whose gestus conceals its visionary, even illusory features, went through notable transformations in Benjamin's theses. In his variants on 'Baudelaire', Benjamin even anticipated them: 'the quotation as principle of discontinuity – "quoting history" – further: discontinuity as regulative idea of the bourgeois, continuity as regulative idea of the proletarian tradition'.[93]

From the viewpoint of historical and aesthetic philosophy, in the debates of around 1930 in which Benjamin and Brecht took part, concepts such as 'smashing [the state]' and 'bursting open' were used. This symptomatic loss of faith in progress, continuity and uniformity has practical consequences. These are the roots in intellectual history for the validation of categories important to the aesthetic avant-garde, such as interruption, 'separation of elements', shock, quotation, detail, fragment, montage, experiment. That historical distance is a condition of knowledge, that what separates past from present should not be blurred, is a functional, pragmatic consideration expressed in Brecht's 'Short Organum', relevant to this context, and is similarly to be found in Benjamin (in his *Origin of Tragic Drama* and in the *Arcades Project*).*

From the contribution of literature to changing the world, there emerged the duty to sift through the past for its unreleased factors, to track down the 'secret agreement between past generations and the present one'.[94] Memory and 'mindfulness' are driving forces of aesthetic and theoretical work, because they can refer to unfinished business and thus construct the 'time filled by now-time [*Jetztzeit*]'[95] outside history.† Benjamin's *Arcades* work is a symbolic attempt at

---

* See Brecht's 'Appendices to the Short Organum' (no. 12), in *Brecht on Theatre*, p. 276, and Benjamin, *The Origin of Tragic Drama*, pp. 53–4. And in the *Arcades Project* we find: 'In order for a part of the past to be touched by the present (*Aktualität*), there must be no continuity between them' (op. cit., p. 470).

† Brecht's *Tales from the Calendar*, for instance, were written in the consciousness of this claim. The function of the calendar, to create 'days of remembrance' 'in time-lapse mode', is described by Benjamin in Thesis XV of 'On the Concept of History' (*SW*, vol. 4, p. 395). Benjamin understood the closing lines of Brecht's poem 'To Those Born Later' ('Think of us / With forbearance') as a challenge to remembrance: 'As an example of genuine historical imagination: Brecht's "To Those Born Later" – from those born later we ask not thanks for our victories but remembrance of our defeats' (*GS* I/3, p. 1240). Similarly, in a variant to the theses of 'On the Concept of History': 'What we should expect from those born later is not thanks for our great deeds, but reflection on our defeats – if any generation should know this, it must be our own' (*GS* VII, p. 783). Tony Phelan establishes the connection between Benjamin's concept of history and the *Svendborg Poems* (in his chapter 'Figures of Memory in the "Chroniken"', in Ronald Speirs (ed), *Brecht's Poetry of Political Exile*, Cambridge, 2000, pp. 172–89).

resistance through evocative recall, through the reconstruction of the past, which corresponds to Brecht's anti-fascist objectives.* 'Today passes into tomorrow, nourished by yesterday,' Brecht was to write in 1954: 'History may make a clean sweep, but fears emptiness.'[96] Culture is, we know from Benjamin, 'never free from barbarism'.[97] 'There is a tradition that is catastrophe.'[98] 'Cultural treasures' carried along in the 'triumphal procession' of the rulers 'in every case have a lineage' which the 'historical materialist' 'cannot contemplate without horror'.[99] At the head of his seventh thesis, in which he developed this thought, Benjamin placed these lines from *The Threepenny Opera*: 'Consider the darkness and the great cold/ In this vale resounding with misery.'[100] In his literary texts, Brecht, who approved these ideas, though with an ironic undertone,† had met in exemplary fashion the challenge 'to brush history against the grain'.[101] In the poems 'Questions from a Worker Who Reads' and 'A Visit to the Banished Poets', from the *Svendborg Poems*, Benjamin himself recognized evidence of a change of direction towards 'the anonymous toil of others who lived in the same period'.[102] And in notes on his 'Commentary on Poems by Brecht' he wrote:

> The tradition of the oppressed is of concern to Brecht ('Questions from a Worker Who Reads'). The tradition of the oppressed is also the decisive factor in his vision of the banned poets. Brecht emphasizes the basis, the background, against which great 'princes of intellect' emerge. In bourgeois representations this background tends to be a uniform grey.[103]

Both saw in communism a way of overcoming oppression; the revolution appeared to them to be the obvious, necessary path − as it is portrayed in Brecht's poem of around 1931, quoted by Benjamin, 'Der Kommunismus ist das Mittlere' ('Communism is the Middle Way') : 'Communism is really the least challenge/ The most obvious thing, the middle way, the most sensible'). Resistance to a new ideology is decisive, as expressed in Benjamin's letter to Werner Kraft of 1934:

---

* Stanley Mitchell stressed the connection between the *Arcades Project* and Brecht's anti-fascist position, as Brecht outlined it for example in conversation with Benjamin: 'In the struggle against them [the fascists], it is vital that nothing be overlooked... Every cell convulses under their blow. So we mustn't forget a single one' (*SW*, vol. 3, p. 340); see Mitchell, 'Big Ideas' (review of Susan Buck-Morss, *The Dialectics of Seeing: Walter Benjamin and the Arcades Project*), in *Oxford Art Journal*, vol. 16, no. 1, 1993 p. 144).

† See *Journals*, 22 August 1942, p. 255. The entry refers to Hans Reichenbach: 'Saving the nation's works of art keeps him awake at night, whereas it puts me to sleep. In vain we explain to him that art-works have assumed the same character as artefacts in general, namely they have become commercial commodities. A Beethoven symphony merely subjects the proletarian to the remaining 'culture', and this is barbaric to him.'

You admit that for the time being you do not want to accept communism 'as the solution for humanity'. But of course the issue is precisely to abolish the unproductive pretensions of solutions for humanity by means of the feasible findings of this very system; indeed, to give up entirely the immodest prospect of 'total' systems and at least to make the attempt to construct the days of humanity in just as loose a fashion as a rational person who has had a good night's sleep begins his day.[104]

In a similar way, in 1936, in his essay 'Die biblische Botschaft und Karl Marx' ('The Bible Message and Karl Marx'), Fritz Lieb wrote that Communist society led 'to the threshold of a period of human history where, as Walter Benjamin well expresses it, "the experience of humanity can first be created"'.* It may have been thoughts such as these that prompted Benjamin to bring to Brecht's attention the work of the dialectical theologian and political thinker Lieb. In August 1936, writing from Skovsbostrand, he wrote to Lieb asking him to send the latest issue of the journal *Orient und Occident*, which Lieb edited, and which contained Lieb's article.† Lieb complied with Benjamin's wish; at any rate, the journal is present in Brecht's library.

In Brecht's journal note, already quoted, about Benjamin's theses on the philosophy of history, he wrote:

> The little treatise deals with historical research, and could have been written after reading my 'Caesar' (which B. could not make much of when he read it in Svendborg). B. rejects the notion of history as a continuum, the notion of progress as a mighty enterprise undertaken by cool, clear heads, the notion of work as the source of morality, of the workforce as protégés of technology, etc. He makes fun of the common remark about its being astonishing that fascism 'should still be possible in our century' (as if it were not the fruit of every century).[105]

Certainly the theses were not prompted by the 'Caesar' fragment, of which Benjamin had hardly taken any notice. Benjamin had preserved the intellectual substance of the theses in his mind for 'some twenty years', and had already revealed elements of them in his essay, 'The Life of Students', of 1914–15.[106] But Brecht probably did not mean his statement quite so literally. However, the

---

* *Orient und Occident*, Bern/Leipzig, new series (1936), no. 2, p. 12. See Chryssoula Kambas, *Walter Benjamin im Exil*, p. 207. The quotation from a conversation with Benjamin in Paris is emphasized in the original.

† Benjamin, postcard to Fritz Lieb, 13 August 1936, Benjamin-Lieb correspondence, pp. 254ff.: 'I am very sorry that, inexplicably, I left the last issue of *Orient und Okzident* in Paris. As it is very important to me to acquaint B[recht] with your work, I would be very pleased if you would send a copy to me here.' Benjamin's postcard to Lieb is missing from the six-volume edition of Benjamin's letters.

correspondence in intention and concept between *Die Geschäften des Herrn Julius Caesar* ('The Business Affairs of Mr Julius Caesar') and the theses 'On the Concept of History' is by no means accidental. Brecht's sentence, 'The triumphs of the commanders were triumphs over the people', is reminiscent of the 'triumphal procession' of the rulers.[107] History books are written by rulers and 'of course show our view of things to the best advantage'.* Like the theses, the novel insists on the meeting of challenges posed in the past.†

The conviction that humanity would not be able to come to terms with misery and the deprivation of its rights was characteristic of the thoughts of both Benjamin and Brecht on the concept of 'happiness'. Benjamin wrote in his theses: 'In other words, the idea of happiness is indissolubly bound up with the idea of redemption.'[108] Brecht's project for an opera, *Die Reisen des Glücksgotts* ('The Travels of the God of Happiness'), of the nineteen forties, corresponds to motifs of Benjamin's such as happiness, disaster, salvation: a messenger with singed wings, in the Brecht, recalls the 'angel of history', even if the latter is nourished from other sources.[109] Benjamin's angel sees in the past 'one single catastrophe, which keeps piling wreckage upon wreckage.'[110] Brecht's messenger, close to earth, materialistic, draws in his train 'a furrow of excesses and manslaughter'.

Brecht tried to encourage the posthumous publication of Walter Benjamin's works. A note among his papers shows that he took part in efforts to collect and publish Benjamin's writings. In one of his notebooks he recorded the addresses of Hannah Arendt, Gershom Scholem and Stefan Benjamin, adding the keywords 'Benjamin' and 'bibliography'.‡ He noted Hannah Arendt's address as 'c/o Jewish Cultural Reconstruction' – the institution on whose behalf she was in Europe in 1949. The note, which also suggests its context, is probably to be dated to a visit by Arendt to Berlin after Brecht's return there. There had already been efforts to deal with Benjamin's literary estate – for example, in a conversation between Brecht and Heinrich Blücher, which Hannah Arendt reported in a letter to Brecht of 15 October 1946:

> Dear Herr Brecht,
>   When Blücher spoke to you some time ago about Benjamin's literary estate, you also discussed the possibility of finding a publisher for Benjamin. Schocken-Verlag, which you presumably remember from

---

* See *The Trial of Lucullus*: 'Always / the victor writes the history of the vanquished' (Brecht, *Collected Plays*, vol. 4, p. 386).

† On the correspondence between Benjamin's philosophy of history and Brecht's *Caesar* novel, see Herbert Claas, *Die politische Ästhetik Bertolt Brechts vom Baal zum Caesar*, pp. 165–70, and Richard Faber, *Cäsarismus – Bonapartismus – Faschismus*, pp. 17–22.

‡ The note is preserved in the Brecht Archive.

Germany, and which is now bringing out a collected German edition of Kafka's work, wants to publish a volume of collected essays by Benjamin in English. For this, naturally, I need your help.

You will probably know that Dora, Benjamin's sister, died this summer in Switzerland. I have not the slightest idea who owns the rights to Benjamin's estate, or if anyone has them at all. Perhaps you know something about this.

For the volume of essays I would suggest the following:

1. 'Elective Affinities'; 2. 'Baudelaire'; 3. 'Kafka' (in an expanded version); 4. 'Kunst des Erzaehlens' (published by Lieb just before the war); 5. 'Karl Kraus' (*Frankfurter Zeitung*, 1932); 6. Perhaps 'The Work of Art in the Age of Its Technological Reproducibility'; 7. The theses on the philosophy of history; 8. The conversations with Brecht. –

I would like to have your views on my suggestions, or additional suggestions. Further, of course, the 'Conversations with Brecht' with your notes (of which you held out a prospect to Blücher). And last but not least, if you would like, an essay on Benjamin (or whatever you would like to call such a thing).

I know that you hardly ever reply to letters. (At least, that is your reputation.) What am I to do? The dead can hardly insist, and I am a poor representative.

Yours sincerely,

Hannah Arendt[111]

What is remarkable about this letter is not only the early plan for an American edition of Benjamin,* which shows Hannah Arendt's very full knowledge of his work, but the matter-of-fact way in which she proposes that the 'Conversations with Brecht' – that is, Benjamin's records of the Svendborg conversations – should be made part of this edition. Brecht's Literary Estate includes the notes of 1931 from the south of France with the story of the dog-rose and peonies, conversations about Trotsky, Kafka, 'living' and 'inhabiting', and Brecht's early years, which were probably already in Brecht's possession in the nineteen forties. It is doubtful whether Brecht would have considered publishing the later records, above all the explosive ones about the Soviet Union and Stalin of 1938; in fact, it is even improbable that he knew they existed at all.

It is clear that Brecht – with Adorno, Scholem, Hannah Arendt, Bloch, Peter

---

* A year earlier Arendt had already mentioned the intention that Schocken should publish Benjamin's posthumous works, without, however, entertaining hopes of the publisher's agreement. See Arendt to Gershom Scholem, 22 September 1945, in Scholem, *Briefe I*, Munich, 1994, p. 449.

Suhrkamp and a few others – contributed, even after returning from exile, to the publication once more in Germany of Walter Benjamin's texts.[112] The reprinting of 'On Some Motifs in Baudelaire' in the fourth issue of the first volume of *Sinn und Form* could have been arranged through Brecht, who followed with great interest the initial phase of this journal.* Benjamin's 'Baudelaire' 'filled one of the gaps that had formed in discussions on cultural politics'; its reprinting had a programmatic quality, and it 'could be read as a polemic against constrictions'.[113] The editor of *Sinn und Form*, Peter Huchel, had consciously juxtaposed Benjamin's essay with 'Odysseus or Myth and Enlightenment' from *Dialectic of Enlightenment* by Horkheimer and Adorno, whose theoretical basis, however, was not destined, any more than Benjamin's, to be of influence in the German Democratic Republic.[114]

Brecht's interest in the publication of Benjamin's works after his death is shown by his comment during a conversation with Werner Kraft and Peter Huchel in the summer of 1955 in Berlin. As Kraft remembered, they had been talking about the literary estates of Georg Heym and Walter Benjamin: 'He was deeply interested in both, and wanted them to be published, whether in the West or the East did not matter.'† An indirect indication that Brecht's high opinion of Benjamin was sustained up to the time of his own death can be found in a letter from Elisabeth Hauptmann to Peter Suhrkamp of 13 October 1955:

> I am most grateful for the attractive little book, *Dichten und Trachten* ('Writing and Striving'), which contains much of interest, including, at last, the work of Walter Benjamin. Perhaps you could tell Dr Unseld that – if it is not a presumptuous request – we would like to have another six copies.‡

It is likely that the request for further copies came from Brecht; certainly he joined in the approval of the publication of Benjamin's writings as announced in the Suhrkamp yearbook.

---

* Brecht's copy of the issue of *Sinn und Form* has its pages cut only up to page 9, but of course he knew the text from conversations, the manuscript, or its first publication in the *Zeitschrift für Sozialforschung*; in any case, he may have had access to another copy of that issue of *Sinn und Form*.

† Werner Kraft, 'Gedanken über Brecht', in *Neue Zürcher Zeitung*, 16 October 1965, p. 21. Gershom Scholem, on the other hand, gained the impression from a conversation with Brecht in 1949 that 'the dead Benjamin was no longer of interest to Brecht' (see Gerhard Seidel, 11 October 1966, evening at Frau Hauptmann's: conversation with Prof. Gershom Scholem [Notes in the Brecht Archive]).

‡ BBA 789/121. See *Dichten und Trachten*, the Suhrkamp Verlag yearbook, Berlin and Frankfurt am Main, no. VI (Autumn 1955), including an essay by Adorno on Benjamin; Benjamin's 'On the Mimetic Faculty'; and a scene from Brecht's *Life of Galileo*.

Among Brecht's papers are the following manuscripts of Benjamin's: the two essays both entitled 'What is Epic Theatre?', two versions of 'Brecht's Threepenny Novel', the essay 'L'Opéra de Quat' Sous', fragments of the commentary on the poems, and in addition notes, journal entries and letters. In his library, apart from the issue of *Das Wort* with the first 'Paris Letter' (no. 5, 1936), there are only the new edition of *One-Way Street* from the Bibliothek Suhrkamp of 1955 and three xerox copies from the period after 1949.* But caution is advisable here: only isolated examples have been preserved even of Brecht's own publications before 1948. Also, manuscripts, copies and offprints that Benjamin had sent him are missing. Finally, it can be regarded as certain that Brecht owned the two-volume edition of Benjamin's writings edited by Theodor W. Adorno, Gretel Adorno and Friedrich Podszus in 1955. After all, it was there that the complete version of the 'Commentary on Brecht's Poems' was published for the first time and, in addition, Brecht was usually sent copies of such books by the publishers, Suhrkamp, who were his publisher too. So the gaps are rather an indication of the fact that the interest in Benjamin's writings was not – unfortunately for Brecht – restricted to him.

Four Epitaphs

The news of Benjamin's death did not reach Brecht until the summer of 1941, a few days after his arrival in California. When he recorded it in his diary, the suicide had taken place more than ten months earlier:

> Walter Benjamin has poisoned himself in some little Spanish border town. The *Guardia Civil* had stopped the little group he belonged to. When the others went to tell him the next morning that they were being allowed to carry on, they found him dead.[115]

Brecht's source was Günther Anders, who owed his knowledge of Benjamin's ill-fated flight to Hannah Arendt.† She herself preserved a reaction by Brecht to the news of Benjamin's death which is not recorded elsewhere: '...recognition came ... from Bertolt Brecht who upon receiving the news of Benjamin's

---

* The copy of *One-Way Street* contains no signs of having been read, or any marked passages. The copied items consist of the version, already mentioned, of 'On Some Motifs in Baudelaire' in *Sinn und Form*, an abridged reprint of the Fuchs essay in the anthology *Deutsches Vermächtnis*, edited by Bruno Kaiser (Berlin, 1952), and a reprint of 'The Task of the Translator' in the reader *Deutscher Geist* (Berlin and Frankfurt, 1953).

† See Arendt, *Men in Dark Times*, pp. 168–9. Günther Anders confirmed the content: 'It is true that it was I who gave Brecht the news of Walter's death. In Santa Monica. I had received the news from Hannah Arendt (to whom I had been married earlier)' (Anders to the author, 23 September 1988).

death is reported to have said that this was the first real loss that Hitler had caused German literature.'[116]

Anders believed this 'alleged remark on Benjamin's death to be very unlikely, since several of the prominent émigrés had already disappeared from our ranks (through suicide) (for example Toller)'.* Certainly, Brecht's remark makes no claim to validity in terms of literary history, since it disregarded the deaths or the literary achievements of notable victims of Hitler: Theodor Lessing, Erich Mühsam, Kurt Tucholsky, Carl von Ossietzky, Ernst Toller, Joseph Roth and Rudolf Olden had fallen victim, directly or indirectly, to the Nazi thugs; in 1940 Ernst Weiss, Walter Hasenclever and Carl Einstein had escaped the Gestapo through suicide. Brecht would not have intended to bring a balance-sheet mentality to bear on such losses, even though Benjamin was undoubtedly closer to him both personally and as a literary figure than any of the others. And yet the subjectivity of the remark is symptomatic. Brecht transferred his grief for his friend into a seemingly objective judgement. This attitude also characterized his poems on Benjamin's death.†

Brecht made Benjamin's fate the theme of four poems: 'Die Verlustliste' ('Casualty List'), 'Wo ist Benjamin, der Kritiker?' ('Where is Benjamin, the Critic?'), 'Zum Freitod des Flüchtlings W. B.' ('On the Suicide of the Refugee W. B.') and 'An Walter Benjamin, der sich auf der Flucht vor Hitler entleibte' ('To Walter Benjamin Who Killed Himself Fleeing from Hitler'). It is not known when they were written, presumably immediately after Brecht had received the news of Benjamin's death, between the end of July and September 1941. The texts, in Brecht's papers, were not published until 1964 and 1990; a possibility for publication that arose in 1942 was, for unknown reasons, not taken up. There had been a plan to ask Brecht for a contribution to the commemorative text put together by the Institute for Social Research in the spring of 1942, under the title 'In Memory of Walter Benjamin'. The suggestion had come from Max Horkheimer, whom Brecht saw repeatedly in Los Angeles at this time, and who wrote to Leo Löwenthal, the editor of the volume, urging him to include 'some pages from Brecht', 'so that the issue would really be an homage to Benjamin. You know that Brecht was an intimate friend of

---

* Günther Anders to the author, 23 September 1988. See also, in the same letter: 'The remark that Br. made, according to H. A., about the meaning of B.'s death is one that I did not hear from Br's mouth; it must therefore have reached H. A. through someone else. Through whom, I do not know.'

† See James K. Lyon, *Bertolt Brecht in America*, Princeton, 1980, p. 37: 'Two poems Brecht wrote about Benjamin at this time (August 1941), especially a four-line commemorative, give the appearance of an objective statement. By refusing to express grief, these poems, like scenes in some of his plays, become that much more powerful through their control of undeniable emotion.'

Benjamin's.'[117] Although Löwenthal welcomed Horkheimer's suggestion,[118] the commemorative volume, in which Benjamin's theses 'On the Concept of History' were published for the first time, contained no contribution from Brecht; it is more likely that Brecht – if indeed he was asked – did not deliver anything, than that whatever he submitted was rejected.*

The first poem is a stocktaking exercise.

Casualty List

Fleeing from a sinking ship, embarking on another sinking one
– with still no new one in sight – I note
On a little scrap of paper the names of those
No longer around me.
My little teacher from the working class
Margarete Steffin. In the middle of the lesson
Exhausted from flight
The little wise one sank down and died.
In the same way *Walter Benjamin* left me –
My sparring-partner, so learned
Always seeking after the new.
At the impassable frontier
Tired of persecution, he lay down.
No more did he wake from sleep...

At the beginning of the list is the description of a situation. It expands the biographical experience into a historical one – Brecht's landing in San Pedro, California, on 21 July 1941: the joy of having solid ground beneath one's feet again, and the doubt as to whether the ground is really solid. The sinking ship from which the speaker in the poem is fleeing is not the *Annie Johnson*, the Swedish freighter in which Brecht sailed with his family from Vladivostok on 13 June, but the old continent, Europe, where war is raging. The sinking ship he boards would then be the new world, America. 'The rats are boarding the sinking ship' had been Karl Kraus's greeting in Austria in 1933. There, the pessimism arose from being next-door neighbour to Hitler's Germany, which was to end in the Anschluss, whereas Brecht saw the lack of future, which he

---

* The mimeographed commemorative publication contained, apart from the theses, the essays 'George und Hofmannsthal' by Adorno, and 'Autoritärer Staat' and 'Vernunft und Selbsterhaltung' ('Reason and Survival') by Horkheimer, as well as a bibliographical note on Benjamin's work. Löwenthal did not remember the plan to involve Brecht in the commemorative publication, and did not believe he had corresponded with Brecht about the Benjamin Festschrift. It was more likely that Horkheimer or Adorno had spoken to Brecht about it (Löwenthal to the author, 7 November 1988).

predicted in the USA, as based most acutely on the war, from which he had just escaped over the ocean, and in the endemically imperialist economy. The lack of perspective – 'No new one in sight' – characterizes the whole poem. Unlike the people named, the speaker can cherish his security, but it is a provisional security; the danger has not yet been forgotten. In view of this experience, the conclusions acquire particular importance. The motif of the naming of friends who have died or disappeared corresponds to Po Chü-i's poem, 'Separation'.* The concept of a 'casualty list' recalls an inventory kept by a bookkeeper. But what follows is not an official record; the list is a little scrap of paper which avoids bureaucratic formality, and the way the dead are described allows the loss to be recognized as a personal one. This summary avoids the grand gesture, and grief is kept under control, like the deaths which the speaker knows to have been 'exhausted' and 'weary'. Lament and accusation are undemonstrative, but unmistakable.

> *Where is Benjamin, the Critic?*
>
> Where is Benjamin, the critic?
> Where is Warschauer, the radio broadcaster?
> Where is Steffin, the teacher?
> Benjamin is buried on the Spanish border.
> Warschauer is buried in Holland.
> Steffin is buried in Moscow.
> I drive along the bomber-hangars of Los Angeles

This unfinished text corresponds to the poem 'Casualty List' without being part of it. The situation and register of the speaker are different, and the people about whose deaths there is certainty are also not the same. The fragment 'Where is Benjamin, the Critic?' is more austere than 'Casualty List'. The speakers' companions are sufficiently characterized by the professional descriptions, 'critic', 'broadcaster' and 'teacher'; these are subjective concepts – Margarete Steffin, as we know, was not a teacher, Brecht only called her one, and 'broadcaster' as a concept is rather unusual. The parallel, artless formulations for inquiring about the friends' whereabouts and naming the places where they are buried are effective. The seventh line, finally, provides a description of the speaker's situation, which is open to interpretation: 'I drive along the bomber-hangars of Los Angeles.' This could at first sight mean: I, unlike the dead, have escaped. But the buildings being passed are not accidentally identified. They show that the resistance to the terrorism to which Benjamin,

* Brecht knew Po Chü-i's poem 'Separation' from Arthur Waley's *One Hundred and Seventy Chinese Poems*, which he used for his own adaptations.

Warschauer and Steffin fell victim requires bombs. The laconic, hopeless ring of the final line, however, suggests that it is doubtful whether the bombs have the power to overcome this terrorism.

On the Suicide of the Refugee W. B.

I'm told you raised your hand against yourself
Anticipating the butcher.
After eight years in exile, observing the rise of the enemy
Then at last, brought up against an impassable frontier
You passed, they say, a passable one.
Empires collapse. Gang leaders
Are strutting about like statesmen. The peoples
Can no longer be seen under all those armaments.
So the future lies in darkness and the forces of right
Are weak. All this was plain to you
When you destroyed a torturable body.

The poems 'On the Suicide of the Refugee W. B.' and 'To Walter Benjamin Who Killed Himself While Fleeing from Hitler' (below) are epitaphs, obituaries in a narrow sense, which pick up elements from the biography of Brecht's dead friend. On the typescript of 'On the Suicide of the Refugee W. B.' is a hasty, handwritten comment: 'Only a strong arm/ is able to lift the weapon'. Rather than a commonplace remark about virtues in the war against the 'butcher', this could be – perhaps with a reference to the opening lines of the poem – a restrained recognition of Benjamin's courage in preferring death to a hopeless situation without freedom. The effect of the poem rests on contradictions and paradoxes, for example, when the border between two countries, in this case France and Spain, is called 'impassable' and is thus less permeable than the passage between life and death, whose finality is called 'passable'. The structure and formulations of speech are similar to those of Brecht's first poem about Karl Kraus, 'On the Meaning of the Ten-line Poem in No. 888 of *Die Fackel* (October 1933)', and of the obituary for Carl von Ossietzky, 'On the Death of a Fighter for Peace'. The apparently succinct communication which in reality already represents an interpretation – the murder of Ossietzky, the message of the eloquent man (in the case of Kraus), Benjamin's suicide – is followed by the equally terse description of the situation, which nevertheless takes on a more general aspect, in paratactic turns of phrase which correspond to the epigrammatic style of the *German War Primer*: 'The gang-leaders / stride about like statesmen. The people / can't be seen for weaponry.' His friend recognized these perversions, saw no way out and killed himself. The poem laments this death.

To Walter Benjamin Who Killed Himself While Fleeing from Hitler
Tactics of attrition are what you enjoyed
Sitting at the chess table in the pear tree's shade.
An enemy who could drive you from your books
Will not be worn down by people like us.

This quatrain is addressed to the dead man, a kind of last letter, in which, as in the preceding one, Brecht changed the 'Sie' form he had used in communication to the second-person, intimate form. The poem refers to Benjamin's habit of wearing down his opponent by extending his pause for thought to the very limit. Margarete Steffin once reminded Benjamin of the summer months spent together in Skovsbostrand: 'As far as your chess-playing is concerned, I still remember your "attrition tactics". Do you still practise them?'[119] A sentence of Brecht's gives an idea of the measure of time with which Benjamin tested the patience of his opponent; he invited Benjamin to 'the northland': 'The chessboard lies orphaned, and every half hour a tremor of remembrance runs through it: that was when you made your moves.'[120]

The epitaph transfers the concept of 'attrition tactics' to the struggle of the exiles against the fascists. Hitler drove Benjamin away from his books, not only in the literal sense (he was able to rescue only a part of his beloved book collection, deposited with Brecht in Skovsbostrand). The dictator forced Benjamin to employ his energies in the struggle against him, thus dictating themes to him, robbing him of his existence, driving him into poverty, isolation and death. This poem declares that persistence against such an enemy is not enough. More is not said, but the omission suggests a challenge to find more decisive forms of resistance. The phrase 'people like us' shows that Brecht was directing it to himself as well; if that were missing, the poem could be read as a distancing of himself from Benjamin. The quatrain form lends an urgency to the poem that makes it stand out from the others: the language of verse, with its rhymes, regular rhythm and vowel sounds, evokes a summer day in the orchard at Svendborg, which is abruptly interrupted by the enemy – the sound and expressive placing of the words disturb the flow of talk.

In Brecht's poem Benjamin's death became a token of the power of fascism, whose end was unimaginable. The wait for a change was unbearable; in Finland Brecht had already coined the term 'in-between time' (*Inzwischenzeit*) for it. The news of Benjamin's death came to him in the period of his mourning for his collaborator and lover, Margarete Steffin, after a dramatically successful flight, newly arrived in a country (the USA) whose mentality was foreign to him: 'Almost nowhere has my life ever been harder than here in this mausoleum of *easy-going*.'[121] That the poems dedicated to his friend are related in tone to poems he wrote about Steffin is evidence of great closeness. The texts develop their effect in their restrained but unmistakable accusation. They bring out Benjamin's opposition to Hitler's dictatorship; his death demands rebellion against his pursuers. 'Was the fight in vain too?' Brecht had asked in his Ossietzky epitaph. 'When he who did not fight alone is done to death/ The Enemy/ Has not yet won.' This hope is not conveyed explicitly in the Benjamin poems, but the texts express resistance to death, which is a triumph by the barbarians, by keeping alive the memory of the murdered man. The historical constellation demanded an individual utterance. It is an utterance that has experienced the loss of a friend as an expression of terror, an utterance that gives universality to the grief of one individual over another individual. The poems, whose personal character as portraits is rare in Brecht's lyrical work, preserve for ever the name of the victim.* The fates of Steffin, Warschauer, Benjamin, must be spoken of if the enemy is not to have power over them. Brecht knew the warning of his friend, who wanted to fan a 'spark of hope' into flame: 'The only historian capable of fanning the spark of hope in the past is the one who is firmly convinced that *even the dead* will not be safe from the enemy if he is victorious. And this enemy has never ceased to be victorious.'[122]

---

* The exceptions are poems about historical or political personalities such as Lenin, Luxemburg, Liebknecht, Dimitrov, Ossietzky and Tretyakov, and above all the series of Steffin poems.

Documentation and Minutes of 'Krise und Kritik'

Author's Note

The following Minutes of the discussions about the projected periodical *Krise und Kritik* (see Chapter III) were never meant for publication. They were taken down by two secretaries from the Rowohlt publishing house to record aims, methods and editorial guide-lines. Despite their occasional fragmentary nature, they still present a clear enough record of what were often very lively discussions. However, it is worth noting that, in printed form, paradox and dogma tend to be reinforced. Moreover, these Minutes do not seem to have been read through, and some references and contexts, which would have been clear to the participants, remain unexplained. It is also not always possible to know if some passages are verbatim quotations, records of a contribution, or summaries of a foregoing discussion; misunderstandings by the Minute-takers have not been corrected, references are sometimes unexplained, and unfinished sentences remain. However, in order not to risk possibly misleading interpretation, these discrepancies, which are in part due to the corrupt or defective state of the original xeroxes, have been retained here. Two short passages in Document 5, where the German original was too unclear to make a translation possible, have been omitted. These are marked '[transcription incomplete]'.

The documents are set out here in thematic, not chronological, sequence. They begin with discussions and statements on questions of content and editorial principle, and they end with often fragmentary, more abstract notes, referring back to the earlier discussion. I believe that the novelty, immediacy and historical interest of this material, certainly never intended for publication, justify its reproduction.

1. Krise und Kritik *Memorandum*

This journal is to appear monthly, with no firm deadline, on the one hand to avoid hurried and rushed work, on the other to leave open the opportunity to intervene where necessary when occasion arises.

Supplements to the journal will appear three or four times a year. Their aim will be to articulate the critical and theoretical basis of the collective undertaking, which can naturally develop only gradually and tentatively in the journal itself.

The following are some of the journal's intentions:

The journal is political. By that is meant that its critical activity is consciously anchored in the critical situation of present society – that of class struggle. At the same time, however, the journal will not be party political. It is emphatically not a proletarian paper, nor an organ of the proletariat. Rather will it fill the gap of a journal in which the bourgeois intelligentsia can do justice to itself through insights and challenges that, uniquely under current circumstances, permit it an active, interventionist role, with tangible consequences, as opposed to its usual ineffective arbitrariness.

As the journal has to establish its own basis, it cannot turn to outside authorities. All the more must it find its collaborators among the bourgeois intelligentsia in the widest sense, in so far as they are specialists in a particular subject and have proved themselves not to be corrupt.

The following is a provisional list of such collaborators:

Benjamin
Borchardt (Hans Borchardt)
Brentano
Brecht
Eisler
Franzen
Giedion
Gross
Ihering
Kracauer
Korsch
Kurella
Lukács
Marcuse
Piscator

Reger
Rerich
Sternberg
Weill
Wiesengrund

Some of the above will from time to time be consulted as editorial advisers for literature, philosophy, sociology, architecture, music, etc.

So much for the journal itself. The aim of the Supplement is – independent from current affairs, but in closest contact with the respective contributions to the journal – to establish a collection of theses which can serve as guidelines for the contributors to future volumes of the journal. In other words, the journal's contributors may well want to criticize individual theses they feel they have to reject, but cannot totally ignore them in what they write. The editorial committee of the Supplement does not have to be in all circumstances unanimously in agreement over the theses or articles it either contributes itself or publishes. All such theses or contributions to the Supplement should therefore be signed by the contributor or contributors on the senior editorial committee who have either written them or declared themselves in agreement with them. It must be the ambition of all contributors to find at least one sentence of what they write in the journal taken up in the Supplement.

Work on the journal will begin in this way. A questionnaire, whose content is currently being drafted, will be sent to prospective collaborators, the answers to which – in so far as they are of interest – will be printed in the journal and, in part, in the Supplement. The questionnaires will have the character of interviews on the contributors' theoretical attitudes to their particular specialities.

2. Krise und Kritik *Constitution*

A. Organization

On 25 January 1931 a two-monthly journal is due to appear, published by Ernst Rowohlt under the title:

KRISE UND KRITIK

Editorial responsibility: Herbert Ihering.

The letterhead to read:

Edited by Herbert Ihering with the collaboration of:

Walter Benjamin Bert Brecht Bernard von Brentano Siegfried Giedion.

Each number will be edited by a three-member working committee to be nominated by the editor in consultation with the above collaborators. If insoluble differences arise in the working committee, the editor has the right to form a new one.

In all editorial matters the editor has an extra vote.

If the work of the working committee meets with the disapproval of the editor, he has the right to announce, in the same number of the journal, an article of his own in the next number or special issue.

B. Special Issues

In addition, a minimum of six special issues are to appear annually, each a maximum of two signatures. These special issues are to retain the same editor and collaborators as the journal. Their appearance will depend on current circumstances and will therefore be determined by the editor. There will be no working committee for special issues; the editor has full responsibility.

C. Administration

The publisher will provide a royalty of 25 Marks per page [to be checked]. Royalties for special issues will be the same – 25 Marks per page. In the case of the bimonthly journal itself, 5 Marks will be deducted from this royalty and paid to the working committee. This payment will be made not later than a week after publication.

For all technical matters, the publisher will put Herr Franz Hessel at the working committee's disposal and, in addition, will provide the editorial secretary Fräulein Siebert to take minutes of meetings.

3. Krise und Kritik *Minutes, c. November 1930*

PROGRAMME

The journal's field of activity is the present *crisis* in all areas of ideology, and it is the task of the journal to register this crisis or bring it about, and this by means of criticism. The entire field of historicizing and aesthetic criticism is disregarded in the process. On the contrary, such criticism is a critical target of this journal.

Topic

Aspirations, Attitude and Effect of Intellectuals in Public Life

Mannheim
Thomas Mann
Frank Thiess – Tucholsky

First essay

The Historical Role of Intellectual Leadership

Comment on the first topic (Brecht)

The intelligentsia floats freely above everything else, can't decide anything for itself, takes up a 'third' position, is influenced by no one, but still wishes to exert influence, and attempts to reconcile differences. This gives it a claim to power on account of its supposed impartiality.

——

Proposals for the first issue:

'Criticism of the attitude of intellectuals to economic questions concerning them' (German Writers' Union)

——

Development of the history of intellectuals.

——

Intellectuals as leaders in their historical attitudes.

——

For Kurella and Brecht

Suggest an author for the first subject: 'The Historical Role and Idea of Intellectual Leadership'

For Dr Benjamin: The commissioning of an essay on Thomas Mann

For Kurella: To take over the subject of [Karl] Mannheim

For Ihering: Possibly to take over an essay on Frank Thiess and Kurt Tucholsky

For von Brentano: The commissioning and editing of reports from medical, pedagogic, etc., journals.

Working committee of first number:

Ihering
Brecht
Kurella

Suggestions for subjects for future volumes of the journal:

Fascism
Anarchism
The Jews
Criticism of the legal system
Education

Special Issue: Newspaper von Brentano

Meeting of 21 November 1930

Present: Ihering, Benjamin, Brecht

First number

Brecht suggests a more 'provocative' article, for example

'Welcoming the Crisis'

or 'How to Capture the World in Five Pictures'

in addition: 'Contemporary Theatre Criticism' (for Ihering)

For the first number, something constructive, to Ihering's taste.

In addition (stimulated by an essay by Köhler):

'Research on the Intelligence of Apes'

to be undertaken by a scholar.

Is there perhaps a chance of having a detailed essay on 'Measuring Human Intelligence'?

Benjamin considers this possibly a very good question, but one which normally arises in the most turgid meetings. Only seldom is anything gained.

Is intelligence useful? The subject is not immaterial, and what we object to about such writers is not that they occupy themselves with intelligence but that they do so in the wrong way.

This subject is also relevant to the Mannheim essay.

21 November 1930

Benjamin:

'What is Intelligence?'

This subject can go together with 'Leadership and Intelligence'. On intelligence's suitability to lead. The subject of this essay can be clarified with recourse to history. Where the intelligence of leaders has sufficed and where not and why not. The subject only makes sense if anything at all can be said about intelligence's basic suitability.

Further suggestions for the first number of the journal:

On the Problems of Criticism

(We apply the same criteria to drama and literature as mathematicians and physicists, etc.)

21 November 1930

Organization
and New Subjects

Co-opting of Kracauer (Brecht initially against)

Brecht: I imagine that a Russian scholar from such-and-such a university is commissioned to write a short cultural – historical survey of the role of thought in history. And that he's been given this task in order to collect together any possible methodological guidelines, aids or tricks by which thought has solved any problems so far, and if so, which ones.

Benjamin: We cannot treat matters of intelligence with the same currency as we treat matters of sport, etc. We must achieve something in our own field, where we are specialists. Then we can say: perhaps you could do something similar in your field.

New Subject: Benjamin

    Criticism of Publishing
    (not criticism of books published)
        Political tendency of publishers

ditto   Why no one any longer writes lyric poetry

ditto   On fashions in recent philosophy
       (subject for Kracauer)

Subject for Brentano:

It is a basic fault to interpret a physical formula as more than a sign, a symbol for something quite specific. The worst fault is to explain this symbol symbolically.

New Subject: Novelists' fashionable ideas (the novel as rhetoric)

Suggestion for the subject: Wassermann (Benjamin's suggestion)

On the subject of Frank Thiess and Tucholsky, Remarque should also be considered.

Subject for Brentano, with the cooption of Korsch and Kurella:

'Current Varieties of Intellectual Leadership'

The professor (Mannheim)
The politician (Hellpach)
The journalist (Kerr)
The freelance (Tucholsky)

Travel Literature

Subject for Ihering Brecht's suggestion

But of course not for the first issue.

The difficulty of theatre criticism – application of criteria not based on taste.

Why the Kerr type of criticism is not sufficient.

If we want something for the first issue, then at best cover the important ground: on the application of systematic possibilities of evaluation, or the necessity for testable criteria for the ever-breaking waves of sentimental slush.

Further titles for this field:

Censorship and Intelligence
Politicization of Criticism
New Directions of Criticism

Today's critic actually represents the theatregoer; he is a theatregoer, with the possibility and duty of being able to make a decisive judgement.

On the subject of Thomas Mann (Benjamin)

Stabilization of the subject 'Thomas Mann' (stance/attitude), ending with 'German Address'.

Benjamin's task would be to ask as follows: To what extent do the highest values of this literature actually coincide with those of a particular bourgeois attitude? Second concept: *Irony/nuance*.

The project that could develop this essay into a wide-ranging exercise – 'The Crisis of Belles-Lettres' – would consist in identifying the extent to which, in a number of belletristic works, irony, nuance and other such phenomena yet to be discovered, can be shown to be – through their political significance for a bourgeois attitude and for bourgeois self-assurance – a bourgeois defence-mechanism. Thomas Mann as most important example.

The political value of nuance for the bourgeoisie is that it allows it to deny all fundamental questions. The public is also enabled, through nuance, to achieve maximum comfort by balancing out highly contradictory and mutually hostile social forces.

Why can't we keep the bourgeoisie and abolish Thomas Mann, or keep Thomas Mann and abolish the bourgeoisie? Thomas Mann is but *one* representative of the bourgeoisie; the bourgeoisie has numerous representatives. What is interesting is that a man like Thomas Mann, for example, is in a strange way unhappy in his work.

Thomas Mann and Feudalism.

Thomas Mann is a rentier. In its defensive position, the bourgeoisie is trying to consume its culture, its rents. (Brecht)

The origin of the genuine bourgeoisie is Calvinistic, hardworking, ascetic and creative. And Thomas Mann is dissolute. The bourgeoisie hasn't been able to create a consumer-culture – that is a representative outward-facing culture. Obligatory nuance is genuinely feudal, voluntary nuance is bourgeois.

Irony (Death wish. Social democracy)

One would have to investigate the origins of this irony and the extent to which it is artificial or, on the other hand, taken over from a feudal attitude. Irony confronted with frivolity. Frivolity of the subject. Irony differs from frivolity in that its corrosive power vis-à-vis institutions reaches a minimum and can only be mobilized against the *self*.

Benjamin's suggestion

An analogy (Thomas Mann) – investigation of Wassermann.

Of incredible importance in Wassermann is the hypocrisy, not subjective but objective hypocrisy – a way of saying things so that, from the very outset, it disturbs no one.

Brecht's suggestion:

Tucholsky is an enormously important phenomenon.

But this subject can easily wait a while.

Benjamin in general for small subjects because they are suited to lead readers to conclusions they're not suspecting. Big subjects arouse all of a reader's inhibitions.

Benjamin on Brentano's task (see above):

It is madness to enforce 'currency' on anyone. There's something forced about Brentano's suggestion.

4. Krise und Kritik *Minutes of 26 November*

Session of 21 November 1930 (actually 26 November 1930):

Present: Ihering, Benjamin, Brecht, Bloch, Kracauer, Glück.

Remarks from the discussion on a topic for the first issue on *Criticism.*

Brecht: We should try to introduce a certain empiricism into our critical attitude, far removed from taste and individuals, to find a scientific basis. In this way, criticism would always be something that could be examined.

Benjamin: If we take the term 'criticism' in its widest sense, in fact as it is used by Kant, then we face a task that is simply insoluble without applying Kantian philosophy. I could write here about drama criticism or literary criticism – such terms are familiar – but if one should wish to express ideas about a critical attitude to events or to the world in general, that would be difficult.

Brecht: This takes us right away from the empirical. For me, this is about class struggle – the other side of class struggle, the melting down of all philosophical facts into commodities. The extent to which ideas have consequences in the social structure – this is what should be investigated.

—

We must move from a historical to a contemporary version. Historical essays must have a contemporary task. The examination of *Thomas Mann* for example should show what Thomas Mann's values are and for whom he writes, where his competence begins and ends, and whether the stance he assumes on the basis of such value is still valid, whether it is correct or not.

Reading out of some topics for the new arrivals. Here already are some remarks from the discussion on the topic of 'the different forms of leadership, etc.'. Discussion on this topic (see later).

Brecht speaks again on the general topic 'Crisis and Criticism'.

In purely bourgeois literature, for example in belles-lettres, we find, after all, enormously progressive results, perhaps even an improvement in the means of literary production. We must definitely look into this. I mean the change in viewpoint rather than the methodological improvements (James Joyce and Döblin in contrast to Mann or Wassermann). What would personally interest me would, for example, be to show that James Joyce and Döblin are to be related to certain other improvements of creative construction. Thinking as a productive force. Then I would want to produce evidence that this improvement of productive forces, as implemented by these literati – by these leaders of belles-lettres – has counterparts in other fields, in which productive forces would also be improved.

Session of 26 November 1930

Brecht: Such phenomena in James Joyce and Döblin are in their way central to the crisis, they are in a certain sense attempts to emerge from the crisis, but they are, regarded separately, also the crisis in themselves.

After all, these are positive things, progressive things, on the basis of which something can be explained. The type represented by James Joyce and Döblin in general regards thinking as method and separates itself from the purely private personal. Döblin, who is progressive, and above all Joyce, already see their method of thinking as something transportable (*Transportables*). This is very obvious. Joyce does not open himself up, he does not express himself simply, but he sets up machinery, which incidentally he is continually changing, and which is saleable and as such can be transported. He is already selling machines. He adopts points of view. It is different with Thomas Mann or even Goethe, who build up their points of view and are not transportable. This is the most important point about modern literature.

Benjamin: This interests me more than you could possibly have wished; from a depth of ignorance, I don't know Joyce, have only heard about him, and have formed a certain very inadequate impression of him that doesn't immediately coincide with what you are saying. I would be very interested to learn more. May I remind you that you once formulated this topic differently and very acutely? Is there a technical obligation, a standard in literature? And where is a technical obligation, a standard, in Joyce and Döblin?

Brecht: This is a factor in objective (provable) criteria that we have to discover. One of the criteria is as follows: writers such as Thomas Mann, in fact the ruling tendency in general, actually do not take up a position with respect to certain things in life, individually, separated out, but they construct a world view, the expression of their personality. Within this expression, everything makes sense; with Wassermann, everything makes sense. Wassermann, for example, creates a public prosecutor who does not exist. And so on. Now if one were to apply a criticism which only from the object, that is from the individual object in each case, monitored the writer's ability to present things, things cut out with scissors, one would have to extract things from their context, squeeze them out, confront them, etc., which would encourage the reader to think actively.

Benjamin: What you have just outlined is precisely the programme of the New Objectivity (*Neue Sachlichkeit*). Kästner, Gläser, Weihrauch, etc. They take up mechanical attitudes to individual things. So this method cannot be correct, as it is the method of these people. I believe this programme to be false. It contains no theoretical criterion.

Brecht: Example of the public prosecutor in Wassermann. In my view, a criterion that can be examined – that is no way to write a book.

Gläser, for example, has a world-view and designs everything so that it conforms to his world-view. Now how can one deal with Gläser and Thomas Mann by the same method?

Benjamin: How does Döblin's method differ from Gläser's? You mentioned Döblin and James Joyce, who no longer create from the 'whole'; you held Thomas Mann responsible for world views. I cannot yet be clear about the difference between how someone like Gläser writes and the way a man like Döblin writes.

Brecht: I will let the second question pass.

The dangerous thing is that everything in Thomas Mann makes sense, because the first sentence is strengthened by the third, the fifth chapter confirms the first, etc. The whole thing is completely closed.

Benjamin: Do you believe you can really substantiate such apparent totality by means of a criticism [incomplete transcription]. Do you want to build this up as a critical method?

Brecht: We have to try. Just name any critical methods that ensure this does not happen. But in itself it is completely closed and dead to suggestion.

Benjamin: In a chapter by Otto Ernst for example – teacher and student – you surely will not say straightaway that everything makes sense. On the contrary, you will be conscious of the utter insincerity of this Otto Ernst.

Kracauer: The description of the sanatorium in *The Magic Mountain* is exactly right, just as Thomas Mann describes it. Out of the sanatorium there grows a 'world in itself', as it says in all the newspaper reviews.

Brecht: If criticism only concerns good writers, other writers and reviews wouldn't belong in our monthly.

Ihering: Then do you also think that writers such as Frank Thiess are unsuitable?

Brecht: Thiess is typical, as is, for example, Remarque. We want to demolish Remarque and cite his influence, which we regard as harmful, as an example.

Nail the bad examples. With the methods of the present criticism, we can demolish him, for example, by placing him with other writers, and within this context you can oppose and destroy the figure of Remarque, the person Remarque.

(In this connection Kracauer mentioned Edgar Wallace.)

Brecht: If, on the other hand, one uses a method by which one approaches the world of Remarque and takes it to pieces, so that the reader finds something that, for example, sabotages him on page 17, this may possibly destroy the magic for the reader.

I have mentioned only one criterion, there could be many. It would be important to work out criteria and make them visible. The intention is not to sabotage fame, but a clear attitude.

26 November 1930

(In this connection Nico Stehr was mentioned, who is not read, and Waldemar Bonsels, who is or was much read.)

Brecht: It would be important in itself to set up studies in this field, because we must say something about the method. We are not obliged to know the whole method, we can cite *one* and try to work on twenty.

We must publish something with this tendency in the first issue.

Kracauer: Can we describe the methods in an abstract way?

Brecht: I am of another opinion. Take Marxism as an example. Marxism is incomprehensible in so far as the method is not stated. The reader should himself be able to apply such methods, in order to work out these things.

Ihering: One could express it in this way: that one uses it in criticism, then abstracts it and afterwards makes it clear. Then the reader can read the article again.

Benjamin: The method that undertakes a comparison of the text with real life conditions, and doesn't allow one concretely to see that that reality is different, I believe in itself to be wrong. There are not many people who try to apply this method. Brentano tries to apply it. He developed this with Wassermann. And I maintain that this lies in their method. Admittedly my opposition is limited. I agree with your theory that one of the definite and most important critical means is the sabotaging and destruction of totality. I believe it is wrong to say that it is the critic's task to compare the conditions represented with reality itself.

We see with Brentano where that leads.

It yields no criticism of the reality of the writing!

Brecht: Döblin once showed how through resistance to the desired goal one arrives at a quite different result.

(Proposal to call the topic of this discussion 'Technical Standards in Literature' ... we must realize that the person in himself expresses nothing.)

Benjamin: I admit that the goal of literature is to capture reality, or at least one of its most important tasks. To that extent I am in agreement with Döblin's statement.

Brecht: Let us assume we are stating that it is a question of the writer presenting an uncritical image of reality. Or, that we now have an urgent need to represent reality... Create people, but go on murdering! This is the objection: you don't give a picture of reality, but you give reality in a work of art.

Reality in works of art:

Benjamin: Do you see any possibility other than dialectical materialism for investigating works of art in their reality?

Materialistic criticism does not show where the work does not agree with reality; it shows the opposite.

It shows the reality which the work is dealing with to be harmful, bad, etc. I absolutely do not see the possibility of monitoring any work with a particular reality, or another reality, and saying it is wrong. Brentano has a method which I believe to be one of the progressive ones, his method is quite incomplete, it is not at all dialectical, but it brings out certain faults.

Ihering: One does not apply a method in order to show faults, but to show how difficult it is... [incomplete]

Brecht: Remarque's book could not be disproved because a criticism has never attempted to show how all that is represented in a distorted way. Döblin could prove that Remarque's book does not make sense on many pages.

A criticism of the idea that people who write have of reality would be an enormous thing.

Kracauer: One would have had to build Remarque up to the point where one recognized how he perceived reality. One would have to go beyond him.

Brecht: That is a fantastic building-up of the consequences.

Basic principle in criticism: 'What is understood is saved'.

For the *first* issue it would be tremendously important to have a topic on *criticism*. Perhaps theories about criticism would be developed which could be carried on in the next issue.

Ihering: We must come to the conclusion that this is not a special topic, but a closed one, and if it is exhausted, in the end it can be presented in formulated theories.

Topic(s) that contain the basic tendency of the journal.

Important for the *first* issue (as a basic theme).

Why does literature no longer give a real picture of reality?

Developed on the subjects: Thomas Mann and Remarque.

Proposal by Brecht: topic

'How does one in fact think scientifically?'

Bloch: replies to this that people think differently in the different sciences....

Topic: 'On class thinking'

Bloch: How far does class consciousness go?

Proposal: On the book by Lukács: History and class-consciousness, writing a report, *very important*. But not for the first issue, topic for [incomplete]

Proposal by Benjamin: 'Sociology of the Literary Project'

(would accept only unwillingly)

Proposal by Benjamin: A debate on what has until now been brought to us from the materialist side about literary criticism.

(Franz Mehring, Lü Merten, etc.)

For the first issue

> Topic for *Kracauer* for the *first issue*
>
> *Döblin*: journal notes
>
> (One would, however, have to wait until the book was published.)

Proposal by Kracauer: Topic: Arnolt Bronnen, Ernst von Salomon, etc. Matters concerning these intellectuals who have gone astray.

(Are these really intellectuals who have gone astray? (Ihering)

'Intellectuals who have gone astray'

suggested as a new topic by Kracauer.

This is a broad topic, it includes the whole student community, not only Bronnen and Salomon.

Kracauer: believes the topics that Brecht has proposed in this long discussion to be far too large.

A uniform way of treating everything must be found; it also depends on the language used whether we have a clear position, even to the point of agreement on method and language.

Topic proposed by Benjamin: How to concentrate when you read a periodical.

Glück: refers to the regularly recurring advertisement:

> 'Seek the world in a book'

as material for a topic.

Benjamin: If we have only three topics, then we should talk purely in terms of technical organization about the way the topics are handled. Then the existing papers will provide material for a fourth paper.

Topic proposed by Kracauer, which he would like to work on:

> The case of corruption.

On this topic, deal constructively with two matters concerning Ullstein, that Urban was dismissed because he allowed himself to be bribed, and secondly that the man at *Tempo* was forbidden to continue as a critic. The individuals here are unimportant. It is a question of publisher propriety and impropriety, and I believe that plenty of decent people may work at Ullstein and that nevertheless the publishing house is deeply immoral because of its behaviour.

As an experiment in thought, this topic would be eminently suitable for a *special issue*.

The topic of the great modes of philosophy intended for *Kracauer* during the second session is declined by him, with detailed reasons.

Bloch is asked what he would like to write for the first issue.

Discussion of the topic The different forms of leadership:

Instead of the scholar (Professor) Mannheim, Kracauer suggests *Heidegger*.

This topic to be offered to *Wiesengrund* (i.e. Adorno).

The topics of Politician and Freelance Writer.

Breitscheid and *Marou* [Marcu?] to be offered to Brentano.

Brentano could perhaps write under a pseudonym.

Instead of Willy Hellpach as a cultural politician, it would be better to choose a contemporary politician. Suggestions were: Rudolf Breitscheid and Rudolf Hilferding. Otto Braun would fit in here. One should be careful that these are not just 'experts' (Brecht). This topic would also be suitable for collective treatment (Benjamin).

Proposal: Divide up the topic and [cover it] in three or four consecutive issues with a recurrent heading.

Benjamin is more in favour of covering the topic in the first issue and dividing it up among several people.

The topic of *Tucholsky* is to be treated later with much more attention (Benjamin).

Topic proposed by Kracauer: Report on literature

> This would be a topic for Brecht.
>
> A general article about German intellectuals' distrust of the radical position.
>
> 'Radicalism as escape' (Tucholsky fits in here as well)

5. *Conversation between Benjamin, Brecht and Ihering, c. September 1930*

Intelligence cannot lead; today one cannot make the claim that it does.

Brecht: You shouldn't put anything on an empty table... Criticism = correct implementation of forces.

Benjamin: Criticism today is the correct stance of intelligence.

Brecht: Dangerous, for then one can say that intellectuals should do nothing. You need a leading position if you want to perform a function. Today, different stance of intellectuals from earlier, for very varied reasons, today no longer leaders but...

Benjamin: No intellectual today should go to a platform and make a claim, *instead* we work under the control of public opinion (*Öffentlichkeit*), we do not lead... Now that the intellectual's old stance has been shattered, do we want to create a new one?

Benjamin: No.

Ihering, Brecht: Conditionally, yes.

Ihering: We are interested in the intellectual, but do not want intellectuality (no matter where it comes from).

Benjamin agrees.

Brecht: I am for the simple production of intellect.

Benjamin: Today's situation precedes the seizure of power by the proletariat.

Brecht (objection): Cannot be assumed.

Benjamin: Two really possible positions:
1st really possible position for intellectuals: joining the ranks of the defensive front of the bourgeoisie. 2nd really possible position: intelligentsia's preparedness to mobilize for the proletarian revolution. What does such preparedness *not* look like: not the seizure of the leadership, but to abandon the intelligentsia and enter into the necessary sociological positions. Benjamin rejects the idea that what is conventionally referred to as the revolutionary intelligentsia is counter-revolutionary. The intellectuals who cling unconditionally to the leadership of the intelligentsia need democracy as a state form.

The 2nd really possible stance: the intelligentsia holds on to its means of production, but fulfils a subordinate function, and renounces its position of leadership, so that, on the seizure of power, the intelligentsia enters the factories and fulfils the functions assigned to it.

Brecht: On the 1st stance: do people like Thomas Mann fulfil such functions? Brecht doesn't believe so. Didn't Mann once point out that he dissolves the bourgeoisie?

Benjamin: 1. Destruction of the solidarity of all intellectual work. 2. Renunciation of leadership claim. 3. The dialectical-materialist method of the work itself.

Brecht: We do not worry about intellectuals at all, they do not exist for us as a class, another kind of intelligentsia must be developed (namely, the confrontation of an intelligent person with a subject) – Benjamin's thesis is: how does one bring intellectuals into the class struggle?

Brecht's theses: 1. There is such a thing as intellect as commodity, which is then produced by intellectuals. 2. The intellect necessary for the class struggle, for the revolutionizing of all observers, and thus for the abolition of the ideological market, cannot be produced as a commodity.

Benjamin: Not every intellectual product has a commodity character. Topic: How does the commodity character of an intellectual product connect with the leadership claim of its producer? Do you, Brecht, want to expand on this topic: today's intellectual is the producer of the commodity called intelligence; no such intelligence as commodity has any value for us?

Brecht: If intelligence does not have change as its aim, it becomes entirely the slave of its commodity character! It is possible to sell intelligence in which the class struggle is contained as a commodity. Products of the intelligence are not class bound, but are and can be found everywhere.

Benjamin: Important production of intelligence everywhere, how does one judge intelligence-value? Today, monopoly of judgement by the intelligentsia, not production by it. The intelligence has *no* stance in the class struggle, but the dialectic.

Theses against Döblin

Benjamin: With you a passionate will to destroy every other unity but the social.

Brecht: At least since man no longer needs to think for himself, he no longer can do so. I hereby defend my demand for the destruction of all other thought than the socially realizable. How to achieve this in practice? By limiting thought and allowing it only so far as it is socially realizable, that is, through organization. I believe in the autonomous correction of thinking by reality, since I don't believe in any thinking independent of reality. Truth is not to be established by digression, by the collection and adding together of all that's thinkable, in other words of all possible consequences, but every stage must be immediately and repeatedly confronted with reality. (Leonardo on the portrait: proposes that an artist should not invent anything, otherwise he'd do nothing but merely repeatedly reproduce himself.)

Benjamin: There have always been movements, formerly predominantly religious ones which, like Marx, start out with the radical demolition of icons.

Two research methods: (1) Theology; (2) Materialist dialectic.

Brecht: Today all thinking is hampered by the suspicion that thinking connected to the present is therefore rendered incomplete. The way that issues in methods rather than results is the atheist way.

(If I deduce my intellectual demands from an actual fact, then I must be careful not to view as a fact the results that my thought will in reality have brought about. Only reality should succumb to the wish that my thought generates, or from which my thought is generated. In short, I need the actual, real revolution; in short, I can think only as far as where the revolution begins; I must omit the revolution from my thinking.)

Division of work into three stages:

1. Formation of capitalist pedogogics.
2. Formation of proletarian pedogogics.
3. Formation of classless pedogogics.

Start with the first stage.

[transcription incomplete]

Three functions of language:

1. Belles-lettres - writing without authority and without responsibility.
2. A manner of writing prescriptive of action.
3. An additive manner of writing, producing an effect [transcription incomplete]

Brecht: Writing number 2 is suggested mainly because of its quotability, and the literature of category 2 consists of quotation; in the third category, the second manner of writing acquires the character of number 3, or practice: the authority has been established.

All literature of category 3 simply corresponds to a stage of social life realizable only through actual revolution, or a totally literarized life. (In China *according to class!*)

That Lenin could believe that a world revolution would come about through a few people running around with pamphlets in their coat pockets about a particular issue, and the cutting of wages in a Moscow factory, this is a belief in the written word such as otherwise only occurs in the Holy Scriptures. This proves the extent of the role assigned to the written word.

6. Benjamin, 'Some Remarks on Theoretical Foundations', c. 1930

Instead of developing them in a systematic sequence, it is advisable to present them in the more manageable form of theses:

Thesis 1. All thinking other than the socially realizable is to be destroyed. Explanation: Truth cannot be established by digression (*Schweifen*), by the collection and addition of all that's thinkable, above all by arbitrary flight from its consequences. Rather must it repeatedly be confronted with reality at every stage and point.

Thesis 2. We must have done with the prejudice that says that thought tied to the present is rendered unfinished (*incomplett*), invalid, by that tie. It is not the formal demands of thought – the consideration of all viewpoints, the exploration of all objections, and the justification of all consequences – that leads to true, that is to say, fruitful validity. Rather is genuine validity guaranteed by the closest possible connection with social reality. Valid thinking means thinking that is socially consequential. That is to say consequential both for life and for thinking itself. Thence

Thesis 3. Thinking should be reduced (*verarmt*). It should only be allowed if it is socially realizable. Brecht says: at least from the time man no longer needs to think on his own, he can no longer do so. But to attain really effective social thinking he must surrender his false, complex variety, namely, the variety of private values, positions, world-views – in short the variety of opinion. Here we come up against exactly the same fight against opinions … against which Socrates fought two thousand years ago.

Thesis 4. Opinions will be freed – in other words, society will no longer try to force certain opinions on individuals, but declare once and for all its total indifference to all private positions and convictions. Their claim to so-called correctness will not even be put to the test. The only thing that the commonality is interested in is their utility.

(GS VII, pp. 809–10)

Endnotes

Notes to Chapter I

1. *Benjamin Correspondence*, p. 350. See p. 219 above for List of Abbreviated Titles and Sources.
2. Benjamin to Scholem, 24 June 1929, in Scholem, *Benjamin*, p. 159.
3. Quoted in Scholem, *Benjamin*, p. 166.
4. Hannah Arendt, *Walter Benjamin. Bertolt Brecht. Zwei Essays*, Munich, 1971, p. 10 (Arendt's essay on Benjamin in this German edition is the basis of, but is not identical to, the version in her *Men in Dark Times*; wherever possible, reference is made here to the latter).
5. 'Walter Benjamin', p. 172.
6. Scholem, *Benjamin*, p. 146.
7. Benjamin to Scholem, 30 January 1928, *Benjamin Correspondence*, p. 322.
8. Arendt, *Men in Dark Times*, p. 174.
9. Scholem, *Benjamin*, pp. 158–9.
10. *SW*, vol. 1, p. 253.
11. ibid., p. 293.
12. ibid., p. 460.
13. ibid., p. 444.
14. Benjamin to Scholem, 7 July 1924, *Benjamin Correspondence*, p. 245.
15. *SW*, vol. 2, p. 215.
16. Benjamin to Scholem, 22 December 1924, *Benjamin Correspondence*, p. 257.
17. Benjamin to Scholem, 21 July 1925 and 29 May 1926, ibid., pp. 276 and 300.
18. Benjamin, *Moscow Diary*, p. 73.
19. Fritz Sternberg, *Der Dichter und die Ratio. Erinnerungen an Bertolt Brecht*, Göttingen, 1963, p. 25.
20. ibid., pp. 22 and 27.
21. Walter Benjamin to Max Rychner, 7 March 1931, *GB* IV, p. 18, *Benjamin Correspondence*, p. 372 (see Chapter III below).

22. Bernard Guillemin, 'On What Are You Working? A Talk with Bert Brecht (1926)' in *As They Knew Him*.
23. *Brecht on Art and Politics*, p. 73.
24. *Brecht on Theatre*, pp. 23–4.
25. ibid., p. 30.
26. Brecht, *Collected Plays*, vol. 3, p. 325.
27. ibid., p. 319.
28. ibid.
29. Brecht, *Collected Plays*, vol. 2, pp. 345ff.
30. *Brecht on Theatre*, p. 28.
31. In *As They Knew Him*, p. 19.
32. ibid., p. 39.
33. Benjamin/Adorno, p. 7.
34. *GB* III, p. 444.
35. Benjamin to Gretel Karplus, beginning of June 1934, *GB* IV, p. 440.
36. Asja Lacis, *Revolutionär im Beruf* ('Revolutionary by Profession'), p. 59.
37. Adorno/Benjamin, 31 May 1935, p. 89.
38. See Benjamin to Gretel Karplus, early June 1934, *GB* IV, p. 440.
39. Adorno/Benjamin, 31 May 1935, *GB* V, p. 89.
40. Benjamin to Friedrich Pollock, draft, *c.* mid July 1938, *GB* VI, p. 132.
41. See Adorno, 'Benjamin the Letter Writer' in *Notes to Literature*, vol. 2, p. 239.
42. 'Walter Benjamin'. p. 189.
43. Scholem, *Benjamin*, p. 159.
44. 'Walter Benjamin', p. 189.
45. Scholem, *Benjamin*, pp. 197–8.
46. Adorno/Benjamin, 4 May 1938, p. 250.
47. Scholem to Adorno, 8 February 1968, in Gershom Scholem, *Briefe II*, Munich, 1995, p. 203.
48. Arendt, *Men in Dark Times*, p. 165 and n.
49. Scholem, *Benjamin*, p. 228.
50. ibid., p. 176.
51. Benjamin to Karplus, after 3 December 1935, *GB* V, p. 205.

52. Adorno, '*The Threepenny Opera*', in Kurt Weill, *The Threepenny Opera*, edited by Stephen Hinton, Cambridge, 1989, p. 133.
53. Adorno/Benjamin, 10 November 1938, p. 284.
54. Adorno, *Notes to Literature*, vol. 2, p. 230.
55. ibid., pp. 82–7
56. Adorno, *Prisms*, p. 234.
57. ibid., p. 241.
58. Peter von Haselberg, 'Wiesengrund-Adorno', in *Text +Kritik* (Adorno special issue), Munich, 1977, p. 14.
59. Adorno/Benjamin, 6 November 1934, p. 53.
60. ibid.
61. ibid., 2–5 August, p. 108.
62. Horkheimer to Adorno, 22 January 1936, *GB* V, p. 225.
63. Adorno, 'Interimsbescheid', in *Über Walter Benjamin*, p. 94.
64. See Adorno, *Notes to Literature*, vol. 2, p. 237.
65. Ernst Bloch to Karola Piotrkowska, 5 November 1930, in Anna Czajka, 'Rettung Brechts durch Bloch?', in *The Brecht Yearbook* (Madison), vol. 18, p. 122 (see Chapter III below).
66. Scholem, *Benjamin*, pp. 164ff.
67. Günther Anders, 'Bertolt Brecht: Geschichten vom Herrn Keuner', in *Merkur* (Stuttgart), vol. 33, no. 6, September 1979, p. 890.
68. ibid., p. 38.
69. Günther Anders to the author, 23 September 1988.
70. Asja Lacis, letter to Hildegard Brenner of 14 November 1967, in *alternative*, nos 56/7, 1967, p. 213.
71. See the letters of Elisabeth Hauptmann to Benjamin in WBA 57, published in part in Geret Luhr (ed.), 'was noch begraben lag', op. cit., pp. 93–114, also Sabine Kebir, *Ich fragte nicht nach meinem Anteil. Elisabeth Hauptmanns Arbeit mit Bertolt Brecht*, Berlin, 1997, pp. 168–79.

72. Jewish National University Library, Jerusalem, Arc. 4° 1706.
73. Hans Bunge (ed.): *Brechts Lai-tu. Erinnerungen und Notate von Ruth Berlau*, Darmstadt, 1985, p. 105.
74. See Anna Maria Blaupot ten Cate to Benjamin, 27 November 1933 (WBA 22/3), in Geret Luhr, (ed.), 'was noch begraben lag', op. cit., p. 131.
75. Blaupot ten Cate to Walter Benjamin, first half of June 1934 (WBA 22), in ibid., pp. 150ff.
76. Dora Benjamin to Karl Thieme, 20 September 1943, in ibid., p. 280.

Notes to Chapter II

1. *Benjamin Correspondence*, 6 June 1929, p. 350 (my italics – E.W.)
2. Asja Lacis, *Revolutionär im Beruf*, p. 49.
3. Asja Lacis, *Krasnaja gvozdika* ('Red Carnation'), Riga, 1984, pp. 91ff. (translated from the German).
4. See *Revolutionär im Beruf*, pp. 41–9 and Scholem, *Benjamin*, pp. 121–2.
5. Lacis, *Krasnaja gvozdika*, p. 87.
6. Benno Slupianek et al, op. cit.
7. See Klaus Petersen, *Die 'Gruppe 1925' – Geschichte und Soziologie einer Schriftstellervereinigung*, Heidelberg, 1981, p. 60.
8. *GB* III, p. 214.
9. See Klaus Petersen, *Die 'Gruppe 1925' – Geschichte und Soziologie einer Schriftstellervereinigung*, Heidelberg, 1981, p. 60.
10. ibid., p. 208. See also Brecht's statement on the Becher Case, GBA 21, p. 225.
11. Klaus Petersen, op. cit., pp. 168ff.
12. ibid.
13. See Brecht's 1926 note on Becher's *Levisite*, GBA 21, p. 165.
14. *GS* II/2, pp. 622–4.
15. GBA 21, pp. 697 and 247.
16. *GS* II/2, p. 623
17. GBA 21, p. 247.

18. Manfred Voigts (ed.), *Oskar Goldberg. Der mythischer Experimentalwissenschaftler*, Berlin, 1992, p. 162.
19. ibid.
20. *SW*, vol. 2, pp. 470 and 469.
21. Benjamin to Scholem, 6 June 1931, *GB* IV, p. 35.
22. *Benjamin Correspondence*, 20 July 1931, p. 380.
23. Brecht, *Letters*, p. 127 (the last phrase is missing in the English translation).
24. *Benjamin Correspondence*, p. 368.
25. Benjamin to Scholem, 6 June, *GB* IV, pp. 35ff.
26. *SW*, vol. 2, pp. 476–7
27. ibid., p. 484.
28. Brecht, *Journals*, 13 August 1938, p. 12.
29. *SW*, vol. 2, p. 482.
30. In 'A Family Drama in the Epic Theatre', in *SW*, vol. 2, p. 559.
31. *SW*, vol. 2, p. 482.
32. *Berliner Tageblatt*, 12 June 1931.
33. GBA 22/1, p. 351.
34. *Brecht on Art and Politics*, p. 85.
35. *SW*, vol. 1, pp. 236–52. See Chryssoula Kambas, 'Walter Benjamin liest Georges Sorel: Réflexions sur la violence', in Michael Opitz and Erdmut Wizisla (eds), *Aber ein Sturm weht vom Paradiese her*, Leipzig, 1992.
36. Bernhard Reich, 'Recollections of Brecht as a Young Man' (1957), in Witt, *As They Knew Him*, p. 39.
37. Fritz Sternberg, *Der Dichter und die Ratio. Erinnerungen an Brecht*, Göttingen, 1963, pp. 36ff.
38. GBA 21, p. 420. This note was first published posthumously.
39. See Benjamin's *One-Way Street* ('Manorially Furnished Ten-Room Apartment'), 'Berlin Chronicle', 'Berlin Childhood around 1900', and *Arcades*, pp. 212–27 ['The Interior, The Trace'], above all the notes I 4,4 and I 4,5 [pp. 220ff.]; and in Brecht's *Threepenny Novel* and in his *Me-ti. Buch der Wendungen*.
40. *SW*, vol. 2, p. 264, translation adapted.

41. *SW*, vol. 2, p. 472.
42. ibid., p. 701–02.
43. *SW*, vol. 3, p. 39.
44. *SW*, vol. 2, pp. 479–80.
45. Adorno/Benjamin, 10 November 1930, p. 7.
46. *Benjamin Correspondence*, 25 April 1930, p. 365.
47. Korsch, *Marxism and Philosophy*, p. 30 passim.
48. ibid.
49. See *SW*, vol. 2, p. 476.
50. See GBA 21, 526–8 and 536ff.
51. ibid., p. 528.
52. ibid., p. 526.
53. See BBA 1518/01. For Mildred Harnack, see Shareen Blair Brysac, *Resisting Hitler – Mildred Harnack and the Red Orchestra*, Oxford/New York, 2000.
54. BBA 1518/04.
55. See BBA 328/84 and 86–90.
56. See, for example, *Benjamin Correspondence*, letters nos 227 (to Scholem), 231 (to Gretel Adorno) and 232 (to Brecht).
57. Benjamin/Scholem, 20 March 1933, p. 34.
58. ibid., 7 December 1933, p. 89.
59. ibid.
60. See Benjamin to Kraft, 12 November 1934, *Benjamin Correspondence*, p. 462.
61. *SW*, vol. 2, p. 786–7.
62. ibid., p. 789.
63. Brecht, *Journals*, p. 10.
64. ibid., p. 159.
65. Benjamin to Alfred Cohn, 10 August 1936, *GB* V, p. 349.
66. Benjamin/Scholem, 30 December 1933, p. 93.
67. Klaus Mann, *Tagebücher 1931 bis 1933*, edited by Joachim Heimannsberg et al, Munich, 1989, p. 179, and Benjamin to Gretel Karplus, 8 November 1933, *GB* IV, p. 309
68. Benjamin/Scholem, 16 October 1933, p. 94.

69. Benjamin to Gretel Karplus, 8 November 1933, *GB* IV, p. 309.
70. Werner Hecht, *Brecht Chronik 1898–1956*, Frankfurt, 1997, pp. 382ff. and 388ff.
71. Benjamin to Gretel Karplus, 16 May 1933, *GB* IV, p. 207.
72. See *GS* VII/2, p. 847.
73. See Brecht to Benjamin, mid September 1934, GBA 28, p. 439.
74. *SW*, ibid., pp. 708ff.
75. See Brecht to Korsch, Brecht, *Letters*, p. 386.
76. See Anna Maria Blaupot ten Cate to Walter Benjamin, 30 November 1933 (WBA 22/5), in Geret Luhr (ed.), 'was noch begraben lag', op. cit., pp. 133ff.
77. Benjamin to Margarete Steffin, after 7 June 1939, *GB* VI, p. 292.
78. See WBA 224.
79. GBA 28, p. 561.
80. Benjamin to Gretel Karplus, 8 November 1933, *GB* IV, p. 309.
81. Brecht to Lisa Tetzner [June 1935].
82. Benjamin to Brecht, *c.* 13 January 1934, *GB* IV, p. 337.
83. Helene Weigel to Walter Benjamin, 7 December 1936.
84. See Brecht to Benjamin, mid September 1934, GBA 28, p. 439. Benjamin's application of 4 July 1934 is reproduced in *GB* IV, pp. 448–51.
85. Hannah Arendt, 'Walter Benjamin und Bertolt Brecht', p. 16, and Gretel Karplus to Benjamin, 27 May 1934, *GB* IV, pp. 442ff.
86. Benjamin to Bryher, draft, mid August 1936, *GB* V, p. 362.
87. Benjamin to Kitty Marx-Steinschneider, 20 July 1938, *Benjamin Correspondence*, pp. 568–9.
88. Hans Bunge (ed.), *Brechts Lai-tu*, op. cit., p. 105.
89. Benjamin/Scholem, 4 August 1934, p. 133.

90. Lou Eisler-Fischer, 'Eisler in der Emigration', in Manfred Grabs (ed.), *Wer war Hanns Eisler?*, Berlin, 1983, p. 448.
91. Benjamin to Bryher, draft, mid August 1936, *GB* V, p. 362.
92. Barbara Brecht-Schall, in Joachim Lang and Jürgen Hillesheim (eds), *Denken heißt verändern*, Augsburg, 1997, p. 18.
93. See Helmut Lethen and Erdmut Wizisla, 'Das Schwierige beim Gehen ist das Stillestehn', in *The Brecht Yearbook* (Madison), no. 23, 1998.
94. Benjamin to Steffin, 2 June 1934, *GB* IV, p. 438.
95. *GS* II/3, p. 1371.
96. Brecht to Benjamin, July/August 1935, GBA 28, p. 517.
97. Margarete Steffin to Benjamin, 20 July 1937, Steffin, *Briefe*, p. 247.
98. Benjamin to Brecht, 21 May 1934, *Benjamin Correspondence*, p. 443.
99. *GS* VI, p. 526.
100. See Hans Bunge (ed.), *Brechts Lai-tu*, op. cit., p. 105.
101. Brecht to Steffin, 28 December 1934 and 17 February 1935, GBA 28, pp. 469 and 490.
102. Brecht to Benjamin, early December 1936, Brecht, *Letters*, p. 238.
103. Benjamin to Gretel Adorno, 20 July 1938, *GB* VI, p. 139.
104. Brecht to Benjamin, April 1936, Brecht, *Letters*, p. 230.
105. Benjamin to Steffin, 18 April 1939, *GB* VI, p. 267.
106. Benjamin to Gretel Adorno, 20 July 1938, *Benjamin Correspondence*, p. 571.
107. Alfred Kurella, 'Deutsche Romantik', in *Internationale Literatur* (Moscow), no. 6, 1938, pp. 113–28.
108. Benjamin to Gretel Adorno, 20 July 1938, *Benjamin Correspondence*, p. 572.
109. Kurt Krolop, *Sprachsatire als Zeitsatire bei Karl Kraus*, Berlin, 1987, p. 261.
110. Benjamin to Kitty Marx-Steinschneider, 20 July 1938, *Benjamin Correspondence*, p. 569.

111. Benjamin to Gretel Adorno, 20 July 1938, ibid., p. 571.
112. Benjamin to Adorno, 4 October 1938, ibid., p. 576.
113. Steffin to Benjamin, 17 November 1938, in Steffin, *Briefe*, p. 288.
114. Benjamin to Adorno, 4 October 1938, *Benjamin Correspondence*, p. 576.
115. ibid., p. 572.
116. *GB* VI, p. 286.
117. Benjamin to Friedrich Pollock, draft, *c.* mid July 1938, *GB* VI, p. 134.
118. See Helene Weigel to Walter Benjamin (*c.* July/August 1939), in Stefan Mahlke (ed.): 'Wir sind zu berühmt, um überall hinzugehen', in op. cit., p. 16.
119. Stephan Lackner, 'Von einer langen, schwierigen Irrfahrt', unpublished Benjamin letters in *Neue Deutsche Hefte* (Berlin), no. 20, 1979, p. 66.
120. Brecht to Fritz Lieb, June 1940, GBA 29, p. 177.

Notes to Chapter III

1. Benjamin, *Memorandum zu der Zeitschrift 'Krisis und Kritik'*, *GS* VI, p. 619.
2. Rolf Wiggershaus, *The Frankfurt School*, Oxford, 1994, p. 66.
3. See Hildegard Brenner, *Die Kunstpolitik des Nationalsozialismus*, Reinbek, 1963, pp. 7–13.
4. See BBA 363/38. The outline for the journal is printed in GBA 21, pp. 330ff.
5. GBA 28, pp. 321ff.
6. DLA Marbach, Bernard von Brentano archive.
7. *Benjamin Correspondence*, 3 October 1930, p. 368.
8. Brecht, *Letters*, p. 127 (the words 'from what I know of him' are missing in the English version).
9. *Benjamin Correspondence*, 3 November 1930, p. 369 (this sentence is not in the English translation).

10. ibid., pp. 371–3.
11. *GB* III, p. 556.
12. See Benjamin to Brecht (after 5 February 1931), *GB* IV, p. 15.
13. *GB* IV, p. 11.
14. See Benjamin to Brecht, *Benjamin Correspondence*, end February 1931, p. 370.
15. ibid., p. 371.
16. See *Neue Augsburger Zeitung*, Augsburg, 12 March 1931, p. 1, and *Neue Badische Landes-Zeitung*, Mannheim, 12 March 1931, p. 2.
17. Pasted into Armin Kesser's diary (Gabriele Kesser, Zürich).
18. See Brentano to Brecht, 18 July 1931, transcribed letter, DLA Marbach, Brentano archive.
19. Georg Lukács, 'Die deutsche Intelligenz', in *Zwei Welten 3/1932*, quoted in Alfred Klein, *Georg Lukács in Berlin*, Berlin/Weimar, 1990, p. 41.
20. Brecht, *Letters*, pp. 127–8. The date of the letter should be corrected from Autumn 1930 to Summer 1931.
21. Undated cutting, presumably from the *Rote Fahne* (c. end of July 1931), BBA newspaper cutting file.
22. See WBA Ts 2468ff.
23. Benjamin to Alfred Cohn, 6 March 1929, *GB* III, p. 448.
24. Information from Wolfgang Glück, Vienna.
25. Scholem to Dolf Sternberger, 30 May 1950, in Scholem, *Briefe II*, Munich, 1995, p. 18.
26. *Benjamin Correspondence*, 28 October 1931, p. 386.
27. See Appendix, above.
28. Brecht to von Brentano, end of October 1930, Brecht, *Letters*, p. 127.
29. WBA Ts 2463.
30. BBA 824/71ff.
31. See *Benjamin Correspondence*, end February 1931, p. 370 (translation emended).
32. GBA 21, p. 331.

33. Max Rychner to Scholem, 2 May 1960, in Scholem, *Briefe II*, op. cit., pp. 6off.
34. See p. 190 below.
35. BBA 332/49.
36. See Günter Hartung, *Debatten über faschistische Ideologie*, pp. 117–31.
37. WBA Ts 2475.
38. *SW*, vol. 1, pp. 116–85.
39. ibid., p. 293.
40. *Benjamin Correspondence*, 8 November 1921, p. 194.
41. *SW*, vol. 1, p. 297.
42. ibid., p. 460.
43. *Brecht on Art and Politics*, p. 90.
44. *Benjamin Correspondence*, 14 February 1929, p. 347.
45. *SW*, vol. 2, p. 406.
46. Heinrich Kaulen, 'Die Aufgabe des Kritikers', in Wilfried Barner (ed.), *Literaturkritik*, Stuttgart, 1990, p. 320.
47. Sessions of 21 and 26 November 1930 (see pp. 191–203 below).
48. Session of 21 November 1930 (pp. 191ff. below).
49. Undated session (*c.* early November 1930) and session of 26 November 1930 (p. 197–203 below).
50. Session of 21 November 1930 (pp. 191ff. below).
51. *GS* II/3, p. 1371.
52. Benjamin to Rychner, *Benjamin Correspondence*, 7 March 1931, p. 372.
53. Session of 26 November 1930 (WBA Ts 2486).
54. Adorno, *Über Walter Benjamin*, p. 98.
55. *Benjamin Correspondence*, 7 March 1931, p. 372.
56. ibid.
57. GBA 21, p. 422 ('On Thinking as Behaviour').
58. Günter Hartung, 'Zur Benjamin-Edition' (Part 1), in *Weimarer Beiträge* (Berlin/Weimar), vol. 36, no. 6, p. 158.
59. *SW*, vol. 2, pp. 305ff.
60. See Bernd Witte, *Krise und Kritik*, op. cit., pp. 15–18 and 33.
61. *SW*, vol. 2, p. 309.

62. ibid., p. 310.
63. Undated session (*c.* early November 1930) (p. 191 below).
64. 87 See Karl Mannheim, *Ideology and Utopia*, London, 1960, pp. 137 and 139.
65. *GS* III, p. 174
66. Undated session (WBA Ts 2490).
67. BBA 217/04.
68. Benjamin to Klaus Mann, 9 May 1934, *GB* IV, p. 421.
69. See p. 193 below and *SW*, vol. 2, pp. 394–6 ('A Critique of the Publishing Industry').
70. See sessions of 21 and 26 November 1930 above.
71. Session of 21 November 1930 (see p. 191 below).
72. WBA Ts 2463.
73. Session of 26 November 1930 (see p. 197 below).
74. *Benjamin Correspondence*, 20 July 1931, p. 381.
75. GBA 21, p. 422.
76. Ernst Bloch to Karola Piotrkowska, 5 November 1930, in Anna Czajka, 'Rettung Brechts durch Bloch?', in op. cit., p. 122.
77. Kracauer to Adorno, 12 January 1931, DLA Marbach, Kracauer Archive, 72.1119/8. I owe the reference to this document to Momme Brodersen.
78. BBA 244/01–37.
79. *Benjamin Correspondence*, end February 1931, p. 371.
80. *SW*, vol. 2, p. 479.
81. Undated session (*c.* beginning of November 1930) (see p. 191 below).
82. See session of 26 November 1930 (see p. 197 below).
83. ibid.
84. See session of 26 November 1930 (pp. 197–203 below).
85. Ernst Bloch and Hans Götz Oxenius, 'Gespräch über die Zwanziger Jahre' [1962], in *Bloch-Almanach*, second series, Baden-Baden, 1982, p. 16.

86. Hildegard Brenner, *Die Kunstpolitik des Nationalsozialismus*, op. cit., pp. 11–13.
87. Fritz Sternberg, *Der Dichter und die Ratio. Erinnerungen an Bertolt Brecht*, Göttingen, 1963, p. 37.
88. Walter Gropius, *Architektur. Wege zu einer optischen Kultur*, Hamburg/ Frankfurt, 1955.
89. Benjamin to Scholem, 3 October 1930, *Benjamin Correspondence*, p. 368.

Notes to Chapter IV

1. *Benjamin Correspondence*, p. 396.
2. *GS* III, p. 183.
3. ibid., pp. 183 ff.
4. See Kracauer to Adorno, 20 April 1930, in Hans Puttnies and Gary Smith, op. cit., pp. 35ff.
5. See *GS* III, pp. 362–3.
6. *Brecht on Art and Politics*, p. 90.
7. *Brecht on Theatre*, p. 43.
8. See *Understanding Brecht*, pp. 7–8.
9. *GS* II/3, p. 956.
10. *Brecht on Film and Radio*, p. 162.
11. *SW*, vol. 2, p. 519.
12. Verbal communication, March 2001.
13. *Benjamin Correspondence*, 5 June 1927, p. 315.
14. Arendt, *Men in Dark Times*, p. 197.
15. *SW*, vol. 2, p. 733.
16. See Kurt Krolop, *Sprachsatire als Zeitsatire bei Karl Kraus*, Berlin, 1987, p. 267.
17. ibid., p. 267.
18. *Benjamin Correspondence*, end February 1931, pp. 370 (translation emended).
19. WBA Ts 417^v.
20. *SW*, vol. 2, p. 769.
21. *SW*, vol. 3, p. 330.
22. *SW*, vol. 1, p. 444 and Thesis XVII, *SW*, vol. 4, p. 396.
23. 'What is Epic Theatre? (1)', in *Understanding Brecht*, p. 6.
24. *SW*, vol. 2, p. 374.
25. ibid., p. 370.
26. ibid., p. 560.

27. *GS* I/3, p. 1042.
28. *SW*, vol. 2, p. 370, and *GS* II/3, pp. 145ff. (see also *GS* VII/2, pp. 808ff.).
29. See *SW*, vol. 2, p. 732.
30. *SW*, vol. 3, p. 339.
31. *SW*, vol. 2, p. 542.
32. See Kurt Krolop, *Sprachsatire als Zeitsatire bei Karl Kraus*, op. cit., pp. 257–61 and Edward Timms, *Karl Kraus: Apocalyptic Satirist*, London/New Haven, 2005, pp. 385–9.
33. *SW*, vol. 2, p. 370.
34. GBA 18, p. 29, and Brecht, *Versuche 1–3*, p. 1.
35. See Detlev Schöttker, *Konstruktiver Fragmentarismus. Form und Rezeption der Schriften Walter Benjamins*, Frankfurt, 1999, pp. 193–203.
36. *GS* VI, p. 182.
37. *GS* II/3, p. 1455.
38. Benjamin to Adorno, 28 April 1934, Adorno/Benjamin, p. 49. See also Benjamin to Brecht, 21 May 1934, *Benjamin Correspondence*, p. 427.
39. *SW*, vol. 2, p. 375.
40. *Understanding Brecht*, p. 25.
41. *SW*, vol. 2, p. 367.
42. *GS* VII/s, p. 655.
43. *SW*, vol. 2, p. 367.
44. See Bernhard Diebold, 'Militärstück von Brecht', in *Frankfurter Zeitung*, 11 February 1931, p. 10 and reviews by Alfred Kerr (*Berliner Tageblatt*, 7 February 1931) and Herbert Ihering (*Berliner Börsen-Courier*, 7 February 1931).
45. See *Brecht on Theatre* ('The Question of Criteria for Judging Acting'), pp. 53–6.
46. *Understanding Brecht*, pp. 1ff.
47. ibid., pp. 1, 3 and 9.
48. ibid., p. 3
49. ibid., p. 9.
50. ibid., p. 3.
51. Benjamin to Scholem, 3 October 1931, *GB* IV, pp. 53ff.
52. See Benjamin to Gretel Adorno, 26 June 1939, *Benjamin Correspondence*, p. 610.

53. Bloch, *Briefe* 1, p. 359 (see also p. 355).

54. *Blätter des Hessischen Landestheaters* (Darmstadt), Leipzig, 1931/2, vol. 5, no. 16, 'Theater und Rundfunk' (July 1932).

55. See Klaus-Dieter Krabiel, *Brechts Lehrstücke. Entstehung und Entwicklung eines Spieltyps*, Stuttgart, 1993, pp. 108–15, and Sabine Schiller-Lerg, 'Ernst Schoen (1894–1960). Ein Freund überlebt', in Klaus Garber and Ludger Rehm (eds), *global benjamin*, Munich, 1999.), pp. 993–9.

56. Brecht, *Collected Plays*, vol. 3, p. 319 (Brecht's italics).

57. *Brecht on Film and Radio*, p. 35 ('Suggestions for the Director of Broadcasting'), and p. 42 ('The Radio as Communications Apparatus') and see further Brecht's texts on radio theory in ibid.).

58. *SW*, vol. 2, p. 585 ('Theatre and Radio').

59. Brecht, *Collected Plays*, vol. 3, p. 343.

60. *SW*, vol. 2, p. 505.

61. See *GS* VII/1, p. 469.

62. Klaus Mann, *Tagebücher 1931 bis 1933*, Munich, 1989, p. 180.

63. Klaus Mann to Benjamin, 2 May 1934, WBA 141/3.

64. Klaus Mann, *Tagebücher 1931 bis 1933*, op. cit., p. 31.

65. Benjamin to Klaus Mann, 9 May 1934, *GB* IV, p. 421.

66. See Klaus Mann to Benjamin, 12 May 1934, WBA 141/5.

67. Heinrich Mann to Klaus Mann, 22 May 1934, SB Munich, Klaus Mann Archive.

68. See Klaus Mann to Lion Feuchtwanger, 19 August 1935, Klaus Mann, *Briefe*, Berlin and Weimar 1988, p. 219ff.

69. See Hans-Albert Walter, *Asylpraxis und Lebensbedingungen in Europa. Deutsche Exilliteratur 1933–1950*, vol. 2, Darmstadt, 1972, p. 199.

70. Benjamin to Kraft, 3 April 1935, *GB* V, p. 69.

71. Steffin to Benjamin, 13 May 1935, Steffin, *Briefe*, p. 136.

72. See Benjamin to Brecht, 20 May 1935, *Benjamin Correspondence*, p. 484.

73. *Benjamin Correspondence*, pp. 472–3, 7 January 1935.

74. *SW*, vol. 3, p. 3.

75. See Paul Haland, 'Zu Brechts *Dreigroschenroman*', in *Unsere Zeit* (Paris), vol. 8, nos 2–3, April 1935, p. 66, and Wilhelm Stefan (Willy Siegfried Schlamm), 'Brechts Lehrbuch der Gegenwart', in *Europäische Hefte* (Prague), vol. 1, no. 30, 8 November 1934, pp. 526–9.

76. *SW*, vol. 3, p. 8.

77. ibid., pp. 8–9.

78. ibid., pp. 9–10.

79. *Unsere Zeit* (Paris), vol. 7, no. 12, December 1934, p. 62.

80. *SW*, vol. 3, p. 4.

81. ibid., p. 8.

82. *SW*, vol. 3, p. 8.

83. Benjamin to Steffin, 26 April 1937, *GB* V, p. 521.

84. Benjamin to Alfred Cohn, 17 November 1937, *GB* V, pp. 605ff.

85. Brecht, *Letters*, p. 271.

86. Steffin to Benjamin, 30 May 1938, Steffin, *Briefe*, p. 286.

87. Helene Weigel to Brecht, [beginning of May 1938], in Stefan Mahlke (ed.), 'Wir sind zu berühmt, um überall hinzugehen', op. cit., p. 15.

88. *SW*, vol. 3, p. 332.

89. ibid., pp. 330ff.

90. ibid., p. 331.

91. See *SW*, vol. 2, p. 560 and vol. 4, pp. 305–6. In 'On the Concept of History' Benjamin used the term 'Chok' (shock) in connection with the 'standstill' of thoughts (Thesis XVII, *SW*, vol. 3, p. 396).

92. *SW*, vol. 3, p. 331.

93. ibid., p. 332.

94. ibid., p. 330 (E.W.'s italics).

95. ibid., p. 332.

96. ibid., p. 332.

97. Brecht to Weigel, beginning of November 1937, Brecht, *Letters*, p. 265.
98. See Brecht to Slatan Dudow, 19 April 1938, ibid., p. 285.
99. Brecht, *Journals*, 15 August 1938), p. 13.
100. Steffin to Benjamin, 24 August 1937, Steffin, *Briefe*, p. 249.
101. 123 Steffin to Benjamin, 17 November 1938, Steffin, *Briefe*, p. 288.
102. Steffin to Benjamin, [mid May 1939], Steffin, *Briefe*, p. 300.
103. Geret Luhr (ed.), 'was noch begraben lag', op. cit., p. 183.
104. *SW*, vol. 4, p. 215.
105. ibid., vol. 4, p. 216.
106. Brecht, *Journals*, 10 September 1938, pp. 16–17.
107. See *SW*, vol. 4, pp. 231 passim.
108. Kraft to Benjamin, 25 December 1935, WBA 74/15ᵛ.
109. *Benjamin Correspondence*, 30 January 1936, pp. 520–1.
110. *SW*, vol. 4, pp. 216 passim.
111. *SW*, vol. 2, p. 214.
112. *SW*, vol. 4, p. 215.
113. ibid., pp. 232–3.
114. Arnold Zweig to Brecht, 18 August 1935, in Heidrun Loeper (ed.), 'Briefwechsel Bertolt Brecht, Margarete Steffin, (Isot Kilian, Käthe Rülicke) und Arnold Zweig 1934–56', in *The Brecht Yearbook* (Madison), vol. 25, 2000, p. 363.
115. See Ruth Fischer, *Stalin and German Communism*, Cambridge, Mass., 1948, pp. 615–25.
116. *SW*, vol. 4, p. 248.
117. See Helene Weigel to Brecht, [beginning of May 1938], in Stefan Mahlke (ed.), 'Wir sind zu berühmt, um überall hinzugehen', op. cit., p. 15.
118. See Chryssoula Kambas, *Walter Benjamin im Exil*, pp. 213ff. On the quotation from the letter, see Walter Benjamin to Fritz Lieb, first half of April 1939, *GB* VI, p. 260.

119. Benjamin to Lieb, 3 May 1939, *GB* VI, p. 273.
120. Elisabeth Young-Bruehl, *Hannah Arendt*, op. cit., p. 150.
121. Arendt, *Men in Dark Times*, p. 242.
122. Brecht to Karl Thieme, April 1948. BBA E 73/250.
123. BBA 1157/68.
124. 26 June 1939, *Benjamin Correspondence*, p. 610.
125. See *SW*, vol. 4, pp. 302ff.
126. Ferdinand Lion to Benjamin, 14 May (actually June) 1939 in WBA, 153/9.
127. See Ferdinand Lion, 'Über vergangenes und zukünftiges Theater', op. cit., pp. 677ff.
128. 'Grenzen des Brecht-Theaters', op. cit., pp. 837–41.
129. See Benjamin to Max Horkheimer, 6 December 1937, *GB* V, p. 617.

Notes to Chapter V

1. Steffin to Benjamin, May 1934, Steffin, *Briefe*, p. 124.
2. ibid., 16 October 1935, p. 151.
3. ibid., end of November/beginning of December 1937, pp. 161ff.
4. ibid., 24 August 1937, p. 249.
5. ibid., 13 May 1935, p. 136.
6. Benjamin to Steffin, 18 April 1939, *GB* VI, p. 268.
7. Steffin to Benjamin, mid May 1939, Steffin, *Briefe*, p. 300.
8. Benjamin to Steffin, after 7 June 1939, *Benjamin Correspondence*, pp. 607–8.
9. Steffin to Benjamin, 22 June 1939, Steffin, *Briefe*, p. 302.
10. ibid., August 1939, pp. 308ff.
11. Benjamin to Steffin, 6 August 1939, *GB* VI, p. 327.
12. Brecht to Arnold Ljungdal, June 1940, GBA 29, pp. 177ff.
13. Arendt, *Men in Dark Times*, p. 165.
14. Adorno, 'Zur Interpretation Benjamins' (notes on a planned essay), in Adorno, *Über Walter Benjamin*, p. 99.

15. *Benjamin Correspondence*, 20 May 1935, p. 485.
16. Brecht, *Collected Plays*, vol. 8, p. 126.
17. Benjamin to Scholem, 4 April 1937, *Benjamin Correspondence*, p. 539.
18. Benjamin to Willi Bredel, 5 September 1936, *GB* V, p. 507.
19. Brecht to Bredel, 5 September 1936, *GB* V, p. 374.
20. Steffin to Benjamin, 9 June 1937, Steffin, *Briefe*, pp. 242ff.
21. ibid., 7 September 1937, p. 252.
22. Benjamin to Brecht, 20 December 1936, *GB* V, p. 444.
23. Michael Rohrwasser, *Der Stalinismus und die Renegaten. Die Literatur der Exkommunisten*, Stuttgart, 1991, p. 1.
24. Ernst Bloch to Benjamin, 30 January 1937, Bloch, *Briefe*, vol. 2, p. 664.
25. GBA 22/1, p. 188.
26. See Benjamin to Steffin, 29 March 1937, *GB* V, p. 503.
27. Steffin to Benjamin, 12 March 1937 (actually 1938), Steffin, *Briefe*, p. 276.
28. *SW*, vol. 2, p. 749.
29. ibid., p. 756.
30. Brecht, *Letters*, Spring 1936, p. 229.
31. *SW*, vol. 3, pp. 72 and 74.
32. Brecht to Otto Neurath, middle of 1933, Brecht, *Letters*, p. 142.
33. ibid., p. 189, Brecht to Johannes R. Becher, end of December 1934.
34. GBA 22/1, pp. 899ff.
35. Brecht to Max (Mordecai) Gorelik, beginning of March 1937, *Letters*, p. 243 (for the Diderot Society, see also *Brecht on Theatre*, p. 106).
36. Benjamin to Alfred Cohn, 14 April 1936, *GB* V, p. 270.
37. See Steffin to Benjamin, 16 October 1935, Steffin, *Briefe*, p. 150.
38. Brecht to Benjamin, draft, April/May 1937, GBA 29, p. 29.
39. *Brecht on Art and Politics*, p. 250.
40. Steffin to Benjamin, 7(–9) November 1936, Steffin, *Briefe*, p. 212.

41. Brecht to Max (Mordecai) Gorelik, beginning of March 1937, *Letters*, p. 243.
42. Benjamin to Alfred Cohn, 10 August 1936, *GB* V, p. 349.
43. See Steve Giles, *Bertolt Brecht and Critical Theory*, op. cit., pp. 133–66.
44. Benjamin and Brecht to Willi Bredel, 9 August 1936, *GB* V, p. 348.
45. *SW*, vol. 3, p. 122.
46. Brecht, *Poems*, p. 299.
47. *Brecht on Art and Politics*, p. 194.
48. Brecht, *Journals*, p. 115.
49. GBA 18, p. 35.
50. *SW*, vol. 2, p. 210.
51. *The Stories of Herr Keuner*, translated by Martin Chalmers, San Francisco, 2001, p. 13.
52. Benjamin to Gershom Scholem, 22 December 1924, *Benjamin Correspondence*, p. 256.
53. *SW*, vol. 1, p. 481.
54. GBA 18, p. 95.
55. *SW*, vol. 2, pp. 367–8.
56. ibid.
57. GBA 14, pp. 376ff.
58. *SW*, vol. 2, p. 368.
59. ibid., p. 783.
60. ibid.
61. ibid.
62. Benjamin to Scholem, 3 October 1931, *Benjamin Correspondence*, pp. 383–4.
63. *SW*, vol. 2, pp. 785–6.
64. See for example *SW*, vol. 2, pp. 800ff. and 807–08 ('Franz Kafka').
65. See Bernd Auerochs, 'Walter Benjamins Notizen über die Parabel', in Theo Elm and Hans H. Hiebel (eds), *Die Parabel. Parabolische Formen in der deutschen Dichtung des 20. Jahrhunderts*, Frankfurt, 1986.
66. See *SW*, vol. 2, pp. 447ff.
67. *SW*, vol. 2, p. 286.
68. Peter Beicken, 'Kafka's *Prozess* und seine Richter. Zur Debatte Brecht-Benjamin und Benjamin-Scholem', in Benjamin Bennett et al (eds), *Probleme der Moderne*, Tübingen, 1983, p. 352.

69. Lorenz Jäger, "'Primat des Gestus". Überlegungen zu Benjamins "Kafka"- Essay', in Lorenz Jäger and Thomas Regehly (eds), 'Was nie geschrieben wurde, lesen', *Frankfurter Benjamin-Vorträge*, Bielefeld, 1992, p. 96.
70. Brecht, *Journals*, p. 10.
71. Benjamin, *Arcades*, p. 363.
72. Benjamin to Max Horkheimer, 16 April 1938, *Benjamin Correspondence*, p. 557.
73. GBA 22/1, p. 450.
74. *SW*, vol. 4, p. 135.
75. GBA 22/1, p. 450.
76. *SW*, vol. 4, p. 92.
77. *SW*, vol. 4, p. 63.
78. GBA 22/1, p. 450.
79. Benjamin to Max Horkheimer, 28 September 1938, *Benjamin Correspondence*, p. 574.
80. *GS* VII/2, p. 755.
81. *SW*, vol. 4, p. 338.
82. Willy R. Berger, 'Svendborger Notizen. Baudelaire im Urteil Bert Brechts', in *arcadia* (Berlin), vol. 12, no. 1, 1977, p. 64.
83. Benjamin to Adorno, 4 October 1938, *Benjamin Correspondence*, p. 576.
84. Scholem, *Benjamin*, p. 206.
85. Hans Mayer, *Der Zeitgenosse Walter Benjamin*, Frankfurt, 1992, p. 42.
86. Steffin to Benjamin, 12 December 1938. Steffin, *Briefe*, p. 289.
87. Steffin to Benjamin (February 1939), ibid., p. 299.
88. Brecht, *Journals*, 9 August 1941, p. 159.
89. *Brecht on Art and Politics*, p. 103.
90. *SW*, vol. 4, p. 394.
91. ibid., p. 395.
92. *GS* VII/2, p. 753.
93. *GS* VII/1, p. 255.
94. *SW*, vol. 2, p. 390.
95. See Thesis XIV (*SW*, vol. 4, p. 395).
96. 'On Looking Through my First Plays' (GBA 23, p. 245).
97. *SW*, vol. 4, p. 394.
98. Benjamin, *Arcades*, p. 473.
99. *SW*, vol. 4, pp. 391–2.
100. ibid., p. 391.
101. ibid., p. 392.
102. ibid.
103. *GS* VII/2, p. 659
104. Benjamin to Werner Kraft, 26 July 1934, *Benjamin Correspondence*, p. 452.
105. 9 August 1941, Brecht, *Journals*, p. 159.
106. Benjamin to Gretel Adorno, end of April/beginning of May 1940, *GB* VI, p. 435 (see *SW*, vol. 1, pp. 37–47 for Benjamin's 'The Life of Students').
107. *SW*, vol. 4, p. 391.
108. ibid., p. 389.
109. ibid., p. 392.
110. ibid.
111. Hannah Arendt (letter headed Schocken Books Inc., New York) to Brecht, 15 October 1946 (BBA 3229).
112. See Günter Hartung, 'Zur Benjamin-Edition [Part I]', p. 152, and 'Zur Benjamin-Edition [Part II]', in *Weimarer Beiträge* (Berlin/Weimar), vol. 236, no. 6, 1990, p. 994.
113. Uwe Schoor, *Das geheime Journal der Nation. Die Zeitschrift 'Sinn und Form'. Chefredakteur: Peter Huchel, 1949–1962*, Berlin, 1992, p. 60.
114. Horkheimer and Adorno, 'Odysseus oder Mythos und Aufklärung', in *Sinn und Form*, vol. 1, no. 4, 1949, pp. 143–80.
115. Brecht, *Journals*, p. 159.
116. Arendt, *Men in Dark Times*, p. 152.
117. Max Horkheimer to Leo Löwenthal, 11 February 1942, in Horkheimer, *Gesammelte Schriften*, edited by Alfred Schmidt and Gunzelin Schmid Noerr, Frankfurt, 1996, vol. 17, p. 267.
118. See Löwenthal to Horkheimer, 18 February 1942, in Löwenthal, *Schriften*, edited by Helmut Dubiel, Frankfurt, 1980–87, vol. 4, p. 241.
119. See Steffin to Benjamin, 27 October 1937, Steffin, *Briefe*, p. 260.
120. Brecht to Benjamin, beginning of December 1936, *Letters*, p. 238.
121. Brecht, *Journals*, 19 August 1940 and 1 August 1941, pp. 89 and 157.
122. *SW*, vol. 4, p. 391.

List of Abbreviated Titles and Sources

Wherever possible references in this edition have been given to published English-language sources, from which quotations have been taken. Where no such English sources have been found, German references have been retained and translations supplied. In some cases (books by Hannah Arendt and Gershom Scholem) it has been necessary to refer to both the English and the German editions of the same work because the German contains items or passages missing in the English. In the case of Benjamin, most of the works cited are conveniently in the four-volume Harvard edition, but that edition only prints the second version of the essay 'What is the Epic Theatre?' Its first version is published in *Understanding Brecht* under the title 'What is Epic Theatre?'

Adorno/Benjamin   Theodor W. Adorno and Walter Benjamin, *The Complete Correspondence 1928–1940*, edited by Henri Lonitz, translated by Nicholas Walker, Cambridge, 1999.

Adorno, *Notes to Literature*, vol. 2   Theodor W. Adorno, *Notes to Literature*, vol. 2, edited by Rolf Tiedemann, translated by Shierry Weber Nicholson, New York/Oxford, 1992.

Adorno, *Prisms*   Theodor Adorno, *Prisms*, translated by Samuel and Shierry Weber, Cambridge, Mass., 1981.

Adorno, *Über Walter Benjamin*   Theodor Adorno, *Über Walter Benjamin – Aufsätze, Artikel, Briefe*, edited and annotated by Rolf Tiedemann (revised edition), Frankfurt, 1990.

Arendt, *Benjamin/Brecht*   Hannah Arendt, *Walter Benjamin/Bertolt Brecht. Zwei Essays*, Munich, 1971.

Arendt, *Men in Dark Times*   Hannah Arendt, *Men in Dark Times* (Benjamin essay translated by Harry Zohn), Harmondsworth, 1973.

As They Knew Him   Hubert Witt (ed.), *Brecht As They Knew Him*, translated by John Peet, Berlin, 1974.

BBA   Bertolt Brecht Archive, unpublished material, Akademie der Künste, Berlin.

Benjamin, *Arcades*   Walter Benjamin, *The Arcades Project*, edited by Rolf Tiedemann, translated by Howard Eiland and Kevin McLaughlin, Cambridge, Mass./London, 1999.

Benjamin Correspondence   *The Correspondence of Walter Benjamin 1910–1940*, edited and annotated by Gershom Scholem and Theodor W. Adorno, translated by Manfred R. and Evelyn M. Anderson, Chicago/London, 1994.

Benjamin/Scholem   *The Correspondence of Walter Benjamin and Gershom Scholem 1932–1940*, edited by Gershom Scholem, translated by Gary Smith and Andre Lefevere, introduction by Anson Rabinbach, Cambridge, Mass., 1992.

Benjamin, *Moscow Diary*   Walter Benjamin, *Moscow Diary*, edited by Gary Smith translated by Richard Sieburt, Cambridge, Mass./London, 1986.

BN Paris   Bibliothèque Nationale.

Brecht, *Collected Plays*   Bertolt Brecht, *Collected Plays*, eight vols, edited and translated by John Willett, Ralph Manheim, Tom Kuhn and David Constantine (revised paperback edition), London, 1993–2003.

Brecht, *Letters*   Bertolt Brecht, *Letters*, edited with commentary and notes by John Willett, translated by Ralph Manheim, London, 1990.

Brecht, *Journals*   Bertolt Brecht, *Journals*, edited by John Willett, translated by Hugh Rorrison, London, 1993.

Brecht on Art and Politics   Bertolt Brecht, *Brecht on Art and Politics*, edited by Tom Kuhn and Steve Giles, translated by various hands, London, 2003.

Brecht on Film and Radio   *Brecht on Film and Radio*, translated and edited by Marc Silberman, London, 2000.

Brecht on Theatre   *Brecht on Theatre – The Development of an Aesthetic*, edited and translated by John Willett, New York, 1964.

Brecht, *Poems*   Bertolt Brecht, *Poems 1913–1956*, edited by John Willett and Ralph Manheim, translated by John Willett and various hands, London, 1976.

Brodersen, *A Biography*   Momme Brodersen, *A Biography*, edited by Martina Derviş, translated by Malcolm R. Green and Ingrida Ligers, London/New York, 1996.

DLA   Deutsches Literaturarchiv, Marbach.

GB   Walter Benjamin, *Gesammelte Briefe*, six vols, edited by Christoph Gödde and Henri Lonitz (Adorno Archive), Frankfurt, 1995–2000.

GBA   Bertolt Brecht, *Werke*, Große kommentierte Berliner und Frankfurter Ausgabe, thirty vols, edited by Werner Hecht, Jan Knopf, Werner Mittenzwei, and Klaus-Detlef Müller, Berlin/Frankfurt, 1988–2000

GS   Walter Benjamin, *Gesammelte Schriften*, seven vols and three supplementary vols, edited by Theodor W. Adorno, Gershom Scholem, Rolf Tiedemann and Hermann Schweppenhäuser, Frankfurt, 1972–1999.

JNUL Jewish National and University Library, Jerusalem.

On Walter Benjamin   *On Walter Benjamin, Critical essays and Recollections*, edited by Gary Smith, Cambridge, Mass., 1991.

Origin of German Tragic Drama   Walter Benjamin, *The Origin of German Tragic Drama*, introduced by George Steiner, translated by John Osborne, London, 1985.

RGALI   Russian State Archive for Literature and Art, Moscow.

Revolutionär in Beruf   Asja Lacis, *Revolutionär in Beruf – Berichte über proletarisches Theater, über Meyerhold, Brecht, Benjamin und Piscator*, edited by Hildegard Brenner, Munich, 1971.

SB Munich   MSS collection, Munich City Library.

Scholem, *Benjamin*   Gershom Scholem, *Walter Benjamin – The Story of a Friendship*, translated by Harry Zohn, London, 1982.

SW   Walter Benjamin, *Selected Writings*, four vols, edited by Marcus Bullock and Michael W. Jennings, translated by Edmund Jephcott, Rodney Livingstone and others, Cambridge, Mass./London, 1996–2003.

Steffin, *Briefe*   Margarete Steffin. *Briefe an berühmte Männer. Walter Benjamin, Bertolt Brecht, Arnold Zweig*, edited by Stefan Hauck, Hamburg, 1999.

Understanding Brecht   Walter Benjamin, *Understanding Brecht*, introduced by Stanley Mitchell, translated by Anna Bostock, London, 1973.

'Walter Benjamin'   'Walter Benjamin and his Angel', Gershom Scholem, in *On Jews and Judaism in Crisis – Selected Essays* [Benjamin essays translated by Lux Furtmüller and Werner J. Dannhauser], New York, 1989.

Walter Benjamin und sein Engel   Gershom Scholem, *Walter Benjamin und sein Engel – Vierzehn Aufsätze und kleine Beiträge*, edited by Rolf Tiedemann, Frankfurt, 1983.

WBA   Walter Benjamin Archive at the Akademie der Künste, Berlin.

List of Works Cited

Theodor Adorno, 'The Threepenny Opera', in Kurt Weill, *The Threepenny Opera*, Stephen Hinton (ed.), Cambridge, 1989.

Günther Anders, *Bert Brecht. Gespräche und Erinnerungen*, Zürich, 1962

Günther Anders, 'Bertolt Brecht. Geschichten vom Herrn Keuner', in *Merkur* (Stuttgart), vol. 33, no. 9 (September 1979), pp. 882–92

Hannah Arendt, 'Walter Benjamin', in *Merkur* (Stuttgart), vol. 22, no. 4 (January/February 1968), pp. 50–65; vol. 22, no. 3 (March 1968), pp. 209–24; vol. 22, no. 4 (April 1968), pp. 305–15

Hannah Arendt, *Walter Benjamin, Bertolt Brecht. Zwei Essays*, Munich, 1971

Bernd Auerochs, 'Walter Benjamins Notizen über die Parabel', in Theo Elm/ Hans H. Hiebel (eds), *Die Parabel. Parabolische Formen in der deutschen Dichtung des 20. Jahrhunderts*, Frankfurt, 1986, pp. 160–73

Helmut Baierl/Ulrich Dietzel, 'Gespräch mit Alfred Kurella', in *Sinn und Form* (Berlin), vol. 27, no. 2 (1975), pp. 221–43

Peter Beicken, 'Kafkas *Prozeß* und seine Richter. Zur Debatte Brecht-Benjamin und Benjamin-Scholem', in Benjamin Bennett / Anton Kaes / William J. Lillyman (eds), *Probleme der Moderne. Studien zur deutschen Literatur von Nietzsche bis Brecht. Festschrift für Walter Sokel*, Tübingen, 1983, pp. 343–68

Walter Benjamin, *Moscow Diary*, edited by Gary Smith, translated by Richard Sieburth, Cambridge, Mass. and London, 1986

Walter Benjamin, 'Theater und Rundfunk' in *Blätter des Hessischen Landestheaters*, Leipzig, vol. 5 (1931/32), no. 16 (July 1932)

Willy R. Berger, 'Svendborger Notizen. Baudelaire im Urteil Bert Brechts', in *arcadia* (Berlin), vol. 12, no. 1 (1977), pp. 47–64

Dietz Bering, *Die Intellektuellen. Geschichte eines Schimpfwortes*, Stuttgart, 1978

Otto Biha, 'Der gefälschte "Brecht". Feststellungen zu dem Vortrag von Ludwig Kuntz und Dr W. Milch, Breslauer Sender, über Brechts "Lehrstücke"', in *Arbeitssender* (Berlin), vol. 5, no. 7 (12 February 1932), p. 4

Ernst Bloch, *Briefe 1903–1975*, Karola Bloch et al (eds), 2 vols, Frankfurt, 1985

Ernst Bloch, Hans Götz Oxenius, 'Gespräch über die Zwanziger Jahre (1962)' in *Bloch Almanach*, series 2, Baden-Baden, Ernst-Bloch-Archiv, 1982, pp. 11–16

Bertolt Brecht, *A Penny for the Poor*, translated by Desmond Vesey, verse translation by Christopher Isherwood, London, 1937

Bertolt Brecht, *Stories of Mr. Keuner*, translated with an afterword by Martin Chalmers, San Francisco, 2001

Hildegard Brenner, *Die Kunstpolitik des Nationalsozialismus*, Hamburg, 1963

Bernard von Brentano, *Du Land der Liebe. Bericht von Abschied und Heimkehr eines Deutschen*, Tübingen and Stuttgart, 1952

Edward J. Brown, *The Proletarian Episode in Russian Literature, 1928–1932*, New York, 1953

Heinz Brüggemann, 'Das andere Fenster: Einblicke in Häuser und Menschen', in *Zur Literaturgeschichte einer urbanen Wahrnehmungsform*, Frankfurt, 1989

Heinz Brüggemann, 'Walter Benjamin und Sigfried Giedion oder die Wege der Modernität', in Klaus Garber / Ludger Rehm (eds), *global benjamin, Internationaler Walter-Benjamin-Kongress 1992* (Munich), vol. 2, (1999), pp. 717–44

Hans Bunge (ed.), *Brechts Lai-tu. Erinnerungen und Notate von Ruth Berlau*, Darmstadt and Neuwied, 1985

G. K. Chesterton, *Dickens*, London, 1925

Herbert Claas, *Die politische Ästhetik Bertolt Brechts vom Baal zum Caesar*, Frankfurt, 1977

Anna Czajka, 'Rettung Brechts durch Bloch?' in *The Other Brecht II, The Brecht Yearbook*, vol. 18, Marc Silbermann et al. (eds) (Madison, Wisc.), 1993, pp. 120–37

Bernhard Diebold, 'Dreierlei Dynamik', in *Die Premiere* (Berlin), vol. 2, (October 1925), p. 4ff.

Bernhard Diebold, 'Baal dichtet. Zu Bert Brechts "Hauspostille"', in *Frankfurter Zeitung*, vol. 71 (1927), no. 316 (30 April)

Bernhard Diebold, 'Militärstück von Brecht', in *Frankfurter Zeitung*, vol. 75 (1931), no. 108 (11 February), p. 10

Alfred Döblin, *Wissen und Verändern! Offene Briefe an einen jungen Menschen*, Berlin, 1931

Hanns Eisler, *Gespräche mit Hans Bunge. Fragen Sie mehr über Brecht*, Hans Bunge (ed.), Leipzig, 1975

Lou Eisler-Fischer, 'Eisler in der Emigration', in Manfred Grabs (ed.), *Wer war Hanns Eisler? Auffassungen aus sechs Jahrzehnten*, Berlin, 1983, pp. 447–51

Ruth Fischer, *Stalin and German Communism. A Study in the Origins of the State Party*, preface by Sidney B. Fay, Cambridge, Mass., 1948

Gisèle Freund, *Photographien. Mit autobiographischen Texten und einem Vorwort von Christian Caujolle*, Munich, 1985

Werner Fuld, *Walter Benjamin. Zwischen den Stühlen. Eine Biographie*, Munich/Vienna, 1979

Helga Gallas, *Marxistische Literaturtheorie. Kontroversen im Bund proletarisch-revolutionärer Schriftsteller*, Neuwied and Berlin, 1971

Steve Giles, *Bertolt Brecht and Critical Theory. Marxism, Modernity and the Threepenny Lawsuit*, Bern, 1977

Peter Gebhardt et al (eds), *Walter Benjamin – Zeitgenosse der Moderne*, Kronberg, 1976

Hermann Greid, *Der Mensch Brecht wie ich ihn erlebt habe*, Stockholm, Stockholm University (German Institut), 1974

Walter Gropius, *Architektur. Wege zu einer optischen Kultur*, Frankfurt and Hamburg, 1955

Günter Hartung, 'Debatten über faschistische Ideologie', in *Wissenschaftliche Zeitschrift der Martin-Luther-Universität Halle*, series G, vol. 38 (1989), no. 2, pp. 117–31

Günter Hartung, 'Literaturwissenschaft und Friedensforschung. Eine Duplik', in *Zeitschrift für Germanistik*, Leipzig, vol. 10 (1989) no. 5 (October), pp. 597ff.

Günter Hartung, 'Zur Benjamin-Edition – Teil II', in *Weimarer Beiträge*, Berlin/Weimar, vol. 36 (1990), no. 6, pp. 969–99.

Peter von Haselberg, 'Wiesengrund-Adorno', in *Text + Kritik Sonderband Theodor W. Adorno*, Hans Ludwig Arnold (ed.), Munich, 1977, pp. 7–21

Klaus Hermsdorf, 'Anfänge der Kafka-Rezeption in der sozialistischen deutschen Literatur', in *Weimarer Beiträge*, Berlin/Weimar, vol. 24 (1978), no. 9, pp. 45–69

Ulrike Hessler, *Bernard von Brentano – ein deutscher Schriftsteller ohne Deutschland. Tendenzen des Romans zwischen Weimarer Republik und Exil*, Frankfurt, 1984

Alexander Honold, *Der Leser Benjamin. Bruchstücke einer deutschen Literaturgeschichte*, Berlin, 2000

Max Horkheimer, *Gesammelte Schriften*, Alfred Schmidt and Gunzelin Schmidt Noerr (eds), vols. 16 and 17, *Briefwechsel 1937–1980*, Frankfurt, 1995–6

Lorenz Jäger, '"Primat des Gestus", Überlegungen zu Benjamins "Kafka" – Essays', in Lorenz Jäger/Thomas Regehly (eds), *Was nie geschrieben wurde, lesen*, Frankfurter Benjamin-Vorträge, Bielefeld, 1992, p. 96–111

Lorenz Jäger, 'Mord im Fahrstuhlschacht. Benjamin, Brecht und der Kriminalroman', in *The Other Brecht II, The Brecht Yearbook*, vol. 18, Marc Silberman (ed.), Madison, Wisc., 1993, p. 24–40

Michael W. Jennings, *Dialectical Images. Walter Benjamin's Theory of Literary Criticism*, Ithaca and London, 1987

Chryssoula Kambas, *Walter Benjamin im Exil. Zum Verhältnis von Literaturpolitik und Ästhetik*, Tübingen, 1983

Chryssoula Kambas, 'Wider den "Geist der Zeit". Die antifaschistische Politik Fritz Liebs und Walter Benjamins', in Jacob Taubes (ed.), *Der Fürst dieser Welt. Carl Schmitt und die Folgen*, Paderborn, 1983, pp. 263–91

Chryssoula Kambas, *Die Werkstatt als Utopie. Lu Märtens literarische Arbeit und Formästhetik seit 1900*, Tübingen, 1988

Chryssoula Kambas, 'Bulletin de Vernuches. Neue Quellen zur Internierung Walter Benjamins', in *Exil* (Maintal), vol. 10, (1990), no. 2, pp. 5–30

Chryssoula Kambas, 'Walter Benjamin liest Georges Sorel: "Réflexions sur la violence", in Michael Opitz, Erdmut Wizisla (eds), *Aber ein Sturm weht vom Paradiese her. Texte zu Walter Benjamin*, Leipzig, 1992, pp. 250–69

Chryssoula Kambas, 'Walter Benjamin – Adressat literarischer Frauen', in *Weimarer Beiträge*, Vienna, vol. 39 (1933), no. 2, pp. 242–57

Alfred Kantorowicz, 'Brechts "Dreigroschenroman"', in *Unsere Zeit*, Paris, vol. 7 (1934), no. 12 (December), pp. 61f.

Heinrich Kaulen, '"Die Aufgabe des Kritikers".Walter Benjamins Reflexionen zur Theorie der Literaturkritik 1929–1931', in Wilfried Barner (ed.), *Literaturkritik – Anspruch und Wirklichkeit*. DFG Symposion 1989, Stuttgart, 1990, pp. 318–36

Sabine Kebir, *Ich frage nicht nach meinem Anteil. Elisabeth Hauptmanns Arbeit mit Bertolt Brecht*, Berlin, 1997

Walter Kiaulehn, *Mein Freund der Verleger. Ernst Rowohlt und seine Zeit*, Hamburg, 1967

Alfred Klein, *Georg Lukács in Berlin. Literaturtheorie und Literaturpolitik der Jahre 1930/32*, Berlin/Weimar, 1990

Lotte Kohler (ed.), *Within four Walls, the Correspondence between Hannah Arendt and Heinrich Blücher, 1936–1968*, New York/London, 2000

Max Kommerell, 'Jean Paul in Weimar', in Max Kommerell, *Dichterische Welterfahrung. Essays*, Frankfurt, 1952, pp. 53–82

Karl Korsch, *Marxism and Philosophy*, translated and introduced by Fred Halliday, London, 1970

Reinhart Koselleck, *Kritik und Krise. Eine Studie zur Pathogenese der bürgerlichen Welt*, Frankfurt, 1973

Klaus-Dieter Krabiel, *Brechts Lehrstücke. Entstehung und Entwicklung eines Spieltyps*, Stuttgart and Weimar, 1993

Werner Kraft, 'Gedanken über Brecht', in *Neue Zürcher Zeitung*, 16 October 1965, p. 21

Karl Kraus, *Die Dritte Walpurgisnacht*, Heinrich Fischer (ed.), Munich, 1952

Kurt Krolop, *Sprachsatire als Zeitsatire bei Karl Kraus. Neun Studien*, Berlin, 1987

Alfred Kurella, 'Deutsche Romantik. Zum gleichnamigen Sonderheft der "Cahiers du Sud"', in *Internationale Literatur* (Moscow), vol. 8 (1938) no. 6, pp. 113–28

Asja Lacis, 'Brief an Hildegard Brenner, 14 November 1967', in *alternative* (Berlin), vols 56/7, no. 10 (October/December 1967), pp. 211–14

Asja Lacis, *Revolutionär im Beruf. Bericht über proletarisches Theater, über Meyerhold, Brecht, Benjamin und Piscator*, Hildegard Brenner (ed.), Munich, 1971

Asja Lacis , *Krasnaja gvozdika, Vospominania*, Riga, 1984

Stephan Lackner, 'Von einer langen, schwierigen Irrfahrt' (from unpublished Walter Benjamin correspondence), in *Neue deutsche Hefte* (Berlin), vol. 26 (1979) no. 1, pp. 48–68

Joachim Lang / Jürgen Hillesheim (eds), *'Denken heisst verändern...'. Erinnerungen an Brecht*, Augsburg, 1997

Leo Lania, 'Brechts Dreigroschen-Roman', in *Pariser Tageblatt*, vol. 2 (1934), no. 355 (2 December), p. 3

N. Lenin, 'Unter der Fahne des Marxismus', in *Die Kommunistische Internationale*, Petrograd, vol. 3 (1922), no. 22, pp. 8–13

N. Lenin, 'Unter dem Banner des Marxismus', in *Unter dem Banner des Marxismus*, Berlin/Wien, vol. 1, (1925), no. 1 (March), pp. 9–20

Helmut Lethen/Erdmut Wizisla, '"Das Schwierigste beim Gehen ist das Stillestehn". Benjamin schenkt Brecht Gracian. Ein Hinweis', in 'drive b: brecht 100', *The Brecht Yearbook 23* (1998), Marc Silberman (ed.), Berlin, 1997, pp. 142–6

Burkhardt Lindner (ed.), *Walter Benjamin im Kontext* [1978], Königstein, 1985

Ferdinand Lion, 'Über vergangenes und zukünftiges Theater', in *Maß und Wert*, Zürich, vol. 2, (1938/39), no. 5 (May/June 1939), pp. 677–89

Ferdinand Lion, 'Grenzen des Brecht-Theaters', in *Maß und Wert*, Zürich, vol. 2, (1938/39) no. 6 (July/August 1939), pp. 837–41

Heidrun Loeper (ed.), 'Briefwechsel Bertolt Brecht, Margarete Steffin, (Isot Kilian, Käthe Rülicke) und Arnold Zweig 1934–1956', in *Helene Weigel 100. The Brecht Yearbook 25*, ed. by Judith Wilke, Madison, Wisc., The International Brecht Society 2000, pp. 349–422

Leo Löwenthal, *Schriften*, Helmut Dubiel (ed.), 5 volumes, Frankfurt, 1980–1987

Geret Luhr (ed.), 'was noch begraben lag', *Zu Walter Benjamins Exil. Briefe und Dokumente*, Berlin, 2000

Georg Lukács, *History and Class Consciousness*, translated and introduced by Rodney Livingstone, London, 1971

Georg Lukács, *Record of a Life*, István Eörsi (ed.), translated by Rodney Livingstone, London, 1983

James K. Lyon, *Bertolt Brecht in America*, Princeton, 1980

Stefan Mahlke (ed.), 'Wir sind zu berühmt, um überall hinzugehen', *Helene Weigel. Briefwechsel 1935–1971*, Berlin, Theater der Zeit / Literaturforum im Brecht-Haus Berlin, 2000

Klaus Mann, *Tagebücher 1931–1933*, Joachim Heimannsberg, Peter Lämmle and Wilfried F. Schoeller (eds), Munich, 1989

Karl Mannheim, *Ideology and Utopia*, translated by Lonis Wirth and Edward Shils, London 1960

Hans Mayer, 'Walter Benjamin und Franz Kafka. Bericht über eine Konstellation', in Hans Mayer, *Aufklärung heute. Reden und Vorträge 1978–1984*, Frankfurt, 1985, pp. 45–70

Hans Mayer, *Der Zeitgenosse Walter Benjamin*, Frankfurt, 1992

Stanley Mitchell, 'Introduction', in Walter Benjamin's *Understanding Brecht*, translated by Anna Bostock, London, 1973, pp. vii–xix

Stanley Mitchell, 'Big Ideas' (review of Susan Buck-Morss, *The Dialectics of Seeing*), in *Oxford Art Journal*, vol. 16 (1993), no. 1, pp. 139–44

Werner Mittenzwei, 'Brecht und Kafka', in *Sinn und Form*, Berlin, vol. 15 (1963) no. 4, pp. 618–25

Soma Morgenstern, *Kritiken, Berichte, Tagebücher*, Ingolf Schulte (ed.), Lüneburg, 2001

Stéphane Mosès, 'Brecht und Benjamin als Kafka-Interpreten', in Stéphane Mosès / Albrecht Schöne (eds.), *Juden in der deutschen Literatur. Ein deutsch-israelisches Symposion*, Frankfurt, 1986, pp. 237–56

Heiner Müller, 'Keuner +/- Fatzer' in *Brecht-Jahrbuch 1980*, Reinhold Grimm and Jost Hermand (eds), Frankfurt, 1981, pp. 14–21

Reiner Nägele, 'From Aesthetics to Poetics. Benjamin, Brecht, and the Poetics of the Caesura', in Reiner Nägele, *Theater, Theory, Speculation. Walter Benjamin and the Scenes of Modernity*, Baltimore and London, 1991, pp. 135–66

Reiner Nägele, *Lesarten der Moderne. Essays*, Eggingen, 1998

Michael Opitz / Erdmut Wizisla (eds), *Aber ein Sturm weht vom Paradiese her. Texte von Walter Benjamin*, Leipzig, 1992

Klaus Petersen, *Die 'Gruppe 1925'. Geschichte und Soziologie einer Schriftstellervereinigung*, Heidelberg, 1981

Hans Puttnies, Gary Smith (eds.), *Benjaminiana. Eine biographische Recherche*, Gießen, 1991

Bernhard Reich, *Im Wettlauf mit der Zeit. Erinnerungen aus fünf Jahrzehnten deutscher Theatergeschichte*, Berlin, 1970

Michael Rohrwasser, *Der Stalinismus und die Renegaten. Die Literatur der Exkommunisten*, Stuttgart, 1991

Michael Rumpf, 'Radikale Theologie. Benjamins Beziehung zu Carl Schmitt', in Peter Gebhardt et al. (eds), *Walter Benjamin – Zeitgenosse der Moderne*, Kronberg/Ts., 1976, pp. 37–50

Willy Siegfried Schlamm, 'Brechts Lehrbuch der Gegenwart' in *Europäische Hefte*, Prague, 1934, no. 30, pp. 526–9

Silvia Schlenstedt, 'Auf der Suche nach Spuren, Brecht und die MASCH', in Brecht-Zentrum der DDR (Ed.), *Brecht 83. Brecht und Marxismus. Dokumentation*, Berlin, 1983, pp. 18–28 and 365ff.

Detlev Schöttker, *Konstruktiver Fragmentarismus. Form und Rezeption der Schriften Walter Benjamins*, Frankfurt, 1999

Gershom Scholem, *A Life in Letters 1914–1982*, Anthony D. Skinner (ed.), Cambridge, Mass. / London, 2002

Gershom Scholem, *Walter Benjamin und sein Engel. Vierzehn Aufsätze und kleine Beiträge*, Rolf Tiedemann (ed.), Frankfurt, 1983

Gershom Scholem, *Briefe I. 1914–1947*, Itta Shedletzky (ed.), *Briefe II. 1971– 1982*, Thomas Sparr (ed.), *Briefe III. 1971–1982*, Itta Shedletzky (ed.), Munich, 1994–9

Uwe Schoor, *Das geheime Journal der Nation. Die Zeitschrift "Sinn und Form". Chefredakteur: Peter Huchel. 1949–1962*, Berlin, 1992

Ernst Schumacher, 'Brecht als Objekt und Subjekt der Kritik', in Ernst Schumacher, *Brecht. Theater und Gesellschaft im 20. Jahrhundert. Achtzehn Aufsätze*, Berlin, 1981, pp. 292–321

Benno Slupianek et al, 'Gespräch mit Asja Lacis und Bernhard Reich über Brecht', in BBA Tape Collection, nr 582/3

Ronald Speirs (ed.), *Brecht's Poetry of Political Exile*, Cambridge, 2000

Fritz Sternberg, *Der Dichter und die Ratio. Erinnerungen an Bertolt Brecht*, Göttingen, 1963

Karl Thieme, 'Des Teufels Gebetbuch? Eine Auseinandersetzung mit dem Werke Bertolt Brechts', in *Hochland*. Munich and Kempten, vol. 29 (1931/32), no. 5 (February 1932), pp. 397–413

Rolf Tiedemann, *Studien zur Philosophie Walter Benjamins* [1995], Frankfurt, 1973

Rolf Tiedemann, 'Historischer Materialismus oder politischer Messianismus? Politische Gehalte der Geschichtsphilosophie Walter Benjamins', in Peter Bulthaupt (ed.), *Materialien zu Benjamins Thesen "Über den Begriff der Geschichte"*. *Beiträge und Interpretationen*, Frankfurt, 1975, pp. 77–121

Edward Timms, *Karl Kraus: Apocalyptic Satirist*, London/New Haven, 2005

Manfred Voigts (ed.), 'Oskar Goldberg. Ein Dossier', in *Akzente*, Munich, vol. 36 (1989), no. 2 (April), p. 158–91

Hans-Albert Walter, *Asylpraxis und Lebensbedingunge in Europa. Deutsche Exilliteratur 1933–1950*, vol. 2, Darmstadt and Neuwied, 1972

Theodor Wiesengrund-Adorno, 'Mahagonny', in *Der Scheinwerfer* (Essen), vol. 3 (1929/30), no. 14 (April 1930), pp. 12–15

Rolf Wiggershaus, *The Frankfurt School*, Oxford, 1994

Judith Wilke, *Brechts 'Fatzer' – Fragment. Lektüren zum Verhältnis von Dokument und Kommentar*, Bielefeld, 1998

Bernd Witte, *Walter Benjamin: an Intellectual Biography*, Detroit, 1991

Elisabeth Young-Bruehl, *Hannah Arendt – For Love of the World*, New Haven/ London, 2004

Erdmut Wizisla, 'Ernst Bloch und Bertolt Brecht. Neue Dokumente ihrer Beziehung', in *Bloch-Almanach*, vol. 10, Baden-Baden, Ernst-Bloch-Archiv, 1990, pp. 87–105

Erdmut Wizisla, 'Über Brecht. Gespräch mit Heiner Müller', in *Sinn und Form*, Berlin, vol. 48 (1996), no. 2, pp. 223–37

Erdmut Wizisla (ed.), '...*und mein Werk ist der Abgesang des Jahrtausends*'. 22 *Versuche, eine Arbeit zu beschreiben* (catalogue of Bertolt Brecht centenary exhibition in the Akademie der Künste, Berlin), 1998

Acknowledgements and Permissions

For the provision of material and permission to use it, for information and for fruitful discussion and all kinds of other support, my thanks are due to the following:

The late Günther Anders, the late Karola Bloch, Willi Bolle (São Paulo), Barbara Brecht-Schall (Berlin), the late Margot von Brentano, Momme Brodersen (Palermo), Michael Buckmiller (Hanover), Margot Cohn (The Jewish National and University Library, Jerusalem), Hans-Joachim Dahms (Berlin), Gabriele Ewenz (Düsseldorf), the late Gisèle Freund, Christoph Gödde (Theodor W. Adorno Archiv, Frankfurt), Lorenz Jäger (Frankfurt), Joachim Kersten (Hamburg), Gabriele Kessler (Zürich), the late Stephan Lackner, the late Fritz Landshoff, Burkhardt Lindner (Frankfurt), the late Leo Löwenthal, Ursula Marx (Walter Benjamin Archiv, Berlin), the late Kitty Marx-Steinschneider, Grischa Meyer (Berlin), Jochen Meyer (Deutsches Literaturarchiv, Marbach am Neckar), Michael Opitz (Berlin), Michel Prat (Paris), Jan Philipp Reemtsma (Hamburg), Michael Rohrwasser (Vienna), the late Hans Sahl, Detlev Schöttker (Berlin), Kerstin Schoor (Berlin), Michael Schwarz (Walter Benjamin Archiv, Berlin), Rolf Tiedemann (Oberursel), Peter Villwock (Berlin), Reinhard Wizisla (Falkensee), Sabine Wolf (Berlin) as well as my colleagues in the Akademie der Künste (Berlin), especially those in the Bertolt Brecht Archive.

I owe special thanks to the late Gerhard Seidel and the late Peter Wruck, supervisors of the doctoral thesis on which this book was originally based, defended at the Humboldt University (Berlin) in 1994. I would also like to thank its joint referees, Chryssoula Kambas and Heinz Brüggemann (both of Hanover), as well as Günter Hartung (Halle), whose constructive criticism played a decisive part in the preparation of the published German version.

Erdmut Wizisla
Berlin, February 2009

Thanks are due to the following for permission to reproduce copyright material: Harvard University Press for quotations from their four-volume edition of Walter Benjamin's *Selected Writings*; The University of Chicago Press for quotations from *The Correspondence of Walter Benjamin*; Suhrkamp Verlag for quotations from their seven-volume edition of his *Gesammelte Schriften*, and from their six-volume edition of his *Gesammelte Briefe*; and Methuen Publishing Ltd for permission to quote from the works of Bertolt Brecht. Bibliographical details of all these works will be found on pp. 219–29 above.

Annotated Name Index

Names found in standard works of reference and those of contemporary scholars, editors, etc., are not annotated.

Index of Works by Bertolt Brecht

Index of Works by Walter Benjamin